FRANCESCO
PETRARCH

LETTERS OF OLD AGE
(RERUM SENILIUM LIBRI)

VOL. 1: BOOKS I-IX

FRANCESCO PETRARCH

LETTERS OF OLD AGE
(RERUM SENILIUM LIBRI)

VOL. 1: BOOKS I-IX

Translated by
Aldo S. Bernardo,
Saul Levin &
Reta A. Bernardo

ITALICA PRESS
NEW YORK
2005

First Published 1992
Copyright © The Johns Hopkins University Press

First Paperback Edition
Copyright © 2005 by Aldo S. Bernardo

Italica Press, Inc.
595 Main Street
New York, NY 10044

The edition was printed on
60-lb Natural Paper
by BookSurge,
U. S. A./
E.U.

Library of Congress Cataloging-in-Publication Data

Petrarca, Francesco, 1304-1374.
    [Correspondence. English. Selections]
    Letters of old age = Rerum senilium libri / Francis Petrarch;
translated by Aldo S. Bernardo, Saul Levin, Reta A. Bernardo
        p. cm.
Translation of: Rerum senilium libri, I-XVIII.
Includes bibliographical references and index.
    ISBN 978-1-59910-004-3 (pbk.: alk. paper)
    I. Petrarca, Francesco, 1304-1374—Correspondence.
2. Authors, Italian—To 1500—Correspondence.
I. Bernardo, Aldo S. II. Levin, Saul. III. Bernardo, Reta A.
IV. Title. V. Title: Rerum senilium libri.
PQ4496.E29E23   1992
851'.1–dc20   91-18097

Printed in the U.S. and E.U.
5 4 3 2 1

Cover Art: Ambrogio Lorenzetti, Good Government in the Countryside. Palazzo Pubblico, Siena. Detail. Scala/Art Resource, New York.

For a Complete List of Medieval & Renaissance Texts
Visit our Web Site at: http://www.ItalicaPress.com

CONTENTS

BOOK III

BOOK IV

BOOK V

BOOK VI

BOOK VII

BOOK VIII

BOOK IX

Volume Two

BOOK X

BOOK XI

BOOK XII

BOOK XIII

BOOK XIV

BOOK XV

BOOK XVI

BOOK XVII

BOOK XVIII

PREFACE

This translation has been evolving over a period of almost ten years. Its roots extend back to the Bernardo translation of Petrarch's *Familiares*, whose third and final volume appeared in 1985. It was therefore natural for the Bernardos to assume that there would be little difficulty in moving from one collection to another. However, they soon learned the value of working from a definitive edition. Whereas such an edition had been available for the *Familiares*, there was none for the *Seniles*. An examination of the manuscript tradition revealed many complexities whose resolution would have required a herculean effort even to consider such an edition. Having been convinced by the arguments of Ernest H. Wilkins that the collective edition of 1501, containing the first complete printed edition of the *Seniles*, was the most reliable, they decided to use it as their basic text. As the project proceeded, the desire to arrive at a text assuring maximum reliability prompted them to consider turning to a limited portion of the manuscript tradition in order to exert some control over the 1501 edition. This unfortunately led to another problem: their limited experience as paleographers.

The transcription of the 1501 edition into machine-readable form was already completed when Saul Levin, an accomplished Latinist, was asked to join the project. He kindly agreed to help with both the Latin text and the translation. This was back in the early 1980s. The three of us have been working together ever since with the assistance of a series of modest grants which have helped simplify our task. These included a translation grant from the National Endowment for the Humanities, two grants from the Marguerite Eyer Wilbur Foundation, a series of grants for computer time from the Vice Provost for Graduate Studies at the State University of New York at Binghamton, and funds for xeroxing from the Center for Medieval and Early Renaissance Studies at Binghamton. We wish to express our sincere gratitude for such assistance.

Our basic text has remained that of the *Librorum Francisci Petrarche annotatio impressorum* (Venice, 1501). All questionable readings have been checked against the following fifteenth-century manuscripts containing all or most of the 128 letters of the collection: Cod. Marciano 17, Clas. 11 (has lacuna between IV,5 and V,2); Bibl. Laurenziana Plut. 78.3 (lacks Books IV–V); Urbinate lat. 331 (lacks Books IV–V); and to a lesser extent Naz. Napoli 8, G. 7.

The editorial principles governing this translation differ somewhat from those used for the three volumes of the *Familiares*, for the *Seniles* present problems of their own, taxing the scholarship and ingenuity of anyone who deals with them. One mundane problem is the paragraphing. We have generally tried to respect that of the 1501 edition, except where a paragraph was so inordinately long that it might have obscured the meaning.

Since the translated text itself is so long, we limit our annotations to the most indispensable details, such as the identification of the addressees and of most of the passages cited by Petrarch, as well as of certain important personages mentioned or alluded to by him. In his monumental Italian version, Giuseppe Fracassetti did not attempt to furnish such bits of information, although at the end of many of the letters he did write a substantial note to date each one and explain the circumstances surrounding it.* We have found his translation very useful, though often too free and occasionally quite mistaken. We have also consulted the few existing translations of individual letters into English, French, or Italian, but gained little from them.

Petrarch deeply loved and endlessly studied the ancient masters. Virgil above all was his model for poetry, Cicero and Livy for prose. He did his best to write like them; and on the whole he succeeded in screening out the influence of his contemporaries, whose Latin style in speaking and writing was slovenly, crabbed, awkward, or stilted. His style not only surpassed theirs but that of all writers since Augustine. Because we as translators have been immersed in his epistles year after year, we in our turn have come to admire more and more his flair for neat and powerful Latin expression; and in our English rendering we profit from it as much as we can. Our combined talents fall short of his—that we cannot help; but we endeavor to give our readers the flavor of his rhetoric, within the

---

* *Lettere senili di Francesco Petrarca*, 2 vols. (Florence: Le Monnier, 1869).

limits set by the great difference between the two languages in their structure and their history. Even granting that his style is not beyond all reproach—for example, his overuse of *fateor*, "I admit" and *ni fallor*, "unless I am mistaken" becomes an annoying mannerism—we have chosen to translate our author faithfully, warts and all.

We could not attempt, in Petrarch's fashion, to recapture the superior English style of some past golden age (say that of Swift and Addison, or Burke and Johnson). Occasionally we do avail ourselves of archaic words or phrases, where they are appropriate to the context as well as the time of Petrarch's discourse, and where—on the other hand—nothing in the current English vocabulary would do; in such passages some readers may have to turn to a dictionary. Otherwise our aim is to make the translation easy to read and understand, which often requires us to split up his very long Ciceronian sentences.

Our respect for Petrarch's classicism extends to instances where he consciously chose ancient terminology for the things around him. The country where he spent nearly all of his old age was, for him, *Gallia cisalpina*, and we translate it "Cisalpine Gaul" rather than the paraphrase "northern Italy;" for something of his mentality is at stake in this geographical fancy. Instead of *Neapolis* he often writes *Parthenope*, the ancient poets' name for the city; we retain his distinction, rather than judge it to be pointless. Of course we give proper names in the standard English form, provided it is widely known—in this case, *Naples* (which came into English through French).

For the sake of consistency, places and persons that are customarily not Anglicized, such as *Alexandria* and *Augustus*, we simply take over from the Latin text. But we have taken the liberty of improving upon Petrarch's spelling, since knowledge of Latin orthography progressed rapidly among the humanists after his time; so we correct his *Cesar* to Caesar, *Eneas* to Aeneas, *Fabritius* to Fabricius, and so on. In the case of Lelius, however, we have decided to distinguish the ancient Laelius (the bosom friend of the younger Scipio Africanus) from Petrarch's own bosom friend, Lelius, whom he had thus renamed. Many of the Greek names are likewise distorted, and these too we restore to their true Latinized form.

When it comes to his favorite authors, Petrarch often writes *Satiricus* (the Satirist) instead of naming Juvenal, and *Comicus* (the Comic [Poet]) instead of naming Terence. To others he refers either by their *nomen gentilicium* or by their *cognomen*; so our readers should be aware that

Tully or Marcus Tullius	=	Cicero
Sallust	=	Crispus
Virgil	=	Maro
Horace	=	Flaccus
Ovid	=	Naso
Annaeus	=	Seneca
Suetonius	=	Tranquillus
Severinus	=	Boethius.

Like other writers of his time, Petrarch Latinized the names of his contemporaries, but the present custom of scholars calls for the Italian or French form (depending on the nationality of the individual and adjusted to present-day spelling)—Matteo Longo, Sagremor de Pommiers. However, persons of international renown—kings, popes, saints—have their names Anglicized: Robert (not Roberto), Urban, Francis. The forms generally agree with Ernest Wilkins's list of addressees.[*]

We usually translate the Latin titles of books, unless the untranslated title is actually more familiar to educated English readers; for example, Cicero's *De officiis*. Abbreviations for names of classical authors and titles of works are taken from the *Oxford Classical Dictionary* (1970). Reference to the Psalms is according to the numbering that now prevails rather than as it appears in the Vulgate. Citations without sources indicate texts we could not locate.

The dates of letters take two forms: a bracketed date indicates the general consensus by scholars as found in Wilkins; an unbracketed date is Petrarch's.[**]

Though compiled by a number of Venetian humanists eager to preserve the writings of the master, the *editio princeps* of 1501 was not well proofread and therefore is corrupt in dozens of passages—most of them quite obvious to any Latinist. A truly critical edition, on a par with Vittorio Rossi's edition of *Rerum familiarium libri* (Florence: Sansoni [1934–42]), is still in the making and may not be published for years to come. The 1501 edition has proven surprisingly dependable; where it is unsound, we have consulted the principal manuscripts accessible to us; and wherever any of them supplies the true reading, we simply follow it without calling attention to the discrepancy between it and the 1501 edition. In the

[*] Ernest H. Wilkins, *Petrarch's Correspondence* (Padua: Antenore, 1960), p. 12.
[**] Ibid., p. 94.

minority of cases where those manuscripts too are all corrupt, we do footnote our emendation of the untenable received text.

We are indebted to a number of colleagues for their assistance in hunting down some of the more obscure references in the letters or in expediting the preparation of the typescript. Among these are Paul Szarmach and Daniel Williman.

The Translators
Binghamton, N.Y.
August, 1990

INTRODUCTION

In the autumn of 1361 Petrarch's collection of *Familiares* (*Letters on Familiar Matters*) had reached such proportions that he decided to gather his remaining and future letters in two other collections. One was to be a collection of letters already written which for a number of reasons he had not included among his *Familiares*. The other was to be a collection of letters yet to be written, to be entitled *Epistole seniles*. In the probably fictional concluding letter of the *Familiares*, XXIV, 13, to his friend Socrates, he states in effect:

> Now, since many and varied letters are calling to be written, since it is uncertain how long my life will last, and since the present volume can hardly hold anything more, I am planning to gather in another volume letters that I still have on hand, and to gather in still another volume, which will take its name from my age, such letters as I may write hereafter.

As Ernest H. Wilkins comments regarding this short summary, "It seems hardly possible that he is thinking here of the little collection, already completed, of the *Epistolae sine nomine*."[*] According to Wilkins, Petrarch must have initiated the *Seniles* before the end of 1361 with the dedicatory letter addressed to Francesco Nelli. It is interesting to note that just as the dedicatory letter of the *Familiares* written to Socrates probably in 1350 opens with a reference to the loss of friends in the plague of 1348, in the same way *Sen.* I, 1 opens with a similar reference to the loss of friends, particularly Socrates himself, in the current plague. The new collection, however, did not

---

[*] Ernest H. Wilkins, *Petrarch's Later Years* (Cambridge, Mass.: Harvard University Press, 1939), p. 17.

prevent him from adding to the *Familiares* letters written after 1361 (XXII, 1, XXIII, 9–10, 14–16, 18–19, and 21); and to the *Seniles* three letters written before 1361 (VI, 6 of 1358, and XVI, 8–9 of 1354) and XVI, 5 of early 1361.[*]

Although Petrarch included 128 letters in the *Seniles*, it is certain that he wrote many more. In *Sen.* XVI, 3, written in 1372, he states that he has collected more than four hundred letters in two thick volumes, discarding a thousand others for lack of space. Twenty-nine letters written in these years, but not included in the *Seniles*, have survived. There is one, *Variae* 15, whose last section Petrarch rewrote and included as the ending of *Sen.* XIII, 13.

In analyzing the criteria probably used by Petrarch in deciding which letters to include in the *Seniles*, Wilkins stresses literary quality, moral value, public importance, and personal reminiscence. Wilkins also analyzes the revisions between the original missives and the final forms of several letters that exist in both forms. His conclusions indicate a relatively complex process undergone by letters before being deemed worthy of inclusion into a collection. While the *Seniles* do show a generally chronological progression from book to book, it is not always so within books. Wilkins's analysis also demonstrates Petrarch's very real concern for the length of books and a tendency to begin and end books with letters having special significance. He likewise points to a number of letters that were never intended as missives, and therefore could be called certainly or probably fictional (VI, 7–8, VIII, 2, XVI, 6–7, and in a certain sense I, 1). A number of letters resulted, furthermore, from splitting longer ones or from combining shorter ones.[**]

The extent to which artistic concern played a decisive role in Petrarch's preparation of his two principal collections of letters in prose may be seen in the fact that while he ended his *Familiares* with a look toward antiquity by closing the collection with letters addressed to the ancients, in the *Seniles* he casts his glance toward the distant future by placing his Letter to Posterity, his unfinished autobiography, at the very end as Book XVIII. As I have noted elsewhere concerning these two endings,

> the very positioning of the *Posteritati* at the end of the *Seniles* was a classical gesture in the manner of the great Latin poets,

[*] Ibid., p. 18.
[**] Ibid., pp. 303–14.

such as Ovid, who ended collections of their works with an autobiographical epilogue. In fact, if the letter was intended to balance the ending of the *Familiares* with its ten letters to the ancients, it follows that Petrarch hoped to be for posterity what the ancients had been for him, and somewhat more: an *exemplum* not only of the learned man, creative writer, moral philosopher and historian, but also of the good Christian standing taller than the ancients whom he chides in the last book of the *Familiares* for not having lived a life commensurate with their learning and creativity.[*]

Furthermore, by having the *Posteritati* preceded by four letters to his beloved disciple, Boccaccio, he creates a carefully orchestrated epilogue in which we see a living exemplar of the new man of letters who must show his generation the way it had lost, an exemplar in keeping with the one projected by Boccaccio himself in his biography of the great master where he proclaims Petrarch to be a born-again ancient. The epilogue reaches a climax at the end of Book XVII with Petrarch's grand and highly personalized gesture of Latinizing Boccaccio's tale of Griselda, thereby raising Boccaccio's famous vernacular novella to the level of a classical *exemplum*, but with Christian overtones.[**]

The scope of Petrarch's total correspondence is impressive indeed. As Wilkins remarks, if we take into consideration the enormous number of letters that Petrarch admitted destroying, he probably wrote more than anyone had ever written before him. He started writing them during his university days and continued until the last month of his life. We know one hundred and fifty correspondents to whom his letters were addressed. These included the emperor Charles IV and his empress, King Robert of Naples, the French dauphin Charles of Valois, members of the powerful Visconti family and of several other ruling families throughout Europe, doges of Genoa and of Venice, several chancellors, two popes, a number of cardinals, many bishops and archbishops, many members of religious orders, courtiers, scholars, teachers, poets, musicians, jurists, warriors, physicians, a great number of friends, and even a minstrel.

---

[*] Aldo S. Bernardo, "Petrarch's Autobiography: Circularity Revisited," *Annali d'Italianistica* 4 (1986): 50.

[**] Ibid., p. 68.

The contents of the letters also vary greatly, ranging from reminiscences, invitations, thanks, consolation, exhortation, reproof, and recommendations, to praises of Italy, discussions of antiquity, poetry, authorship, scholarship, books, fame, fortune, friendship, and solitude, and to such subjects as astrology, diet, dreams, gout, pestilence, servants, pleas for peace, and arguments for the return of the papacy to Rome.*

Being the letters of Petrarch's later years, the *Seniles* truly project his mature judgment on matters that reflect the centrality of his role at the dawn of humanism. In them, for example, we find more letters addressed to Boccaccio (eighteen), with whom he shares his ideas on culture and literature, than to anyone else; we find two whole books (VII and IX, in addition to several other letters) addressed to Pope Urban V and to his secretary, Francesco Bruni, regarding a host of concerns over the rightful location of the Church, its structure, and its proper role; and we find the equivalent of nearly two more books (in XIII, XIV, XVI) addressed to powerful rulers of the day (Pandolfo Malatesta, Francesco da Carrara, and Charles IV) and dealing with matters of statecraft and political rectitude.

Also of considerable interest are those letters interspersed throughout the collection dealing with personal matters, down-to-earth, everyday concerns, and personalized philosophical and spiritual reflections. Among these, the most common themes include the strong awareness of the passage of time and the sense of approaching death, which in turn lead to meditations on the meaning of life; the sadness resulting from the loss of dear friends and the desire to have them closer; the sincere concern over the return of the Church to Rome from Avignon and an unwavering faith in divine providence and life after death; and the disturbing onset of the illness that was eventually to prove fatal. In this regard, Petrarch's skeptical view of doctors and their treatment of patients, especially with respect to their dietary advice, reflects the conviction that nature is a better healer than medicine.

Among the more interesting letters dealing with the human side of Petrarch are the following:

---

* Ernest H. Wilkins, *A History of Italian Literature* (Cambridge, Mass.: Harvard University Press, 1954), pp. 87–88.

In the previously cited letter XVI, 3 Petrarch exclaims: "I am putting an end to this epistolary habit, lest it always keep me from better studies, since I see that replying to all who write me is an endless task. . . . After this, even if a letter comes, even if the Roman emperor writes me—which he often has done—I would not reply otherwise than in the vernacular." The Latin epistle was thus a special kind of artifact requiring the creative energy that diminishes with age. Considering the very few vernacular missives that have been identified as written by Petrarch, the age of classical humanism had clearly dawned.

A.S.B.

Letters of Old Age

—————————

VOLUME ONE

Sen. I, 1.

Proem, to Simonides [Francesco Nelli].*

Writing some time ago to my Socrates [Ludwig van Kempen], I had complained that the year 1348 of our era had deprived me of nearly every consolation in life because of my friends' deaths. For I remember with what grief I gave vent to uncontrollable laments and tears. Now what shall I do in the sixty-first year of this century, which has snatched away, together with nearly every other treasure, even my dearest and most precious one, Socrates himself? I have no wish to weary my pen describing the loss of other friends, lest the sad memories make me weep anew, and lest this plague-ridden year force me once again to do what I would rather not—burst into plaints unworthy of my years, of my studies, unworthy of me altogether; this year has not only equaled but even surpassed the earlier one in many regions, especially here in Cisalpine Gaul, and has almost completely emptied along with many other cities the most flourishing and populous Milan, untouched until now by these disasters. Earlier I had allowed myself much that I now reject. I do hope that Fortune will never again catch me in tears; I shall stand erect if I can, and if not, she will lay me low, tearless and silent. A groan is more shameful than a fall.

I shall continue with what I began to say. My book, *Letters on Familiar Matters*, is dedicated to Socrates; vast in its bulk, it would become still more so if I were to allow it. Now I see just what I then guessed: nothing but the end of my life will bring an end to my letter writing. Therefore, if friends' demands or circumstances wrench more of them from me in the future (for, aware of my situation, I seek not to add to my burdens but to lessen them), I intend to dedicate them all to you to whom prose is more congenial than poetry. It is uncertain how much of my writing or of my life lies ahead. However little it may be, you will take it in good part because it is all yours, even if very little. And do not be upset at being second, or believe that I preferred Socrates to you, but keep in mind that I had not yet met you when that collection was begun.

---

* Prior of the Church of the Holy Apostles in Florence when P. met him in 1350; later served the Kingdom of Naples as royal secretary. He was P.'s principal addressee in the *Familiares* (27 letters). According to *Sen.* III, 1, P. called him Simonides because he considered him, like the ancient Simonides, "both priest and poet."

There are still many letters in it addressed to you, though I had yet to name you Simonides; however this collection of letters turns out, I am giving it to you, in effect, like the catch of a net—the later you receive it, the more welcome it will be. The gifts of old age are generally more balanced and unusual than those of youth.

[1361].

Sen. I, 2.

To Francesco [Nelli] of the Holy Apostles of Florence,* that the flatteries of fortune must be rejected with a noble contempt.

Even before the arrival of your brief letter, I was saddened to hear of the passing of our Zanobi [da Strada] and happy to learn of your becoming a Neapolitan. I honestly rejoice that you, like half of my soul, as Flaccus says of Virgil, are where I cannot be in person, assuming that, wherever you may be, you are well and happy, which is my desire and hope. I am convinced that it could not possibly be otherwise, considering your host [Niccolò Acciaiuoli, Grand Seneschal of the Kingdom of Naples] (that Maecenas to us all), your intellect, and lastly your wealth of virtues so profuse, so constant, so unique.

As for the warm entreaty with which that Maecenas, and yourself after him, now invite me as well to Campania, what else shall I say except to marvel not at your love for me, which I well knew in the past, but at your tireless insistence in pressing for something so often refused. You tire neither of asking nor of waiting, whereas now I am weary not only of refusing you but of remaining silent and even of living. Nothing new can be said about this on either side; it has all been said.

Putting this aside, I shall say one thing to make you realize what flattering snares the world also weaves for me even now, were I not careful. Yet let it tempt me! I cannot be fooled, being so well versed in such games, and, as they say, steeped in them. For at the very moment when our illustrious and truly dear friend sends me this invitation, whereby—were it not for other obstacles—I am being summoned to no one else's home than my own, the Roman emperor [Charles IV] summons me from the one side and the competing French king [John II] from the other, with promises and gifts sent in advance, which any attempt to list will take too long and will seem unbelievable. Why two warrior princes should be concerned about a lone cleric, unarmed and already elderly, is truly astonishing. Most recently, in fact, the Supreme Pontiff, the same one who used to consider me a necromancer [Innocent VI], also officially

* See I, 1.

summoned me, having already conferred two benefices, and offering more if I would obey. There is nothing really surprising in this since the reason is obvious. He wants me for the office of secretary which our Zanobi formerly held, and which he or his predecessor would never have held, had I not refused it when so respectfully offered to me many years ago.

But old age is suspected of avarice, and perhaps they hope that I, old and richer than I used to be, which makes greed all the keener (so they figure), will embrace something that I never wanted when I was young and poor; but they are mistaken, particularly since I have now nearly run out of needy friends whose welfare then deeply concerned me. Among these (not to launch into my tale of woes which I would rather cut short, lay aside, and forget if I could), was my Giovanni [Petrarch's son]—yours, ours, or rather Christ's, to use Jerome's words; that Giovanni who used to pay you homage in the Babylon of the West [Avignon] has completed the harsh, brief journey of life before evening, indeed even before midday when he had shown signs of a change for the better, I believe, so that his death should be even more painful for me. But it is not, for what most people would turn into the high point of their loss and a spur for sobbing, I have turned into a consolation: because he died a better man, I live more contentedly. To all who beckon me I thus offer my excuses, which are surprising indeed, but the principal one—my very real old age—I do not deny but emphasize by speaking about it. With God's help I am still strong enough for worthy and peaceful labors; for the hateful ones I have become feeble and powerless. I count it among my natural endowments that I cannot do what I do not want to be able to do, nor do I ever lack an honest excuse, but my chariness in using it has often unexpectedly caused me many embarrassments and grave difficulties.

When I made my excuses to the latest invitation of the Pontiff [Innocent VI], I recommended you, my friend, and I did so to honor you. You will forgive me if I erred. I thought that, if they considered me a suitable choice for that great office, and if my advice were fittingly heeded about another person's skills, you would have either the rewards for accepting the position—admittedly demanding, yet honorable—or the distinction of a dignified refusal. But if they were furious with me for not listening to them and scorned my judgment of you, too, I still believed it my duty to honor your name with praise—that was always true but particularly then. I would rather have you learn of this from someone other than me, but I am writing so that you will be better prepared to respond, should you hear anything about it. Nor did I fail to praise our Maecenas when praising you. For I wrote that you were with him and that he had to be asked to let you go; this I did in order that it might be evident in this matter as in many others what kind of man he is, nourishing the Church with men of talent; he would long ago have given Zanobi and would give you now, if requested. I shall say nothing of the praise due our common fatherland which, as the fount of all its citizens' glory, gave birth to him and to both of you, and produced the benefactor and his protégés.

As for the rest, I must tell you that troublesome rumors have been driving me every which way; not at all happy, but with reason's aid I stand fast. What to do about myself still remains in doubt. Unless something new turns up, it is likely that you will hear before many months elapse that I have returned to my transalpine retreat. I have had my fill of things Italian. Farewell.

[1361–62].

Sen. I, 3.

To the same person,* an appreciation of his friendly consolation.

Your most gentle and truly expert hand has applied a welcome salve to my wounds, consoling me over the passing of my young son, about whom I talked as if I hated while he was alive; but now that he is no more I cherish him in my thoughts, hold him in my heart, embrace him in my memory, and, alas, seek him in vain with my eyes. This, like everything else, you do most lovingly. Yet, O vast power of love, exempt from the rule of reason! You, my comforter, also weep, and love compels what reason would not allow. You weep for him, and well you may. For whatever else he may have been, he loved and admired you, and turned out to be a tireless supporter of your good name. For me, this was one indication among many that he was changing from day to day, and that with much effort he was shedding the vices of his young years. I call Christ to witness, for whom he now lives, to whom I often pray, sighing for my final resting place and recommending the soul of the one taken from me, that neither in love nor in admiration did he place me over you, for he thought no mortal your equal; thus did you stand at the summit of his esteem: such was his love, his conviction, in short, his unchanging opinion. Because of the instability of his age, he was fickle about other things, but constant about you. If anyone happened to be compared to you, he would express his opinion with bowed head and silent smile, fearful of speaking frankly with his elders. And if youthful ardor sometimes compelled him to speak, you could see respect struggling with love, and modesty with loyalty. It is fitting, then, for you to weep for him and to miss him as a son since he would have wept for you as a father and missed you as a son.

But since it is right for Fortune to strike but once and not to overwhelm its victim with repeated blows, you too now weep with me over a second wound, my Socrates [Ludwig van Kempen], who was born for me in another part of the world. At our very first encounter, his countenance, talent, and virtue so made him of one mind with me that afterward I never felt his spirit waver even a moment with regard to me, nor did his loyalty flag, something truly rare in a man of barbarian birth. For our lengthy association, contin-

---

* See I, 1.

uous relationship, and mutual love had imbued him with our ways and feelings as if he had been born in the heart of Italy. He was one of us, he admired everything of ours, and, almost oblivious of his roots, sighed for nothing on earth but Italy. What would you have me say? So great a transformation of his nature and activities amazed everyone and delighted me immensely, especially because it somehow seemed to redound to my glory since beyond any doubt he thought me the foremost of mortals. Originally I met him in the first bloom of his adolescence, about seven years before my son's birth; it was, in fact, during the time we lived most contentedly not far from the Pyrenees, enjoying the pleasant comradeship with other young men under that incomparable man of grateful memory, Giacomo Colonna, the illustrious bishop of the region. O king of heaven, O creator of the ages, O ruler of the stars, why this tremendous flight of time? I would have said that it was the other day except that, aside from Lelius alone [Angelo di Pietro Stefano dei Tosetti] (and I am not even certain about him), I now believe that no one from that group is still alive. O treacherous life of man! Never do we cease embarking toward distant hopes that cannot be realized in such a brief period. O harsh field of toil, O inscrutable labyrinth of straying, grim arena of groans, here, yes, here we unhappily carry on, here we struggle bruised and harassed; and the final madness, here we take our pleasure, exult, and become arrogant; here we labor for power and honors, for wealth and authority; here we launch insults, here we plunder, here we take vengeance, though unsure in the meantime of what the present hour, let alone the coming day, has in store for us; and nothing is gained by a long life except to grow old alone and sad, weighed down in body and soul, amidst griefs and tears and the loved ones we miss.

I really ought to have said "today" rather than "the coming day," for what is this life if not a single day, and a short, stormy winter's day at that? And just as it is cut off for many in the morning and for many at midday, so for very few does it extend to the evening. Today, I say, after entering this racecourse with so many joyful teammates, here I am already tired of the road, moving almost alone toward the finish line. Nor do I see anything in dragging out a slightly longer life, so desired in everyone's prayers, except perhaps that we die more resigned because those who once made life sweet for us have been sent ahead; they have left behind nothing to rouse the spirit, unless it were, on the contrary, a troublesome, wretched state: to grow old, always weeping in perpetual sorrow, as the Satirist says, and dressed in black or, more explicitly, to die many times with your friends' deaths, ultimately leaving behind none of them on whose lips and in whose memory you shall live after meeting your end. Now despite the good intentions of a loving father you do me wrong to wish for a prolongation of this toilsome, sad business in saying that you tremble and shudder at the thought of surviving me. But I want you and these very few, who are now the only ones left of all that host of friends, to survive me. May there be someone to receive my final behests as I depart! May there be someone to close my eyes and bury me in the ground, though death will accomplish the one well enough and nature the other; but it is sweet to be buried by the hands of friends. I have no weightier grievance against my fortune than that I, harder than a diamond, slower than a tortoise, and more lasting than a phoenix, have been kept waiting until now, while my friends were carried off before their time—if there is a right time for such an obligation to be paid. And to add insult to injury, I was not allowed to be present at the burial of those whose hands I had hoped would lay me to rest.

But I return to Socrates who returns not to me. Although in body he has withdrawn, I do not believe that he has abandoned me in spirit, since he had completed thirty-one years of faithful friendship with me. The other for whom I weep [his son Giovanni] never finished the twenty-fourth year of his life. What shall I say now? "Woe is me!" I would say three times and more, except that I am determined to banish mourning; I wish I could do the same with grief; I shall try anyhow. In this I see that I must make use of your advice, that virtue is above human vicissitudes and that He who gave has taken away. We must forgive death, which was within its rights, nor must we accuse fortune or nature. We must not seek order where none ever existed, and we must avoid what we sometimes blamed others for, lest we be justly blamed in turn. Nor should we marvel because one man died in callow youth and the other at maturity while still vigorous. For both of them the span of life was completed; for us it remains to be finished, following those we have sent on ahead.

We must, after all, keep in mind what we have said a thousand times: an education in speech alone is trifling, for we must be philosophical in deeds too if we are indeed eager to be delivered; let us fix our attention here and feel the force of our words. We shall follow our dear ones. Who can doubt this? We shall follow them soon, right away, perhaps now; we *are* surely following them now. What else are we doing, I ask you, even when we seem at rest, except to hurry and run? We are really all running, each of us crowding upon one another. What need have we of a spur? Our very nature drives us, even rushes us, joining us with those who went before. There is no respite. What good is there in burdening the soul with grief or tormenting it with regret? Alas, we shall forthwith catch up with those we seek; for we are on the way to them and they will not return to us, even for a moment. This journey is inescapable for us, but irreversible for them. This being the case, we must cease our groaning and useless complaints and turn to holy offerings and prayers for their salvation which you, an intimate daily guest at Christ's table, promised to offer frequently for one of them. I implore you again and again, out of consideration for me and for true friendship, to do it for both of them every time you come to your Lord's table and enter into conversation with Him. These are more useful remedies for our grief, a sizable portion of which you squeezed into a small part of your letter, being by habit and style more lavish with meaning than with words. I gladly repeat them in my own words for this reason: transfused into my spirit through your pen and then flowing back to you through my pen, they may become mine without ceasing to be yours; like a nail driven in by repeated taps, they are fastened firmly and equally in our memory. I shall willingly make use of this gift of yours, for nothing more fitting to this time could have been offered and nothing more helpful to one in need. For the doctor most effective at curing is the one in whom a patient has the most confidence.

There remains for me to mention that since my Socrates is snatched from me for a time, since too there seems no end to this kind of letter writing except the end of my life (as you can see and I have often said), it is still unthinkable for me not to reply to friends who demand attention, although I do yearn more than usual for rest. Nor could this happen without some taint of unmannerliness which I utterly dread. Let all my earlier letters to friends, and now the letters of my old age, pass on to you; and let all my talent, which in the first collection was dedicated to a foreigner, henceforth be dedicated to Simonides, my fellow citizen and an inspired poet, and therefore dear to me. For you are that Simonides of mine to whom the first letter of this work is addressed; it has yet to reach you, however, and indeed will not arrive alone. Undoubtedly when you read it, you will understand what is missing in this one.

Finally, I must add that, in the interest of honor for you and rest for myself, I left Padua on the tenth of January and made my way to Milan to be better prepared to cross the Alps. For I hated the turmoil in Italy and wished to leave there as soon as possible in order to gaze once again upon my transalpine Helicon [Vaucluse], left behind nearly ten years ago; both my yearning and my disgust were sufficiently conveyed to you in a few words at the end of my previous letter. If the Pontiff has any trust in me, I would give you to him as my replacement in person, as I have already done at a distance in writing, both for that office so often offered me, which I should like to see not only well but magnificently filled, and for you or your needs at least, which you want to hide from me but cannot, despite the distance of time and place that separates us. I believed that both of these things would be accomplished. But with everything everywhere aflame with war, our small unarmed group could not get through the armed bands. I therefore stayed here, awaiting the Pontiff's [Innocent VI's] reply, which I have yet to receive either because his people are involved in their own war—there are many alarming rumors about it—or the messengers have been captured en route, as we have heard in many cases. This one message has been addressed to my compatriots, merchants in Milan on business: namely, that the Pontiff had answered through his staff that, if I did refuse his offer, I should at least come, bringing with me whomever I judged fit for the position. Whether this is true, I know not. But if so, be prepared to go there either with me or with my letter. If all else remains blocked, the sea route lies open to you.

As for me, impatient at the delay and watching the new seeds of war being sown all around, with nearly all routes impassable, I entrusted myself to the Po, and returned on the eleventh of May to Padua where in this state of affairs a bird could scarcely find its way. From here I intend to go next to the emperor [Charles IV], who has been summoning me so frequently and insistently that he can no longer be ignored without arrogance or disrespect. Thus, after preparing to go west, I went north, which should give you some idea of how much constancy there is in human deliberations. Here too I unexpectedly found all routes blocked by war. Venice, this corner of Italy once the dwelling of peace, and the Noric Alps are in as much turmoil as the rest of Italy, while that area of Germany bordering the Alps is aflame with its own troubles; thus does Mars now beset every part of our world at the same time. Although these troubles cannot help but disturb a mind desirous of peace, I would almost call them welcome because ultimately they promise me a summer of repose; indeed they make me draw in my wings that were stretched toward the west and the north, and stay in a familiar site between the Alps and the Apennines, near a gulf of the Adriatic Sea. If you are going to write me anything now, write to me here. Since I suspect that you have been wrenched from the Sicilian shores because of the death of the king [Robert of Naples], do not keep from me, I who am anxious to know everything about you, where and how fickle fortune has happily deposited both you and your, or rather, our patron.

Finally, delay not in sending the highly prized gift of your diligence, the promised ornament of this library, in which dwells all my repose and my mind's delight, and now the sole solace of my life. Hurry, I beg you, by all the saints in heaven, and have trust in my little strongbox; when it reaches me I shall scarcely wish for anything more on earth. Indeed I am in rapture with the mere anticipation of it. Even if no other book is added to those in my possession, which are neither few nor insignificant, I believe I am rich enough, for I have outdone Croesus in wealth and disparage all the lands and coffers of our magnates. Enjoy good health and farewell, and remember me.

June 8 [Padua, 1361-62].

Sen. I, 4.

To Cardinal [Elie de] Talleyrand, Bishop of Albano,* a refusal of the burdensome appointment offered him.

With respectful joy and astonishment, most loving Father, some time ago I read your letter containing the apostolic summons, but your servant's haste did not allow me enough time to reply. Nevertheless, I did reply as best I could, very briefly at that, but quite truthfully, and what was not in my letter I happily conveyed to your messenger of proven reliability. Here I am now, overwhelmed with still more letters and messengers on the same subject, which compounds still more my astonishment and joy. For who, may I ask, would not be astonished and at the same time overjoyed at being a friend of Jesus Christ's Vicar [Innocent VI], who not only used to suspect me in the past of magic but reaffirmed this false opinion of me and always obstinately defended it against your eloquence and that of many others wishing to rid him of it; now suddenly he has not only dropped his opinion but exchanged it for another so different that he seeks with gifts and entreaties my confidential advice and loyal service when he once shuddered to speak to me or even to see me. Great is the power of truth; it can be pushed around and laid low by lies, yet it cannot be extinguished. After lying abandoned for a time, of its own accord it will rise higher and brighter.

May God forgive the one who is the source of that false opinion. He was a great man, granted, not the least in your order, and, what is more, well versed in the law, a man of broad experience and quite advanced age, all of which make his error still more astounding, unless perchance it was not an error but simple hatred, though there can be no error greater than that offense. Nor does anyone err so shamefully, no matter how ridiculous or tasteless something invented through ignorance may be, as the one who knowingly hates God or his neighbor. In short, whatever the cause, he did call me a magician. Nor did he blush to give as his reason that I read or had read Virgil's works—and he was believed. So much for the intellects

---

* A member of the noble and wealthy family of the Counts of Périgord; he was so learned in law and the sciences that John XXII elevated him to cardinal at the age of thirty. He was one of the most powerful members of the Curia under Clement VI and Innocent VI, and often sought to engage P. directly in the service of the pope.

in charge of the world's affairs! You know how often we joked about this, sometimes in the very presence of the one whom my slanderer had convinced, until he was elevated to the papacy; then the matter ceased being funny and began arousing your anger and my grief. Not that I wished much of anything from him! All my ambitions are known to you. Yet since Benedict had known my adolescence and Clement my youth as being, I shall not say innocent, but recoiling from shameful pursuits or evil arts, I could not help but grieve that my old age would seem blemished to Innocent. Therefore, at the time of his elevation, as I left there without knowing whether I would ever return, you wanted to take me to him to say goodbye, and he wanted it too, but I refused lest my magic offend him or his credulity offend me. You know that I am speaking the truth, and that more than once you tried in vain not to let me leave without paying my respects to him.

See what the venomous tongue of one man who had no reason to hate me has done, yet nothing is without cause. He hated not me personally but him who he remembered was my close friend; he hated you too because of the same man. Aware of the injustice of his hatred, the cunning hypocrite feigned friendship with both of us. I am recalling details well known to you and to the one in his grave; unappeased even by the death of this man, he declared war against his ashes. O sad and blind rage of the mind, O deadly propagator of hatreds! Surely if divine commandment bids us to love our enemies, what is in store for those who find it insufficient to hate an enemy even after he is gone, unless they pursue all his friends with undying hatred. Whether the cause was stubborn hatred or shame at retracting what he had said, he nurtured this allegation as long as he lived, and irrigated what he had planted; but, thank God, truth conquered the lie and death the liar. Of course the Pontiff does not believe that the one he wants for a secretary is a magician, nor that the one whom he considers worthy of the secrets of his innermost chamber and fit for his sacred correspondence goes in for sorcery. I am deeply grateful to him for such lofty honors as well as for laying aside such a false opinion. For while steadfast minds cannot be shaken by haphazard, false opinion, still in my mind the opinion, however false, of such an eminent man was bound to cause some distress. Nor would I ever wish it to continue so long that his last day or mine would find him feeling the same about me.

I know, however, that he is awaiting my reply; and while there the Pope's goodness, your kindness, and friends' entreaties and tears strongly attract my humble person, and here the advice of my people urges me to accept, still I stand firm in my original intention. There is absolutely nothing that will change my mind. Dealing with someone else, I would undoubtedly need more words. With you, in matters involving me, brevity, even silence, is enough, for with you I fittingly apply to myself David's saying, "O Lord, before You lies every yearning of mine" [Ps. 38:10]; and not, to be sure, "my groan" (I give none over transient things), but my sigh is certainly not hidden from you. What I want, what I crave, solicit, or sigh for, is as well known to you as to me. What need then of further words? I see myself called to struggles, to honors, to toil, to what nearly all mortals desire, but I do not agree at all with the many. Consequently, neither my fortune nor my spirit needs money; my profession and way of life do not need such honors, nor do my busy days and declining age need the toil. Once again, offer my apologies to the Pontiff so that he does not attribute to arrogance what is in fact modesty. Let your eloquence defend me now as it honored me so often in the past.

I have recommended two compatriots of mine [Boccaccio and Nelli]; if I was deemed worthy of such a high office, I reckoned I was a worthy appraiser of others for it. Either man is most deserving. Since I am eager for a quick and happy resolution of this matter, I decided to contact each one by letter, and found what I guessed to be true. One rejects the burdensome honor. The other is available, if asked. Where to find him, and whatever else is involved, is known by this messenger of yours. In conclusion, say this to the Pope: if he has this man [Nelli], he will get me and whatever he was seeking from me, and something besides. We have one homeland, one name, one spirit, one talent, one style, but his life is more renowned and he is distinguished by the priesthood. Farewell, O you who are a glory to the Church and to me.

[1361–62].

Sen. I, 5.

To Giovanni da Certaldo [Boccaccio],* on the prophecies of the dying.

Your letter, dear brother, filled me with great alarm; as I read on, tremendous surprise vied with enormous sadness. Yet, by the time I finished reading, both had vanished. For completely ignorant of the events, with only your words to look at, how else could I read the account of your tears and approaching death, except with tearful eyes? When I finally focused and concentrated my inner vision on the matter at hand, my state of mind immediately changed, banishing astonishment and sadness.

First of all, I shall pass over your very modest and respectful statement at the beginning of your letter that you dare not disapprove of the plan of your famous preceptor, as your excessive humility calls me, to carry off the Muses and, as you say, all of Helicon (of which, as you know, I had been a poor, lowly dweller, and from which now, driven by foreign interests, I have almost become an exile), and to emigrate to Germany and most remote Sarmatia (to use your word), as though damning the Italians and judging them unworthy of the fruits of my labors. You rebuked me, I confess, much more effectively than had you poured out the full stream of your eloquence in satire. I do congratulate you for the spirit and zeal that cause you, "fearful when all is safe," in Maro's words [Aen. 4.298], to overflow with fear rather than fall short of love. But, dear friend, since I do not want any of my plans hidden from you, I am revealing the whole secret of my aggrieved spirit: just as I cannot have enough of the sight of Italy, at the same time, as I recently wrote to our Simonides [Francesco Nelli], I am, by heaven, so disgusted with Italian politics, and often have had a mind to betake myself not even to Germany but to some hidden corner of the world. There, far from this rumbling and the whirlwinds of envy, to which not so much my destiny (in my opinion it perhaps deserves contempt but certainly not envy) as my renown, gained far and wide, has exposed me, there, well hidden, I might live well if it

---

* A close friend of P.; they first met in 1350, the year of the Jubilee, when he hosted P. in Florence. He became P.'s chief correspondent in matters dealing with literature, philosophy, and culture. Of the thirty-three letters P. addressed to him, eighteen are in the *Seniles.*

be granted, and die well. And I would have done so had fortune not blocked the path where my inclination was pushing me. But why was I heading north? What you have heard was not the reason. Surely I do not seek tranquillity in that barbarous nation or under those inclement skies and in that uninviting land, but I do it out of a respectful, humble deference; for were I not to pay a short visit to our Caesar [Charles IV] who has repeatedly invited me with such insistence, it would seem not only pride but a kind of rebelliousness or sacrilege. In Valerius you have read that "our forefathers considered capable of any crime anyone who did not know how to honor princes" [*Fact. et Dict. Mem. Lib.* 8.5.6]. Lay aside your fear and your complaints. Here, too, I was not sorry to find the road blocked by war. Strange to say, where I was willingly going, even more willingly I do not go. My willingness to go should suffice to prove my loyalty and to satisfy the prince's desire; fortune will be blamed for the rest.

Bypassing all this, I come to what I said shook me so forcefully upon first reading your letter. You write that a Pietro [Petroni] of Siena, renowned for his manifest piety and even more for his miracles, who recently passed away, made many predictions about many people, and among these some about both of us; and you go on to say that this was reported to you by the person to whom he had entrusted it, and you asked him more precisely how the holy man knew us, though we did not know him; whereupon the messenger replied that, as he was given to understand, Pietro's intention was to do a good deed. Seeing that he could not carry it out, I imagine because he was forewarned of his own death, Pietro beseeched God with fervent prayer, certain to reach heaven, to designate substitutes fit for the undertaking; to them the Divinity would vouchsafe the completion, denied to him, of the task which had been begun or projected. And while, with that intimacy existing between God and the soul of the just man, he understood that he had been heard, to leave no doubt, Christ Himself appeared to him, upon whose face he saw all "that is, was, and is soon to come," not as Proteus in Maro [*G.* 4.393], but more fully and much more perfectly and clearly. For what, I ask, would he not see who sees Him by whom all things are done?

It is a great thing, I admit, to have seen Him with mortal eyes—if it is true. For it is an ancient custom to draw the veil of religion and sanctimony over lies and invented stories in general so that belief in divinity covers human trickery, about which I say nothing more for the present. When the messenger of the deceased comes to see me, the one who, you say, came first to you because you happened to be closer, next went on to Naples after delivering his message, then by sea to Gaul and Britain, and eventually will visit me to deliver in turn my full share of the message, then I shall finally see how much credence he will win from me. The messenger's age, face, eyes, manners, dress, gestures, gait, and way of sitting, even his voice, his delivery, and especially the upshot and thrust of his words will all figure in my judgment. Now here is what I gather from what was said to you: as the holy man [Pietro] departed this life, he had a vision of us two and some others, and entrusted some confidential information for all of us to this executor of his last will whom you believe conscientious and loyal. Unless I am mistaken, this is the gist of the story.

Whatever others may have heard from this man is in doubt, but these two things regarding yourself you heard (for you prefer to withhold the rest): the first is that the end of your life is at hand and that you have a few years to live; and the second and final pronouncement was that you are forbidden to cultivate poetry, whence all your consternation and grief which became mine in reading your letter. But I put them aside after some pondering, and so will you if you listen to me, or if you heed yourself and your inborn reason, realizing that you have been grieving over what ought rather to be cause for rejoicing. I am not belittling the import of the prophecy, for whatever is said by Christ is true. It is impossible for truth to lie. But the question is whether Christ is the author of this or whether someone else, as we have often seen, assumed the name of Christ to lend support to a fiction. Suppose, however, that this happened to people ignorant of His name. If pagan poets and philosophers are to be believed, both Greek literature and our own say that the dying often make many prophecies. See how Homer's Hector prophesies death to Achilles, Virgil's Orodes to Mezentius, Cicero's Theramenes to Critias, and Calanus to Alexander; and to mention something more like the cases worrying you, in Posidonius, the most famous philosopher of his time, a certain Rhodian names six of his contemporaries who will die shortly after him, and furthermore adds the order of their deaths. This is not the place to discuss either the truth or the cause of these things. But even assuming that this and things like it that are reported by others, and finally the pronouncements by this alarmist of yours are true, what is there to disturb you so? We make light of the ordinary and the well known; the unexpected shakes and upsets us. I ask, did you not know without him telling you that what remains of your life is brief, something that even a newborn infant, if he could reason, would know?

The life of all mortals is short, and the life of old people shortest; although often contrary to men's expectations and hopes (as we daily complain and lament) death reverses the order of birth in that those who came here last leave life first. Indeed the life we live here is only smoke, a shadow, a dream, an illusion, in short, nothing but a threshing floor for grief and toil. Its one good is that it leads to another life; otherwise life would be not only contemptible but hateful and wretched, and then it could be said with good reason that "it is best by far not to be born, and next to die as soon as possible" [Cicero, *Tusc.* 1.48]. And lest this brief thought of a pagan be suspect, the wisest of the Hebrews agrees with him. Indeed, as even Ambrose, in his grief over his brother's passing, methodically showed, and as it is proved by analyzing the chronology, Solomon does not follow the philosophers; they follow him. I shall copy the thought for you from Ambrose rather than from Solomon in order to have a double authority for the one saying. This then is what he says. "It is far preferable not to be born, in the opinion of holy Solomon. Those too who viewed themselves as excelling in philosophy followed him, for before them but after our [biblical] writers, in Ecclesiastes he said: 'And I praised all the dead who have already passed on, more than the living, whoever lives to this day, and, far beyond these two, whoever is yet unborn and does not see the evil being done under the sun.' Not much later he says, 'Who has said this, if not he who sought and gained wisdom?' " After interjecting a few comments about Solomon's wisdom, Ambrose says, "Thus, how could mortal things be hidden from the one to whom celestial things were not hidden, and how can he err or lie about a condition of his nature, which he has felt in himself? Yet not only he felt this, even if he was the only one to express it; he had read that holy Job had said, 'May that day perish on which I was born.' He knew that birth is the beginning of all ills, and therefore wished the day on which he was born to perish in order to remove the source of his troubles." Adding then the testimony of David and Jeremiah, Ambrose concludes as follows: "If, then, saintly men flee from life (whose life is reckoned useless to them although useful to us), what ought we to do who cannot be of use to others and feel this life to be like deadly money lent in usury, weighing us down with a mounting accumulation of interest in our daily traffic of sins" [*De excessu fratris sui* 2.32–34]. If Ambrose said these words, if such men before him said them, what shall I say, whose wretched life is not only heavy and weighed down with sins but consists altogether of nothing but temptation and sin?

But although much is being said here by others and may even be said by us whom experience with evil men has taught a great deal, nevertheless this is more than enough for you. For I need not teach you but only rouse you to remember how holy men and you yourself felt before astonishment—you recall—wrenched your memory from you. Still I shall dwell a little on the subject that has brought us to this point in our discussion. Although, as I have said, these points have been so debated and upheld by men of great stature as to overwhelm me not only with their arguments but with their authority as well, it will perhaps not be out of place to hear how others have felt about these very things. There are two positions: one is that this thing of ours, which is called life, is death. The youthful Cicero wrote this in the sixth book of his *Republic*. In his old age, he repeated it on the first morning of his *Tusculan Questions*. The other idea he also placed in the first book of the *Tusculans*—that it is best by far for a man not to be born, next best to die as soon as possible. Perhaps Cicero stated both ideas elsewhere, as many others did. Indeed although the first idea seems not just true but eminently true because of the innumerable evils of life, nevertheless to call life simply death is clever, I believe, rather than completely true or well balanced.

What then? I like Gregory's moderation in one of his weekday sermons. He says that temporal life, compared to eternal life, should be called death rather than life. I think this is more tenable and sound. Although the greatest authors, as you see, have treated the second idea (in fact both of them), it still seems not irrelevant to cite a book of the *Institutions*—I do not remember which one—by the learned and eloquent Lactantius Firmianus refuting human impatience. He says, "What, then, shall we say, if not that they err who either seek death as if it were a good or flee life as if an evil, and that they are most unfair who do not balance fewer evils against more goods? For when they have spent their entire life in far-fetched and varied pleasures, they wish to die if any bitter experience happens to overtake them. What is more, they behave as though it would never be well for them if ever any ill befalls them. Thus, they damn all of life, and think it full of nothing but ills, whence was born the absurd opinion that what we consider life is death and what we fear as death is life. The first good, then, is not to be born; the second is to die early. In order to give this view greater authority it is attributed to Silenus. In his book *On Consolation*, Cicero says 'Not to be born and not to crash against the reefs of life is by far the best; if you are born, however, the next best

thing is to escape, as from fortune's raging fire, as soon as you can.'
That he believed in this empty saying is evident in his adding something of his own to embellish it. How can he think, I ask, that it is best not to be born when there would be no one at all to feel this? For feeling makes it possible for something to be good or evil. Furthermore, why should he think that all of life is nothing more than reefs and fire, as though it were in our power not to be born, as though fortune, not God, granted us life, or as though life's course seemed to bear some resemblance to a fire" [*Inst.* 3.19]. These are the words of Lactantius.

But see, I have knowingly and willingly woven together contrasting authors and opinions before your eyes so that you would not think me bound to anyone's opinion. You, too, will choose as you see fit, and the truth will stand in its proper place. To return to the subject, I do wish to say this one thing: regardless of which of the many things we have said is true, still while we are not to love this life too much, we must bear it to the very end, and throughout this life aspire to the other, as though it were a very rough road to our longed-for fatherland. In any event, we cannot now be unborn.

But if life is two-faced, dangerous, evil (and I believe no one living doubts this, unless, blinded by vain pleasures, he has lost true awareness and judgment of himself), it follows that the end of an evil thing is good and desirable; and if life is to be lamented, which I would not deny if it is considered in itself, what ought to be lamented is not that it ends but that it began. We have learned that some peoples are accustomed to doing this: they have—I can properly say—a natural philosophy, weeping at their children's birth and rejoicing at their death, which is to be feared not because of the brief joy of living as much as the dread of eternal punishment. This may be postponed, but it cannot be avoided except with the aid of virtue and mercy; indeed it cannot even be postponed. It is not death, then, that is to be feared since it is feared in vain; it is life that must be reformed. This alone will enable us not to be afraid of death, and in the meantime we must acquire a certain familiarity with death itself. Not only the horrifying word but the contemplation and image of the fact itself should be daily confronted so that when it comes we shall fearlessly accept it as something often meditated upon, and not shudder at it as something unknown. This is the teaching of Plato and of the finest philosophers after him. They define philosophy itself and the entire life of the wise as a rehearsal for death. Paul the Apostle felt this too when he says that he died each day [1 Cor. 15:31]. No one can naturally die more than once. Frequent meditation, not nature, will allow us to die more often and to relieve through practice something the multitude considers hardest. How the philosophers did this is for them to explain. Now much more clearly than before, our meditation—that is, Christian meditation—is through Christ and Christ's life-giving death and victory over death. I cannot leave out something that comes to mind on this topic: Ambrose's advice in the same book on his brother's death. You will not be surprised at my using this author since for almost ten years I was a Milanese and his guest for fully five of them. He says: "What is Christ, if not the death of the body and the life of the spirit? So let us die together with Him that we may live with Him. Indeed let our practice and our eagerness for death be with us daily so that, through what we call separation, our soul may learn to retreat from bodily desires; and, as though nestled on high where earthly lusts cannot reach and catch hold of it, it may take on the image of death in order not to incur the pain of death" [De excessu 2.40].

I pass over other points, and if the ones here are more than you would have liked, forgive me. For they are meant to draw you back to the point from which sadness had misled you; then you will neither cherish life greatly nor hate or fear its end, nor at your advanced age be dumbfounded that death is near since it was never far away from childhood or infancy, even if it was imagined as very far. Rather you should marvel that what I doubt ever happened throughout the centuries to anyone else but King Hezekiah has happened to you, so that through your prophet's pronouncement you are assured that several years of life still remain for you now. For they cannot be so few that there are not at least two! Thus, whereas no mortal can be certain of a single day or even an entire hour, you have a guarantee of years, unless perhaps we are to believe the man when he declares that death is near, but not when he predicts the length of your life. The nuisance in all this rubbish is that fear and certain grief arise from the evil predictions, empty joy and uncertain hope from the good ones.

Whatever happens, we ought to recall those verses of Virgil:

Each one has his fixed day; the time of life
Is brief for all and cannot be brought back.
But to extend one's fame through deeds—that is
The task of virtue. [Aen. 10. 467–69]

Through deeds, I say, that seek not the faint sound of fame but virtue itself, which necessarily projects the shadow of true glory. I would call this salutary advice, I would call it the only advice in this perplexing world; yet knowing that it was a poet's, I will spare your ears that were barred from any such consideration. This has astonished me much more than the first prophecy. I could accept this with an untroubled spirit if it were said to an old man, as they say, first learning the alphabet: "You have grown old, death is now near, concentrate on the things of the soul. The world of letters is untimely and bitter for old men if it is set before them as something new and unfamiliar. But nothing is sweeter if they have grown old in it. Give up this task then; it is too late. Renounce the Muses of Helicon and the Castalian fount. Many things became the boy that are unbecoming to an old man. In vain do you exert yourself; your intellect is numb, your memory slipping, your eyes blurred, and all your bodily senses are dull and too feeble now for a new labor. Reflect upon your strength and measure what you are getting into, lest death interrupt your useless efforts. Do rather what is always beneficial and appropriate at any age but necessary at the end." All this, and the like, might of course be gravely and eloquently said to an old man about to begin, but I do not know why it is said to an old man who is learned and reasonable. "Here you are close to death, so leave your worldly cares, banish the remnants of pleasure, flee evil habits, reform your mind and your ways into something new and pleasing to God, and now pull out by the roots those reborn vices which until recently you used to prune. Among the first is the pursuit of avarice (I wonder why it is linked and peculiar to old people). Concentrate only on this and meditate on it so as to reach your last day prepared and unworried." Excellent, I say, and sensible. "Leave literature, whether poetry or whatever, in which you are no longer a recruit but a seasoned veteran, in which you know what should be kept and what rejected, and finally in which there is no longer toil but delight in life and pent-up joy" [Sen., *Ep.* 36.4]. I see nothing in this but taking away solace and comfort from your old age.

What if something like that had been said to Lactantius? What if it had been said to Augustine, and he believed it? I shall say what is on my mind. Lactantius would not have so forcefully stripped away the foundations of pagan superstitions, nor Augustine so skillfully built the walls of the City of God. It would have been up to someone like Jovinian to answer Julian and other ranters of equal impiety. Furthermore, what if it had been said to Jerome, though he does recall that it was said, and wants us to believe that it was also said to Vigilans? And what if he had always kept away from poetic and philosophical and oratorical and historical literature? Never would he have crushed with such persuasive ease the calumnies of Jovinian and the other heretics. Never would he have taught Nepotian so well while he lived, nor lamented his passing. Finally, never would he have imbued his letters and books with such oratorical light.

Just as truth is the source from which anything true must be sought, where else, I ask, must a fine artistic way of speaking be sought if not from eloquence, that province of poets and orators, as Jerome himself would never have denied. This is too well known to need proof. I am hastening over the details. But, in short, I fail to understand why it should be forbidden to use soberly, even in old age, studies absorbed since childhood. I do not mean for the old man to be steeped in them, for nothing is well done that is not done at its proper time. I am speaking of the one who knows how these studies can contribute to general knowledge, character building, eloquence, and, finally, the defense of our religion, which, as you see, was done especially by those mentioned. He knows too what is due Jove the adulterer, Mercury the pander, Mars the murderer, Hercules the robber, and finally—to bring in the more innocent ones—Aesculapius the physician, his father Apollo the lyre player, Vulcan the smith, besides Minerva the weaver, and, in contrast, what is due Mary the Virgin Mother and her Son our Redeemer, true God and true man. If we thus shun the poets and others who had never heard Christ's name (and therefore never said it), how much more dangerous must it seem to read the books of heretics who name Christ and at the same time fight against Him. Yet defenders of the true faith do this with the greatest zeal. Believe me, much that is due to laziness and sloth is attributed to seriousness and counsel. Often men despise what they despair of getting. It is characteristic of ignorance to condemn whatever it could not learn and to wish that no one should reach what it has failed to reach. Hence the twisted judgments on the unknown, where the judges' blindness is as evident as their envy. We must not be scared away from literature either by the exhortation to virtue or by the pretext of approaching death. If literature is harbored in a good soul, it arouses a love of virtue and either removes or lessens the fear of death; if abandoned, it will suggest a suspicion of diffidence, which used to be the accusation against wisdom. Literature does not impede, but rather helps a man of good character who masters it; it advances the journey of life, it does not delay it. What happens with foods—many that upset a nauseous, weak stomach nourish a healthy, hungry one—also applies to studies, especially if in both food and learning the power of discretion is present: many are salutary for the bright, healthy mind but deadly for the weak one.

If this were not true, the many who unwaveringly persist to the very end of life would not be so highly praised. Besides, Cato learned Latin literature when he was growing old, and Greek literature when really old. Varro, who was still reading and writing at a hundred, gave up his life before his love of studies. Livius Drusus, a victim of age and blindness, did not cease interpreting civil law, in which he was very useful to the Republic. Appius Claudius, who suffered the same hardships, persevered all the same. Among the Greeks, Homer, though suffering the same ills, persevered and demonstrated equal energy, although in another sphere. Socrates turned to music when he was already quite old. Chrysippus barely completed in extreme old age a brilliant work begun in mid-youth. Isocrates wrote a book of oratory and Sophocles one of tragedy, both very fine works, the one at ninety-three and the other at nearly a hundred. An overpowering love of study made the aged Carneades heedless of food and Archimedes heedless of life. The same love drove Cleanthes among the Greeks to struggle first against poverty and then against old age, and Plautus among our people against both at the same time. Love not of possessions, which motivates many, but of learning, drove Pythagoras, Democritus, Anaxagoras, and Plato over land and sea, oblivious of dangers and toil. Plato, though old yet still devoted to philosophy, on his final day—which was also his birthday—gave up his ghost while reading or, as others would have it, writing. Philemon surrendered his Pierian soul while mulling and bending over a book as his colleagues waited for him, although there is another ridiculous version of this. Solon, whom I have often had occasion to mention, was constantly learning something new as he grew old and neared the end, nor did death quench his noble desire for learning.

Besides these and countless other examples like them, did not all our forefathers whom we wish to emulate spend all their lives with literature, grow old with literature, meet their end with literature, so that their last day found some of them reading or writing? Nor has excelling in secular studies ever harmed anyone I have heard of, except Jerome alone whom I mentioned; whereas for many, it was a source of glory, particularly for him. I am aware that Gregory praised Benedict for abandoning out of a love of solitude and a stricter way of life those studies that he had begun. But he had turned away, not from poetry, but from all literature in general. Would his eulogist be praised had he then done the same? Not at all, I think. There is a difference between having learned and having to learn, just as there is between a boy giving up a hope and an old man giving up the real thing. The boy gives up a nuisance, the old man an ornament; the boy renounces the toil and uncertain effort of acquiring knowledge, the man the real fruit of labor and the delightful, precious treasures of literature gained through study.

What else can I say? I know of many who have attained the highest saintliness without literature; I know of no one excluded from it by literature. Although I hear that the Apostle Paul [Acts 26:24] was taunted with madness due to literature, everyone knows how justly . Rather, to speak frankly, I believe that the road to virtue through ignorance is level perhaps, but too easy; and while all good men have the same goal, many are the ways to it and great the variety among those headed in the same direction. One man walks more slowly, another faster; one unobtrusively, another more conspicuously; one takes a lower path, another a higher one. All have a blessed journey, but surely the higher, the more conspicuous it is, the more glorious; whence it follows that uncouthness, however devout, is not comparable to literate devotion. Nor can you give me an example of a saint from the unlettered mass whom I cannot match with a greater saint from the other group.

Although the subject tempts me, I shall detain you no longer today on this because I have often had to treat it. If you cling to your resolution to reject these studies we put aside so long ago, and all literature,* if you desire to get rid of the very instruments of literature by selling your books and are utterly determined to do so, I am grateful, by heaven, that you have offered them to me before anyone else since, as you say and I do not deny, I am so greedy for books; if I did deny it, my own writings would refute me. Although I seem to be buying what is already mine, I still do not wish such a great man's books scattered here and there or in profane hands, as so often happens. Therefore, just as we have been one in spirit though separated in body, so after we are gone, this paraphernalia of our studies should—if God seconds my vow—come intact and undiminished to some pious, devout place in perpetual memory of us. This I decided after the passing of him who I had hoped would take up my studies. I cannot, however, set a price on your books as you so graciously asked me to do since I do not know for certain the titles, the number, or the value. Do send me a list, with the

---

* The Latin *quantum in imis* is corrupt.

understanding that should you ever decide to spend with me what little time remains, as I have always wished and you have occasionally seemed to promise, you will find your own books together with these that I have collected, which are yours as well; then you will realize that you have lost nothing and gained quite a bit.

Finally, for my part, I deny what you say about being in debt to many, me among them, and I wonder at this superfluous, even silly, scruple of your conscience. I could object in Terence's words: "You are looking for a knot in a bullrush" [*An.* 942]. You owe me nothing but love. Even that you do not owe, for you have long since in good faith paid it in full, unless perhaps you always owe what you go on receiving. But what you constantly repay, you never owe.

As for your all too usual complaint of poverty, I have no wish to offer consolation or examples now of famous poor people; they are well known to you. What then? My reply is always the same, loud and consistent. I praise you for preferring liberty of spirit and peaceful poverty to the great wealth I sought for you, although late; I do not praise you for repulsing a friend who so often invites you. I cannot make you wealthy from here. If it were possible, I would speak to you not with words or pen, but with deeds. I have, however, the resources for one that would abundantly suffice for two with a single heart and home. You do me wrong if you disdain this; you do me more wrong if you mistrust me. Farewell.

Padua, May 28 [1362].

Sen. I, 6.

To Francesco Bruni,* against his friend's excessive loyalty, a sincere expression of his insignificance.

The tone of your letter, distinguished sir, is sweet and its taste sweeter, had it been written about someone else. Instead, along with the sweetness, it made me blush, ashamed, since you prefer me to those whom I wish I were worthy to admire. I would fear this to be mockery, were it not for your well-known virtues and sincerity. I would rather believe you mistaken than myself misled, since the former has the excuse of being full of kindness, the latter a slur incompatible with friendship.

Nevertheless, not to be verbose under this weight of undeserved praises, for fatigue is the friend of silence, I shall simply say this. You have the right to place whatever price you please on what you own, but, believe me, your estimate of me will scare off the bidders. You will reply, "What I praise is not for sale"; I agree. No one, however, will listen open-mindedly to you praising a small thing so highly. If you have regard for my shaky reputation and your own good name, say what is so, and less than that—if there is anything less than the least. I am ashamed to touch even superficially upon what love, in blinding you, made you say amply, profusely, unashamedly. You make me an orator, a historian, a philosopher, a poet, and lastly a theologian. This you would not have done without the persuasion of Love, whom it is very difficult not to believe; so perhaps you deserved forgiveness, had you not, after burdening me with brilliant titles, put me in the end above the greatest men with whom I do not even deserve to be compared.

So that you may realize, my friend, how far I am in my opinion and in reality from this judgment of yours, I am not any of all the things you attribute to me. What then am I? A scholar? Not even that, but a backwoodsman, a hermit in the habit of mumbling something dull amidst the lofty beeches, and—the height of arrogance and rashness!—handling a frail pen beneath a laurel sprout, not as fruitful in results as fervent in labor, more in love with letters

---

* A learned Florentine who, though late in striking up a friendship with P., became one of the principal correspondents in this collection. In 1363, with P.'s support, he was named Apostolic Secretary by Urban V, a position P. had turned down. He was used by P. as his main conduit to the Pope for his letters urging the return of the papacy to Rome.

than rich in them. I am indifferent to sects, greedy for the truth. Since the search for it is arduous, I, a lowly and feeble seeker without self-confidence, often embrace doubt itself in place of truth to avoid becoming entangled in error. Thus, slowly I have become a squatter in the academy, one of many, and the latest in the humble throng, granting myself nothing, affirming nothing, doubting all but what I consider a sacrilege to doubt. Here, then, is your Hippias who once dared to profess all things in philosophical circles; with you he professes nothing beyond the anxious search for truth, nothing beyond doubt and ignorance.

And now you introduce the illustrious Pandolfo's [Malatesta] testimony to support your judgment so different from his. You will realize the validity of such testimony by weighing not the man's worthiness and virtue, which are truly great, but his affection. To be sure, if you seek a true judgment, you must find an independent court and an independent mind. A mind controlled by love is not independent, and you should not believe one who loves any more than one who hates. One of them errs more honorably, but in judgment they are equal. Therefore, trust him completely in matters of government. Trust him about war, strategy, and especially the qualities of a leader—command, fortitude, foresight, sternness, clemency, perseverance, constancy, magnanimity, glory; regarding others' talents, trust him even more than a soldier does his commander. Only when his speech descends to my level, seek someone else to believe: already he has deceived many, many people on this subject, and, if you do not know it, I am quite undeservingly dear to him, to my astonishment. Yet a generous mind is fed by love, it gives love freely. Love is its food, its delight, its comfort.

I thought to control my pen, but, caught up and driven on one side by your praises and exhausted on the other by my own affairs, I cannot rest, but must insert in the letter a rather lengthy story that will make you share my amazement. Many years before that gentleman met me, but attracted just by reports of my fame, he hired a painter for a considerable fee, and sent him where I then resided, a journey of quite a few days, in order to bring him on a panel the longed-for face of an unknown man. Long after this had been done without my knowledge, the war that was then upsetting everything in Italy forced him to come to Milan, where I then lived. And although he was constantly distracted by various developments and dangers which you would say were too much for one person, he considered nothing more pressing, nothing more important than studying the face of the man whose image he had seen. I am omitting what cannot be briefly told: how often that great man and general of such great armies came to visit me, how eagerly he conversed on equal terms with one so far beneath him; the last time, after recovering from a grave illness caused by a summer spent under the burning sun, a winter in heavy snows, and the excessive toil and anxieties of war, he sought me out, leaning on his servants' shoulders and still unable to put weight on his feet. He had seen me daily at his bedside throughout his illness, but enjoyed more seeing me among my books, as he said, in my own place. The fleeting years will never erase from my memory nor will all of Lethe's eddies ever wash away that man's enormous kindness. Finally, at war's end, when he had won and was ready to return with much glory to his native land, he brought in another painter [Simone Martini], one of the very few in our age, because the first painting had not satisfied his wish and my appearance had changed over the years; indeed he would have brought in Zeuxis or Protogenes, Parrhasius or Apelles, had our century been endowed with them. But every age must be content with its talents. Therefore, he sent the one he could, truly a great artist as they go nowadays. When he came to me, disguising his purpose, he took the liberty of sitting down with me as I was reading, for he was an intimate friend; and as he stealthily did something or other with a pen, I recognized the friendly deceit and unwillingly allowed him to paint me openly. Notwithstanding all his artistic skill, he could not do it. That is the way it seemed to me and to others. If you ask why, I do not know, except that often things attempted more aggressively succeed through carelessness, and too much eagerness kills the result. Despite this, that great condottiere took the painting with him and treated it as his favorite solely because at least it bore my name.

So go and trust the praises of such an enthusiast! The remembrance of him and concern for you has forced me to write so much in this terrible place and time so that you may recognize his powerful love for me and realize that you too err no less if you believe him. Let the first pledge of my friendship be that I have freed your mind from a friend's false opinions. I have told you in good faith what I am and what I am not; believe me rather than another about myself. No one knows me more intimately, and if I love myself, still I love the truth, so well known to me in this regard that I am hardly more ashamed to speak against him than to agree even silently with what people say. Yet at times I keep silent, not agreeing at all but hating to argue and bored with words. In this case I could not keep silent because of the unbearable weight of the praises on the one hand, and on the other the rare splendor of his eloquence. Others perhaps thought that I was won over; though everyone were to acquit me, I would consider myself inexcusably guilty if I yielded in silence to such a fluent and artful eulogist. Therefore, on this subject alone, I have come into conflict with the man with whom I would like to agree and be of one mind in all else. I admit I am accustomed to praise from others, but not like this; that is why I have never had such a fight with my friends, never, to my knowledge, done anything like this because I have never undergone anything similar. From now on, love me as you do, but judge me more objectively.

Finally, whatever I am, however slow in intelligence or dull in judgment, or drab in expression, uncertain of almost everything and hesitant, I still am—I believe—quite constant in friendships, unless I am wrong to claim even this. I am not speaking of those perfect, very rare friendships requiring great virtue (very few such pairs throughout the ages, as you know, are recorded as meeting that standard), but of these others which I, being average, can maintain. Just as my spirit yields to no one in the act of loving, it yields to many in everything else; thus, whatever either your love imagines me to be or truth itself makes of me, know that I am your friend, and have no doubt that what I have promised you is firm. Your virtue deserves this, my nature requires it, the good sponsor of our friendship ordains it. Believe that this is said to you not by the Delphic oracle, but by a heavenly one. And so, farewell. Since you cannot remember the face you have not seen, at least remember my name.

[1362].

Sen. I, 7.

To the same person,* that the end of life is near and uncertain, that there is no flight from death, and that astrologers tell many lies.

I am grateful that you urge me to flee death. You would not be doing so unless you loved the opposite of death—my life. You thus love one whom you do not know, or, to speak more truthfully, whom you have not seen. And no wonder! If we were to love only what we have seen, no one would love God or his own soul, and, to go further, no one would love his brother, son, or friend whom, even when we think we see, we are seeing not them but their dwellings; this too I shall say more truthfully: we see their prisons. Indeed what we call bodies are chains, which would have made human misery eternal if they could not be unclasped and broken. For this reason those words of Plotinus, speaking of God and men, are rightly praised: "The merciful Father made mortal chains for them."

But I return to your love. Just as what you have in mind for me is in itself quite friendly and brotherly, so too, it is vain if you consider the nature of the thing. For there is no flight from death; or rather, it has very often happened that a flight from death is a flight to death. Thus there is nothing better, nothing safer when we are between the yearning for death and the fear of it, than neither to anticipate nor to postpone whatever it shall be that we are bidden from above. You recall that old man, harried by many ills but driven out of the citadel of patience, who said, when speaking with God, "You will call me and I shall answer you" [Job 13:22]. Let us too pay heed to our Summoner lest either our reluctance or precipitousness displease Him. For just as not responding to the Lord's call is arrogance, responding to Him when He is not calling is madness. It is equally vain to fear or to wish for death too much. The one is cowardice, the other impatience. The one is a futile fear, the other an empty wish, for it is useless to fear what cannot be avoided, useless to wish for what will soon come about. Let us be brave and calm of spirit. Nothing is less worthy of a man than fear, nothing less worthy of a wise man than anxiety.

From the day we were born, we have been surrounded by dan-

---

* See I, 6.

gers and troubles, labors and snares, all of which ought to have been foreseen earlier by any man. If they have not been, then we are really ignorant of what arena, what ring, what struggle we have entered, and indeed what world we have come into. The gatekeeper has deceived us unless He forewarned us at the threshold of all the sufferings awaiting us. He who does not know he is exposed to human misfortunes does not know he is a man, and he who does not contemplate death and expect it at every hour and in all places, forgets his mortal nature. This is our lot, which we can weep over and lament as learned men did throughout entire books, as I myself in the past have done in lengthy letters. Yet tears and laments accomplish nothing; the laws of nature are like steel. God spoke once,

> When we were born, our Maker told us once
> For all, whatever He would let us know, [Luc. 9.575-6]

and whatever He said is all fixed forever. In the the words of another poet:

> Heavy and immutable the weight
> Of holy words; the fates follow that voice.
> [Stat., *Theb.* 1.212-13]

And indeed, if the word *fate* derives from *fari* [to say] which I know to be the opinion not only of this poet [Statius] but also of the holy doctors, particularly Augustine, then our fate, if we are allowed to use that word, lies not in the movements of the stars but in the words and providence of God. Therefore, whether we are confident or timid, we will undergo what nature, what God's inflexible edict has ordained; no one doubts that we must die. When, where, and how remains much in doubt, just as with virtually everything in the future. Nor is there only doubt, but also ignorance and the deepest, thickest darkness which our vision will not penetrate.

What need is there of a soothsayer? Why does the astrologer torment himself? What does vain curiosity for a horoscope labor over? Although I am fully aware that these fellows can be annoyed by words but not reformed, without hope of success I often attack them thus: Stop it, O madmen, let the stars follow their orbits. For either the stars have no power over us or they reveal nothing about us, or we understand nothing of this. Your lies, if nothing else, certainly reveal to the world that at least one of these possibilities is true. Choose whichever you like! To choose anything else is not allowed, to argue about nothing is foolish, to argue about inaccessible things is vain. Why then do you overwhelm us with the weight of your lies? We are weary of listening, weary of waiting since nothing comes of all that you murmur as if dozing and drunk, except perhaps some rare, fortuitous truth such as slips sometimes even from the mouths of those who want to lie. For no one can say everything false, no matter how much he wants to; often through a liar's unwilling lips truth comes forth from his breast. And so you boast of the one instance of truth slipping out among a thousand lies, whereas honest spirits blush over a single lie among a thousand truths. Tell us one thing for certain before it happens; and so that it may not seem accidental, add another to that first one. Why do you feign futile prophecies after the fact or call chance truth? Why do you weary heaven and earth and mankind in vain? Why subject the glistening stars to your foolish laws? Why wish to make us, who were born free, slaves to the senseless stars? O ridiculous rashness and unheard-of impudence, to want nothing whatsoever from those to whom you sell the human race and yet to want, to demand, to extort a price from the foolish and wretched men who are being sold! Strange transactions, a new kind of trade, with people who are ignorant of the present and the past but wish to know only the future, which alone cannot be known! Yours is a profitable and easy game. The more educated laugh at your tricks. What has Mars or Venus, Jupiter or Saturn to do with you? Why do you bring back those names long since renounced, and why do you so boldly delude us either with unholy talk or shipboard coarseness? The names of those whose souls were in Tartarus have been transferred to the heavens by those about to follow them to hell. Shall we, who have been promised heaven, place hope in these names, unless perhaps Maro's words are more believable: "Then a sailor gave the stars their names and numbers" [G. 1.137]? Certainly not the names He long before coined—"He who counts the multitude of the stars and names them all" [Ps. 147:4]! Happy indeed is anyone privileged to know such things! For me, that man would really be a true, famous astrologer, and not Ptolemy or Archimedes or Julius Firmicus, but one much loftier and more dependable.

Therefore, this mortal invention of star names, a punishment for impiety, an aid to sailors, cannot be a help in our lives, nor ought it to be a punishment. Why do you enchanters labor in vain? Do as you please with the multitude, but we are alert to your tricks, we are prepared and armed against them. You want us to join your ranks so as to be with you among those whom the Lord threatens through Zephaniah. "On their rooftops they worship the heavenly host" [Zeph. 1:5], which is displayed up there—namely, the sun, the moon, and the rest. Those people rise up against the knowledge of God, ascribing whatever happens in the world to the stars' rising and setting; they swear by the Lord and by Molech; they wish to please two masters, God and the world, which cannot be done under any circumstances because of discord between the masters. Truly we worship under the roof of our closed and pious breast, not the host of heaven but the almighty King of heaven Himself, who is God the Father and His only son, Jesus Christ, the crucified, and the Holy Spirit, the Paraclete proceeding from the Father and the Son; this one and triune God we cherish and trust; in Him we do believe, by Him and no one else we swear. Why do you involve us in foreign superstition? We obey Him who created us and rules over His creatures, who at the same time created the heavens and the stars and rules over them; nor does He need the stars' aid in creating and ruling us any more than He needs ours in creating and ruling the stars. If there were any room in us for another power, we would cherish it with due reverence, but as it is, we know we owe nothing to anyone else. If there is any good in us, it is from Him. On the other hand, any evil in us comes from no one but ourselves; otherwise it would not be punishable since it would originate elsewhere.

Do not confuse, then, the Creator and the creatures! Finally, if you still choose error, leave open the way to truth and to life for those aspiring to Him who is the Way, the Truth, and the Life. O blind stargazers, mercenary slaves of the stars, and—what is still more amazing—brokers and forgers who ensnare souls, what are you after? What are you trying to do? Why do you engage as our guides either unstable fiery globes or dead sinners? One greater than Jupiter, One you either do not know, or do not believe in or love, moves and controls the heavens, governing as creator His own world. To Him and not to Jupiter is sung, "In your hands is my destiny." You can resolve to forget those shining lights which, if valued in themselves, caress the eyes and blind the soul, and to raise your thoughts to Him about whom it is written, "In Your light shall we see light" [Ps. 36:10], and to begin at last to believe that, while your Jupiter can do nothing, our Christ can do everything; the sun and moon shine for the eyes but their Creator shines for the mind. Why do you turn that incorporeal, divine light back upon bodies, however lustrous? You are dazed, perhaps, by these lights that adorn the heavens and the days and nights, and are useful if only the world knew how to use them wholesomely. But the upright soul that gazes on high is charmed by an inner light; when we turn to it, we feel no need for wizards and these false prophets who empty gold from the coffers of the credulous, and fill their ears with nonsense and their minds with error and horror, and upset the present condition of life with promises of the future.

Dear friend, I have often said all this and the like against these triflers, so hateful not only to me but to Christ and to His believers; and now, to clear up your puzzlement, I have been speaking as though talking to them and almost oblivious of you, because these days I have been besieged and vexed contrary to my expectation by the very people from whom I hoped this noble city would be free. These are certainly a few of the many things that I wished to say, more than this time would call for or this narrow space can hold, except that the anger I felt in speaking about them for the past two days inflamed me anew as I wrote.

I return to the subject. If, then, there is anyone disturbed by these things, who, uneasy about the future, has too little faith in the King of the ages to whom he owes everything, let him know that he is taking a pathless journey at night without light, and listen to that divine poem of Flaccus:

> God purposely wraps up in murky night
> The outcome of the future, and he laughs
> At mortals shuddering more than they ought.
>
> [*Carm.* 3.29.29–32]

Let us be confident, O worried mortals, and not fret lest He laugh at us and our fretting, and what matters most, lest He, whose love is the one sure happiness, hate us. Let us be still and control our anxieties, let us stifle our complaints and quietly await the bidding of the most provident and clement Lord; in fact, let us rather hasten to meet Him, unencumbered and eager. Death does not come to us, we go to her; not by chance, says Maro, "each one has his fixed day" [*Aen.* 10.467]. Oh, why does he say "his fixed day"? It is we who are running, and while we try to flee and to halt, we fly toward it, and when we arrive, that day will no longer be standing still for us, but will vanish with all the others, as if it had gotten what it was waiting for.

Someone perhaps views this differently because of what is written in a psalm about the sinner, "The Lord will laugh at him since He foresees that his day is coming" [Ps. 37:13]. And in another place,

"The day of perdition is at hand, and the times are hastening to arrive" [Deut. 32:35]. Surely it is futile to argue about the words when there is agreement about the substance. Let each man choose the way of speaking he likes, provided he remembers that the day is near; if it is set, we must go to it with courage, and, if it is approaching and hastening toward us, we must await it with equanimity. To face either prospect fearlessly, however, does not suffice. It behooves us to face it joyfully, and this advice applies to me especially, whom nothing, or little, delights any longer; with nearly everyone sent on ahead who used to make life happy for me, I now hate the solitude I have so often praised, and this lingering on earth, which is futile and perhaps very brief. For what we speak of may perhaps be close by. Why do we place in doubt something that is most certain? I meant to say "near" with the Psalmist, for who will doubt that it is close? Can what is never distant from those who enter upon this journey be further from those who have been moving forward? And can what was close in the morning be far in the evening for those who have hastened toward it without halting? It could happen, nor will it be strange or unusual if it does, that what we drag out in time with flickering hope is going to happen this very day. And who knows whether what we suspect of being the worst in human existence we will find to be the best? So that what we feared so much, we will be ashamed not only to have feared, but even not to have hoped for, when the day breaks to dispel the mists of our errors, and we go forth into that light from which we are now kept by this dark prison.

But, as you yourself say, much has been said about this subject by me, yet much more can be said by others which neither the time nor the place allows; I have rambled enough today. There is one thing I would like you to know so that you will cease worrying. I did do what you warn me about, though for a different reason, and have long since left Padua where the plague was raging, and come to Venice, not to flee death but to seek some peace, if there is any on earth. Farewell.

[Venice, 1362–63].

Sen. II, 1.

To Giovanni da Certaldo [Boccaccio],* a defense against criticisms of his style.

I ought either to have said nothing or gone into hiding, or better still, not to have been born so as to avoid these barking Scyllas. To come out in the open is not a game. Strong dogs rage with their teeth, weak ones with their bark; there is danger from the former, annoyance from the latter. My intention was to evade both by silence and concealment. The surge of events has carried me where I did not wish to go. Now whenever I am seen in public, those people whose acquaintance is bad for anyone's reputation point me out. I am not Scipio, whom the dogs never barked at as he climbed the Capitoline at night; I remember seeing this written about him, although some people believe this can be done by drugs or spells. Wherever I walk in broad daylight, a vulgar pack of dogs howls around me. Wherever I turn, every alley teems with them. I would not be as afraid of the ones with a pedigree, for these are few and far between, and rarely attack unless their masters sic them on. The others, however, are innumerable, restless, hoarse; they endlessly pester those whom they cannot bite. As Annaeus elegantly puts it, after enduring the same sort of thing: "Like puny dogs you bark at the approach of people you do not know" [Ep. 19.2]. And truly they are puny and I am unknown to them, even though not unseen. They are dogs, used to barking or biting out of fear. There is no reason for such fear here. For I do not have Theon's teeth [Hor., Ep. 1.18.82], and, to keep from being bitten, they have continued with amazing skill to remain ever silent and ever hidden. They do not realize how impudent and arrogant it is to want to judge others when they do not want others to judge them. Whoever throttles his voice in obstinate silence lets no one in to judge his words.

This is a new breed, or rather an ancient one, a nuisance not only to me, the least of men, but to the foremost and greatest men, and to Jerome above all, who says in a book to his friends about these types: "Do not express yourselves in public, do not offer food to the finicky and the snubs of those who know only how to judge others and not how to do anything themselves, although this in itself suffices to judge them, in my opinion. What they engage in to cover

* See I, 5.

their ignorance becomes proof of it; and what they use the most to conceal them betrays them because, in silently avoiding the judgment of men, they stand condemned by the silent judgment of learned men" [*Praef. in Ezram, Patr. lat.* 28. col. 1472]. If that great man feared them and gave warning to avoid them, what would you think that I or others should do? Really not so much from fear, but out of hatred and contempt for them so as not to furnish such wanton tongues the material and tools with which to dig, I often warned myself and my friends—myself not to write anything new, and them not to make public anything that I happened to have already written. I have no reason to complain about others—I did not follow my own warning; if I were so inspired to write, I should have written and erased it, and since it was on my mind, I would have derived the pleasure from composing, yet avoided envy's bite and bark. Perhaps I would have done so, except that the delight in writing made me quick to write, but compassion made me slow to erase. I felt sorry for the harmless novelties, and too it is hard to kill the one you love; I seemed about to do violence with my own hands to my offspring—that is, the offspring of my mind. And yet I did to my writings as Abraham did to his son in his zeal for God; speaking as a poet rather than as a Catholic, I viewed it as a pleasing sacrifice to Phoebus and Pallas, thinking at the same time that this would deprive my detractors' impudence and wantonness of much material. Had I been able either to write nothing or to burn what I had written, I would have given them perpetual hoarseness and myself peace. But I could not. Again, had I been able to hide what survived rigorous pruning, I would at any rate have had peace as long as I lived, but I was incapable of this as well, since I have learned to hide nothing from my friends and to deny them nothing—the prime root of my problem.

Listen to one of many examples. Many years ago, after the death of our great king [Robert], the Roman Pontiff [Clement VI] sent me to Naples when my dear Barbato da Sulmona was there—a welcome and delightful antidote to the tedium of waiting—a man most interested in everything literary, and so exceedingly taken with my writings as to seek in them no seriousness of subject, no beauty of words, in short, nothing but whether they are mine. But even more, he can recognize their very odor from a distance; and since I did not spend a day apart from him throughout that period, it chanced that he liked some verses in my *Africa*, which, though new at the time, was already better known and more famous than I wished, but later waned under the weight of many grave preoccupations. Afraid to ask me for them outright—for no one was more shy, no one more respectful—he sent a friend, who was also one of my best friends, to request them with a humble entreaty, as if they were a very special gift. Contrary to my usual way, I refused, and reproved the untimely request frankly but kindly. He blushed and for a while remained silent, then begged me to forgive his overwhelming love. Nor did he cease pressing me day after day with additional intercessors, with ingenuous, modest pestering, since his sensitive face and shy, deep blush could not bear the harshness of my refusals. Thus, there were always substitutes in his stead, since it is more honorable for anyone to be demanding on behalf of someone other than himself.

I think you can already guess the outcome. I refused as long as I could without damaging our friendship. Because either way I would be doing something amiss, I was eventually defeated, for I never fight with friends without surrendering; I gave in and handed over to that friend, to whom in the end I could deny nothing, thirty-four verses, unless I am mistaken, still lacking polish and the time needed for revision, on condition that they should not fall into anyone else's hands. Since intense longing is ever ready to make promises, yet not as firm in remembering them, he did not reject any condition so long as he got his wish; he gave me his word, which I believe he broke that very same day. Thus, from that time I have scarcely stepped inside any educated man's library without meeting those verses on the threshold, like the epigram on Apollo's tripod confronting those entering the temple; and scribal errors have been added to their original roughness. Although this complaint is not so much mine as common to all writers, in this instance that friend of mine, while seeking to praise me and to make me as illustrious to others as I am to him, scattered the verses around and exposed them to many criticisms—pardonably, I admit, because the impulse of honest love drove him to it. Yet I am not surprised; I recognize their voices, I understand their accents, they are our fellow citizens, very keen and quick to attack other things but otherwise quite slow; so as not to say anything more sarcastic about them, I love everything about them except their behavior.

This is a good place to digress. I have heard that Frederick, who lived very near to our time, the last of this name to rule the Roman Empire, a wise prince of German origin but Italian in spirit, who learned fully the customs and talents of both peoples, the first through birth and the second through long residence, used to say that these two are the outstanding nations of the entire world, yet differ diametrically from each other; both ought to be equally rewarded for their merits but not equally punished, for both are spurred toward virtue by reward, but Italians improve when pardoned and recognize their fault and their ruler's clemency. But Germans are puffed up by impunity, and ascribe mercy to fear; the more you pardon them, the more daring they become. Thus, you can often safely spare Italians, indeed not only safely but advantageously, whereas for Germans even postponing a deserved punishment is a matter of grave peril—in short, Italians must be treated with honor but Germans with kindness. Italians enjoy honors, Germans affection and comradeship; with these devices both peoples are drawn toward friendship and loyalty. One must avoid intimacy with Italians because they are curious about things and, when it comes to other people's vices, too eager to criticize everything, not only what is true but what they have imagined, however falsely. Therefore, they ridicule whatever is done differently from how they think it should be done, for each is so self-confident as to believe himself a fitting critic of everyone else. On the other hand, however, one can indulge in social intimacy with Germans since they never find any fault in their friends; they seek nothing in friendship but to be loved, and believe that there is no greater proof of love than intimacy.

I wanted to tell you all this so that you might see how that great man felt about our intimacies and our passion for passing judgment. I am not disputing how true this opinion is, but I do think that what I am about to say is true: nothing truer, nothing graver could be said if he had said it not about Italians but only about our fellow citizens who do not go in for intimacies or friendships but only find fault. This is not gentle and kindly criticism but implacable and bitter, for there is not one of them who is not more indulgent than Sardanapalus in daily life, yet more severe in judging than Fabricius or Cato. To skip over their criticisms of other things that concern me less, they criticize literature as though nothing can be properly expressed if it does not fill their big, gaping ears, or comfort them when ruffled, soothe them when hostile, refresh them when weary, stroke them when tender, and attract them when busy; this would be a difficult task even for Cicero or Maro, or, as I rather think, impossible for the two together. I suppose they have not attentively read what that author said (I do not like much of his, but this I like very much): "He who shows off with someone else's book is a rascal" [Mart., Pref. *Epigr.* 1]. How much more of a rascal, however, is he who is most clever and fussy, to the point of disdain and loathing, when dealing with others' works, yet with his own is not

only stupid but mute, silent, and lifeless. I congratulate these genius-
es of ours as much as I can.

Those few, innocent little verses of mine traveled over the Apennines, the Po, and then the Alps and the Danube; from what I hear,
nowhere did they find a critic except in my fatherland. O talents
more strident than solid, more bitter than ripe, what flames burn
you? What poison infects you? What spur urges you onward? For
you, neither the madness of seething Etna or Charybdis nor the
crashing of the angry sea or the thunder sounds forth more dread-
fully than the name of one of your citizens. Nor does this affect me
alone. Whoever strives to rise above the general public is a public
enemy. Why—tell me? Are Seneca's words also true perhaps? "We
are better off," he says, "if no one seems good, as though anyone
else's virtue were a reproach to everyone's misdeeds" [*Ep.* 19.2].
Believe me, my friend, you who share my indignity and my wrong,
we have been born in a city where to praise one is to insult many,
especially if applied to to their laziness, wherefore they hate no one
more than their fellow citizens who have excelled at something. Why
do you think they do so, if not because in their eagerness to lie low,
they find the light all the more annoying the closer it is.

Do you want this made plain as day to you? Consider how often
within our memory, how often within the memory of our fathers
and grandfathers, when troubled by grievous wars, they searched
now Cisalpine Gaul, now the Piceno and other lands, for the condottieri, when at home they always had an abundance of the bravest
men and the most skilled in martial arts; they chose to be conquered under foreign leadership rather than to conquer under their
own. Success gained by their own leader is so shameful that they
would rather have the enemy win a victory over them than their
own fellow citizen win glory over the enemy, whence this envy or
fear arising from envy lest the virtue of illustrious men, made
known through outstanding deeds, would reveal the laziness lurking
in themselves. I have no idea where they got this habit of admiring
every exotic idea and foreign custom, while resenting the wholesome examples of our forebears—surely not from our Roman ancestors and founders. It is, therefore, right that, while the trophies for
Roman victories were inscribed with the names of famous citizens,
the unhappy titles of foreign condottieri and the weight of imported
disgrace stick to our defeats.

O envy, worst of all diseases of the human spirit, you are said to
have brought death to the human race, and you still do not let up!
What else are you seeking? What else will satisfy you, if to have

destroyed it does not? O sad and wretched dilemma for bodies, yet even more wretched for spirits! It is said that lions have a daily fever; although much nonsense is told about them, as about other animals, especially unusual ones, what Pliny says following Aristotle—that the lion's only sickness is squeamishness—contradicts this popular opinion [*Nat. hist.* 8.19.52]. A doctor friend of mine who had a son in his teens, swore to me that, anxious with fatherly concern over his health, he had never at any time found him free from fever. Whether this is possible, I leave to the physicians. But to make it credible, there is Pliny's statement in the seventh book of his *Natural History* [52.172] that Maecenas had a perpetual fever. Furthermore, Varro, no lowly author but by far the most famous and learned, maintained in his book, *De re rustica* [2.3.5,7], that the goat is never without fever; he believes that *capra* derives from *carpo* ["pluck, seize"], as though it were *carpa*. Yet, oh, how much more oppressive is the fever of envy, oh, how much more parched, since it cannot be fed grass or leaves, nor curbed by shade or springs but only by the ruin, death, and disgrace of one's neighbor. Just as the law of lease stipulates that a tenant may not let a kid graze on the farm, as Varro attests [*De re rust.* 2.3.7] was in effect in his time (even today a prudent head of a family does not ignore this), would that Nature—the best mother—had stipulated by eternal law that no son of envy, drawn by evil intent, should intrude in her domain and the round of human life, or feed upon the commonwealth. As it is, since all pastures are trampled, especially by such flocks, and the wounds of envy are inflicted most hungrily upon the nobler legs, what else shall the scars from such teeth be taken for if not marks of glory? But what am I to do with the carpers, my feverish, smelly, butting goats? They jump upon my silence and fly into a rage at my rebuttals; they are enemies of truth, they scorn patience.

Now, as happens at the start of a courtroom speech, in the urge to let off steam I have said a great deal about the character of my accusers. Let us now come to the point. The section of my poem that was snipped off prematurely and made public too hastily is the death and lament of Mago the Carthaginian, Hamilcar's son and Hannibal's brother, who was sent with an army to Italy in the Second Punic War. At sea, off Sardinia, while making for home, he perished of a wound received in Liguria. So as to reprimand me more freely without suspicion of envy, my critics begin with plaudits, and praising the verses themselves to the heavens, they call them fine in themselves, but given by me to one whom they did not become. Such criticism, if true, would be neither rude nor offensive.

For we know that nothing, however powerfully and skillfully expressed, could avoid well-deserved criticism when not in keeping with the speaker's rank and character; in fact, the more eloquent an inappropriate speech, the more wrong it will be. This is the poetic canon of the speaker discussed by Cicero in *De officiis* [1.28.97] and by Flaccus in the *Art of Poetry* [119ff]. If it is ignored, you can expect nothing Pierian, nothing divine. Let us now see, however, how much skill and judgment my critics have used to carry out the calumny so cunningly broached.

In case you do not know, for a long time I was galled by these trifles and whisperings but bore them silently—I hope—hearing here and there what this one or that one had spouted without yet understanding the thread of the accusation; this very day, for the first time, I learned the whole thing in detail from a young religious, our fellow citizen, who strongly disagrees with them and battles their envy out of love for me since he thinks it almost a sacrilege for such—to him—ignorant men to show off their knowledge against my work; this, he claims, so disturbs everyone in my country who loves my name that they are saying much in defense of the truth, but my critics persist so forcefully in what they have begun that now they seem to be seeking not the truth of the matter but only my disgrace. Today he told me all this, with eyes flashing and words halting and shaky; finally, his anger so welled up that he could scarcely hold back his tears. I recognized the impulse of youth and love in him; to allay it, I told him to be of good cheer: those who strive for glory by the straight path must not spurn the same lot as the greatest philosophers and poets, but wish for it, since things lying idle are subject to rust while anything bright and solid, when rubbed and scoured, shines like gold. In the end, having barely curbed his anger and fervor, he revealed what my Aristarchi are quibbling about.

First of all they say—not in these words but in their own, which barely express that what they mean to say is this—that such great power of speech and mass of complaints do not really become a dying man, nor does the hour of death warrant such weighty sentiments. As you see, then, the first part of their attack is twofold: a dying man's breath is inadequate for voicing such words, and his mind inadequate for conceiving them. To these I shall now reply, laying aside the customary rule among disputants before I am distracted by anything further, while the impact and my memory are fresh. For a warrior does not wait until the enemy has had his fill of striking him in order to begin returning the blows; instead, returning wound for wound, now anticipating the enemy, now warding him off, he has his mind on winning and not on getting even.

First then, I am not ignorant of the fact that a dying man's strength is spent and therefore unequal to lengthy or artistic, elegant speeches. I know how Christ breathed his last while crying out something marvelous and unmatched in a loud voice, causing those about Him to realize that there was in Him something more than human. Startled by this miracle, the centurion acknowledged that He was the Son of God. Dealing with this passage in the Gospel of Mark [15:39], Jerome remarks, "We who are of the earth die with a single word or without a sound, but He who came down from heaven expired with a shout" [*Patr. lat.* 30, col. 640]. Anyone can see what I am about to say, unless conceit or envy closes his eyes.

I confess I am ashamed to answer such abject stupidity, but the facts force me to. I do not make a dying man speak, but one who is near death and already staring it in the face. Who is not aware that in such a state not only learned men but unlearned ones often say many things of grave and wondrous import, sometimes containing some presage and divination? Therefore, even if actual death crushes the mind and cuts off the life breath, impending death helps and rouses both, as if reminding one who will soon cross the threshold of his prison to look back and see how much toil and misery is being left behind. Indeed no one can better judge anything than the one who has long experience with it and has a spirit unhampered by passions, one now past all fear or hope. I could cite many examples from philosophers, many from historians, but I would rather say what I have seen with my own eyes and heard with my own ears, for about this I cannot err. There was a man with whom I ran part of the course of this life, which though short is strenuous. I spent many years with him, as it happened; never, or very seldom, in all that time did I hear from his lips a word that was not ribald, rash, arrogant, envious, stormy, or gloomy; he spoke of nothing but feuds and scandals. Nor will this surprise you—such was his life, and such besides was his voice which befit his words. You would have called him a boar gnashing its teeth or a bear raging, not a man speaking. Eventually, he had to face what no man will avoid; if my critics would look ahead to it, they would not worry about my style, I believe, but their own life and death. We eagerly hastened to him out of pity, but also to see how a man would die who had lived as he did. When he realized that he was very near death (you will hear something amazing), he immediately began to speak with the looks, gestures, and voice of a different man; he thus began to talk, to accuse himself, to urge and warn us, one moment altogether and another moment singly; and he prolonged this talk until his very last breath with such deep sighs that, although I had never approved of the fellow's character or loved him, he left me and, I believe, the others who were there, forever grateful to him and kindly disposed.

What shall I say of Robert, King of Sicily? Although the tenor of his actions and words, in life and death, was always the same, he nevertheless voiced something more splendid and sublime in death, for as he met his end he achieved the proverbial swan song, truly philosophical, regal, and divine. He made so clear to those listening the impending danger to the kingdom and all the misfortunes, that you would conclude that what was future to others was present to him; if only his tongue had found ears and minds like his, unhappy Campania and once Greater Greece—now lesser Italy—would not have fallen so suddenly from such an enviable, peaceful state to the present restlessness and wretchedness. Thus, at the very time when these professors of an arcane, new philosophy crush and bury the voice, talent, and all the energy of a man not yet dead, fallen men rise up and, having risen, soar higher than usual. Thus does hardship polish and sharpen the mind, thus does impending death shock laziness and arouse virtue, a time about which I shall tell you what I have admiringly read in Tully. "More than ever," he says, "they are eager for praise, and those who have not lived as they ought will most repent of their sins" [*Diu.* 1.30.63].

These words from a pagan's mouth will suffice for the second quibble, which goes as follows: what I attributed to the man about to die [Mago] seemed not his own thought but more like a Christian's. I really marvel no less at this stupidity than at the first one; and I would scarcely have thought, I confess, that anyone born into this world would prate that stuff so hoarsely and so weakly. Such attacks, betraying only the assailant's sickness and impatience, are indicative of a base, sterile intellect. In Christ's name I ask, what is Christian in those verses rather than human and common to all nations? What, if not grief and groaning and repentance at the last moment, about which you have heard what Cicero wrote? But why limit ourselves to one witness when everyone, indeed the whole world, would answer with one voice? Nowhere in that poem is Christ's name mentioned, which although holy and awesome in heaven and in hell, had no place in the poem because chronology blocks it. No article of faith is found there, no sacrament of the Church, in short, nothing of the Gospel, nothing at all that could not occur to a man of much experience, now speeding toward the end of that experience, by way of his natural intelligence and innate reason, in which I wish we were not so often outdone by those people and others.

A non-Christian, too, can recognize his error and sin, and blush and grieve just as much, not—to be sure—with equal reward but with equal repentance. If this were not so, Terence's character would never say in the *Phormio* [217], "Young as I am, I know myself and my sin." If a healthy, unimpaired man confesses this, what do we believe a sick man will do with death facing him? Furthermore, about this recognition, confession, and repentance of one's sins, it is worthwhile hearing not what Anaxagoras or Cleanthes felt, nor Cato and Cicero among our people, but Naso, the naughtiest of poets, or Epicurus, the flightiest of philosophers, as they say. The poet says,

> I rue it. If any wretch e'er be believed,
> I rue it and am racked by my own deed.
>
> [Ovid, *Pont.* 1.1.59–60]

The philosopher, too, says, "Recognition is the beginning of salvation" [Sen., *Ep.* 28.9–10], words that I see pleased Seneca not undeservedly. After closely studying them, he says, "He who does not know that he has sinned does not wish to be set right; you must catch yourself before you can reform." Immediately after that, he adds, "Criticize yourself, then, as much as you can, examine yourself. Assume the accuser's role against yourself first." What else does he seem to you to be saying if not what Solomon said in Proverbs [18.17], "The just man is the first to accuse himself," or what else does the same Seneca mean in saying to Lucilius [53.8], "It takes a wide-awake man to tell his dream, and to confess his vices is a sign of sanity," if not what David says in the psalm, "I said against myself, I shall confess my wrong-doing to the Lord" (note the confession!), "and you forgave the impiety of my sins" (note the saneness of the confessor!) [Ps. 32:5].

Thus, although no one but a Christian knows to whom and how he must confess, nevertheless the awareness of sin, the prick of conscience, repentance, and confession are common to all reasonable beings. And if we look at the words, how does what the lover in Terence said a while ago differ from what David himself said in that most famous psalm, mindful of his illicit love and crime, "Since I know my iniquity, my sin will stand ever against me" [Ps. 51:5]. But my critics seem to me to have studied too little either these few passages I have mentioned or those by many philosophers, particularly Plato and Cicero, about God, the soul, the miseries and sins of men, scorn for this life, and longing for the next; if the author's name were missing, you would swear they were written by Ambrose or Augustine. Since these are too many and too widely quoted, I shall not cite them, though I do know them. Yet if my critics wish to be as intent on learning as they are about attacking, they will find no end of examples from which to realize that it is as I say, and perhaps to be ashamed of having trumped up such frivolous stuff.

There remains a third accusation: that I was not judicious enough in giving a young man such weighty words, which most aptly fit a more advanced age. This charge, I say, is not only juvenile but childish. Let them read once again all the treatises on this point. Unless I am mistaken, they will find no one who put the beginning of old age earlier than Cicero. For him this was forty-six, an opinion I would not have mentioned except for my belief that nothing from that great man should be overlooked, and that Cato himself, through whose mouth Cicero speaks the truth, says that it was also their ancestors' opinion; and thus a triple authority comes together in one. This being the case, since nothing favors my adversaries' position more closely, will not one dying at forty-one—for example, Titus, Vespasian's son and certainly an excellent prince—be allowed to speak anything witty and mature? On the one hand, Titus noted the flight of precarious life, and, on the other, the shadows of error being dispelled at the approach of death. For Augustine, however, old age is much later than for Cicero. There is his book entitled *Diverse Questions* where he says that it begins with the sixtieth year. Let those who contend nothing serious can be said except by a decrepit old man determine how much force or weight this opinion shall have, considering either the author or the matter itself. In fact, I do not embrace this opinion so stubbornly as to discard all others. I do know that people have felt very differently about this, but it is laborious to collect their feelings and words. Therefore, though more could be cited as witnesses, I have brought in a few who happened to come to mind.

Among these is Isidore, whom I rarely use as an authority; dividing a lifetime into six ages, he states, "The fourth is the prime of life, strongest of all ages, which ends in the fiftieth year" [*Etym.* 11.2.5]. What do my backbiters now say? Do they at least like this witness who is most recent in time, but intermediate in opinion? Or someone else? For, believing in my cause, I reject no one unless he cannot distinguish between a youth and a child, as these whom I am dealing with seem to do: they argue as if I were speaking of a child or a baby rather than a brave young man and a military leader. The young man's mind, mature and steadfast, was at that age when, if one does not know how to speak, I would not advise going to a school of eloquence. I called him the young Carthaginian because, if I had merely called him a Carthaginian, he could at first have been mistaken for Hannibal who was older and more celebrated. Because of his age and the comparison with his brother, it was proper to call him young, for he was young in age and younger than his brother, yet still a man who had so many times known both kinds of fortune in crises.

But why do I defend a most powerful cause as though it were weak, when it is so easy to point out in frail youngsters what astonishes them in the sturdiest, most mature age. I leave out Diadumenus Antoni[n]us, who was elevated with his aged father to imperial power when he was not a young man but a child; as it was customary for new rulers to address the people, his speech, when his turn came, is reported to have been more statesmanlike than his father's.

I will not mention Clodius Albinus, about whose youth such impressive things are related that could seem amazing in any old man whatsoever. For perhaps these count as unknown to my critics, not being as devoted to history as to satire; but they know, do they not, the Roman prince Alexander, who is described as acting so prudently and soundly in the tightest circumstances, making such measured responses, quelling disorders so effectively, deliberating with such foresight, that he proved a long life unnecessary for wisdom? Indeed, he lived no more than twenty-nine years, three months, and seven days. Was this an old man? Or when he had borne the weight of that great empire with such high praise for his words and deeds in spite of fortune puffing him up (which kills prudence and begets arrogance), will they say that he could not have spoken a few well-chosen words at death, which stifles vanity of the human spirit? We find all this written about him not in poems where there is a little more license, but in histories. So severe was he with his troops that he often discharged entire legions, calling them "citizens" instead of soldiers; nor did he ever fear the army. And the best reason for this fact was that nothing could be said against his way of life. The historian Aelius Lampridius comments about this prince at this very age: "He was enormously sagacious; no one could prevail upon him" [*Hist. Aug.* 18.29.6]. What then? Is this man, who took over an empire in his early teens and ruled it from beginning to end with such wisdom and justice, who countless times delivered such memorable speeches, to be imagined mute at the end, if he had met a natural, tranquil end and not a sudden, violent one? But perhaps chance has brought to my attention, though I am a random scholar, what is unknown even to serious scholars. Are they, indeed, also ignorant of the acumen of the boy Alcibiades, who gave to the wisest elder of then flourishing Greece the famous advice that the Greek and Latin elders equally admired. That, however, was not the cast of his mind, but its bloom, and thus exemplifies not virtue but nature. Yet it does indicate that not only a young man but a child can speak effectively and admirably.

But is there anyone in the world who knows his own name but is ignorant of Scipio, whose virtue and glory earned him above anyone else the surname of Africanus? At the furious and disastrous battle of the Ticinus [Ticino] he saved from certain death his father, at that time the celebrated commander of the Roman army but recently defeated and severely wounded, and this, according to Livy, when he was just entering puberty, or had barely gone beyond boyhood, according to Valerius, thus earning the triple honor of having saved a citizen, a general, and a father, and the crown entwined with triple praise after that battle where brave men hardened to the ways of war and veterans in the use of arms hoped or sought for nothing but flight. Neither the power of adverse fortune and the spectacle of the frightful slaughter nor the weakness of his age withstood his precocious determination. For true virtue does not measure the danger or count the years. As Livy testifies, the same Scipio not long afterward, while still very young, with the utmost presence of mind and incredible courage demolished the utterly shameful and cowardly proposals to abandon Italy. Again, later, after the commanders had been either paralyzed or wiped out, he alone, at the age of twenty-four, was not afraid to assume upon his youthful shoulders the defense of the republic; he accepted before his time the command in Spain, where the warm blood from the slaughter of his family and of his people was still oozing; and after that, when consideration of his age was arousing fear and the people had begun to regret having thoughtlessly voted, without any discussion he summoned all the tribes to an assembly, and overcame all mistrust with a magnificent speech that awakened the deadened élan of their spirits and filled every mind with the most certain hope of victory. When more advanced in age, though still young, he would not have the slightest idea, I suppose, how to speak to himself on his camp-bed—he who, in his teens, had spoken in public and so easily won over to his thinking the greatest people on earth, discordant and contrary; and lest the daring of a youth seem to have filled their spirits with false hope, the whole world has been told how bravely and successfully, he soon avenged his father, his uncle, and his fatherland after setting out for his province.

And lest his martial virtue alone take all the praise, what continence he showed during those days at Spanish Carthage [now Cartagena], what trustworthiness toward the enemy too, and what severity blended with clemency in his dealings at Suero! In the former, his assiduous respect for married women whose chastity was untouched even by his men's eyes bears witness, and in the latter, the army silenced by a simple nod, the guilty ones punished, and his speech to the soldiers! Note too how, upon returning home from his victory, he stood out among the the people and in the Curia when he defeated with a glorious speech, despite senatorial opposition, Quintus Fabius, at that time the greatest leader of the Senate, the wisest and most famous elder, who disagreed with him about the highest affairs of state. In the debate he boasts, and the facts prove, that a young man had bested an elder, at least in his restrained use of language. And soon after that, when he was about to cross from Sicily to Africa, with what skill he armed and trained that squadron of the bravest cavalry! To pass over what could be called audacious or fortunate rather than well-planned (though nothing was done by him, even in battle, without sound counsel), and to mention only what takes planning and skill, what charm, what graciousness, what power of eloquence he displayed to win over not only Syphax, an uncivilzed king (to use Livy's words), unaccustomed to Roman ways, but even that most implacable enemy, Hasdrubal! What humaneness, what chastity when he returned a bride of peerless beauty untouched to her husband, or sent back the captured boy of royal blood, laden with gifts, to his uncles! With such devices he conquered both men more readily than he would have by war. What dignity, what saintliness, whereby without giving offense he prevailed upon Massinissa, his contemporary and dearest friend, but wild and distraught by love! Later, to cheer up Massinissa, who was frantic with excessive grief, he distracted him with consummate skill from the sense of an overpowering blow with other concerns. Finally, what intelligence, what confidence he showed in the ultimate crisis in answering Hannibal who sought peace!

Speaking at length about my Scipio is a sweet and rich subject since there is no statesman that I love more, no one who can better blunt the nonsense of these people and their stinging envy. For without doubt (I often repeat the same thing so that my deaf friends may hear), without doubt, I say, it is more prodigious for a young man, especially when prompted by illness and impending death, to murmur softly a little about our common nature and men's hazards and fortunes than for a young man to mollify enemies and prevail upon friends with his talk, to discipline armed legions and refute in open debate—the most demanding branch of eloquence—the most eloquent leaders of the Romans and Carthaginians! I omit other deeds of his even though they were done in his prime. Everything I have said was really done by a lad in his teens or on the border between adolescence and young manhood, before or around the thirtieth year. But my young man, as I called him, was either past forty or approaching fifty, and so had not yet lost his right to be called a man in his prime.

If I have not convinced them even with all this, and human conjectures are of no avail, who will resist divine truth? Indeed, if God, having been made man in the fullness of time, though eternal and immense in His divinity, presiding over all and undergoing neither diminution nor increase, still grew up subject in His humanity to His parents (that is, to His real mother and His putative father), gained in strength as Luke the Evangelist said, and advanced in wisdom and age until the beginning of his preaching, as God He was aware of everything from eternity and had no need of time, as a man He deemed the thirtieth year suitable to begin, who would dare call this age, consecrated for us by our Leader's choice, imperfect? Who was there to forbid Him to wait until then—Him who could neither be born nor die except when He willed it? He could have shown the road to heaven later, he could have shown it earlier; for Him any time was suitable. Lest you doubt that this is so, already in His boyhood, at the age of twelve, sitting and disputing among the teachers of the law, He astonished everyone. He therefore waited until thirty and no longer, not for His own need, but as an example for us, for as Augustine says in his *Book on True Religion*, all of His life on earth in the human form that He deigned to assume is a model of behavior. By His deed, then, He set the bounds for all those desiring to undertake something grand, so that we would neither claim mastery too early nor defer until old age the exercise or teaching of virtue. Let my judges be quiet, I beg, and not torture themselves in vain. I did not say a baby, nor—for that matter—a child or a teenager, but a young man, that is, one not yet old; in fact, he who is not tolerably wise at this age will be crazy in old age. I admit there are many, or rather countless, people who spend all their lives amidst pleasures, vanities, and groundless delusions in the hope that the years alone, not learning, not study, will bring wisdom to make them wise at the end of their lives. It is like the farmer who, after wasting all the time for sowing in sleep and playing, hopes for a rich harvest the coming summer!

But there is already enough of this extraneous matter to throw my barking critics "a mouthful spiced with honey and exquisite fruits," and lull this Cerberus bristling with serpents. But if envy is utterly implacable and sleepless, I have satisfied, I believe, the truth and its devotees, and above all others you who I know are the first to have tired of these dogs, with the letter which, tame as it is to our friends, barks back at our antagonists.

By heaven, I know not whether the fourth and final accusation moves me to anything but laughter. They say my style is more lofty in the *Bucolics* than the humbleness of a pastoral poem requires. Would that everything that I have written or will write may avoid every other fault! I will gladly accept guilt for this because I am not unaware that there are three styles for poets and orators, and that blame cannot be avoided if one style is transferred into the sphere of another. Usually, however, something is said to be lofty or lowly or medium by comparison, rather than in an unqualified sense: small hills stand out on a plain, and great mountains lie hidden when ringed by greater ones. Olympus itself, victor over the clouds, is conquered by the heavens. The moon, very high for us, is lower than all the stars. I wrote that poem as a youth, and with youthful daring, as Maro says about his *Bucolics*; I thought I was then on the verge of writing something else, and had already begun what I hoped, and still hope, will turn out so lofty that it will make anything else look lowly and base next to it. Furthermore, to put an end to all comparisons, many things too that are accepted in themselves appear—depending on differences between judges—lofty to one and humble to another, whence it is written in the psalm [104:18], "The high mountains are for stags," and then, "the cliffs are a refuge for hedgehogs," and the mole, once it touches the earth's surface, rises no higher. And among the birds, the eagle, to soar on high, scales the clouds, the peacock the roof-tiles, and the cock the dung heap, and so forth. I will freely absolve a style whose only shortcoming is loftiness, and, if necessary, gladly suffer this disgrace. In my opinion, however, it is unnecessary; those who see it that way are perhaps of too modest talent. To me, nothing in that poem is loftier than is proper or than I wish.

Finally, my friend, let us hear these detractors of ours some day saying or writing something pleasing in Latin instead of always belching forth their puzzles in the vernacular at street corners among silly women and fullers. For these are the schools where they philosophize, these the tribunals where they pass judgment without justice or discrimination. Whoever is absent is put on trial, no one is shown any favor, no one unable to defend himself is spared, the reputations of the ancients and the moderns are reviled, the names that have been made to shine through long vigils are disfigured. Present a man of letters to such muggers, and they are dumbfounded and harden into flint as though the Palladian Gorgon had come upon them. Just let them write—that is all I ask—so they will understand that we have teeth too, if we feel like using them. But why do I call for it? They are as cautious as they are ignorant and envious. They have protected themselves against such attacks, once and for all. They always hiss and hide; and to conclude with Jerome, who suffered many attacks, they think themselves learned if they detract from others. Farewell.

Venice, March 13 [1363].

Sen. II, 2.

To Francesco Bruni, that both in want and in wealth there is room for virtue and glory.*

To your earlier letter about my fleeing death and changing location I replied that the cause was the very move from that most wretched place and the confusion arising from the move, although you could have found sufficient answer to that letter from mere hearsay—that I had escaped from the wreckage and by drifting with the current had landed in Venice, a city located nearby, yet now far off because of its healthy climate. Since I knew that these plagues have wings, that there is no escape and the end remains fixed and unshakable, I did this, I confess, not from an eagerness to escape but to rest. As for your latest letter, though advice about things past is useless, I would still like to say this one thing. In my opinion, you chose the best course; as the last of your friends, not in loyalty but in time and place, I give my assent if you think my opinion carries any weight. I feel that the Most Holy Father [Urban V], truly liberal and "urbane," who I happily hear knows you very well, has ascended to the highest rank of human excellence with God's distinct approbation, to the advantage of you and of all good men, and for the salvation of the world—and all the more blessedly, the more unexpected it was. So go auspiciously, then, under Christ's guidance, and return more auspiciously.

While men who despise transitory things may be most justly praised, those who seek them out of necessity should not therefore be blamed, provided they take care in their zeal for possessions not to overlook justice, moderation, compassion, and decency. For although Diogenes the Cynic was famous for being content to drink from cupped hands after his wooden dipper broke at the spring, and for living in an adaptable home [a tub!], yet no less known was Democritus with his great riches, or Cicero and Annaeus among our people, both of whom we know were reproached for their wealth. In *De officiis*, the one says, "An enhancement of one's property that harms no one must not be condemned, but wrong-doing must always be avoided" [Cicero, *Off.* 1.25]; the other says in his book where he portrays the blessed life as well as he could, "Stop forbidding money to philosophers. No one has condemned wisdom to

* See I, 6.

poverty. The philosopher will have ample wealth, but not taken from anyone, nor gory with others' blood, nor acquired by wronging anyone" [Sen., *Ep.* 23.1]. Can you hear Cicero's opinion, expressed in Seneca's words, that enhancement of wealth, unless dishonest or harmful, is permissible for the good, conscientious man and even for the philosopher? There Seneca said much to excuse himself and those charged with the crime of being rich. Most pertinently he says, "I deny that wealth is a good, for if it were, it would produce good men. Now what is found among evil men cannot be called a good. I deny this name for it. Yet I admit that we must have it, that it is useful and brings great comfort to life." I omit anything further, lest like another Crassus or Croesus, I seem today to be launching a defense of wealth, which I am scarcely under obligation to do, except perhaps in passing.

But to come rather to our own people, are the wealth and honors of Ambrose and Gregory any less renowned because Francis' poverty and humility are very much so? One of them was the bishop of the wealthiest city, the other was the the prince of all bishops. And so, to compare not only several persons in each category but one and the same man with himself, Plato and Aristotle were no more renowned, were they, before they sought or accepted money than afterward—for admittedly both of them were criticized for it. I am aware that a base or relentless quest for wealth does harm to famous names, although not the honorable possession of enormous wealth. Thus, was Virgil less distinguished after Caesar's gold made him wealthy than when he headed for Rome, a poor exile, driven from his original village home? Or was Silvester less saintly because of Constantine's immense gift than when he lived poor and naked in the woods and mountain caves? That bestowal perhaps has harmed, and will harm, his successors. Yet it took away nothing whatsoever from his sanctity or glory. In general, nothing can budge a spirit well based and firmly rooted, whereas in the midst of fortune's shifts, light breezes shake a poorly moored spirit and the slightest pressures crush it.

Finally, not to philosophize forever in the clouds, but breaking out of the shadows, to succeed at long last in understanding and being understood, let others do as they like; for me, the best path in life is moderation. If forced to shift from it to an extreme, I would certainly rather be rich than poor, but I am speaking of that fearful, ugly poverty, overwhelmed by dire want and rank filth. Just as nothing is sweeter than a simple, honest poverty, so too nothing is more vexing than extreme want. I make one exception—the poverty assumed in the name of Christ. This kind alone can overcome difficulties and ease troubles, lighten burdens and lessen hardships so that, without it, all the labor of philosophers, like an empty, sterile luster, feeds the eyes but fails to drive away hunger.

Lastly, let this be the brief resolution of the problem: riches must not be sought too eagerly nor rejected too haughtily, in short, neither praised nor reviled, but rather numbered among indifferent things, as wise men agree. I feel just the same about poverty, for it is the use made of poverty or of wealth that deserves praise or condemnation. Therefore, you should not now fear any taunt of ambition. It is not ambition, nor even cupidity, to accept happily, if offered, the gifts—I will not say of fortune, as the multitude does, but of God—and to lose them with equanimity if they are taken away; to use them gratefully and soberly, to do without them calmly, just as your spirit is the same no matter whether everything of yours prospers or fails, and always emerges unconquerable with undiminished superiority over what is below it.

When you ask me for a letter of recommendation to the Supreme Pontiff, that is certainly a sign of your love rather than of your judgment. You feel so warmly about me that you trust that anything from me will do you good; if I too believed this of myself, I would not be hesitant to give a few lines to such a friend who begs so modestly; for I have often dashed off so many letters either because of an urge to write or the pestering of thankless people. But believe me, it will not only be called naïveté, which good people do not look at askance, but madness or a lot of nerve, if I—such a nobody, so unworthy—approach such an august Father on behalf of one so deserving; and besides, I who recommend am a total stranger to him. Though I thank you for your error, I have no doubt that your opinion will be no different than mine, if you remove for a moment the veil of your love, which places me high in your estimation, and begin considering how things really are. Instead, when you approach the sacred feet, if you think it proper and are not ashamed of my drab name amidst such splendor, make mention of me. For although, as you know, I am not just personally unknown to him, as with you, but totally unknown, what has me bewildered is that several times in the past few days, and most recently yesterday evening, I learned from my friends' impassioned letters that the Pontiff wants and bids me to come to him, at once.

A great hope has been instilled, one that will perhaps stir great spirits—all through some rumor about me, they think, but they are mistaken; rather, only God's mercy, which unbidden looks out for one so unworthy, is doing this. I will confess to you that if I rated myself so highly that the Vicar of Christ could wish to see me, I would already have dashed off on my journey, not simply on foot or horseback, but borne all the way by litter, if necessary, or by ship, I swear to God, considering not so much his papal office as his virtue, about which I learn much either from your letters or from those of friends abroad whom I mentioned, or from the common report of upright, truthful men everywhere. This stands out in them: he loves good men; though I am not among them anyhow, I would still be happy to be numbered with them, particularly by such a fine judge. Unless I am mistaken, I am now being summoned to do work, honorific no doubt and profitable too, if that concerned me, but by now too contrary to my age and the leisure I have always longed for. Farewell, etc.

[Venice, 1362].

Sen. II, 3.

To the same person,* how laborious and dangerous it is to write, yet one must write, and in what manner.

The great power of eloquence, flavored with charm and reason together, and abounding in words and ideas, has often been recognized and proven. Never were Milo's or Hercules' arms so powerful that Cicero's or Demosthenes' tongue was not mightier still. The strong men, to be sure, perhaps moved with great strain a boulder, an ignoble weight, but the orators moved minds, the noblest thing, utterly fickle and divine. Now you are bringing all this back to me. I had scarcely read your letter when I began, as if drawn by some great power, to go helter-skelter in opposite directions, so that, strange to say, I felt sorry for you, and at the same time rejoiced with you.

I am indeed glad that you have safely arrived at your destination and have found apostolic clemency just as you had hoped and wished for. Nothing is harsher or more bitter than an unrealized hope. Besides the faith I have in your letters and in those of many others, his name, Urban, had long since been a sure presage of his kindness, gracious ways, and angelic conversation. A name voluntarily assumed is, for me, a token of one's attitude, a witness of one's intentions. He has obviously chosen the best path, pleasing to God and to men, the one which is going to lead him without fail to a happy haven; although the way is unknown to many and overlooked, yet for him, and especially for his stature, it is destined. And although nothing is loftier, nothing more illustrious or venerable than the Roman Pontiff, or rather, although the world has nothing equal to him, nevertheless, exalted by such great honor and subjected to such a weighty burden, he must match the reverence and admiration of the faithful with his humanity and piety, and, unless I am mistaken, be even more gentle and humble than before.

Perhaps this will astonish the many who become arrogant through success, however slight, but not Urban himself who realizes, as his actions prove, that he is the vicar on earth of Him who says, "Learn from me because I am gentle and humble of heart" [Matt. 11:29]. It is quite unbecoming and incongruous for the vicar of a humble Lord to be arrogant. Therefore, I neither demand nor

---

* See I, 6.

expect any greater testimony about him than what you write me and what his fame says. For, I ask, what more certain sign of the unconquerable spirit, founded on solid rock, could you require than that he is not cast down by Fortune's threats nor uplifted by her allurements? Or from where could you seek loftier proof than the loftiest place? In fact, nothing else will move this man who has reached the pinnacle of human dignity without being moved. O noble spirit, unshaken by such things! Happy is he with these qualities, happy is the world with him at its head, happy are you with this master! This I say: he is happier for these qualities than for his rank, and you are happier with this master than with freedom. There are times when freedom means toil, when ruling means slavery, when slavery means ruling. Therefore, I congratulate your fortune and glory, though I do pity your labor. Your situation is good and your time of life vigorous, the work is meritorious and noble. Your superior is the best, and there is nothing more desirable than that for worthy talents on their way up.

Under him, then, with God's favor, you will take on eagerly, tirelessly, manfully whatever it will be, recalling those words of Flaccus: "Life gives nothing to us without great toil" [Serm. 1.9.59–60]. Rich as you are in faith and able of mind, you will find nothing too formidable to approach, nothing too difficult to carry out. Faith even moves mountains; for those who really will it, everything is simple. You lack neither skill nor intelligence; if newness brings something unfamiliar or novel, you will attack it with your mental pincers and drag it into the open; shaped on your anvil, dipped and reheated in the furnace, it will become yours, and not only that, but better. Do you not recall that from the same block of stone Phidias sculpted one image, Praxiteles another, Lysippus another, and Polycletus yet another? Set to work, do not mistrust yourself, mix the new with the old. If you do it right, it will fetch its own price. It is silly to trust only in what is old. Those who invented these things were just human beings, too.

If we are too frightened to follow in the footsteps of men, for shame! It is women who hold first place in this honor. A woman was the inventor of the letters that we use. Let us not be influenced either by that trite, vulgar saying that there is nothing new, or nothing new to be said. Since Solomon and Terence wrote this, how much luster has accrued to philosophy, how much improvement to poetry, how much light to history! How many arts have been invented, how many laws passed in different nations! What grace has been added to human life! What proficiency with things! How much awareness of the divine! Nothing is so refined, so perfected that something cannot be added to it.

Rise and exert yourself, for work is the food of the healthy mind, just as pleasure is of the sick one. First rehearse alone in silence, then confine your ideas within the cage of your memory and lock them up, quietly and earnestly mull them over and examine them objectively. Then let them gradually come forth to the mouth's threshold and to your pen without anyone yet witnessing them, let them pause from time to time and, like those who deliberate, appear to be both doubtful and confident. Doubt will render your speech circumspect, cautious, sober, and modest. Confidence will render it joyful, rich, magnificent, and attractive. Once your concepts have broken forth into words or into letters in a continuous text, let them sound as if you were hearing them not as their creator but as a critic. Call upon your ear and mind for counsel, and consider what you would have had to say if your enemy had written it. How do you know whether your words will fall into enemy hands? "Whose?" you will ask; envious ones who have declared eternal war on virtue. Anyone who has begun to rise a little higher will encounter many enemies, not only those striving outright to do the same, but also the sluggards (which will surprise you), and those slumped on the ground—in fact, these in particular. No vice is lazier than envy. The enemy of light, a stranger to joy, it dwells in base, sullen spirits.

You see how toilsome and dangerous it is to write, yet we must lest envy seem to have made us hoarse, as the wolf did the peasant. But we must so write that those who gnaw at our works will find them hard, glowing, shaggy, stiff, and bristling, and thus realize at the price of their broken teeth that he spoke truthfully who said that envious men are nothing but self-tormentors. Let them admit that our expression was not offhand and callow, but mature and truly princely. And this we shall achieve more successfully if we come out as honest, truthful, and severe critics of our own inventions, considering nothing in them of less importance than their author and loving nothing less than the fact that they are ours. For we must not love our style because it is ours, as a misshapen, uncouth son is lovable because he is a son; the issue is not whose it is, but what it is in itself, what truth, what depth, what beauty it has. You must most rigorously see to it that any brilliance of one word or another, any charming expression—yours or another's—will not mislead you. On some people's lips, there is nothing that does not sound sweet. Put it on another's lips instead, and you would think that you had a different personality. Writers must search for tasteful language and shrink from harsh language. To please at all times, look to your meaning. If neat, noble, and graceful, it will delight, even if bare, and it will be easy to clothe. You will be able to do much in either direction, unless you give up. You do this alone or with a few people at first; then turn to a few more frank people who are not so much your friends as friends of truth, although if they are your friends, and not friends of your fortune, they would give nothing but honest advice. Thus your works, a little rough at first and kept at home, will gradually come out into the open well polished. When you have done it once or twice, you will feel your toil diminish from day to day until it becomes a habit, and no longer toil but delight in the doing.

I am not teaching you, dear friend, but myself, and in addressing you, I admonish myself and learn by listening to myself. You will forgive me; I am being long-winded. It is experience, Aristotle says, that has begotten art. That he is telling the truth none of the arts would deny, especially the one that I have right before my eyes, I mean navigation. Next to justice, this has brought so much varied growth to this great city, where I recently moved to flee the storms of the world. You remember how loudly the Greek poets and ours lauded that solitary, primitive vessel laden with demigods (as the story goes) which left the Thessalian shores, and entered the Euxine Sea through the nearby, almost contiguous straits of the Hellespont, the narrow Propontis, and the Thracian Bosphorus (terrible names!), and with great hope of glory or gain forged onward to Colchis, as if to another world: that a ship had reached the Phasis was worthy of the applause of all nations and immortal celebration, O great accomplishment! Experience was beginning to make an art, but the art was still lying in the cradle. From there it has grown so much that you would think it justifiably said that a son greater than his father was going to be born of Thetis. While this did happen in all the arts, in none is it more apparent [than in navigation]. See now, countless ships set sail from the Italian shore, some in the dead of winter, some today while spring still is uncertain, more like winter than summer; some sail toward the east, others toward the west, some northbound and others southbound for the Libyan Syrtes. Some will leave behind Gades [Cadiz] and Calpi [Gilbraltar], the western boundary of the world, some the two Bosphori, Colchis, and Phasis, not drawn, as long ago, by the miracle of the Golden Fleece, but still urged and spurred onward by gold, so that through so many risks and perils on land and sea, over here our wines may be delivered to the cups of the British and over there our honey to those of the Scythians, still others—you would scarcely believe this—transporting our timber to Greece or Egypt, our saffron, our oil, our linen to Syria and Armenia, to Persia and Arabia; and in turn something comes here from there.

I shall force you to stay awake an hour with me. While, heavy with sleep, I was writing these thoughts to you, the night was stormy and the atmosphere sodden. When my weary pen had reached this point, such a loud shout from some sailors suddenly struck my ears that I rose, remembering what that means, and rushed to the upper floor of my house which overlooks the harbor. I looked out; good God, what a sight, what a scare! Heartwarming, tremendous, delightful! Here, at my door, a number of ships were anchored to the glittering shore for the winter; equaling in size even this huge mansion, which this free and munificent city has provided for my use, their mastheads rose strikingly above its two corner towers. As the clouds veil the stars, as the wind shakes the walls and rooftops, and the sea bellows with an infernal roar, the largest of them is setting sail this very hour, and I do wish it Godspeed. Believe me, if Jason or Hercules could see it, they would be utterly amazed. If Tiphys sat at the helm, he would blush at having gotten such a great reputation for nothing. You would call it not a ship, but an image of a mountain floating on the sea, so weighed down with cargo that the waves hide a good part of its hold. It is going to call at the river Tanais since navigation in our sea does not extend there. Some passengers will disembark at that point, but it will not halt until, crossing the Ganges and the Caucasus, they arrive in India, farthest China, and the Eastern Ocean. Behold the burning and insatiable thirst for possessions that engulfs the minds of men! I was sorry for them, I confess, understanding then why the poets justly say that sailors are wretched. When I could no longer follow them with my eyes through the shadows, I returned to my pen with my mind deeply shaken. Silently I kept turning over this one thought: alas, how costly and, at the same time, how cheap life is to mortals.

There you have, dear friend, my story which this letter may not need, but I relish it, and our subject and the moment made me recall it without even trying. It does indeed concern what I had begun to say. If experience really makes art, then practice begets, nourishes, and makes art perfect. What Afranius thinks turns out to be true—that knowledge of things is the daughter of practice and memory. You remember his words:

Practice begot me, mother memory bore me.
The Greeks call me Sophia, you call me Wisdom.

[frag. 79 (Diehl)]

Augustine seems to have been thinking of this and the like when he defined art as the memory of things experienced and enjoyed. You too get experience—and so often what was experience becomes practice. Replete with this, memory will soon bear you the most beautiful offspring: ease of action, confidence, delight, and glory. In the meantime, though a crowd of vulgar minds may perhaps clatter about you, which is very bothersome, yet common in such circumstances, nevertheless you, in answering to so great a judge, will easily despise the empty clatter and extinguish envy with virtue, learning, and study.

But now my heavy eyes, my weary hand, and the hour of the night that leans toward dawn, sleep's messenger, all demand an end; only my sleepless mind, still unsatisfied with this conversation, shrinks from closing. It compels me to give some response to what you wrote about some people around you who are passing judgment not only on you, but also on me and my talent. I beg you, do not become indignant, do not struggle against them, do not waste your energy, for you will make enemies for yourself without getting rid of them for me; you will instead annoy and madden them all the more. If I may say so, for me this has been a longstanding and fatal plague. Many pass judgment on me whom I neither know nor wished to know, nor do I consider them worthy of meeting; who could have made them judges of my doings? I cannot deny that I am astonished at this. And I suffer as much from that as from our common fatherland and our fellow citizens, who I wish were as competent and just judges as they are hasty and careless. I do not know, however, why this breed has this peculiar trait: the more uninformed one of them is, the bolder and rasher his judgment. This might be because knowledge of a few things blocks them from looking at many and the emptiness of their minds make them more flighty, and so the process of passing judgment is shorter and quicker. Or it might be because with men's reputation, where the primary concern, however tenuous and unstable, depends on many different arts but especially on arms and letters, the same thing happens as in nearly everything else, namely, the one who has nothing of his own worth grabbing or plundering is always more prone to grab and plunder what belongs to others.

That effrontery from my townspeople, however, has just drawn a huge letter from me. This other, from a distance, I will bear in silence out of respect for him whose dogs—not to mention friends—one must defer to not only when he jokes, but even when he rages. Of course, it behooves us to tolerate impartially the judgments of all, for just as spurning fair comments is arrogance, so fearing unfair ones is weakness. Usually a lie is not long-lived; often too, fault-finding fabricated with much zeal is transformed into great praise for the one attacked and great shame for the attacker. The light of truth can be covered, but not quenched, for it lives on when it is thought to be quenched. And its unexpected splendor breaks through the clouds thrust in its way. Wherefore, even if sometimes I feel annoyed and galled—it is quite disgusting to endure so many critics of that ilk—ultimately I reject no judge except envy and hatred. Finally, there remains for me to urge you, although it is superfluous and well known to you, never to trust in your own powers, whatever you do, but to ask and hope for help from above. The pious, humble realization and constant awareness of earthly frailty will earn you divine aid and heavenly strength. Nothing is more certain than this strategy for doing things, nothing more effective. Embrace this trustworthy advice of your older friend, and farewell and remember me.

Venice, April 9 [1363].

Sen. II, 4.

To his Lelius [Angelo di Pietro Stefano dei Tosetti], *
whether it is worse to deprive authors of credit
for what they have written or to give them credit
for other men's works.

What need is there for flatterers' lies, since they do not make dim
talents shine, and brilliant ones have no need of such aid, which
harms rather than helps them? A lying supporter lessens rather than
enhances the glory of the one being praised, inflicting the suspicion
of falsehood upon true praises. I am not, I admit, one of these, but
whoever I may be, it behooves me to speak of myself. The subject
itself requires it. You write that recently you have seen a number of
short works, some in the vernacular too, bearing my name. You sent
me the opening lines as well as enough lines of each for me to
discern whether they were mine or another's. I laud your diligence,
but marvel at your uncertainty. For when I glanced at them, I not
only realized at once that they were not mine, but grieved and
blushed, astonished that others could think them mine or that they
caused you any doubt. Therefore, the people attributing them to me
are doubly in the wrong: they rob their author of his work and
burden me with what is not mine. If it is asked whom they are
treating worse, that is rather difficult to decide. But if it involved
some illustrious writer, obviously the one to whom some such thing
is attributed against his will would be hurt more than the one from
whom it was taken. For the one you rob of his work you would
deprive of no more of his reputation than whatever that writing
could have brought, whereas the one to whom you attribute another's work you will readily subject to undying disgrace and the judgment that whatever else he might have written well was accidental.
It is one thing to take away from someone's praise, and quite another to pile dishonor on him; a great man will disdain the first, but
hate the second. As for me, while I have a bit of the glory I hoped
for and none of the glory I sought, still I would rather be dimin-

---

* A supporter of the wealthy and influential Colonna family of Rome, where P.
first met him during his journey with Giacomo Colonna in 1330. Because of the
intimate friendship that developed, P. classicized his nickname Lello in memory of
Scipio Africanus's beloved friend, Laelius. More than a dozen of the *Familiares* are
addressed to him.

ished by this kind of robbery than thrive through one such gift; for I would rather that any grace of my own be hidden away than that another's disfigurements be stuck and stamped on my face, which already has far too many of its own. There are many things that certain people have tried in vain to take away from me. Please, let them be no more successful at this kind of harm than at the other, nor achieve by bestowing what they cannot by stealing. Say with a resolute spirit and demeanor that what they say is mine is not, and that I, burdened with my own things, reject anyone else's.

I am not unaware that this is an old outrage, inflicted upon many great talents in the past, whether through error or love or hatred. How many works are attributed to Aristotle that he had nothing to do with! I would not doubt that the little book entitled *On the Four Virtues* was ascribed to Seneca against his will. All the multitude eagerly read that short work, and include it among Seneca's books. And they cite and admire Seneca in something Seneca never saw. There are those who among all the works of Seneca himself love this one because it most suits their intelligence. For in fact, even if against Seneca's will and if he could disown it, the work has become his by adoption, not his own progeny; yet to this day the multitude has liked it more than the learned, even though the majority of the more learned—truth succumbing to error in this case—are unaware of what I am saying; and they feel as the multitude about its authorship, but cannot agree with them about the work itself, which the multitude either prefers to his better works or makes it their equal. I myself do not disparage this, but I do become a little annoyed with these untoward, loquacious pedants who muddle everything quite wildly.

That book is really by a certain bishop, Martin, who dedicated it to a certain King Miro as a guide for honorable living. For those who do not willingly err, all this is stated in a brief preface to the said work, long since deleted from our copies but extant in copies in the libraries of Gaul, where it is believed to have been written. They are robbing of what is his, an ungifted writer who perhaps has this alone to glory in, only to burden a prolific writer with another's work when he is laden with his own riches. And not content with this, they foist Seneca's own works on him twice, as can be seen in the book *On Morals and Proverbs*, which is said to be by Seneca: everything in it is indeed by him; however, what he wrote was scattered in other works, only to be culled and dumped ineptly in one place. Seldom indeed does he treat anything but morals; and what are the brief, pithy sayings in which he abounds above all others, if not proverbs? That was, however, no reason for this confusion to arise out of sayings well separated and aptly arranged, nor for this snatching from others' works—as though it were unseemly for that poor Martin to think and write about the virtues, which he could have cultivated and perhaps did, and as though everything ought to be attributed, even falsely, to one author, and virtue and honesty cannot be anyone else's subject when it is every mortal's, Plato's and Aristotle's above all others, and Marcus Tullius's among our people, to whom Marcus Brutus's most celebrated book, *On Virtue*, is addressed by name, which Seneca also mentions in his own works. How much better, then, it would have been to search for the lost work against superstitions by the same Seneca, an illustrious work, unless a sample from it misleads me, or to rescue it from being lost, and to bring into the open *On Consolation to Polybius*, which, as I have noted and marked in many copies, is not lost but combined with the one entitled *On the Brevity of Life*, so that they will not appear as one book but the two that they actually are, and so that the book's title, regardless of the book itself, will not perish. This matter has caused no little confusion for duller readers.

It is reputed that many works are attributed to Origen, even to jeopardizing his reputation, and some to Augustine. In a large, ancient volume belonging to the Church of St. Ambrose in Milan, where there are a good number of Ambrose's writings, I myself saw a book in someone else's style attributed to Ambrose. This nearly misled me while I was writing my book entitled *De uita solitaria*. Finally, I realized that it was by Palladius, not by Ambrose. There are many such cases. I know that nothing of the sort happened to Cicero and Virgil because their style, I suppose, is inimitable and always consistent. The book called *The Little Old Lady* is ascribed to Naso. It is surprising who would have thought of this, or why anyone would, except perhaps to seek fame for an obscure work with the lure of a well-known name, and by doing the opposite of what is often done—putting peacocks' eggs under hens—those people hope that a noble brooder will ennoble cheap eggs. And this could have happened with the authors' consent, if they loved their works more than their reputation. If we believe this, it is nothing short of a miracle since the first and most important concern for most authors is their reputation.

To return to our subject, I have nothing from anyone else, no one has anything from me—such, as I see it, is my hope. Let no one, then, steal what is mine, let no one foist upon me either what is his or another's—this I beg. This is the gist of it: if I must undergo one or the other, I would more calmly bear being robbed than being weighed down. Farewell.

[1362-63].

Sen. II, 5.

To the same person,* concerning useful and harmful silence.

I consider it good, if it can be done, to live in freedom, obliged or subject to no one except the laws of charity; I have called it good, whereas it is the very best since human life has nothing better. Nothing, therefore, will shake this conviction of mine: not the hope for riches, the glitter of gold, the splendor of finery or gems, nor their opposite, the squalor of poverty or a harsh life. A free poverty is much better than enslaved riches. Nor do I take freedom to be that we rot in shameful idleness, but that without being forced we willingly take on labors—I do not mean welcome ones, but honorable for us and useful to our country. I understand Cicero's saying in *On the Orata*, "To me a man does not seem to be free who is not at some time doing nothing" [2.24], to mean that he does nothing in the manner of busy people who are driven by the goad of a stern command, but that he is always doing something inwardly with himself while often outwardly idle and doing nothing with others. For to do nothing at all is typical of the sluggard rather than the free man. If, however, "chance controls all things," as Virgil's shepherd states [*Ecl.* 9.5], and if one must indeed live under another's rule (which the power of fortune, or rather the will of God, has made necessary for you now, for me formerly, and often for many of the greatest men temporarily), much must be avoided and much foreseen on all sides. Time does not allow, nor does the subject require, that we discuss all this now.

I shall touch on the two points most relevant to your situation; first, to be silent, and second, not to be silent. You marvel, so I shall say it more clearly. Long ago when you had followed to Rome that lord of both of us, who so quickly deserted us in this vale of woes, I sent from Gaul that querulous letter explaining, among other things, how much the Persians observed the cult of silence; if you remember it, as you usually do with anything of mine, there is no need to say more, except that you should realize that in this regard all lords are Persians, not only lords but friends too. The loyalty we owe them is none the less because their vengeance for breach of

---

* See II, 4.

faith is less prompt, for virtue unleashes honor and not punishment; nor is virtue any slower to give an honor that is snubbed without retaliation than an honor that incurs retaliation if snubbed. For virtue acts on its own and, to use Tully's words, "attracts the mind by its charms" [based on *Rep.* 6.25]. As the philosophers like to say, it is its own reward. Our thinkers look higher: to have sinned is a harsh punishment, inasmuch as no punishment is more severe to a good man than sin, and impunity detracts nothing from it—it adds much to his suffering. Certainly a good man will rather be tortured, even though innocent, or die, if necessary, than live and rule while guilty.

But since our discussion is about lords (although good ones are rare and bad ones are everywhere, and although it is as certain that there are more bad servants than bad lords as it is uncertain whether there are fewer good lords or fewer good servants), still if your lot has subjected you to any lord, good or bad, if indeed your servitude is such as to offend the greater Lord, then free yourself, with pride shake off the yoke, and weigh not the consequences, whether poverty, exile, prison, punishment or death. Nothing other than fleeing the worst thing of all, God's wrath, should seem truly useful and desirable. But if your situation is tolerable though harsh, endure it. And until the Lord of all has decided something else for you, remember that you are subject to that lord, whoever he is, by order of Him from whom flows all power. Being especially loyal to him in this one matter about which I am speaking, as in others, always maintain an unshakable trust of holy silence about all his affairs. Let it not be jarred by flattery, threats, violence, anger, drunkenness, hope, fear, or torture. So much for the first point.

As for the second, just as you keep your lord's every secret, so there is no secret against your lord that you should not immediately reveal and bring to his attention; any delay is dangerous and suspect. Innocence is no excuse for tardiness. There are times when it is not enough to be innocent; nor does the person guilty of several crimes ever free himself by being cleared of one. Many stories about this from our own times are on hand, but what is more famous sinks deeper in the mind. What is more, it is difficult to give weight to what is new or to shed light on what is dim. Therefore, one ancient story will be enough; Alexander alone provides sufficient example. The downfall of Philotas, which I am going to tell, is not the best known: though an illustrious Macedonian, always holding the highest rank in the army until that day, he suffered the extreme penalty because a plot to murder the king was reported to him and he kept still about it. Neither his own bravery and the memory of his deeds nor the luster of his father's glory could rescue him from such a sorrowful end. He was punished not only for concealing a conspiracy against the king but for being an accomplice, not only for silence and inertia but for plotting and treachery. A Persian named Sisenes, who first served under Philip and then under his son, was equally dear to both of them. A letter to Sisenes from a general under Darius, the Persian king, appealed to him as a compatriot who might dare to do something memorable for his country, but it was discovered and taken first to Alexander. In it, the general urged Sisenes to earn glory for himself and his king's gratitude by some brilliant and magnificent exploit. After reading it, Alexander affixed an unfamiliar seal and had it delivered by a Cretan soldier to the addressee. Upon reading it, the loyal, innocent man immediately rushed to the king to show him the letter; but finding him engrossed with his concerns and councils of war, he halted, hesitating whether to interrupt the king's deliberations as an untimely harbinger of bad news or to wait until he saw him at leisure. Finally deciding with disastrous shyness to postpone it, he kept silent that day. Upon his return the next day, he found the king in the same state. With a clear conscience and thus fearing nothing for the king or himself, and not understanding the danger in postponement, he again left without saying anything. With these little delays, for he did the same thing over and over, several days slipped by; and so, the king, who was quick to suspect, ordered the innocent procrastinator put to death. You will find both stories in Quintus Curtius: the first warns us of the need to keep faith, which must be rooted in us by nature, the second to banish any postponement of loyalty lest anyone think it is all right to wait in the midst of peril to our masters, since not only hours, but moments, are likely to bring crises of life and death, and often tardiness gets the punishment that treachery deserves. Farewell, etc.

[1362-63].

Sen. II, 6.

To Roberto, Count of Battifolle.*

The splendor of your name, distinguished sir, as well as love for our friend in common, has made me briefly shift my pen from other matters to address you, whom I know only by reputation; I seldom do this. I hear many magnificent and delightful things about you, your studies, and your character, for which I congratulate you and your country. No one will ever tell me that the birthplace of such men is wild and empty, when great cities are barren and no longer producing them. I congratulate the Apennine hills, lofty, shady, dewy, which have given you to our age. Yet, to be perfectly honest, I envy you because of them and them because of you, and I am gripped and held by a yearning for you and for them. Your excellence of mind and the mountainous scenery draw me to know you, for I too was born near those very hills, though under a lesser star. But since business stands in the way of my wishes, use me at this distance as you see fit, if anyone so insignificant can be useful; consider me there with you in spirit, if you think I am not completely unworthy, amidst the shady slopes of the mountain, the grassy shore, the verdant banks of your ancestral river, and the bed of a roaring stream still untainted by bad city ways, the dense, green forests hiding the sun with their leafy vault among the brooks and ice-cold springs that temper the Lion's [the constellation Leo] fury. I have you here with me, among the gilded palaces and marble churches, between the rivers of Padua and Treviso and the deep inlet of the Adriatic Sea. Farewell, be happy, and learn with me to cherish even what we have not seen.

Venice, July 24 [1363].

---

* A Florentine captain general and lord of the Casentino, who in 1370 liberated the city of San Miniato from the Visconti. He was also a distinguished soldier and orator whom P. had not met personally at this time, but had admired from a distance. In 1364 P. accepted his invitation to visit the Casentino, where he was deeply moved by the singing of the nuns at the Camaldolensian convent of which Roberto was a patron.

Sen. II, 7.

To the same person.*

The style of your letter, illustrious sir, has tremendously heightened the expectation that I already had of you. To be sure, the man whom I, on the word of others, had credited with being a master of strategy I now know for myself is most learned, so full is your whole letter of philosophical and poetic flowers. Why, then, should I not congratulate you and your country again and again, and the Apennines, that king of mountains, for producing talents more profuse than its springs, more burgeoning than its forests, loftier than its peaks?

With trepidation I had begun writing to you, I confess, not because I hold anything in life sweeter than the friendship of good and illustrious men, but because I am fearful, considering your fortune and your age, that you shrink from these studies, now abandoned by the public; what is more, I had little trust in common talk, which likes to tell many lies, or an enthusiast's judgment, which stands convicted of blindness according to an ancient proverb. But now I do know to whom I write, and thus write confidently and eagerly, with no fear of wasting words, which is a slight loss according to Naso, but a serious one according to people who value their silence; on the contrary, I am anticipating great and welcome benefits from your responses and conversations. You have said much about yearning for me and not only your expectation but the noble, sweet-sounding allurements of the region; my appraisal not of any excellence of mine but of your nobility keeps me from doubting that this is true. Thus, if ever my business allows, I shall try to fulfill this recent wish of yours, which is a longstanding wish of mine.

I would rather have said nothing about the following, for it is quite distasteful to me, but in my opinion it is wrong to overlook anything that comes from the mouth of such a man. I should like to respond with one brief, heart-felt sigh to your astonishment, shared by many others, about why I flee and forsake my native land. O you who revere your country, O you who love me, since you want it so, and pay attention to a man whom you do not know! I did not desert her, but she deserted me, whom at one time she seemed to embrace. And if you will allow me to boast humbly to you, at this very

---

* See II, 6.

moment not only Italian cities but even transalpine and foreign cities invite me with futile entreaties and wait for me, not because I deserve it, for I know better, but because it has been granted to me by heaven to find in this one good—perhaps useless and inconstant— such comfort as I can for my many troubles in the vicissitudes of life. Farewell, and pardon my bragging; I did not want to say this, but sorrow forced me; with confidence I have laid a sad burden on a friendly ear.

Padua, October 6 [1363].

Sen. II, 8.

To the Grand Prior of the Camaldolensians [Giovanni degli Abbarbagliati].*

For your kind letter full of true charity and of much that I was unworthy of hearing, but you were worthy of saying and writing, I send my deeply felt gratitude; as for your humbly taking the trouble of coming to bring me to your monastery, since it is inappropriate for you and undeserved by me, to me it is just as though you had come, for since the nobler part of you has come, I have no doubt that you would come in person unless I resisted. For me, it is enough, if I do come, to find the heart of such a man so well disposed. In the meantime I ask you to grant something more useful to me and easier for you: every time you approach the table of Christ pray for me. Pray that the rest of my life be safe and happy. Pray, too, that He not remember the transgressions of my youth and my follies. Lastly, pray that, when I am ready to depart from this prison of a frail body in order to take that long, uncertain journey, He Himself may come to meet me and answer "I am with you" when I call Him time and again, or else that He bid one of His angels, preferably Michael, to attend me and guide on a level path through the demons' snares my unhappy soul, despairing of her merits and presuming only on God's mercy. Farewell.

Padua, October 8 [1363].

* Grand Prior of the monastery at Camaldoli from 1348 to 1387.

Sen. III, 1.

To Giovanni Boccaccio,* concerning this latest plague and the nonsense about astrologers.

I have always wished for your company, so pleasing to my heart, and I have known and experienced it as much as you chose. That it was also a lucky thing I did not then realize; during these few, fleeting months when you decided to remain on in this house (which is called mine but is really yours), I seem upon my word to have had a truce with Fortune who dared nothing dreary during your stay. I was amazed that not one blow of sad news struck my ears, always so exposed to the arrows of unhappy rumors, and silently asked myself, "What is my enemy doing now? Is she tired, or has she forgotten me? Or rather, has she succumbed, crushed by my patience?" None of these, I now understand. The cause of the brief, unusual respite was more subtle and far different: was she perhaps ashamed to try her old tricks on me under the eyes of such a friend? And as long as she was not sparing you, she spared me for your sake? The truth, I should think, was harshness and trickery in which she abounds, not respect, which she totally lacks, or mercy. Not daring to harm someone with such a companion for support, she postponed it until your departure, lest you confront her, if she attacked me earlier, by giving me your right hand were I laid low or your shoulder were I to stagger. Thus, she did not spare me but clung to me; and as she waited for the time to strike, she sharpened her deadly arrows on a gory whetstone. And so, you had scarcely cast off from the shore when my enemy struck me with an unexpected blow as I was alone and heedless, accompanying you in spirit with my sighs. And she would have instantly felled me, had I not embraced a resolution, and stood fast.

Though nearly too late, it was based on firm conviction, and so I grasped at it, though exhausted by many tempests, as the one helm in my storm-tossed life. God willing, I shall not abandon the resolution that death and all mortal things must be calmly borne by mortals. Still, as so often in the past, a cruel lot just recently jabbed me.

[O] what say I? Where am I? What craze perverts my mind?
[*Aen.* 4.595]

* See I, 5.

This fits the one to whom Maro attributes it less than me, whom grief compels to speak against a well-known truth and my own opinion as well, and to accuse Fortune as though Penthesilea or Orithyia had struck me with a cudgel or pierced me with a javelin. A large part of human complaints are, in fact, not so much unjust as foolish. It is wiser and more fitting, then, to admit and believe that nothing happens to men except by the hidden but fair judgment of God; and so, we must not lash out at unknown and guiltless Fortune. But I return to the story I began.

Well, in the very same hour you left, the priest to whom I had given my letter for Lelius [Angelo di Pietro Stefano dei Tosetti] returned with it still unopened. There was no need for words; his face delivered the message. Sadly I grabbed the letter and recognized my handwriting and seal. "What is the matter?" I said. "What does this letter mean? Why has it come back here? Why is it unanswered? Why does it return unopened at that? What is wrong with my Lelius? Where is he?" At these words, he kept his eyes fixed on the ground without answering. I understood what long and frequent experience has made me sensitive to: I know my losses even before they are reported to me. My very dear friend was gone, or rather had surely preceded me, who will follow him, or more exactly am following and hastening at a rapid, steady pace. My Lelius had passed on then, a man unique in intelligence and eloquence and virtue. To speak of our friendship is futile, so well known is it to all. This was the thirty-fourth year of our friendship, a long time, considering life's brevity, but a short one, considering our yearning for life.

But now, while I am stroking this recent wound to soothe it and to keep my spirit up, a new wound is inflicted upon poor me; I am stabbed once more: the passing of our Simonides [Francesco Nelli] is announced by the one in whose bosom he had expired. O happy souls, you who were of one mind while here, you who departed hence at the same moment, all is well for you, I hope. For us who have remained, the course of our life, now that you are gone, has veered as though from a delightful, level pathway to bumpy ruts and deep, tangled thickets. Such are the games, my friend, that Death plays with us, doubling her fatal blows, nor does it spare us except to have a lingering death again and again, overcome by prolonged anguish, as we behold the ashes of all our dear ones. But let her do as she will, for I have now become numb and have begun to feel nothing; grief, which had become a habit, is no longer grief, but a tearful habit and second nature. It is said that some animals live on poison. But I feed upon my misfortunes with a certain savage delight; my groans have become my sustenance. Fulfilled in me is either David's saying, "My tears have become my bread day and night" [Ps. 42:4], or Ovid's saying, "Worry, tears, heartache—these have been my food" [*Met.* 10.75]. I have grown old in the midst of this, nourished by this; the words of that tormented old man come to mind, "More swiftly than a runner my days have fled, and have seen no good" [Job 9:25]. What would you say? I am utterly beside myself. It is an unusual metamorphosis: I have cast off my mental habit and tenor, and my image alone remains. Thus have the swift years, few indeed and evil, transformed me; thus have they engulfed with sad clouds on all sides, arising from nothing else than friends' deaths, that serenity with which old age, still happy at first and easy, though according to the poet always grim, had adorned me. I live dying in their deaths, so that even if my lot were to give me cause for joy, I believe I have forgotten how to rejoice.

Come now, let us rally our beaten and straggling spirits. O dearest Lelius, I speak to the two of you as though you were present and truly alive; I say you are really Lelius to me, though I am not Scipio to you. How much you wept for me this very year, as your letters bear witness, believing the rumor about my passing! O excellent Simonides, to me you are deservedly my Simonides, both priest and poet, and both equally—a sacred poet. How much had you recently written that you shuddered and trembled lest you outlive me whom you prayed should survive you. Against my wishes you have been granted your prayer; heaven has been closed to my prayers, but open to yours. O vain concerns of men, idle fears, empty hopes! What did you fear, O dearest ones? Why were you troubled? Here am I whose rumored death, or even the thought of it, had so shaken your hearts. I who wished to die before all of my friends now dread being the last to die. And this is my first complaint, that both of you scorned for yourselves the very thing that you had warned me about in your letters: shunning the infected air and places notorious for pestilence.

But I am vainly reproaching those who will not respond, in order to unburden my spirit. How I wish, dear friend, that they had followed you and were with you now in the flesh, just as they always were in spirit! How I wish that they had been willing to retreat in the face of the plague, so devastating for Rome in particular and Naples, and thus would now be secure under divine protection. I rejoice that you did do this, and I am grateful, too, that you deemed my home a fit place for you to rest while your fatherland labored under the same disaster. Both of them, however, who loyally advised me, would not apply the advice to themselves—perhaps I should say more truthfully, could not, for it is hard to tear loose what is fixed. And if they had to die now, Lelius's bones rightfully belonged to Rome, where they had first been bound together and clothed with sinews and skin, but the other's remains belonged to Florence; yet Naples took them. Thus the earthly part of Simonides, that love and delight of ours, will lie near Virgil, which to a lover and cultivator of the Pierides is some comfort for a foreign burial. But the spiritual part of both of them has gone to heaven. Thus am I persuaded, thus do I pray, thus do I wish, and surely thus it must be. Such souls cannot go elsewhere, for the ruler of heaven delights in lofty and gentle spirits. But alas, why does the last of our companions to cross the harsh threshold of this life exit first, except to help me understand through redoubled evidence? If I were now to begin to realize this for the first time, I would be slow-witted: that nothing human happens in any order.

I see, dear friend, that lamentations now return to my pen, though my reason condemned them and my mind cast them out. For some sick people endless complaining is a kind of remedy, as if they would relieve the feeling of illness by their laments. Others in their weariness cannot rest without sighs and faint murmuring, as if that groaning fluffed their pillow more comfortably and those quivering cries served for soft feathers. Regardless of where my old habit has pushed my tongue or pen, I have recently made a resolution and fixed it in my mind with much effort, I confess, but determined by the great storm of events: to disdain hope and fear, joys and griefs. It is these that generally upset even stable characters and noble plans. The day is approaching, moreover, when none of those things, which now so powerfully cloud or brighten our lives, will matter to us at all. Meanwhile, as things are, we must resist fear and oppressive gloom with all our strength. Contrary to these, uneasy hope, or that mad cheerful joy, which casts many people down after raising them on high, has brought us no trouble in these times, thank God, and does not seem about to bring us any; for it is long banished and withdrawn from our sight.

But laying these aside, I return to you and to our Simonides; of the two you are nearly my only intellectual comrade still surviving. Though departed, he is present, and never more so than since his departure. For before his end, I used to anticipate his absence, but since death has snatched him from me, I do not think now that he is about to return; yet he has returned, and I take comfort in his imagined presence. I used to consider you and him as another Varius and Tucca, should anything happen to me because of the human condition while my works remained unfinished. Now, since heaven likes this sequence of events, it is fitting, unless I am mistaken, that I should do for him what I had decided that he should do for me. Therefore, if any of his works and letters of any kind remain unfinished, divide them fairly between us. And inasmuch as our fortune also separates us, and considering our individual talents, send my portion to me; keep yours for yourself. We owe this to him, I admit, and you surely would not say no. Let him live in heaven and in our memories as long as we live; after us, however, let him live in the memory of posterity who, if they know him, will hold him dear—and I am not being misled by love. Whatever is required, though weighed down by my own burdens, I promise my assistance humbly, conscientiously.

I am not changing my dedication, which he joyfully accepted after the passing of my Socrates [Ludwig van Kempen], of all my correspondence—and only with my death do I see any end to that. Insofar as this is concerned, nothing is changed by his death, nor is there any need to be silent. I can no longer write to him. Yet surely no one will prevent me from writing and thinking about him, and remembering him as long as I remember myself. Accordingly, my first dedication will never change. What I promised to the man long ago while he was alive and healthy, I shall fulfill to his dry ashes, I shall fulfill to his name alone. Whatever it will be, it will be for my Simonides. I know not how long it will take and how little it will be, but doubtless it will equal the span of my life; nothing is more uncertain than that, but certainly it is already beginning to be longer than I hoped and wished. At that age when everyone is most eager to live, I too wished to live, but not alone without my proven and longstanding friends; I have, as you see, outlived nearly all of them so that very soon I must either live without friendships—an inhuman and wretched kind of life—or seek new ones, a risky and difficult business.

But not to return to complaints, which are suggested by every word and press upon me on all sides in spite of myself, let us turn to another, yet related, subject. I believe you can see the state of human affairs, for certainly anyone who does not must be either asleep or blind. The year 1348 of this last age was one of mourning for us. Now we realize that it was only the beginning of our mourning, for since then this evil force, unequaled and unheard of in human annals through the centuries, has never ceased, striking everywhere on all sides, on the left and right, like a skilled warrior. Having marched across the entire world several times leaving no area immune, it has struck some places two, three, or four times, and plagued a number of them with an annual blight. The city of Milan, the Ligurian capital and metropolis, was long untouched by this ordeal to the point of envy, boasting of its healthful skies, mild climate, and large population, but it too became empty and filthy in the sixty-first year of this century. You know what I, too, lost, while absent through God's will, to that deluge. The following year was kinder to the Milanese, but even crueler to me: it snatched away my best friend on earth [Ludwig van Kempen]; just as there was no man like him, so there is no loss like mine. I shall not name him lest it bring tears to my eyes against my will, and for you it is unnecessary since you understand of whom I speak. The same year so depopulated Verona that our age anyhow will never again view it as it once was.

O savage heart of that cruel ruler who we read used to lament his times for not being distinguished by any public calamities, and to wish for some universal woe and memorable pestilence! How I wish that you had seen something similar, O mad Gaius [Caligula], so that we might not be seeing so much of this daily! And would that the sorrowful spectacle had spared our pious eyes and instead entertained your impious ones! I pass over not only events abroad but our own as well; it is too long and sad a story. In a word, the world is empty of men and full of crimes. Thus does the entire heritage of misdeeds descend upon a few people; let us not marvel if the fewer we are, the worse we are. For inevitably this poison of minds and this fury, this extravagance and this kettle of vices, which are all set atop fires ever refueling, with nothing being taken away but something being added daily, boil up all the more deadly, the more narrowly they are confined.

But to continue: this is the third year in a row, the sixteenth since the calamities began, that the plague has once again invaded many noble cities. Among these was Florence too, which has been so harried and tormented this summer that it nearly equals the summer of fifteen years ago. The internal destruction has been aggravated by the raging foreign war, waged with varying success against the Pisans, but with great devastation on both sides, and with greater danger; the outcome now hangs in great doubt.

Amidst these evils, you have heard what the astrologers dream; they extend the evil influence of the malignant stars into the sixty-fifth year of this century. After that, all the happier things are in doubt with which the charlatans are deluding those able to survive. Yet they keep promising, and the day is so near that it cannot long be doubtful how much the promise is worth—I mean among the people who hang upon the promises not just of astrologers but of any soothsayer or madman that comes along. But for us it ought to be no less sure today than in the future, if we recall their promises of old. Well, they maintain that Mars and Saturn are coming together somewhere among the stars and that conjunction—to use their word—after the year's end will last for a full two years. Quite astonishing that from the beginning of things stars have never been in these locations as long as they have traveled their courses throughout the heavens! But if they were there, it is astonishing that from those same conjunctions and constellations have come such different effects. The astrologers must then concede one of the following: if they deny that anything like it has been seen, read, or heard since the creation of the world or—since they usually deny creation—in man's memory, let them come out with it, or if they cannot deny it, let them remain silent and allow others to, or at least let them not be so confident of deceiving us with their wiles.

We do not know what is happening in the heavens, but impudently and rashly *they* profess to know. Yet we do know in part what has been happening on earth, unless perhaps heaven has its own alterations and discords, and the heavenly bodies, confounded by old age and upset by hatred, have forgotten their paths, and the stars, now truly astray and wandering without laws or the curbs of nature, pursue their courses, so deadly to mortals, outside the zodiac, reckless as Phaethon. For they are going to say this and any nonsense at all rather than confess their own ignorance. Theirs is not only ignorance but blindness and total madness, which many times in the past was evident to everyone, but never more clearly than during this present plague. And now it would be shameful to confess finally that they do not know what they do not know; what is more, there is no one who does not know what they do not know. In this regard, the doctors are more modest; for in my presence even the ones considered most experienced have confessed that the remedies of their art do not extend to this secret of cruel nature; I could forgive their ignorance, were they to admit it likewise in other matters.

Yet astrologers, who are said to be ignorant of everything, would rather die than say they are ignorant of that. Of course, habit and shyness, obstinacy, a little money, and the rashness of madmen, who are ever hanging onto future expectations, all this makes them so tongue-tied that you would need a rack to squeeze the truth from them. No one, unless prompted by a strong sense of modesty, willingly confesses his ignorance. They themselves do know; and if they have doubts, let them learn from that heaven of theirs, which contradicts so many of their lies that what they wave in front of them, what they have for sale, or what they stuff into parched minds and thirsty ears is nothing at all. Yet they strive to keep that nothingness from others for fear that, if it came to light, they too would be nothing. For whatever a man finds delight in, that he is; there is much affinity between art and artist. The overwhelming reason for their obstinacy is this: they fear to appear what they are and they long to be what they are not, since inside they are nothing, and shackled by evil habit, they can no longer be anything else; so they consider this the only possible escape: they choose to appear something that they cannot be, and yet in vain, for they are fools. Certainly if they were to discuss the movements of the heavens, or to predict the winds and the rains, heat and cold, storms at sea and eclipses of the sun and moon, they ought to be listened to, often to advantage and ever with delight. But when they prate about the affairs and vicissitudes of men, things known only to God, they ought to be spurned as fabricators of dismal lies, and refused intercourse not only with scholars but with all good men. With a certain perversity of spirit and remarkable obstinacy, they neglect the possible to concentrate upon the impossible, unashamed, even declaring it easier to know.

Perhaps it has come to your ears that, during the recent expedition against Ticinum [Pavia] when that admirable man, now the ruler there [Galeazzo Visconti], was provoked into making the decision to attack that strong, well-fortified city, all the astrologers began to clamor. Among them was the one we know who is so much more famous than the others that he was commonly believed to have foreknowledge of the future, rather than foreboding. For many days he halted the departure that was ready and the standards raised to do battle, saying that they must await the coming of the auspicious hour. But when it had arrived, he bade the armies to move out and go into battle in full force. Although an extraordinary drought had held sway both in heaven and on earth for many months before that, on that very day the floodgates of heaven were suddenly opened. Such a downpour began to fall, and increased for many days and nights on end, that all the fields and especially the camp surrounding the enemy walls were flooded by an amazing, unusual deluge. There was great danger that those ready to conquer with arms would nearly be conquered by the rain. And if later they engaged in battle with better omens, it was due to that man's courage and good fortune, relying upon God's protection without consulting the stars, that the city was captured and the war ended. Then, intolerant of the lie, I challenged that diviner in a friendly way. He was otherwise a good man of greater than average learning, very dear to me, but, I confess, he would be dearer if he were not an astrologer. Why had his judgment about this important matter so flagged as not to see so dangerous and so immediate a change in the weather? He answered that it was most difficult to foresee the winds and the rains and the other so-called "impressions of the air." To which I replied: "So it is easier to know what is going to happen just to me or another person in years to come than what is threatening and ready to erupt today or tomorrow in heaven and on earth and throughout all of nature, whereas the latter occur naturally and the former supernaturally with God apportioning to each its lot." His answer was, "It is easier beyond any doubt," but he said it in such a way that you could detect on his face the shame in his heart. He knows I am speaking the truth, nor would he, I believe, deny any of this, although from the very founding of the present principality he and I, who was there at that time, disagreed about an even greater absurdity.

Having chosen with a rather detailed horoscope the time for the insignia of sovereignty to be transferred more propitiously to those three illustrious brothers,* he interrupted me and my speech, which I had been bidden to make on that solemn occasion, and the attention of the new lords and of the people, to say that the hour had come which could not be allowed to slip by without grave danger. Though fully aware that it was nonsense, I nevertheless did not oppose the foolish prevailing opinion and halted my speech before it was half-finished. Hesitating and looking stunned, he stood there, saying that some time remained before the arrival of that auspicious hour and began to urge me in the meantime to speak. I replied with a smile that I had finished, that there was nothing after the ending, and that I could think of no pretty story to recount to the Milanese public. He was flustered and kept scratching his head; when all fell silent, some angry and others laughing, after a while he shouted: "Now is the time." Then an elderly man-at-arms in charge of the

---

* Upon the death of Archbishop Giovanni Visconti on October 5, 1354, the Milanese succession passed to his three nephews, Matteo, Bernabò, and Galeazzo.

three straight, white, and gleaming staffs which are now the scepters of our city, placed one in the hand of each brother with joyful words and best wishes and congratulations. But he did this with such long pauses that, if there is any truth in the wheel of Nigidius with which the astrologers reveal their ignorance while wishing to conceal it, then it could well be believed that a different kind of fate loomed for each brother. Nor, by Jove, was it otherwise! It is common knowledge that within the year, the eldest lost Bologna, a noble part of his realm, and soon afterwards he lost his life while still in his prime. The other two have enjoyed better success and longer life, flourishing for more than ten years, now more than ever. All this I have often brought up jokingly with my friend, the soothsayer, although his reply is always the same: that nothing more could be expected from his art. And, by Jove, I believe he speaks the truth. His age and his dire need to raise a large family—which sometimes bends even great talents to unworthy expedients—make me hold him a little less to blame. That this has driven him too into this nonsense I am led to think by one of his responses. While friendly to him and to his reputation, I used to discuss the same thing with him again and again, although he was much senior to me in age and knowledge. One day, as though he had awakened, he sighed deeply and broke into words, "Dear friend, I feel exactly as you do in this matter. But this is how I have to live." I felt the golden chain of need, and out of pity remained silent from then on.

To return to my point, however, such is the custom of others, such is the shame of confessing, such is the desire of minds to gain some power over us, over our fortunes, as they say, and over the liberty of our spirits, no matter how. Hence, they earn the dark infamy of deceit and error instead of the fair praise for honorable study, which they have scorned. Any falseness in their statements you ought to impute to their deceit and ignorance, any truth not to their knowledge but to mere chance. What else did that good counselor once tell Augustine, who was then quite young and thus least inclined to believe it, while later he was not only to believe it, but soon to persuade others of it too and to be throughout his lifetime a strong opponent and a relentless eradicator of this nonsense? That it is the power of chance [so his counselor told him], diffused throughout nature, which does all this. That is why the best-laid plans are thwarted, while others, which slipped out by accident, are often established with real success, and truth not found by long study reveals itself like a game to those occupied with something else. The astrologers, however, proclaim with the greatest insolence whenever one or two things prove true by chance; they find excuses for constantly lying and fly into a rage at whoever questions the basis for their prediction. Surely it is brazen not to blush at the opposite of what you would boast about. I could forgive their error or their poverty, were they to lie more shamefacedly. What man does not detest impudent ignorance and arrogant lying?

I realize that often, to refute them, I hurled many accusations in writing and even more in conversation. These admittedly resulted not from any hope of prevailing, but from hatred of falsehood. It has been a waste of my time, but I am in good company, and that comforts me; for what friend of truth does not hate and refute those fellows? Yet, it is always quite in vain. Words are to no avail; what is needed are blows and the full rigor of the law, not books by learned men. Though ignorant of the past and the present, the astrologers are determined to foresee the future or, more precisely, to foretell it, as though foreknown, to those who believe. Not only the infidelity and impiety, but also the intellectual immaturity and incapacity for any truth is evident in those who put their faith in them; against them truth, reason, experience, not only of holy men but of weighty philosophers, do battle in entire volumes. I leave aside the most painstaking and powerful treatises, the lengthiest disputations by Cicero, Ambrose, and Augustine, which neither time nor space permits, nor any able reader needs. Certainly they are all well known, but do let me give one sentence of Ambrose himself since it was written separately. It is so true and so brief; it is from the book he wrote on the death of his brother, Satyrus. He says, "Philosophers who argue about heaven do not know what they are talking about." What will these "philosophers" say? They will laugh, I know, for they are as foolish as they are rash; but let them remember that anything said against him is said against the Holy Spirit that inspired him as he said these words.

But here I go again. Can those who scorn the Holy Spirit not despise the words and pens of saints, those instruments of the Holy Spirit, or listen more reverently to Isaiah saying: "Predict what is to come and we shall know that you are gods" [41:23]? As they accuse of ignorance the writers of the New Testament, so do they accuse the prophets of madness. In sum, they curse everyone but Ptolemy the Egyptian or Firmicius the Sicilian. But let their madness harm them, while profiting us, so that the more shamefully we see them falling away from the truth, the more tenaciously we cling to it. Finally, to make an end of them once and for all and to cease wasting futile words on the deaf, if you want my brief opinion of their threats and promises, I will make you a diviner by an astonishing shortcut: observe what they predict on anything at all; it will be the opposite. Whoever wishes to use this kind of prophesying will indeed turn out the opposite of them, that is, very rarely a liar, nearly always speaking the truth.

I believe you can now see what hope I hold in their promised end to our ills. If you dismiss their prophecies, hateful and at the same time silly, and want to know once again your simple friend's opinion, you should consult not the stars, not lightning or entrails or birds, in short, no divination at all, but just the mind deliberating in silence, and if there is any truth in my foreboding, this is how I feel, inasmuch as it is God's wrath that overwhelms the human race. This I have long believed, I confess, and it will all finally end when either our spirits are softened and bent to another way of life, or else well-deserved punishments have crushed human hardness which, as you see, reveals itself inflexible and has shaped itself until now with hammer and anvil; in this situation there is no other remedy but to live prepared for the time when we shall be called, and thus, it shall not frighten us as if something new and unexpected. In any case, it goes far back; and unless we are fools, we ought to have foreseen it long ago, especially since we have beheld the general ruination of the world and nearly all our dear ones crushed beneath it and anything on earth that had been quite dear to us. If by chance any were left, by now the survivors have perished. I feel this to be the sole remedy for such ills, and urge you to agree. There is no escape from death. This I wrote long ago to a concerned friend, and I have not changed my mind.

Close your eyes to prophecies and your ears to nonsense, avoid doctors, flee astrologers; the former harm the body, the latter the soul. Worship the true Savior and Creator of the stars. If some variation in nature or the air infected by unknown causes or a certain constellation—if we absolutely must speak thus—unknown to mortals catches up with us, it will end when the corruption is burned off and dispelled by the sun's rays or dispersed elsewhere, or when the pollution is all spent. When either or both of these will occur no sky-watcher knows, but the Creator or perhaps some pious wise man to whom He reveals it, not Saturn or Mars. It is mad chatter to make authorities of *them* and to impose them as lords over us, eluding God's plans as much as possible and killing free will (which the egregious charlatans think they can subsequently revive with quack formulas, by saying that the wise man rules the stars); they blatantly mask their infinite lies with one word, or rather pile lies upon lies. For this too is false. Neither does the wise man rule the stars, nor the stars the wise man, but God rules both. Indeed from where, if we believe *that*, did this wise lord of the stars get his wisdom, except from the stars? O base and fragile pastime of obscurity, O proverb so long cited amiss, for sane ears to block out! How can one rule the stars when he has nothing except what the stars have bestowed upon him? What law has ever made a vassal the lord of the one from whom he holds the fief and not rather made him answerable and subject to himself? The wise man rules himself as long as he obeys God, and, looking to Him, steers the ship of his life to God with the helm of reason; but he can neither rule the stars, nor does he even want to, for there is one Ruler of stars and men. Aware of Him, and content to serve Him and be free of others, the wise man does not seek dominion, I won't say of heaven, but not even of the very earth that he inhabits. For him, tenancy is enough. Let us assume, however, that the wise man does rule the stars, as these people would like, and that he gets that rule either from the stars themselves, or from wherever. Do they not see, or do they ignore how many are slaves to the stars, if only the wise man is either their lord or exempt from slavery?

I could cite many quotations from the Scriptures to show how few have ever been wise, and how true is Solomon's saying that the number of fools is infinite.* I believe, however, that proof for this ought to be left to experience. For my part, let anyone search large cities for himself to see how many wise men he meets each day and ponder how many wise men he has dealt with. Provided that he judges the wise man that we seek by the merit of his life and not by popular repute, that is, not by others' words or even one's own but by the facts and the reality, then adding them all up, I think you can count them on the fingers of one hand. I certainly do not consider a man wise, as foolish people call lawyers wise, nor as even the learned call wise someone who knows a great deal. It is one thing to be wise, another to be eloquent. Wisdom demands character and not letters. When combined with a well-principled mind, letters will be an immense adornment and resource, but will never help the wicked man inclined to evil, and often will be a hindrance to it.

This would be easy to prove with many clear examples, but even the multitude realizes that men of letters have overthrown republics through evil counsel, and have nourished deep discords with their

---

* Based inaccurately on Eccl. 4:16.

words, and driven armed forces to destruction; or, to mention their worst deed, they have infected souls with the dire poison of their doctrines, and the world with their manifold errors. Therefore, good will, not talent, his life, not his speech, make the wise man. But there have been those who say there is no wise man, there have been those who say just one. That honor was conferred upon Cato by our people, but among the Greeks upon Socrates by Apollo. The Greeks themselves count seven. Let those who say it and those about whom they say it see how true it is; their names are common knowledge, of course, in every school. Others perhaps say there were more, but that loquacious nation, so taken with its own accomplishments, was content with this number; nor was there any lack of criticism and ridicule of it. It is much easier to be called wise than to become so. Therefore, if one's eyes could see into the very people who take pride in being called wise, many things would be lacking before they could begin to be what they are said to be; I believe even the multitude, ignorant of shame, would be ashamed and say "there are fewer wise men than reputation would have it." Certainly in my opinion a wise man is, I will not say rarer than the phoenix, reborn every five hundred years, but a rare bird just the same: he does not fly in flocks nor build his nest everywhere, he does not perch on any old bough, nor is he born every springtime. In fact, Cicero views his birth as rarer than a mule giving birth, whose very rarity causes it to be numbered among the prodigies.

Therefore, were this wise man, who either is not or is very rare, to control the stars, what will others do, or what will everyone do? What, I repeat, except to serve the stars not only with their bodies but with their minds; and nothing can be more wretched than that. Yet that does not move these people who, scorning men's salvation, are drawn only by the profit. They only gape after plunder, and since they can hope for nothing from free men and are unable to make them their own slaves, they make them slaves of the stars, as we have already said; they want to be called the confidants and almost the counselors of the stars, and claim to be mediators of the secrets between the slaves and the masters. O brazen outrage of those who promise, O foolish fear of those who believe them! But the greatest brazenness of all is that, to excuse mens' sins, they accuse the justice of God by saying, in Augustine's celebrated words, "The inevitable cause of your sinning comes from heaven and Venus has done this, or Saturn or Mars for that matter; thus man— his flesh and blood and arrogant rottenness—may be blameless, but the Creator, the controller of heaven and the stars, is to blame. And who is this, if not our God, the sweetness and fount of righteousness?"

But now to put a bridle upon the wrath which snatches my pen, and to quit here as I promised above, and to tear away from these cheats: if here too, where there is a quite natural cause of the present evils, you ask my advice, nothing is more certain to me than what you have heard: from this mortal, wretched life where we are endangered, we must flee to Him whose presence is the flood of joy and fount of life. For what else, I ask, may a traveler do, realizing that his limited water supply in a cracked jug is leaking out and fearing to perish of thirst, except to turn at once where he may find a perennial stream or a spring of unfailing water? Yet I would not rule out a certain amount of human precaution, and in particular a change of residence, so that we leave behind for a time the places where the pestilential star has more violently raged and go to a healthier place. Thus does the sailor avoid a storm by entering port, or a farmer the rain by finding cover, thus does the wise man skirt danger by entering a respectable inn; although undaunted by such perils, if forced to choose, he would prefer death itself to wickedness.

Those two friends had, in fact, given me that advice, which—alas, why is everyone a better counselor to others than to himself?—they neglected to heed for their well-being, if indeed it was up to them and they were not held there by dire force. With a reliance either on human judgment or, as seems certain, on God's guidance, you left Naples and, passing by Florence, came by a longer route to my house, even though both cities remained unscathed until that time. Your choice was lucky, as it deserved to be, and certainly touching; I am flattered at your preference for me to your native land, and I rejoice at your prudence or good fortune. My only complaint, as I said to you in person, was your haste to depart too soon. For although the plague was said to have subsided there, you know the multitude has a way of imagining or anticipating what appeals to it. I understood though: either love for your country spurred you onward or the pleasure of my company was already assuaged by three months' stay and did not detain you. And so, you could not be talked out of leaving, nor could I accuse you of unfairness or be angry at taking second place to the country to which you had previously preferred me. Yet since love has the eyes of a lynx or the ears of a boar, I hear that some fear and danger of remnants of the plague still persists there. If it is so, dear friend, I beg you to return for your own sake. Take this worry away from me, to whom you have become, in case you don't know, even dearer than ever. And if you ask why, the shortage itself is the cause. To no one is light dearer than to the one-eyed; as I was saying, you are practically the only one I have from among my old friends. I am uneasy about what to expect from our Barbato [da Sulmona], now that death is so devastating the Peligni and the Abruzzi.

Come then, you will be more than welcome. Here is the mildest season of the year, no cares except delightful Pierian ones, and a house safe from disease, which I would perhaps describe to you in writing but you know it well; here is the best company, I doubt whether anyone could wish better: Benintendi [dei Ravagnani], whose name comes from his accomplishments, chancellor of this celebrated city, very attentive to public affairs and private friendships and noble studies, when freed of his daily concerns, comes in the evening to meet me in his ever-ready gondola with a happy face and affectionate heart. Recently you saw for yourself how nice it was—the nightly boating and conversation—and learned too that there is something so sincere and well seasoned about this man. There is also our Donato Apenninigena [Albanzani], whom the Adriatic shore has sheltered for many years since he broke away from the Tuscan hills. I speak of our Donato who voluntarily gave himself to us, the successor to that Donatus of old both in profession and in name; no one is more pleasant, no one more faultless, no one more devoted to us, no one better known to you than he. I will not mention anyone else; these will suffice. For although I have never liked total, inhuman solitude, and I cannot agree with what is written about Bellerophon (he ate his heart out avoiding all human contact, and long ago I wrote in my two books on the solitary life a great deal about him as best I could in my own solitude), still I have always believed that the wise and learned man needs few companions, since he has learned, if forced by the situation, how to be his own companion and interlocutor. But if lingering here becomes tedious or the changeable autumn weather untrustworthy—although in my opinion northerly or westerly winds cannot becalm and cheer the heavens better than happy faces and welcome conversations of friends—we will leave here, and you will be perhaps a useful but certainly a delightful instigator and companion of my journey. We will go to the Capo d'Istria and to Trieste where the climate is reported to me, in a trustworthy letter, to be perfectly mild.

Finally your return will have this good result at least: as I have been thinking for a long time, we can trace the source of the Timavus, celebrated by poets but ignored even by many learned men, where it is and not where they search for it, namely, in the territory of Padua. A verse of Lucan prompted the error by placing it near Euganean Aponus, but more informed cosmographers place it instead around Aquileia,

> Whence, through nine mouths, he goes—a bursting sea [the
> Timavus].
> Loudly the cliffs resound, and splashing water
> Covers the fields. [Virg., *Aen.* 1.245-6]

Farewell.

Venice, September 7 [1363].

Sen. III, 2.

To the same person,* to find out how he is.

No doubt you have learned of our misfortunes and have mourned the passing of my Lelius [Angelo di Pietro Stefano dei Tosetti] and our Simonides [Francesco Nelli]. Before your departure, you knew about the first one, but preferred to have the blow to my ears delivered by someone other than you. You learned about the second right after that on your own doorstep. Sadly I dictated a lengthy letter to you about them and about other things that concern both our present calamity in our land and that of the world. My reason for not sending it was not so much the exertion or my laziness—although both reasons are true—as the fear of wasting this exertion too, just as the one to Lelius, whom I am speaking about, and to Simonides. After I had written at length to them, the letters found the ashes of both of them still warm, and returned to me at nearly the same hour, though from different directions, still bearing my seal. The very sight of them made me consider them bearers of sad tidings—so they were—and I threw them into the flames as an offering to those dear spirits.

To be honest, a terrible fear for you gripped both our Donato [Albanzani] and me, lest you too be gone. It does not seem possible that you would not have written, if you were alive, to those friends who we think you know are anxious and worried. If you are alive, then, there is utterly no excuse for not writing. As Maro says,

> But if your life is over, and the turf,
> Dear brother, of our country holds you fast
> [*Aen.* 1.555]

you obviously are excused. The excuse, I believe, is as happy for you as it is wretched for us, and from the depths of my soul it will wrench a lingering groan, if any are left there.

Farewell, if you live, and if you are no more, farewell forever.

Venice, December 20 [1363].

---

* See I, 5.

Sen. III, 3.

To Niccolò [Acciaiuoli], Grand Seneschal of the Kingdom of Sicily, a complaint.

Long have I wanted to tell you something, noble sir and dear glory of mine, but my love and your kindness, poured upon me in sweet words, have always stopped my tongue as I began to speak. But now I blame myself because a spirit such as yours, so lofty and so dedicated to the truth, has up to now been treated by me, also a friend of the truth, not as it befits you to hear or me to speak, pleasantly rather than manfully. What I would like to say to you now is brief in words but great in substance. Long have I deemed you the most welcome and trusty refuge for my stormy life, and a truly sweet solace for my spirit; and you too have chosen me as the first among all, as you say, and not the last, as I expect. And now suddenly nearly all who were devoted to you and the best of brothers to me have passed away at the same time, faster than the wind: Socrates [Ludwig van Kempen], Zanobi [da Strada], Lelius [Angelo di Pietro Stefano dei Tosetti], Simonides [Francesco Nelli], and, as I heard lately, Barbato [da Sulmona], all our dear ones who considered you like some god and loved me beyond all human bounds. I leave out the others; it is too long and tearful to count them.

And what do you think? We too shall be going when our time comes, in no time, without any delay, swiftly, instantly. Perhaps we shall die this very day and overtake those whom we sent on ahead; your virtue or good fortune will not exempt you, my learning will not exempt me. We must pay our debt to nature and die, we must depart and yield to those who follow us, we must go the way of our fathers. Death will equally enter your palace and my solitudes. In this shortest of pathways of this most wretched life to whose end, as you see, we are fast approaching, running, indeed flying, especially in these years closest to the final one, you—whom I have honored above many other statesmen and who have preferred me above many others, with a judgment that is otherwise excellent—how much, when we come either singly or together to our end which

---

* A favorite of King Robert of Naples, who made him Grand Seneschal. P. had great admiration for his diplomatic skills, especially during the unstable period following the king's death when Acciaiuoli acted as guardian and adviser to Louis of Taranto, Robert's nephew.

must occur and cannot be deferred, will you grieve that you, distracted by some concern or other, perhaps greater and, for all I know, handsomer, never did anything for me, although at any time you could have and often promised to? Though not indebted to me for any merit of mine, you would still be indebted to your promise. So many times you allotted to me, proferring a binding oath, the best portion of your most ample patrimony and all your possessions, the one nearest my holdings; you reserved for yourself the smallest and most remote part which I would leave for your own use. I have more than one letter written in your own hand. When you were finally asked, you would not supply to that "esteemed and cherished" friend of yours, not, I may say, those portions of your inheritance nor anything at all from your possessions—which I did not in the least seek—but not even a single, rightful, respectful word, worthy of you, that would have sounded most becomingly on your lips and in the ears of listeners. Do think about this. I feel that I would be doing you and myself an injustice not to remind you of this neglected duty that is so becoming to you. What do you think has made me put this off until now, except the numbing pain? When the pain finally overcame the numbness, and chance recently brought me this man who has been so fond of me lately and of you much longer, it forced me not to put it off any longer. I unloaded on him all my disappointments, complaints, and anguish as if I saw you present in him, and complained about you to yourself—which I very often do in silence.

Therefore, believe him, and listen to him, I beg you. Unless it is dishonorable to you, listen to him with patience, but arm yourself with it before he begins, and in a kindly mood confront the overly harsh words. You will hear things said against you. Do not take sides but take the case itself. You, the defendant, witness, and judge, pass sentence on yourself. See how it befits your reputation to have had for so many years a man whom you call friend, whom at times you used to address as a superior because of your inborn humility, forgetful of your own greatness, although he acknowledges himself far from your equal in everything, and to have conferred on him nothing in such a long period beyond the empty name, the éclat of an illustrious friendship. In brief and simple words, you could have long since performed your duties as a friend. You must see what you will respond to this charge before the tribunal of Him who bids us to be good not only to our friends but to our enemies. Twice I asked you. Would that you had either quickly refused it or fulfilled it, albeit late, or at the least been slower to promise. Here now is my third and final plea—how effective it will be is up to you. I have not yet ceased hoping for something from you. If you disappoint me now, I shall be yours nonetheless. The one whom I have once cherished, I cherish forever, but I shall no longer be a nuisance. I shall add this last thought to what has been said: the praise of friendship will be great and special, but it is based on many great things. It is easy to be called a friend, but hard to be a friend. Farewell. And if I speak too intimately, forgive me.

Padua, October 13 [1363–65].

Sen. III, 4.

To a certain unknown person,* concerning the mind and character of Barbato da Sulmona.

The name of my Barbato—scarcely has there been another name dearer to me, or sweeter-sounding even now—arrests my pen in the midst of its preoccupations, petty perhaps, but certainly many. For you ask and, as though it were a duty, demand that I write a short work or panegyric for posterity on that gentleman's life, character, and deeds, which you assume are known to me. I readily admit that he deserves to have his praises sung, that you are the proper person to make such a noble request, and that I owe him such a courtesy; and I do not deny that his virtue, as it is dear, is best known to me. The sun has beheld no one more kind, more sound, and more honest, no one more enamored of letters. He used to relish them as the finest food for which he hungered; he was indifferent to all other pleasures; he fled vainglory; he was incapable of insolence or envy. In addition, he was an intellectually penetrating and elegant writer, extremely learned, with ready memory. This is what I know about the man. If posterity is to have any faith in me, I swear that he is so, and even greater than either the lack of time or this humble style could allow. Moreover, he so cherished me that, unless I am wrong, he not only preferred no one to me, but considered no mortal my equal. And yet my lot begrudged me his company. Thus has it been since the star of Italy and great honor of our century, King Robert of Sicily, was taken from us by a death, harsh not to him but to his country—he through whom we had been united under the yoke of friendship. While the king was alive, my Barbato and I could not be separated from each other in body any more than in spirit. He had brought us together. He would have kept us together, as he bound many things securely and firmly, like a keystone. When Robert was borne off, we too were physically separated, and as every bond of unity was undone there followed such a wretched collapse that all Sicilians realized how much the public welfare had depended on the wisdom and virtue of one man. Upon Robert's death, therefore, my Barbato returned to his Sulmona as

---

* Francesco Sanità, a minor poet from Sulmona who became an intimate of Barbato da Sulmona when the latter returned from the court of King Robert of Naples. This is the only letter to him.

though he already knew of the impending disasters. And I, freed from admiration of the royal majesty whose bond kept drawing me back, captive, to Parthenope [Naples], I thenceforth remained either in Gaul, where I was then, or between the Alps and the Apennines, where I am now. So it has come about that as certain as I was of my excellent friend's love and virtue, I did not know his domestic habits, his way of life, his household routine, his political responsibilities. In short, I have learned nothing of his doings during the twenty-two years that I did not see him, or what he said or wrote, although with his ample talents he doubtless could do many things. Even if I had leisure—which I do not—to write about this, I would be unable to write with any confidence of the facts anything other than what you have heard.

The best I can do comes down to this: many of my letters addressed to him bear witness that his name has mattered to me, as does my youthful work, a book of letters in verse, all dedicated to him. You, who grew up under his tutelage, and are fully informed about his wealth and deeds because of your long-continued association and are favored by age, leisure, and talent, carry out by yourself what you ask of me—successfully, I pray, so that I may learn from you what I am eager to know. You will thus be celebrating not only the memory of the friend we share, but the glory of the country you share with him. Unless love deceives me, with all due respect to Naso, in no age did your country have a greater citizen. Naso had a bright talent, but a dark character, although he tried in vain to cleanse with one short jingle the many stains on his long life.* Your friend had a good talent and led a better life. Farewell.

[1363].

---

* Petrarch perhaps is referring to Ovid's autobiographical poem (*Tristia* 4.10), which is quite long as elegies go.

Sen. III, 5.

To Giovanni Boccaccio,[*] on the discomfort of the scab and the remedies of physicians.

We have gone long enough, and more, without a word, and there is a certain pleasure in peaceful silence as in friendly discourse. But we must take care that it not drag on unduly. I shall not say that I had nothing to write about, lest I tell a lie. For how could that be, when heaven, earth, the sea, and all therein, and man above all—that astonishing product of Mother Nature, at once the best and worst animal, now nearly equal to the angels, now more monstrous than the grisly serpents—is an inexhaustible subject, ever thrust upon our eyes and ears. I can truly say that I lacked only the time, and I had, and I have and know not how long it will last, a rough, dry scab, uncomfortable at any age but considered dangerous at mine. Yet, far be it from me to let any outward trouble worry me, so long as I shake off the mental itch and disease. But this affliction has so taken hold of me for some four months now that it has snatched my hands not only from my pen but from my food in order to scratch and dig at it. We know from experience what remedies or advice for that matter, I can expect from my doctor friends. They have made a game and profit out of men's ills; and professing to be helpers, they become spectators of the sick and of sicknesses; having tried all remedies in vain, while I endured rather than approved or hoped for anything from them, they finally decided, in order to appear as forecasters at least, even if not healers, that I should expect help from the approaching summer—harsh and serious straits that drive me not to ask or hope for help against an enemy, except from another enemy. I, however, do not believe the doctors, nor hope for anything from the summer, but I do hope for everything from Him of whom it is written, "Summer and spring You fashioned" [Ps. 74:17]. This alone I know and accept as the most certain prognosis of my disease: either I will forsake it soon or it will forsake me, for we cannot be together for long. This is my consolation not only in this affliction but in all my troubles, for Providence has so disposed matter that while the torments of mortal life may be countless, none can last too long. I even hear there are some who say that the scab is a sign of exceptional health. I will not grant that, but wish it to be

---

[*] See I, 5.

taken from me and given to them. Certainly if this is health, no one is healthier than I, so much so that with this extreme good health, I have scarcely written these few words. But there was no need for many; it is enough to have broken the silence. Now I have written something, and you should write something in reply. Meanwhile this enemy of mine will perhaps disappear, and we shall revert to our old way. Farewell.

[1365].

Sen. III, 6.

To the same person, * *on the instability of mortal purpose.*

Since I had nothing serious to write, yet determined to write something, I grasped whatever was closest in my memory. Our Leontius [Pilatus] is really Calabrian, but would have us consider him Thessalian, as though it were nobler to be Greek than Italian. While he may be a Greek among us, however, I believe he is an Italian among them, evidently renowned in both countries for his foreign origin. Well, this Leontius, wherever he is from, is a great fool. After your departure, he left here against my wishes; though I tried long and hard to dissuade him, he was deafer than the cliffs where he went. You know the man and you know me; it would not be easy for you to judge whether he is more forlorn or I am more joyful. I let him leave because I was afraid that perhaps his continued presence would corrupt me, for sickness of the mind is no less contagious than sickness of the body. To hold him would require something other than the chains of entreaty. As a companion for his journey I gave him Terence, the comedy writer, whom I had noticed he enjoyed tremendously. I was often suprised at what that gloomy Greek could have in common with this joyful African, yet there is hardly ever a dissimilarity so great that it does not have something similar, just as on the contrary, there is no similarity that does not have something dissimilar.

Well then, toward the end of summer, he left after uttering many bitter insults in my presence against Italy and the Latin name. You would say that he had scarcely arrived when unexpectedly a letter, shaggier and longer than his beard and hair, came to me. Among other things, he praises and loves Italy, like a heavenly land, when he had recently damned it; he hates Greece which he had preferred, and curses Byzantium which he had praised. And he asks me just as insistently to invite him to return, as the drowning Peter begged Christ, who calmed the waves. I laugh, wondering at his great change of heart in such a brief period of time. Rather I do not even wonder at it, for I know nothing is less stable than the mind that has not taken root in wisdom and virtue. Perhaps there are other reasons for this, but you can read one that is not bad, for a pagan, in Seneca where he consoles Helvia [his mother]. "I find some," he

* See I, 5.

says, "who say that there is a certain natural restlessness in the heart to change one's residence and to move one's household. Man was given a changeable, flighty mind. It can remain nowhere, it spreads itself around, lets its thoughts go off into every thing, known and unknown; it wanders, is impatient with repose and most happy with novelties. You will not marvel at this if you think of man's origin, for he descends not from an earthly, heavy body, but from that heavenly spirit, and it is the nature of heavenly things always to be in motion" [*Ep.* 6.6]. He then proves this, but needlessly, for the thing is evident to the senses. To his words I shall add this, and call this astonishing but true, unless I am mistaken: when virtue and wisdom are lacking, in which I require the spirit to be rooted, letters not only do not make for steadfastness, but interfere with it.

Letters give us boldness, teach about geography, reveal a variety of paths, earn our passage, give rise to various thoughts, which as stimuli they arouse the appetite to see many things; they do not bridle a mind that is naturally flighty, but instead impel it, drive it, and twist it about. If ever this was evident in any one man, it is most evident in this Leontius of ours. A Libyan lion, suffering from fever, does not pace more restlessly and more continuously in his cage than our "Leone" crosses entire provinces; and I suppose if poverty had not taken over instead of reason, he would not be a lion but a bird. I rejoice, by heaven, that he who distrusts words has been set straight by facts, and his hard head softened by experience. Yet, I have no faith in his steadfastness, and do not think that either his nature or his age, even were he to promise something different, has what it takes to change his ways. Furthermore, he tacks on to his requests one that will make you laugh: that I intercede for him by letter with the Emperor of Constantinople [John V Palaiologos], whose face I have never seen, whose name I have never heard. Nevertheless, because Leontius is *eager* for me to be acquainted and intimate with that emperor, as I am with the Roman Emperor [Charles IV], he also supposes that I *am*—as if those who have the same imperial title were one. With the title, he is nearly right, for the Greeks call Constantinople another Rome. They have dared to call it not only equal to the ancient city, but greater in monuments and graced with riches. But if this were as true on both counts as it is false (I would say it without offense to Sozomen who wrote this), surely no little Greek, however impudent, would dare to call them equal in men, arms, virtues, and glory.

Finally, so that this verbose mention of our volatile friend not be in vain, I must not forget to ask you for a favor. Send me as soon as you can, since I am in great need of it, that part of Homer's *Odyssey* where Ulysses goes to the Underworld, and the description given by Homer of the places in the vestibule of Erebus, which this man about whom we have been speaking translated into Latin at your urging. Copy it any old way with your own hand. This is all for now. In the future, however, if you love me, I beg you: see whether it can be arranged through your effort, at my expense, that all of Homer in Latin may enter this library where he has long dwelt in Greek. I am not unaware of what I am imposing on your shoulders, already so burdened with a heavy mass of your own concerns, but I am selfishly relying on you. Farewell.

Venice, March 1 [1363–65].

Sen. III, 7.

To Neri Morando of Forlì, on the rumor of his [own]
death which is quite often fabricated and invented.***

Your astonishment—I confess to you, my good sir—I share as I do
many other things, and unless I am mistaken, so do almost all,
whoever they are, that consider my petty affairs worthy of their
thought. Who, I ask, would not be astonished to hear that a man
envied by no one, dear to all, as rumor has it, and living not in
India or among the Seres [Chinese] or in remote Taprobane [Cey-
lon], but in Italy among the Italians, is reported dead every day? It
is now twenty years since, at the command of Clement, who then sat
on the throne of Peter, I set off for Naples; after I had spent some
time there, my death was publicly announced throughout Liguria
and all of the Veneto and Emilia, and adding to the lie it was said
that I had passed away in Sicily. That friend of ours at the time, a
man of considerable talent, but erratic, composed that plaintive ode
about the event, which you heard. As you see, he has gone before
me, I know not by how much time, to the very death which he had
bewailed for me. But the poem itself and the general rumor spread
about on every mouth and into every ear, and had such success that
people viewed me upon my return with amazement and doubt, as if
I were a dead man's ghost. They could scarcely believe their eyes,
having believed their ears to the contrary. During that hocus-pocus,
there were several who, like Thomas, did not believe that I was alive
until they had touched me with their hands; and embracing me as
though I were a miracle or a ghost, they discovered a solid body.
Thus, finally, what they had previously heard barely gave way to
sight and to touch and to hearing the opposite. I marveled, I confess, for although death is common to every age, I was still of an age
which usually shuts out, not death to be sure, but in the majority of
mortals, the thought of death. From that year, however, scarcely
another has passed without the same rumor circulating at least
once. It practically divided the coastline of our world so that the

---

* A high official of the Republic of Venice under Doge Andrea Dandolo. He
subsequently joined the staff of the Emperor, whom he accompanied on his
coronation journey to Rome. Accomplished in both literature and arms, he helped
court the favor of Charles IV in a number of requests made by P. in behalf of
friends.
** The Latin *et figmenti* is corrupt.

truth reigned where I was, rumor reigned where I was not. Thus, I was considered alive in Italy and deceased in Gaul, or on the contrary, alive there, dead here. Even in Italy, perhaps because it is so stretched out and split by the Apennine ridges, I have already told you what has sometimes happened to me—namely, one section of it was feeding me, the other had me buried.

But never did rumor so take advantage of me as recently. While I was alive here, in Gaul and Italy, or rather everywhere, I was dead according to public opinion, with this result: the Roman Pontiff, Urban V, used to say that he was eager to set his eyes on me, and having already summoned me three times, he was keeping in reserve for me an ecclesiastical benefice that he believed would please and influence me. But believing the rumor, he granted to those who understandably sought them not only that benefice but others in addition, which I have long held, and the ones which I had relinquished ten years earlier to certain friends who were then in need and now are deceased. In short, there was a great bustle in that Curia for these few small benefices, with those men running to and fro in order to obtain letters of favor, as if for large spoils; their clamor pervaded the entire city, for in some way or other, my name spurred their greed all the more, and added to the value of the benefices. In this business I suffered the loss of one expectation, but I take comfort in the fact that their passion for gain turned the insolence of vultures or ravens, seeking to feed upon another's death, into trouble for themselves. Sighing for a living man's benefices and exchanging gold for lead, in the end they achieved nothing but toil and shame—if there were any shame in avarice!—and costly, laughable letters. Just as the false rumor drove them to empty spoils, so did it drive you, friends, sad with weeping, to needless grief; and others wept whom I hold dear in Milan and who were concerned about me. Leaving aside more distant places, I was mourned here in nearby Padua, where they practically should have heard my very last breath—if it were true.

So, to continue what I have begun: while it is given to men to die only once according to the Apostle, the wiles and lies of these mountebanks make me die many times. Hence that astonishment that I was speaking about—yours, and at the same time mine and many others'. From what source, I ask, do these figments come forth? Or what do these tricksters want? Is it perhaps that I am such a nobody and my name so obscure that my life and death are equally hidden? Whence, therefore, that concern? To what purpose that zeal for pursuing anxiously such a dark and humble matter? For the breath of fame usually scorns the lowly and strikes only the outstanding and lofty. On the other hand, might it perhaps be that some brilliance and splendor of which I am certainly still unaware is the cause? Yet if this is so, why is it that rumor speaks so falsely of me? To come right down to it, if I am so worthless and unknown, why am I dragged to the forefront? If I am grand and famous, why am I not seen in full light? If, I say, my obscurity is so great, whence such a great fuss of rumors? If my fame is so great, whence this error? It is truly surprising and unusual—so many lies about a well-known man or so much talk about an unknown one. Once in Spain, when the death of Scipio Africanus was reported and believed, it brought the Roman army into extreme danger, but a very grave illness had made that rumor credible. He was an outstanding and incomparable man; I am lowly and humble. He was surrounded by his enemies and widely feared; I am attended by friends, suspect to no one, without an enemy, they say, without anyone that wishes me ill. Finally, nothing depends on me, whereas the fortunes of Italy, Spain, and Africa then depended on him. Yet, to him it was a one-time evil; to me it is frequent, annual. I am understating it. You know how in one year such a rumor twice arose and twice was squelched.

But we know the author of this last fabrication and sense* the reason for it. Our astonishment over the others still remains unanswered. Is it perhaps a certain perverse pleasure of the mind which feigns for itself more eagerly those things that will make it shudder more, not only in thinking but in speaking and circulating what it does not wish at all to be true? Let's suspect that this is the case. As a result, I, a man without enemies, rich in friends, am often imagined lifeless by those who most wish me alive. Surely, unless I am in error, there is no one for whom either my life is damaging or my death useful. Even my heir, if it will be the one whom I want, or whom I have named, has a little more to expect from my life, I think, than my death. He knows that I have a great deal of good will and kindness toward him, but little patrimony out of which to make a bequest; and he sees that he may obtain something from me daily while I am alive, but nothing or very little once I pass away.

But perhaps the cause of this evil is more hidden; it may be that I am not so free of enemies as many believe; rather I have enemies not because of hope or fear or insult—these are indeed the causes of

* The meaning of *committimus* is uncertain.

hatred—but envy, the worst and most hidden thing. Without question, for many this has been the root of undeserved and unexpected ruin, since those who they hoped held them dear, they found hateful by dire experience. See, dear friend, how by reasoning we have arrived at the truth. So it is; I have put my finger upon the sore spot. They fashion these lies, not provoked by any injury, not fearing nor hoping for anything from me, but hating me without reason; and hoping that some ill befall, they believe that nothing is worse than death—wrongly, to be sure, for there is nothing better than a good death. Indeed they themselves do not distinguish between a good death or the best death, and the worst one, as long as it removes me from their midst, freeing their diseased and swollen eyes of this presence, which is perhaps more glorious than they would like. If they wished for this in the right way, by heaven, I would join in their wish and feeling.

For, I ask you, who knows whether it is more advantageous to live a long time or to die today? If living long made us happy, the happiest of all would have been Methuselah, which no one has ever said or believed. Not the quantity, but the quality of a life must be considered, nor do the length of years matter but the splendor of the deeds, and especially the end of life. Hence as uncertain as I am whether it is better to live or die, I am absolutely certain that to die well is safest and best. But those men, to whom every death is equal because every death is bad, want but one thing: that I die. Since this comes about more slowly than they wish, they anticipate it and impudently invent what they wrongfully desire, enjoying as a true report the ring of the rumor blown up by them, just as a theater audience is charmed by dramatic performances which it knows to be false anyhow. What shall I do with these people, except spur on my willing and predisposed mind so that it will hourly be more prompt and more eager to do everything that adds to their envy and pain. And how do we know, but that through the hand of Him who is the source and beginning of life, of whom it is written, "If I have looked upon iniquity in my heart the Lord will not hear me" [Ps. 66:18]. I shall be all the more healthy amidst their most foul wishes, so that I may thus torment them longer. Certainly the life they want ended will seem longer to them; this one kind of punishment they will not avoid.

Although what these men often feign to have happened must eventually happen one day, nevertheless what was so often false, even when it begins to be true, can seem false, so that I, who am called dead while really alive, shall be believed alive when really dead; and they will credit the one untruth opposite to many untruths. Thus, those who seek an untimely and false joy from me will oppose the true joy; and being full of false delight, they have no room for true delight. Furthermore, since this plague breaks out anew every day, I cannot, I know, survive all these who kill me in their talk, but perhaps I shall survive many; doubtless I already have. Why then, I ask, do they struggle and sow vain lies in barren furrows? With all their poisoned, hissing tongues, they cannot snatch away one moment of the time allotted to me. For impiety is not mightier than piety. Neither can the pious prayers of friends increase the time allotted to my life, nor the impious words of enemies diminish it. Let them, therefore, do as they please, for all I care; let them invent things, let them talk and lie; nothing will change the fact, and whichever way my destiny falls, they in the meantime torment themselves for nothing. While I am here, I am tormenting them, and I shall torment them, yet never more bitterly than after my death; then, as I hope indeed, I will live. For if we believe Cicero at all, and the great men both before and after him, what we call our life is death. I have expressed more fully in my recent letter to our Giovanni [Boccaccio] what not only I, but others, have thought about this saying. Therefore, being then truly alive and protected, I shall pierce their jealous hearts with real arrows from the citadel of my tomb. It will happen, I believe, that those who so envy me while alive will envy me more and more when buried, since they can then do nothing to harm me and will rather have alive the man that for so long they wished dead.

My anger has set forth all this against envy. I now return to you, for there remains that section of your letter where you do what no one except a good and learned man can: you most magnificently incite yourself to virtue and to a happy end. I was especially delighted with it, if it were not that where you choose me as the guide for your plan and the exemplar of your life, you caused this friend, conscious of his own weakness and blindness, to blush too much. I would rather have you as my guide, or if you decline, we shall both eagerly travel what remains of the journey, together with Christ as our leader, forgetting with the Apostle what is past and stretching toward what is before us, since it is nearly evening and there is no room for sluggishness. Farewell, my Neri, be happy and remember me.

Venice, April 25 [1363].

Sen. III, 8.

To Guglielmo da Ravenna, physician,* a dissuasion from the study of eloquence.

With sweet and powerful hooks and snares you draw me into your friendship and, like one trying to force friendship, you likewise cast a network of arguments upon me. In vain; for I cannot be forced into it. No one is forced when he is willing; I am willing and eagerly throw open the door of friendship to you as you bang on it; and meeting you at the threshold, I embrace you in spirit; your virtue, loyalty, and insistence deserve it. One cannot shut out a man who demands so forthrightly and so firmly to be let in, who seeks to be a friend of mine, and is already a friend of my Donato [Alban-zani]. Whatever you are to him, you ought to be for me also. We both liked the idea that I should hold all things in common with that gentleman; and it was agreed upon not in word, so often misleading, but in deed and in spirit—and among the most important of these, the very best one: friends.

I would expand upon the subject at this point, for it is broad and agreeable, if I did not fear that by speaking, I might incite you to study eloquence, from which—speaking to you as a friend from now on—I wish to discourage you. Take the doctor's word for it. Whoever dreams that a doctor's eloquence is of any use to the patient is sadly mistaken. To the patient everything is grievous and bothersome except the treatment or lessening of his illness. I speak from experience. One time in Milan, I remember, afflicted by a nasty, difficult illness, I was visited twice daily by all the doctors who were esteemed there, for such was the will of the man in power. However love for me moved some of them, it was nevertheless the lord's command that moved them all. Among them were two unequal not so much in skill as in manner. One would quietly approach my bedside, feel my throbbing pulse, and outside my bedroom, with my close friends, do what was needed. Then returning to me, he would encourage me to be of good cheer, and would leave. Therefore, I view him as a father and deliverer. The other would sit down, and as though rooted there, beat my weary head with words as much he could, indeed much more than he could; intent upon eloquence, he

---

* A physician of some note and friend of P.'s fellow humanist, Donato Albanzani. This is the only letter to him.

would weave astonishing and impenetrable arguments; hence I often had to pretend something new beside the real pains so that he would go away. This man, though a friend when I was well, I hated when I was ill, and I would have him kept out except to spare his reputation, for the man's devotion was pleasing to me, but his conversation unbearable.

But you will say, "This appears so only to you perhaps, but differently to others." Believe me, no sick person likes a doctor that harangues, but one that heals. A well-turned and pleasant speech charms healthy, untroubled people at leisure, but it has nothing to do with a doctor; and any verbosity is certainly hateful to those who are sick, shaky, worried. No one hires a doctor for eloquence but for health. For this, herbs, not words, are needed, and smelling salts, not figures of speech, in short, medicine, not rhetorical arguments. Your responsibility is to heal the body; leave the healing or influencing of the mind to real philosophers and orators. If you attempt to do both, you will perform neither properly. For they are so different and disparate that it is very difficult for one mind to master both at the same time. One is enough; how difficult it is to attain even to that, through intense study, is proved by the scarcity. What, I ask, are the flowers of rhetoricians to physicians, or the subtlety of dialecticians, or the hyperbaton of grammarians, or the riddles of poets? When Maro called it a mute art, in order to exclude all loquaciousness from it, he was not insulting the profession but looking at its basic nature. I speak against the opinion of many, as usual; many things are necessary for a doctor, but fancy eloquence is not only unnecessary but harmful. For it distracts the doctor and disturbs the patient.

What then? Working efficiently and having a remedy ready are the earmarks of a physician. His speech, however, must be brief, grave, and sober; few words, but to the point, to steady the trembling heart of the anxious patient and not to trouble the brain of one who is faint; simple, unlabored words, falling from the pure fount of the spirit, full not of artifice but of trustworthiness, and, as far as the patient is concerned, of good hope—I mean, so long as it can be done without dangerous falsehood. Otherwise, cutting off hope of this life and instilling a concern for a better one is preferable to leading the unsuspecting patient on with empty promises and deceitful hope to the threshold of death, where both life and hope collapse. Hope is indeed good and useful as long as it helps the body without harming the soul. The patient—I am speaking of myself—will get this when he believes the doctor learned in his science, skilled from experience, single-minded in diligence, and distinguished in his charity and faith rather than in his speech, as long as he thinks him mindful of his profession, that is, disposed not to persuade but to heal. Unless I am mistaken, it is this that engenders and sustains hope in a patient; it is this that bestows and enhances the doctor's authority. You doctors, however, are wont to say, I hear, that the more people pin their hopes upon a doctor, the more people he heals. But superfluous words confer nothing upon the patient, nothing upon the doctor, no hope, nothing real. It cannot be told how many thousands have perished while their doctors were disputing or winding up a speech. These many things, put so frankly, are so that you may understand that I am your friend. Farewell.

[1363].

Sen. III, 9.

To Brother Bonaventura Baffo of Venice,* on the sufferings of his troubled fatherland.

A single hour brought two very welcome letters from you which reached me here at the same time though dispatched at different times. Upon seeing them I was right there with you. For although my heart is by nature most tenacious in friendship and indifferent to vulgar concerns, each day I am occupied not only with you or with these few whom my lot has left me, but even with those it has snatched away. And lest anyone find it astonishing that absence cannot do to me what death cannot, nevertheless, a friend, while always present with me in all places, is particularly so in these letters; thus, a well-trained hand has learned to depict a longed-for face by writing no less than painting. I would like to make this reply to your letters: while I do painfully miss you, I rejoice that you have safely moved to a lovely, healthy area. On the other hand, I am sorry that the gift of nature is spoiled by the perversity of men, and that the serenity of the heavens is disfigured by the smoke and dust of war. This happens, I believe, in order that no perishable attraction impede our journey, nor the loveliness of earthly paths render us perhaps unmindful of our heavenly fatherland. The heavenly observer, in order to rid us of our laziness, at times driving us now with coaxing prods and now with harsh ones, mingles and tempers the sweet with the bitter, the joyous with the sad, safety with concern.

I am not surprised that the books I seek are not there, for while I put you to that trouble, it was an attempt rather than an expectation. I enjoyed finding out whether, as sometimes happens, the outcome exceeds the hope. Although this search for books is often futile, I do not know how to stop. It is so sweet to hope for what you crave, and indeed we shall get the ones we can, for rank laziness will not block the noble search. We shall patiently wish for the others, and so continue, content with those our lot has granted us. We shall control with the recollection of mortality our bent for reading and ardor for learning. As for your mentioning that I also have friends there, I am surprised and proud, for that is one part of Italy where I thought myself least known. See to it, though, that you do not adorn a name,

---

* A Venetian friar who, upon being transferred to southern Italy, had agreed to search for certain books requested by P. This is the only letter to him.

which is even now obscure, with a friendly, flattering lie.

Finally with regard to your question about my condition and that of my country, take it from me: there is no end to evils, no hope except in the mercy of God. Beware of those who imagine that what they desire is already at hand, and believe that they have seen whatever they have dreamed. Perhaps for a little while, the plague became less intense than it had been, but still it rages widely and horribly. From all sides, wailing and lamentations strike the ears; from all sides, the dead, still warm, and open coffins strike the eyes. Maro's words about a captured city are true of this one:

> everywhere bitter
> Mourning, and panic and death's every image.
> [*Aen.* 2. 368–69]

And everywhere you turn, Libitina [the goddess of undertakers] still bustling about. Not fear of these things, I confess, but disgust keeps me at home, often missing the pleasant camaraderie of your faithful friendship that I used to have. So much for domestic matters.

The war has never been more onerous or more deadly. We hoped that it would be over, but it is intensifying; and stirred, so to speak, by the bellows of hell, it daily becomes more enflamed. Thus, the wrath of God in heaven provoked by men's sins, and the madness of men on earth provoked by demons' goads have covered the journey in this world with a dust of mingled suffering and terror, and have enveloped the blue sky of this life with a dense cloud of miseries. Passing over the evils of all mankind, which are hard enough to think about all together, not to mention bewailing them one by one, passing over too the storm closer to us, swamping us, in unhappy Italy, I will touch upon that sickness of our very marrow, the ulcer inside us. I shall say something that perhaps you have not yet heard; you decide whether I say it with greater pain or shame. In recent days, the Venetian fleet set forth for Cyprus and Alexandria as it usually does once a year. When it was driven from the shores of Crete, until lately loyal and subject but now hostile, to a city named Sittia on the island's furthest side where it looks toward Asia, toward Lesser Armenia, a troop of our young men, kindled by righteous hatred of the wicked rebellion but, as the outcome proved, showing more zeal than strategy, disembarked either for the purpose or the pretext of getting water. When they were prevented from doing so, they split into two companies and attacked the walls with such force that the section of the city which the admiral of the ships bound for Alexandria had invaded, though protected* by strong fortifications, both natural and man-made, turned to humble entreaties; and, with hands outstretched like suppliants, they placed all hope of safety in surrender. In short, it was all over, except that the other company, led by the admiral of the Cyprus fleet, as if they were not bound for Cyprus but born in Cyprus, spied on the nearest hill a few armed, or rather, unarmed little Greeks, and turned tail with a rabbitlike, vile, and unworthy fear, without a wound, without a show of arms, indeed without any outcry. During that rout, the townspeople, at first astonished by the novelty of the event and scarcely believing their eyes, thereupon regained their courage and sallied forth; some of our men were killed by the sword and others by the waves. The scattered remnant sought out the ships; thus, the others' virtue, useless because of the cowardice of these men, failed to have the effect it had already won, and new shame was heaped upon the old loss. Yet if this company had either stayed at home or moved up along with the other one, there would have been an enormous difference, with little risk, not only for that day but for the entire war that was still pending.

I wanted you, dear friend, to know these things that are grievous to know, yet even more grievous not to know. That it was all so was reported to me in a letter from there by that friend we share, who saw everything from on high on the stern; it is confirmed here by the murmurings and laments of the angry people. Amidst these evils I have this one comforting thought: just as Rome avenged the Caudine dishonor upon the Samnites, the punishment of Atilius upon the Carthaginians, the disgrace of Mancinus upon the Numantines, the deaths of her citizens upon Mithridates, the truce and detestable flight of Aulus upon Jugurtha, so may this city, now more than any other the friend of justice, embittered by the repeated wrongs and consequently forgetful for a little while of her innate kindness, rise up more sharply and powerfully as an avenger of bloody treachery against those traitors to the fatherland whom we considered Venetians. What is there that the passage of time and the change in climate cannot do? We find the Cretans infamous not only by our present testimony, but also by the poet and apostle of yore. Their outward appearance deceived us, and it is not given to mortal eyes to penetrate the shadows of the heart. They were Venetians in dress and name, but enemies in purpose and spirit.

---

* We emend *diffusa* to *defensa*.

May Christ the avenger of lies and inquity damn them to perdition alive and dead.

What you ask of me last can be briefly treated. It cannot be well for me privately when things are going badly for the republic. Just as a righteous man lives on faith, so do I, a sinner, live on hope. Destruction came whence we did not fear it; help will come whence we do not expect it. The king of hell sent us a destroyer, the King of heaven will send us an avenger. For the most just war, the most stalwart leader is being sought—not to keep anything from you, it is our modern Fabricius from Verona [Luchino dal Verme], second to none in our day in the arts of war; this is the one subject of all deliberations. To this end your country deigns to use my assistance, since it is well known that he is a close friend of mine. Consequently, when our Lorenzo [Celsi], that illustrious doge, nicknamed the Tall and taller in prowess, summoned him by letter in the name of the republic, I was bidden to add mine so that, the public authority, supported by friendly advice and private counsel, would more easily sway him. If you hear he has given his pledge, rest assured that with a general like him victory has crossed our threshold. As for the rest, if I could be free of this heartsickness, I am well in body, although you know how I am. I apply contrarily that famous quality of Hannibal's, "equally tolerant of heat or cold" [Livy 21.4.6]. It is not otherwise with me, but he could endure both, I can endure neither. The summer exhausts me; if not completely, then the winter finishes me off. Both are so antipathetic that when one of them returns I long for the other. It is thus with human things: the present is always more hateful, as the past was hateful too when it was there, as the future will be hateful when it arrives. Only the remembrance or anticipation of things is pleasant. Thus, it is easy to judge how much value should be placed in those things that are pleasing only if absent. O joyful heavenly dwelling, forever the same, where nothing is either past or future, but everything present; where nothing is sought or hoped for, but a true and present good is enjoyed; where what once pleased will always please, eternal and unchangeable, which so soothes the longing of those who partake of it as not to diminish that longing, so fulfills that it never ceases, so refreshes that it enflames; in short, no feeling of satiety steals over them or ever can, and no defect, no change, no anxiety or trouble is feared. Happy is that wayfarer who at last arrives there guided by mercy! We remain here, where all things are different; we are indeed wretched unless hope and patience comfort our spirit. Farewell.

Venice, December 6 [1363].

Sen. IV, 1.

To Luchino dal Verme of Verona, Venetian military commander against rebellious Crete, the qualities necessary for a supreme commander.***

I have no fear that you will laugh at me, as Hannibal laughed at Phormio, for I do not speak either to teach you or to show off. But since I saw you put in charge of a cruel, difficult war with the consensus of a great and mighty people, and although I knew you to be endowed with every virtue, especially those of war, I could not refrain from writing you something now. While perhaps useless to you because of your manifold familiarity with such things, it surely seemed not unbecoming to me as evidence of my loyalty, and I am confident that what I have often liked to read will also be to your liking, at least at this time when such things may particularly affect you. Hardly any part of your life since adolescence to the present has gone by that you were not under arms; how often, in the meantime, did you gain eminence both as a commander and a soldier, and with how much success! I do not know, however, whether such a weighty responsibility as this ever fell to you before. The most powerful and most magnificent city in our world has chosen you alone, out of everyone, to be in command of this supreme effort. The great opinion of you, the great confidence in you have seized the public imagination. From the very first day you took the burden upon your shoulders, everyone has believed that the war is won. A strong spur presses from one side, righteous indignation, righteous wrath from the other. In our age there has scarcely been a more righteous war. Slaves have rebelled against masters, children against parents; for they must have been both, servants and children, whom fear on the one hand and love on the other restrained from evil deeds. Neither availed. And it is astounding to recall how those people, bound by so many great benefits, forgot all human and divine law; these are the motives, then, that impel you there, draw you from here.

---

* Famous condottiere from Verona, whom P. compares to the Roman Fabricius in the previous letter. He served with distinction in military campaigns not only for the Veronese Scaligeri, but for the Milanese Visconti and for the Venetian doge. P. first met him at the court of Galeazzo Visconti.

** In many manuscripts and some editions, this letter appears as a separate treatise entitled *De officio et uirtutibus imperatoris.*

If the obvious justice, however, did not offer you the certain hope of victory, you are embarking on a war that is no trifle, but perilous and demanding. You are going to the distant island of Crete. I pass over the discomforts of a sea voyage which no prose can do justice to and no one understands unless he has experienced it. The very length of the journey is one part of the difficulties, even if you were undertaking such a journey on land as a traveler, not as a soldier. It is a large island, indeed the largest island in our sea after Trinacria [Sicily], a famous and powerful island with a hundred cities at one time, where there was Jupiter's palace and tomb, and the horrible Minotaur, and the pathless Labyrinth. None of our islands, unless I am mistaken, lie so far from the continent; it is surrounded on all sides by a vast sea, and its shores are harborless. On land, the inhabitants are turncoats, cunning, false, and were always considered not only by ancient Greek and Latin poets, but even by the Apostle Paul, as liars, evil beasts, lazy bellies. I mean slack in everything except deception; in this alone they are restless and sleepless. With these, then, you will be dealing, with people to whom treachery is not foreign, nor crime unfamiliar. No kind of wickedness is new to them, but every kind has been practiced, and long since become a habit through frequent doing and long custom, and—what I would not place last!—aggravated beyond measure by awareness of their crimes and extreme despair.

Why mention that a large part of the island is mountainous, wooded, waterless, arid, with barren countryside, stark, inhospitable, the paths impassable, unsafe, confusing, ideal for ambushes? And if—heaven forbid, but I realize nothing is impossible in the vicissitudes of warfare—if, I say, anything unfavorable does happen, there is no retreat, all the approaches being blocked, the way out is rocky, the sea-water shackles you, and the deep is a prison around you. For these reasons I rejoice at your glory while sympathizing with your hardships. I contemplate your victory without forgetting the danger. Nor am I unaware that since the beginning of things nothing famous, nothing lofty, nothing memorable has been accomplished without toil or danger.

Great hope, furthermore, arises in me from your virtue which has been tested in difficult straits, and even more from the very justice of the cause whose defense you undertake, and the divine favor which will not abandon it. For energy battles against fickleness, religion against superstition, truth against falsehood, loyalty against treachery, innocence against crime, clemency against cruelty, hope against fear, foresight against blindness, a sound mind against madness, conscientious hearts against a guilty conscience, the most honest judges against the most dishonest thieves, pursuing and avenging masters against fugitive slaves. Therefore, in so unequal a contest I would have thought that arms were hardly needed; whips will suffice, for the fact is at one time in Scythia the masters used them against rebelling slaves and were victorious in the first onslaught.

Nevertheless, as you set off for this war, perhaps some will offer you horses and trappings, others swords and helmets, still others bows and quivers. I have no such things; so with the prince of the Apostles I offer you this: "In the name of Jesus, rise and walk" [Acts 3:6]. Rise, I say, and walk with courage, walk with prudence, and since all have chosen you as their leader, you choose God as your leader with the heavenly hosts of angels as your standard-bearers. Against you, of course, will stand the infernal demons, the contrivers of this treason and rebellion, but they will not withstand the encounter with those enemies by whom they were driven from heaven, nor the arms of avenging justice; but with mere needless words and appeals I distract your mind intent on things. It will suffice to give this one warning: do as you always do, follow your own example. Recall what you did in like circumstances; I offer you yourself to imitate. Use also the examples of illustrious ancients, known in abundance either from reading or hearing. And remember that this very island where you hasten to do battle, was conquered in an easy campaign, at a time when it was wealthier and much more powerful, by Metellus, who was therefore called Creticus. Would that a similar nickname from a similar outcome be in store for you! But let this suffice.

Now I come to what you will receive from me, who cannot give anything great, as a token of loyalty from a poor friend or a gift fit for a soldier; indeed, it comes not from me, but from Marcus Tullius who first said this. If you are hearing it for the first time, I think you will enjoy it. But if you had felt the same thing in the past, you will be glad that your mind on its own arrived at the same conclusion as a very great man. It may well be, and indeed scarcely can be otherwise, that you already know by yourself what I tell you. For how can so great a general not know the things that pertain to a general? Indeed you could not know it was said by Tully or any other writer, especially since this very piece of Tullian eloquence is hidden in a certain obscure passage. If this is so, what will be added to this information of yours, if we search for it? A great deal indeed. For when through reason or experience we have persuaded ourselves about something, yet not completely, if then this is unexpectedly complemented by the authority of some illustrious man, it happens that what was opinion becomes certain knowledge, and what was creeping upon the threshold of the heart penetrates to our very marrow. But if perchance you knew that this was so and that it was said by Tully, you will still listen to me with unprejudiced ears if I expand a little on him.

For he said this about you and other outstanding military commanders who were commonly called generals: "I think this: the greatest general must have these four qualities—a knowledge of the military art, virtue, authority, and luck" [*Leg. Man.* 10]. From this you see, O distinguished gentleman, even if I add nothing to this, what is necessary to fulfill the responsibility of your profession. Some of these are acquired through determination and diligence, but others, unless they are a gift from heaven, cannot ever be acquired with any effort. I shall go over them in order, so as to serve somehow as a mirror revealing you to yourself, as Annaeus Seneca says; and you may rejoice that all these have come to you in full, or if perchance you feel that even now you lack some, which I doubt, you may achieve through noble striving what is humanly possible, and succeed, unless you refuse, by using this model for that undertaking. For if any defect is lurking in anything whatever, there is no clearer way to reveal it than by a precise enumeration and examination of its parts. Nor must you think that it is ever too late to do what is useful and what is honorable. Rather take it from me that, whatever is wrongly postponed, is even worse left undone. Therefore, an improvement of character is always desirable, and the pursuit of virtue praiseworthy until the last breath. But I return to my order, and shall do my best to fulfill my promise.

The first quality, then, of a supreme commander is knowledge of the military art. As with other arts, this one is acquired through learning and practice, both of which are multifaceted. For there is a certain skill in arms and horsemanship, which can be practiced even in peacetime, or rather learned especially in peacetime. Julius Caesar is praised above others for this, as for almost everything else; I am speaking of things concerning war and military service, in which no one ever shone more brightly, according to most and surest authorities. There is also a loftier military science which, no matter where it is learned, cannot be practiced except in battle. This is established primarily in those books on what we call military matters and the Greeks call strategy, some of which, at my urging, you decided to have copied, and likewise from the record of all history, especially Roman, for none is so rich in famous models.

Often indeed, models touch the mind no less than reason, especially the advice and teaching of the finest past masters who have learned much either from reading or experience. The military art is not so easy as some may think, nor haphazard, but is based on many rules, great talent, and long study; and if any rule is overlooked, nowhere is the punishment for negligence more certain. This is that discipline or art which, vigorously maintainted, as Valerius says, "afforded the Roman people primacy over Italy, bestowed on them sovereignty over many cities, great kings, and the strongest nations, laid open for them the straits to the Pontic gulf [the Black Sea], pried open and delivered to them the passes of the Alps and of Mount Taurus." And as if wearied not by what he had said but by what remained to be said, see what he added: "It made of the Roman people, which issued from Romulus's little hut, the pillar of the entire world" [V. Max. 2.8]. Valerius did not see what became of the empire of that same people once it was neglected; we see it.

And this art is in three parts. For it considers what must be done before a battle, what during the battle, and what after the battle, to determine whether one comes out the winner or the loser. You understand how many things are involved in these parts, and all of this is learned either by reading or through experience. Experience seems surer; reading, however, seems to go further, for it is faster to read about many, many things than to experience very few, whence it follows that while a human lifetime is short for experience, a short time suffices for reading—provided the intellect and the memory lend support; without them reading is either wasted or fleeting. Good commanders, however, learn from reading and from experiencing in turn, and verify their reading with experience and confirm their experience with reading. It is reported that Caesar never let a day go by without reading or writing something. He thus produced books in the midst of the great hardships of marches and in the midst of the heat of battle—which I admit others can more readily admire than imitate.* Whoever were the finest commanders are said to be, and have been, the best read too. Hardly any, especially among the Romans, who serve as model for all the others, will be found to have been unlettered, with the sole exception, perhaps, of Marius. For so great was the learning of some men that you would say it was uncertain whether they were more famous for arms or for letters. This could easily be proven to you except that it would take

* We emend *mutabile* to *imitabile*.

too long. Let our commanders hoot and jeer, and our kings and princes who have declared war on virtue and letters, and who with the pretense of contempt mask either their mental slowness or their laziness. At one time letters were the royal and imperial attribute and the adornment of leaders, and they would still be so today if the minds of emperors, kings, and leaders had not degenerated. Because of their fecklessness and pride, the world itself has degenerated, following them. And these few remnants of letters that have devolved upon commoners and country people dwell so shamefully and scantily, not according to their majesty but the need of the times, that I foresee them shortly being driven even from these shelters upon the arrival of the new guests—pleasure and luxuries. How different, then, these so-called leaders of ours are from those true leaders is easily decided if you compare the glory and the deeds of the past leaders with the slumber and carousal of the present ones; and this is determined to be so not only by impartial judges but also by these same despisers of letters and devotees of lust, unless they have fallen into a daze and are totally shameless.

But we have often spoken of this before, and have said more today than was necessary. The facts, their speech, their dress, their character, their conduct, the beginning and the outcomes of their wars, all of these together and each of them singly speaks and pronounces very clearly the difference between these practitioners of the military art, and those. I have always liked you primarily for this one reason: in the midst of so many honors won by military exploits you never displayed a contempt for letters; and if you had had more leisure, I have no doubt that you would have striven to equal your predecessors also in this. Yet I do not mean to suggest that generals need philosophy or poetry, but they do need at least that literature from which to learn military precepts and historical events, which will either not enter the mind or not remain there unless constant reading puts them there and reinforces them. For as moths are to clothing and rust to arms, so forgetfulness is to literature and the knowledge of things; it taints everything and eats away at everything except what is often shaken out and polished through frequent study—and there is a rotting of the mind, as of other things, without unceasing care. In this military science, which we have seen is based on reading and experience, the Athenian Themistocles and the Theban Epaminondas stand out in the first, but in the second the Achaean Philopoemen. In both, however, Roman commanders stand far above commanders of all nations in number and accomplishment.

But lest I play Phormio teaching Hannibal, or, as the saying goes, a pig teaching Minerva, I lay aside these arguments and come to virtue, which Tully assigns second place. Virtue is twofold, as far as the present argument goes; one kind is bodily, including strength of limb and dexterity and sound senses. For a frail commander, though learned, will not be held fit for carrying out the duties of warfare; he will be good for counsel, not battle, more useful in the chamber than in the field. It was for this reason that the son of the great Africanus was unfit for war, though his equal in mental power and even superior in learning. On the other hand, neither will the strongest man, if burdened with too much weight, be able to be here and there, where the situation requires him to encourage his soldiers or to ward off dangers. Then again, neither can a blind or deaf man estimate the enemy's condition or that of his own men, nor determine from the bedlam of combatants' screams and shouting what they needed in the way of direction and action, and where. On this point, those who have an illustrious, powerful, burning, and untiring virtue are, among our people, Julius Caesar and Papirius Cursor (who got his surname from his speed), as well as the Roman king, Tullus Hostilius, both the Africani, and Marius, and among foreigners, Pyrrhus, Hannibal, and Massinissa.

The other virtue is of the mind and, as everyone knows, divided in four parts. For one must know what to do not only in battle against the enemy, which the military science mentions above, but everywhere and with everyone. In fact, commanders are not always in battle, but often—through a truce or by happenstance—they lay down their arms and parley with friends or enemies, where it is shameful to be fooled or to say something churlish or inept. A natural kindness and affability, in which the elder Africanus was the foremost of them all, followed by Augustus, Vespasian, and many others, will take care of this, or else, a higher prudence, for which the Roman king Numa Pompilius, and Fabius Maximus and the two Catos among our people are famous. Add to these Marcus Aurelius Antoninus—I call him by far the wisest—who preferred the surname "philosopher" to Caesar. Among foreigners, there were the two Cyruses, Hannibal the Carthaginian, and Mithridates of Pontus. This virtue is three-pronged, inasmuch as it remembers, discerns, and foresees, fixing its three eyes on the past, present, and future, a marvelous connection between separate events.

There follows fortitude, which teaches how to scorn death and how not to fear terrible things. I shall say little on this subject, for it is common knowledge, and many consider this alone to be the proper military virtue of commanders whereas it is everyone's, even though it is more prominent in wartime, in the midst of the deaths and wounds. The unrivaled abode of this virtue was Rome, followed by Sparta and Carthage. Among our own there come to mind Julius Caesar, mentioned often, and deserving to be still more, the two Scipios, who succumbed to ambush in Spain, the two Africani, the two Paulli (the victor over Macedonia and the one who fell at Cannae), Claudius Marcellus, Claudius Nero, Tiberius Gracchus, Gaius Marius, Drusus and Germanicus Caesar, and the emperors Titus and Trajan. Among the most ancient, there are the first and third kings of Rome; also, from the knightly order, Horatius Cocles, Lucius Dentatus, Marcus Serius, Marcus Scaeva, and countless others. It is easier to count the stars in the heavens and the sands in the sea than the brave men of the city of Rome.

Foreigners include the Lacedaemonian Leonidas, the Athenian Miltiades, and the pair of brave men mentioned before, Themistocles and Epaminondas, and from more ancient books Hercules, Theseus, Achilles, Hector, Tydeus, Diomedes, Ajax, and, to please Maro, Aeneas and "all the shades who," the poet from Cordova says, "owe much to poets" [Luc. 9.963]; there was Hannibal too, his father Hamilcar, and his brother Hasdrubal, Alexander the Macedonian, and his father Philip as well, and his uncle, Alexander of Epirus, and Pyrrhus, likewise king of Epirus, whom we mentioned above, and also a number of Hebrews, especially David, Joshua, and Judas, whose military virtue was so seconded by the Divinity that it seemed to detract something from their human glory. Nor am I unaware of the fact that, although Aristotle himself put courage first, to some I may seem to have forsaken the philosophical sequence of the virtues by putting fortitude before justice.

I have abided by the military order of importance according to which fortitude is considered by far the outstanding virtue; but really justice is no less appropriate for commanders: it teaches them to keep faith not only with friends but with enemies. For there are those who believe it permissible to deceive an enemy by fair means or foul, relying on Virgil where he says: "A ruse or valor—'gainst the foe, who cares" [Aen. 2.390]. This is spoken not by the most authoritative poet but by a passionate adolescent. Other commanders who are truly prudent and alert against the enemy, rage recklessly with violence and plunder against their treaty allies or their subjects. This evil is both ancient and modern, whether because of the commanders' nonchalance or the insolence and mad greed of the soldiers; both qualities must be eradicated from the minds of soldiers and commanders, so as to observe good faith toward enemies, kindness toward friends, and justice toward both, doing no harm to the former, unless it is consistent with honor, or doing no harm at all to the latter. For what anywhere is more shameful or more criminal than to harm those for whose safety and defense you are responsible, or to change in some way from guardian to robber and from dog to wolf? At the vanguard of such a glorious reputation stand Fabricius, Camillus, and Regulus: the first two would not win by trickery, though they could, the third chose the most painful death rather than do harm to his country or break faith with the enemy. Among those who kept faith with an enemy Cassius must not be passed over.

As for the other kind of justice, there are those for whom it was not enough to abstain from harming their own; they even died for them of their own free will. Among these were Curtius in Rome and the two Decii, as well as a third one added by Cicero, but he seems less known to the historians. In Athens Codrus comes to mind first, in Carthage the Philaeni brothers. They voluntarily went to their death, Curtius to calm the people's terror, the Decii to seek victory and brace the crumbling battle line, Codrus to snatch the fatherland from imminent destruction, and the Philaeni to extend their country's borders; for the well-being of their fellow citizens, they gave up their very being. But the great Pompey excels in both kinds. Although Cicero attributes to him alone all the martial virtues, and whatever we have said or are going to say commanders need in order to be the greatest—and Cicero is right, for Pompey deserved it—yet, if each is given his just due, the great Pompey is praised most fittingly for martial justice at the same time as self-control in the midst of victories and triumphs. This must be related to another virtue, which I am about to address here, once I have added one that now applies to justice too: beneficence and liberality are the finest garments under which commanders can hide many, many unbecoming traits. In this glory Julius Caesar outdoes all, for no one, if I remember Seneca's words, used victory more liberally, claiming nothing for himself from it but the power of giving everything away. In first place among foreigners is Alexander, as the Greeks would have it and our authors do not dispute.

Now there remains for me the fourth virtue, moderation, also called temperance and bordering on continence, which I mentioned a short while ago. Without it not only no commander, but no man was ever good. But since I am speaking now of commanders, I ask what good is skill or magnanimity, or any other qualities for a commander if, controlled by lust or gluttony, he lets go of the bridle with which he controlled the army, and hurls himself and his legions headlong, and draws them into ruin. Thus have many often perished with all their forces.

This then was Pompey's unique and characteristic virtue; and had his colleague Crassus cared to imitate him in this, he would never have fallen together with his son and with so much harm to the empire. The very opulent temple of Jerusalem attests to this restraint and moderation of the Roman commander, having been left intact by him and despoiled by another commander. Many other things as well attest to it; part of them appear in Cicero's words which I shall soon cite. This same virtue was also characteristic of many others, but especially the elder Africanus; in the flush of youth and good fortune, both of which more than anything else thwart the virtue that we are discussing, and every other virtue, he gave proof of restraint and chastity.

Added to these virtues is a certain gentleness, sweetness, and affability of mind, in which the same Africanus and Julius Caesar excel; there is nothing more effective for winning over the minds of men. Akin to this is a certain fellowship and comradeship with the army, which must endear commanders to their soldiers. For this Valerius Corvinus and Marius* among our Romans, and Hannibal among foreigners, were celebrated. These arts control the army and other subjects with kindness and love, and the opposite ones, severity and autocracy, control them with fear. The best known for these arts are Manius** Curius, Quintius Cincinnatus, Papirius Cursor, and Fabius Maximus. But no one is equal in this to Iunius Brutus and Manlius Torquatus; the first was so driven by love for the people's freedom that he put his own sons to the ax, after beating them like slaves, because of their support for the tyranny he had overthrown. The second was such a stickler for military discipline that he ordered his son, an extraordinarily gifted youth, to be killed because he had attacked the enemy without his approval—and this although he was his only son and had been the victor. Matching this supremely stern deed was Postumius Tiburtius [Tubertus] whom I would mention, so as not to seem to have left out such an enormity rather than vouch for it; for in some authors, the matter is certain, while in others the story of his deed remains in doubt.

---

* We emend Marcus to Marius.
** We emend Marcus to Manius.

To all these many qualities must be added patience, which is manifold. One kind bears bodily ills calmly. Another endures the equivalent wound in the ear and the mind—insulting words; both kinds are suitable for commanders and soldiers: the first is related to fortitude, the second to civility and that very moderation about which we are speaking. Considered outstanding in the first quality are Mutius and Marius and Pompey himself, as well as Atilius, one of Caesar's soldiers who distinguished himself at Massilia [Marseille], and Marcus Sergius, along with their peers cited above. Among foreigners, Cynegirus the Athenian is celebrated in Greek histories. Outstanding in the second quality are the Roman emperors Julius and Augustus among our people, among foreigners Philip and Antigonus, kings of the Macedonians, and Pisistratus the tyrant of Athens. Finally, Pompey the Great surpasses all—our people and foreigners.

I am here reminded to copy, as I promised a little earlier, Cicero's words from the book that praises Pompey and ends with the self-control of generals or commanders and the four things we require in a commander; I trust this will be either useful or pleasurable for you. He says: "A commander's virtues are not just the ones generally esteemed: tirelessness in his work, courage amid dangers, energy in action, speed in execution, wisdom in foreseeing." After that he says: "For we are not only to expect skill in warfare in a consummate, perfect commander, but many eminent qualities that are relatives and companions of this virtue. First, how great must be the commanders' incorruptibility! How great their moderation in all things, their trustworthiness, their good nature, their intellect, their kindness!" Not much later he says: "Who does not know what terrible distress our armies suffer wherever they go because of our commanders' greed? Recall the marches in recent years our generals have made into Italy through the lands and towns of Roman citizens; then you will more easily figure what is happening in foreign nations. Do you think that more enemy cities have been destroyed these past few years by our soldiers' arms, or more allied cities by their winter billets? For a general who does not control himself cannot control an army, nor can he be strict in judging others when he does not wish others to judge him strictly." Turning then to praise Pompey, he says, "And we wonder that this man much surpasses all others when his legions arrived in Asia so disciplined that not one hand in such a large army, not even one footstep is said to have harmed any peaceable inhabitant? Every day now, talk and letters indicate how the soldiers behave in their winter quarters; not only is no one forced to spend money on a solider, but no one is permitted to do so, even if he is eager. For our ancestors wished the roofs of our allies and friends to be a shelter for our soldiers in winter, not a refuge for the greedy.

"Come now, consider his moderation in other matters. What, do you suppose, was the source of that tremendous speed and such an incredible dash? For it was not the rowers' outstanding strength, or unheard-of skill in navigation or some new winds, that bore him so swiftly to the most distant lands; but those things that usually delay others did not slow him down. No avarice lured him from his intended route in order to plunder; no lust lured him to pursue pleasure, no charming location to bask in it, no city's renown to make its acquaintance, not even toil to rest. Lastly, as for the statues, pictures, and other embellishments of Greek cities, which others see fit to take, he did not think that he should even go to see. Consequently, in those countries, everyone now looks upon Gnaeus Pompey not as one sent from this city, but come down from heaven. Now they are finally beginning to believe that once there were Romans with this same integrity, which to foreign nations has hitherto seemed an incredible and false tradition. Now the splendor of our dominion truly shines upon those nations. Now they understand that not without reason did our ancestors prefer being subject to the Roman people, when we had such temperate magistrates, to being lords over others. All private individuals have such easy access to him, their complaints of injuries from others so unrestrained, that he who excels in dignity the heads of state, seems in affability on a par with the lowliest. How mighty he is in counsel, in the weightiness and fluency of his words—and that, too, shows the dignity of a general—you, O citizens, often experience in this very place. But how highly do you think his good faith is prized among your allies, when the enemies of all nations have judged it most sacred? His humanity is such that it is difficult to say whether the enemy feared his valor more when fighting, or loved his mildness more when conquered" [*Leg. Man.* 11–14].

Thus for Cicero, whose huge mass of words I have added to a letter which I realize is already weary of its own weight, yet I know of no other place where the good qualities of commanders—restraint, humaneness, and affability—are described more clearly. Although you have perhaps no need of these qualities now, since you are not going to march through allied territory but transport your army on ships, and since upon your arrival on the island you will encounter nothing friendly but everything hostile, you will be able to use these qualities in another place and time, since I see you were born for war—whatever the star under which you were born.

Third, there remains the authority that issues mostly from the aforesaid qualities. It is enhanced, however, by the reputation and popularity derived from the commanders' virtues and success. Physical appearance does contribute considerably, "not fashionably dapper," as Livy says [28.35.6], "but manly and really soldierly," as does nobility of blood and military eloquence, something for which Julius Caesar, the elder Africanus, and Pompey the Great are the most celebrated. So great was their authority and the trust of their troops under them that their men believed they were being led not into battle and danger but to victory and booty. Nothing is more conducive to the desired and favorable outcome of a war—which takes the opposite turn through the soldiers' distrust, due to the commanders' nonchalance and laziness. The first of the three that I have mentioned was so eloquent as not only to surpass all commanders in military eloquence but even to equal the greatest orators in forensic eloquence. With admirable skill the second added something immeasurable to the authority that either virtue or nature had bestowed upon him, by neither denying nor confirming his divine origin, so as not to shake with a lie the opinion fixed in the citizens' heart, or to destroy it with the truth, but to strengthen it instead with his silence, and also by certain singular habits over and beyond the customs of men—his lingering, secretly and solitary, in temples, and his utterly certain hope in crises for future events, no less than present ones, as though he had daily conversations with the gods and divine assurances. In this he was following Numa the Roman king and Minos the king of Gnosus [Knossos], except that he adapted to war what they had practiced in peacetime.

The fourth and last quality is good luck not only in campaigning but in life. Naturally, everything relates to this, but no one can give it to himself or increase it; clearly it is a divine gift, yet so necessary for a commander that if he lacks this one thing, though he abound in the rest, no one would declare that an unlucky commander, however learned and valorous, should be appointed. For just as the soldiers' confidence follows from their commanders being lucky, so does their dread from their being unlucky, and nothing is closer than that to disaster.

Of our people the last three stand out in this by far—I say this with the exception that Pompey had a little more life than luck, and also the younger Africanus, Camillus, Titus, Trajan, Theodosius, as well as Sulla, Marius, and Ventidius Bassus, a man of the humblest station yet with surprising good fortune, to whom fate granted an incredible victory over the Parthians and revenge for the Crassi. But all are, as fame has it, outdone by Metellus, called "the lucky," although in the opinion of those who search profoundly for the truth, no one is lucky here; but we are speaking only of military luck, and call lucky the commander who usually is victorious and never tastes defeat. On the battlefield he requires fortune on his side, though it may be harsher at home. Thus, the same person may be a lucky commander and an unlucky man. In this category, among foreigners, are Alexander the Macedonian, Cyrus the Persian king (had he not gone on to Scythia), and the Carthaginian commander Hannibal, had he believed Maharbal or met his end a little earlier. Nor do we exclude Charlemagne who, last in time, will not feel offended at occupying last place in this letter.

That you lack none of these qualities discussed your reputation declares and events prove; and that none fail you in the greatest crises, I pray, I wish, and I hope; but you do have one thing that all but two of those named lacked—Christ the King. Now go with good luck and return in triumph, and by your outstanding faith and energy earn God's love, immortal glory, and the everlasting gratitude of that great republic. Farewell, and remember me.

Padua, April 1 [1364].

Sen. IV, 2.

To the same person,* felicitations on his speedy and bloodless victory.

What I feared does not always happen, I admit; what I hoped sometimes does, for you have won and, what is even better, your victory is bloodless.** In war, no success is so great that it may not have been at too high a price; this one, bought with no bloodshed, is worth not less, but more on this account. I can believe that armed justice was at the forefront of the battle, at whose appearance the hostile spirits fell and the army in the wrong was routed by the prick of conscience. Otherwise, how could so many armed men have turned tail in terror at the mere sight of you? Within their hearts were diffidence and fear from the memory of their crimes. You had many supporters in the enemy camp. In the judgment of some, the victory could have perhaps seemed more illustrious, had it been steeped in more blood. But, by Jove, it would not have been more blessed and more useful to the republic, nor more glorious for you or more admirable in itself. For no army is so well deployed that it cannot suffer defeat by a headlong charge and the powerful assault of spirits resolved to perish. To conquer without striking a blow and with no bloodshed is, after all, a true victory that subdues the enemy and saves your fellow citizens. The death of the enemy, when this is achieved by the death of many citizens, must not be reckoned worthwhile. Well known is that renowned commander's saying that he would rather save one citizen than kill a thousand enemies; for an enemy, either defeated or pacified, can be drawn into friendship, but a citizen, once killed, can never be brought back to life. Taking much into consideration and fearing much, as a lover does, I had warned you of many things as you set forth in battle array, certainly hoping for victory but not expecting such an easy and speedy one. Therefore, I had a feeling that just as much remained for me to do, and I believed that I would have no less to write after the victory or during the war than before the war began. I am grateful, then, for the conscience and fear of the Cretans which free me from this labor.

Indeed from all I wrote then, you picked one thing in particular

---

* See IV, 1.
** Contemporary historians dispute that the victory was bloodless.

for yourself—to vie with Metellus in speed of conquest; you thus overcame the enemy in war and Metellus in swiftness. For your part, you went off to war in the Roman way and certainly with a Roman spirit, that is, as Cicero says, prepared either to conquer or to die. When they beheld you, on the other hand, they were overwhelmed by sudden fear, like the local goats, stricken and paralyzed by great terror; they took refuge in the victor's mercy, as though it were dittany, the herb familiar to them and salutary for wounds. Thus, the glory of your name, the Venetians' well-known valor and power as well as their equally known clemency, brought an end to a grave war with incredible ease.

But whereas everything with the enemy proved favorable and smooth, with your worthless and disloyal soldiers there was the utmost difficulty and danger. Blinded by greed and envy, they had dared not only to incite the army to rebellion with speeches, but also to attack you, their leader, with the sword, under whom they had successfully served—perhaps so that you could not boast of a victory without danger. With great valor and firmness you quelled the mutiny, truly dire even for great commanders, thus proving yourself greater than the great; and, while ignoring the wrong done to yourself,* you avenged the injured republic by justly punishing a few, by immediately restoring the peace, and by calling the army to obedience. In this also, as in many things, you magnificently imitated those incomparable commanders, Africanus the elder and Julius Caesar.

Since all that, though great and memorable, was brief and swift, it is not fitting that the account be any longer than the events that it describes. Yet, whereas there was no need to write at length, I did feel obliged to congratulate you publicly on the one hand for your valor and on the other for your good fortune, and to welcome you, the returning victor, with joyful and triumphant words.

Hail, therefore, Metellus Creticus, or our Scipio from Verona, savior of citizens, victor over the enemy, punisher of the guilty, restorer of military discipline. You bring us a glorious victory without bloodshed, an army safe and sound without strife. You restored to warfare its law and to captured citizens their liberty, to our country peace and its lost dominion. Although the honor of the laurel and the civic crown for such merits has long fallen into disuse, and though you may lack snow-white steeds and golden

---

* The text is corrupt; we follow Fracassetti's conjecture.

chariots and the Capitoline summit, those ancient rewards for victors, you will still triumph most gloriously in the minds of the lovers of virtue, than which no theater is more majestic, absolutely no citadel more lofty. Farewell; and return as soon as possible to your people who long for you.

Venice, June 10 [1364].

Sen. IV, 3.

To Pietro Bolognese [da Muglio], rhetorician,[*] on the Venetian victory.

Even if you, being present in spirit and near in body, could almost drink in the din and applause with your ears, and the smoke and dust of the games with your eyes, even if word of mouth by those continually coming and going could supply any report you might lack, I still believe that you would eagerly learn from my letter what you would have still more eagerly seen in person, were it not that sickness begrudged you this finest delight. For, I ask you, what finer or more deserving spectacle can be imagined than to look at the most deserving city rejoicing for justice alone and not for the harm to its neighbors, not for its citizens' feuds or plunderings? I would not have you think that the most august city of Venice—today the one abode of liberty, peace, and justice, the one refuge for good men, the one haven for ships of those wishing the good life, yet continually buffeted on all sides by the storms of tyranny and war, rich in gold but even richer in fame, mighty in wealth but even mightier in virtue, built on solid marble but held firm by the still more solid foundation of civic harmony, surrounded by tricky waters but secure from still trickier counsel—boasts and rejoices over recovering the island of Crete, which, though great in the antiquity of its name is still a little thing to great minds (all things are little except virtue, though they seem very large), but rather over the outcome as was befitting, that is, not over her victory, but the victory of justice. For to stout men of might, with this power and this general, and these masters of warfare on land and sea, what is great in having defeated unarmed little Greeks and villainy on the run? It is great that, even now in our age, treachery yields so quickly to fortitude and vices succumb to virtues, that God cares even now and watches over human affairs. "I am the Lord," He says, "and I do not change" [Mal. 3:6]. And again He says, "I am who am" [Exod. 3:14]. But He would not truly and clearly be, if any change were in Him; He is the very thing He was, and not by chance does the Psalmist attribute this quality to Him. Moreover, what He was and what He is, which perfection is either the sole or the main

---

[*] Professor of letters at Bologna and Padua, who often consulted P. on historical and literary matters.

result of his virtue, He will always be; or rather, neither "was" nor "will be" properly fits Him, but only "is." Likewise, what He knew he knows, what He willed He wills, what He could He can. If this were ever unclear to anyone because mortal things seemed neglected sometimes either through the manifest guilt of men or by God's hidden judgment, see how he has been enlightened by the extraordinary speed of the recent bloodless and easy victory. Such was the speed that now the war against the Cretans has ended before the news was heard in Venice that it had begun—just as once, long ago, the news about the war against the Illyrians was heard in Rome. Hence the joy, hence the triumph.

It would take too long for my humble and busy pen to describe in words the whole series of joyful and solemn celebrations. Accept a summary. Around the sixth hour of June fourth of this year, 1364, I happened to be standing at the window looking out at the high sea, and with me was my erstwhile brother, now my most loving father, the Archbishop of Patras, who will be proceeding to his very own see at the beginning of autumn, but, out of love for me, which remains unshaken despite the favors of fortune, is spending the summer here in his house, the one that is called mine. Suddenly, one of the long ships, which they call galleys, garlanded with leafy boughs, rowed into the harbor mouth, interrupting our conversation with its unexpected appearance. We at once had the premonition that it was the bearer of some happy tidings; it was clearing the channel with sails trimmed; the nimble sailors and young men, crowned with leaves and smiling broadly, waved banners aloft from the very bow and hailed the victorious fatherland, still ignorant of the news. Now the watchman on the highest tower signaled the arrival of the ship from abroad. And so, without anyone giving orders, but out of curiosity, there was a general concourse to the shore from all over the city. When the ship came closer and details became visible, we noted enemy banners hanging from the stern, and no doubt remained that the ship was a messenger of victory. We were hoping for victory, not yet in the war, but in some captured city, and so our minds were incapable of grasping the reality. But when messengers came ashore and reported to the Council, all was joyful beyond our hope and beyond belief. The enemy was conquered, killed, captured, and routed, our citizens released from bondage, the cities returned to their allegiance, once again the yoke was imposed upon Crete, our victorious arms lain down; in short, the war was ended without slaughter, and peace achieved with glory.

When all this became known, Doge Lorenzo [Celsi], truly a noble man—unless perchance my love for him deceives me—and memorable for the greatness of his mind, the gentleness of his manners, his zeal for virtue, and, above all, a singular piety and patriotism, knowing that nothing goes right and nothing succeeds unless it begins with religion, turned with all the people to praises of God and thanksgiving. Throughout the city, but more prominently in the basilica of blessed Mark the Evangelist—which, in my opinion, none anywhere is more beautiful—everything was done that can be done for God by man. Lavish rites and an extraordinary procession were held before and around the church where not only all the laity and clergy were on hand, but also foreign prelates whom either chance or curiosity or so much talk about the ceremony had kept in town.

After the religious ceremonies had ended in splendor, everyone turned to games and spectacles. It would be tiresome to enumerate the many kinds of games, their forms, their cost, their solemnity, and their sequence; there was no disorder, no confusion, no ill-will, very rare and wonderful as it is in such a case, but everything was full of joy, courtesy, harmony, and love. Magnificence and pomp held sway, but without banishing modesty and sobriety; they governed and checked it as it reigned in their city and in their festivity. The celebration continued in varied pomp throughout many festive days, and at length the entire affair concluded with two spectacles, for which I have no fitting Latin words, but I shall describe them for you. One can, I believe, be called a race, the other a contest or joust. In the former the participants each ride along a straight course; in the latter they dash helter-skelter against each other. Both games are equestrian; but the first is unarmed, except that the riders with spears and shields and silk banners fluttering in the wind reflect a certain warlike image, while the second is armed, a kind of duel. Thus in the first there is the most elegance and the least danger; in the second, however, there is as much danger as skill. Not properly, the French call the first "spear play" when the name would be more fitting for the other; in that they really play, whereas in this they fight, but in both is something that I would scarcely have believed another telling me, but now I do believe with my own eyes: the great and marvelous industry not of a nautical and seafaring people, as the world has come to believe, but of a military and martial one that excelled in the art of horsemanship and weaponry, as well as in that endurance of heat and hard labor that would be enough even for the fiercest warriors on earth.

Both spectacles were held in that square which I doubt has an equal in the world, before the church's marble and gold facade, and no outsider participated in the first contest. They chose for this part of the celebration twenty-four noble youths, striking in appearance and dress, and summoned Tommaso Bambasio from Ferrara. So that posterity may briefly know about him, if I am to have any celebrity or credit with them, throughout Venice he is today what Roscius was in Rome; and he is as dear and congenial to me as Roscius to Tully, although, while there is a very great similarity in a certain aspect of these friendships, there is much dissimilarity in another. In any event, under his direction and planning, the performance was so skillfully staged and completed that you would conclude you were not seeing men riding, but angels flying—a marvelous spectacle, so many youths dressed in purple and gold, reining in and whipping on so many fleet-footed horses, so aglitter with ornaments, that their feet barely seemed to touch the ground. And they followed their captain's orders with such precision that when one reached the goal, another sprang from the mark. Another made ready to race, and with this alternating, perfect coordination within the circular formation, there was a continual race as one man's finish became another's starting point; when the last stopped, the first began again, so that, though many raced throughout the day, you would have said in the evening that only one had raced. At one moment you would see spear splinters flying through the air, at another purple banners rustling in the breeze. It is not easy to say nor credible to hear what a crowd of people was there day after day; neither sex, nor age, nor station, was missing.

By this time the doge himself [Lorenzo Celsi] with a huge retinue of nobles had taken his place before the church facade above the vestibule; from this marble dais everything was beneath his feet. It is the place where those bronze and gold horses stand, as though copied from life and stampeding from above, of ancient workmanship by a superb artist, whoever he was. To shield us from the heat and glare of the setting summer sum, the whole area was provided with varicolored awnings. I was invited there—as I am often honored by the doge—and sat at his right; but after having my fill of the spectacle for two days, I excused myself from the rest because of business that no one was unaware of. Down below there was no empty spot, for as the saying goes, a grain of millet could not have fallen to earth; the huge square, the church itself, the towers, roofs, porches, windows were not only filled, but packed. An incalculable and incredible crowd of people covered the face of the earth; and the many large and well-dressed families of the flourishing city, spread before our eyes, doubled the joy of the festival, so that there was nothing more delightful to the populace in so much rejoicing than the sight of itself. On the right was a wooden grandstand, like a huge platform, built hastily just for the occasion, where four hundred young married women sat, of outstanding beauty and attire, selected from all the flower of the top nobility; and they provided elegance at midday to the spectacles, in the morning to the daily banquets, and in the evening to the entertainment under the stars. And something else that refuses to be shrouded in silence: certain high noblemen from Britain, earls and kinsmen of their king, who had lately arrived in this country by chance, took part. An overseas journey had brought them here to celebrate their recent victory and to refresh themselves meanwhile after their seafaring labors. This was the end of many days of racing games whose only prize was honor, and the same honor so equally that it could be rightly said that every man was a winner and no one a loser.

For the other tourney, however, because it was to be conducted with greater danger, and some foreigners were to come, other prizes were posted: a weighty crown of pure gold and sparkling gems to honor the victor, and then a silver belt of splendid workmanship as consolation prize for the one who earned second-place honors. Earlier, an invitation in military form and in the vernacular, but authenticated with the doge's seal, had been sent to neighboring and distant provinces to summon all those tempted by the desire of such glory to that equestrian tourney—as I called it. And many assembled, not only from different cities, but with different languages, yet trained in fighting, bold in prowess, and hoping for distinction. After the other competition came to an end, on the fourth of August this one began and continued for four days with such huge crowds that in man's memory nothing comparable can be recalled since the founding of the city. On the last day, in the unanimous judgment of the doge, the nobles, the foreign knights, and especially of the one who had been commander in the war, and, next to God, was the author of the victory and the rejoicing, first prize was awarded to a citizen and second to a visitor from Ferrara. Let this be the end of the games, but not of our joys and successes; let this be the end of this letter through which I tried to make present to your eyes and ears what sickness robbed you of, so that you may know, one after another, the events here, and may understand that even among seafaring men there is an army and a sense of pomp, lofty spirits, a contempt for gold, and an appetite for glory. Farewell.

Venice, August 10 [1364].

Sen. IV, 4.

To the same person, [*] *on the obstinacy of servants.*

That venerable lady, your mother-in-law, came to see me; for her, if there were nothing else to reinforce it, the fact that she gave birth to a daughter worthy of you was more than sufficent not only to let her be admitted but embraced—so to speak—and cherished and attended with due honors.

But why am I going roundabout? You know my servants, or rather my domestic enemies. But why should I dishonor my servants who wish to be called the best of all and perhaps are the best of servants, yet unquestionably the worst of men; so much so that, while some people envy me, I detest them like an intestinal illness and a poison poured into my bowels? In any case, you know all my servants. There is no need to describe them. After professing to serve, they, or rather an intolerable and unworthy tyranny takes control; I omit other matters—material for a book, not a letter. A hundred times I have begged them, not to say ordered them, that if anyone who comes to visit while I am absorbed in the divine office, they should tell him to wait, unless he is very distinguished or the matter is urgent; that while I am busy studying, they should neither admit nor exclude everyone indiscriminately, but use their discretion, if they have any, about the persons and their reasons. But when I have taken time for a meal or a nap, whoever it may be should enter immediately, since I am eager for excuses to cut short either of these; and besides, it is possible to return to either one after a conversation. Well, in all this, as in everything else, they always do the opposite of what they know I want, whether this is their disloyalty or my lot, or perhaps because they think that I too am overcome and enslaved by the same feelings as they know they are, drowsiness and gluttony—although neither my words nor, I think, my life is open to such suspicion.

But to return to the account of today's story. It was the sixth hour, and as is my custom in the summertime, I had retired to my bedroom for the afternoon to compensate for the sleep lost last night. This is our inheritance from that forefather of our race, who was not as useful to his descendants as he was notorious: hunger, thirst, weariness, and sleep—whether this brief sleep or that unend-

[*] See IV, 3.

ing one. Thus I had scarcely begun to let my eyes graze on this daily image of death called sleep, when she came to this house of yours where I live, eager to see me whom she has not seen up to now and loves without seeing. These splendid guardians of mine replied that I was asleep, and the pack of liars were not lying about this; yet it was neither the sleep of death nor one that could not be recouped. What could the tired and elderly woman do, for I surmise that she was both? What made it more difficult was that she was being dragged by her companions in a hurry and in a great city, always crowded; the populace is now utterly overflowing with hordes of foreigners which this day has drawn here—and not, I hope, the desire for sightseeing or viewing a most beautiful city, but the pious hope of the annual indulgence and the wish to ascend interiorly to heaven with Christ. She therefore departed, blaming her luck for being unable to see me. When I awoke, what do you suppose I did, what remedy did I take, except to resent it in silence? Of course, as they say, what we are used to does not torment us; or rather, it does, but more sparingly; habit produces a callus, hardened to be sure but not impervious to pain. I was sorry, and I thought of having her paged, but it is easier to find a small fish in the surging Adriatic than one person in this Adriatic city, especially on this day. I beg you: tell her this in my words, lest she or her companions attribute to my arrogance what was my servants' villainy. Farewell.

Venice, on Ascension Day in the evening [1363-66].

Sen. IV, 5.

To Federigo Aretino,[*] on certain creations of Virgil.

Among juvenile trifles that I dashed off in the heat of youth is a poem written in haste, at that time with burning enthusiasm, but now oudated, as things go, and scarcely mine any longer, in my judgment. To tell the truth, it was prompted by anger at that great, envious rival; in it I wrote against him who, while seeking so doggedly the highest literary honor that he could not bear an equal—certainly not in Italy—nor an aspirant, was the enemy of nearly all literature except for the little that he has chosen not for its quality of content but its pleasure to the ears. Among other things it befell me to defend the poetry he was bitterly attacking, to which I was then dedicated because of my age; and so, when Virgil, deservedly the most praised of our poets, was the target of his pen, and mention was made of the stories that are so numerous in Virgil and in the rest of them, which that man was said to be most in the habit of damning, I lightly touched upon some of them, to reveal them to that arrogant fellow as gems wrapped in a napkin and at the same time to lay bare to him his own ignorance, and to shove it in his eyes, so that he would have to recognize how foul it is for an intelligent man to condemn what he does not know.

Here, after so long a time, you have found occasion to ask and to trace humbly what is the first step to virtue and knowledge, what those stories mean, once the veil of allegories coating the truth is removed. I dare say you are fit to have them revealed, and I am fit to lend a hand to any honorable desire. Heavens, I would gladly undertake it, if I had as much free time as inclination; and it would give me pleasure to aid your youthful curiosity with the remains of my youthful studies. Yet if I begin speaking of what I used to think once upon a time in my youth about these and similar matters (for I have long since put them behind me, concentrating on far different things), my memory will not suffice to recall them, nor time to describe them. Yet if I want to pursue others' opinions and conjectures, an immense series of things opens up, so rambling and so mottled that the writers' diversity and outspokenness would be monstrous. For the difference in intellects is also infinite, with no

---

[*] A minor poet, much younger than P., known for both his Italian and Latin verses.

one to check the boldness of new opinions, while the subject itself is such as to fit many varying interpretations. If they are true and will stand literally, they should not be rejected even though they never entered the mind of those who created the stories. Who would dare proclaim amidst so much obscurity what the truth is in something deliberately hidden? Who would affirm unhesitatingly that those authors, thousands of years ago, meant this, not something else. It is enough to elicit a particular meaning from the words or more meanings that are true, regardless of whether the author had in mind more meanings or the very same ones, or fewer meanings and not all the same, or none of them whatever. For it is not as easy to know what each one thought as to know what is true. In his *Confessions* Augustine examines many such things in regard to Moses. Since you now ask me, however, and draw me back to my early concerns as the day wanes and I wearily contemplate my final resting place, I shall briefly tell you whatever is still accessible to me without taxing my memory—not what I contend is the truest or the finest, but what occurred to me at that age where you now are, when I was busy with the same concerns and studies as you are now. In keeping with that age, I was variously moved by ideas, now in one direction, now in another, now this notion would come to me, now that one; and I would quite often discuss them with my comrades.

Now take in hand the letter that prompted you to probe this, and what I remember to be written there. Look at Virgil whom I defended against that slanderer, who, it is agreed, meant something loftier than what he says in that divine work, which for him was the last, but for all who sip from the Castalian fount the first and foremost. Not only is this the common opinion of devotees of poetry, but a letter of the poet himself, written to Augustus Caesar, confirms how he had entered upon the greatest thing, one requiring extensive study beyond what appears necessary. There are many things besides; indeed I cannot recall them all, but only the ones that over all clearly hint that what I say is so. Since—as I myself maintained then and do not change my mind—hardly any verse is without a disguise, I shall come to your question in order not to weave an endless and inextricable web; and if I give more than that, you will thank my generous pen, but if I omit something, you will excuse me for being busy.

At the beginning, those dark brothers who he says take orders from Aeolus, are the winds, "brothers" because they were born of the same father—the air, "dark" because of the whirlwinds, squalls, dust, rain, hail, and storm-clouds that these brothers stir up by alternating blasts. They are brothers, therefore, but wild and hostile to each other, and restless and rebellious even against their father. Aeolus was king of the nine windiest islands near Sicily, which are named Aeolian after him. He is said to have had, without any particular experience or skill, such knowledge of the winds that he could predict with certainty from the color and the flow of the air and from mountaintops that the winds were about to break forth or abate. Consequently, he was called and esteemed the king of the winds not simply by rude, ignorant, gullible folk but even by the poets, particularly by Homer in that exquisite tale where he has Aeolus shut the winds in a leather pouch and make a present of it to Ulysses who was wandering. Of course, this is literal and historical, and known to all.

There are those who seek a moral sense in Virgil. This is how it goes: each one tends toward his own goal, and concentrates upon it, and thus from one and the very same thing several interpretations are obtained because of variation in those dealing with it; in Annaeus' words, "In the same meadow the ox seeks grass, the dog a rabbit, the stork a lizard" [*Ep.* 108.29]. I admit it is hard work either way, whether we seek the natural meaning or the moral one, under a poetic mist—that is, if a passion for knowledge stretches the search from the beginning to the end of a work. For it is scarcely possible for a human intellect to make everything fit, nor was that in my opinion the writer's intention. Leaving others aside, however, I shall return to Virgil, the very one you ask about, whose goal and subject, as I see it, is the perfect man. Such perfection consists either solely or primarily in virtue. I deem a moral consideration of his work very useful because this is the most matchless jewel in life, and because it follows the writer's main intention. And what I have said about Virgil, I would say about Homer, for both walk the same pathway with matching strides.

Thus, to solve finally what you are seeking in the passage you ask about, to me those winds have always seemed to be nothing but the impulses of lust and wrath, and the emotions dwelling in the breast and beneath the heart, disturbing the serenity of human life, as there are storms that disturb the calm sea. Aeolus is reason itself, controlling and restraining the soul's appetites toward wrath and lust. As Virgil himself says,

> If he did not, they in their rage would snatch
> The seas and lands and lofty heaven above.
> [*Aen.* 1. 58–59]

That is, they would snatch up our blood, flesh, bones, and finally the soul itself, the former being all of earthly origin and the latter celestial—evidently to hurl them to death and destruction. The dark caverns where he has them hidden, what are they if not the hollow and hidden part of a man, the chest and innards where, according to Platonic doctrine, the passions have their seat? The superimposed boulder is the head, which Plato likewise declared the seat of reason. Aeneas is the strong and perfect man of whom I spoke a little earlier. Achates is worry, the companion of illustrious men, and anxiety and diligence.

The wood is this life, full of shadows and pitfalls, confusing and unsure byways, inhabited by wild beasts, that is, beset with many hidden trials and perils. Sterile and inhospitable, at times it confronts and soothes the ears and eyes of the inhabitants with the lush greenery, the songs of birds and the murmuring of waters, that is, the short-lived and frail image, the empty and deceptive sweetness of things that pass on and slip away. As the light dims, the wood becomes horrifying and terrible, and with winter's approach, it turns ugly with mud, scruffy in its bareness, bristling with stumps, and stripped of foliage.

In the midst of the wood appears Venus. She is lust, which is hotter and keener around midlife, and assumes a maidenly semblance and garb to deceive the unknowing. For if anyone were to perceive her as she is, the mere sight of her would no doubt make him flee in horror, for though nothing is more attractive than lust, so too nothing is more foul. She is portrayed with her garments girded because she flees swiftly, and therefore is compared to the swiftest things. Whether you consider it in general or in particular, nothing passes more swiftly than pleasure. It ends very quickly, and while you are engaged in it lasts but a moment. Finally, she wears the dress of a huntress because she hunts for the souls of the wretched; she carries a bow and tosses her hair to the winds so as both to wound and to charm, indicating also that the charm itself may be flighty, inconstant, and that, in the end, all is fleeting like the wind. In fact, she is depicted befriending the Trojans, either because they worshipped her with more devotion or they preferred the last of the three kinds of life understood and described by poets along with philosophers—the first is the life of wisdom and study attributed to Pallas; the second, the life of power and wealth is given to Juno; the third, the life of lust and pleasures sacred to Venus.

What is more, the Trojan judge who had won fame among the beasts for his fairness and justice appeared unjust and foolish on a greater issue; for, when summoned to render judgment in the very famous contest of the three goddesses that I have just mentioned, he obeyed not reason but passion, ruling in favor of naked Venus. As a fitting reward, he got a passing pleasure, and soon a long travail and a series of ills, and finally not only his own death but that of his whole family and ultimately the slaughter, in short, of the entire people loyal to him. She is called the mother of Aeneas because even great men are begotten of lust, and because he had such rare comeliness that, though a poor exile, he is said to have been attractive even to chaste eyes. It was this same Venus who presented her Aeneas hidden in a dark cloud with only Achates as a companion, after being buffeted by great calamities and surviving fire and shipwreck, to a beautiful widow—as beauty causes lust and widowhood fosters a freedom to sin. That cloud is hidden under this mystic cloud, for often it happens that, roused by the reputation of virtue alone, minds are at first prone to bring help to needy wretches under the pretext of humanity and compassion. Later, when their nobility and beauty have been viewed and examined, the veil is torn open, and Venus's son is left exposed, and becomes the object of base love. At times he too is tempted because it is difficult even for a perfect man not to be swayed by the preeminent beauty of things, especially when he realizes that he is loved and desired. Or rather, as Jerome says, "It is impossible for man's senses not to be stirred by the heat in his marrow," but, the same writer says, "That man is praised and called blessed who, as soon as he begins to think, kills the thoughts." This is nothing more than what David had said earlier, that "he takes and dashes his babies against the rocks" [Ps. 137:9];* or because not everyone is capable of this, he too is blessed who, though he has consented and succumbed to sin, or worse yet, is stuck with the glue of a bad habit, bound tight with chains and stooped under the burden, nonetheless eventually either through God's silent prompting or the warning of someone, declaring it God's will, rises and returns to the straight path of virtue and glory, leaving behind the pleasure that held him.

Then, Mercury, the god of eloquence, sent by Jove, warns Aeneas to change his ways. Though under passion's sway and shaken in spirit by his great love, he still obeys the command from heaven, despite the vain opposition of pleasure itself and ingratiating habit which leaves nothing untried to keep the beloved tied down. For it

---

* P. misunderstands this verse.

can scarcely be told with what flattery seductive pleasure engrosses and delays the mind, as it contemplates escape, or what sweetness dangles before him if he lingers, what bitterness if he departs. When all has proven hopeless and he has finally left, Dido weeps alone and wretchedly. Then she sends away for a while her aged sister, Anna,* that is, the custom and memory of the past which she has often dispatched in vain to keep him there, whose presence did not allow her to die; finally she commits suicide, for foul lust evidently perishes on its own when the mind, according to the Apostle's advice, forgetting its sins, is converted to honest pursuits. Granted that he wavered a long time in making up his mind, and then, when things were ready and he had resolved to go, he falls asleep "on the ship's lofty stern," that is, within the depths of his lofty mind and in his firm purpose he found repose since, as we know, arriving at a firm decision is the end of distress. At length he sails away, although from time to time turning to view what he has left behind; he continues nonetheless and heads for Italy through the waves whipped up by the north wind—that is, steering the ship of his persevering mind through the midst of difficulties with the rudder of his reason, and pressing forward with the sails and oars of actions and words, he finally reaches the destined shore.

There he attends first to religion; sacrificing in the traditional way, he pays his respects to his venerable father—a verse that the Catholics adopted and the Church has carried over to the high altar of Christ. Following the divine rites, he turns to things human, which are nothing but games where, according to fortune's whim, the first are often last and the last first, where slow and constant old age overcomes the fickleness and arrogance of youth. Yet at the end, mourning replaces rejoicing, as is often the case. This upsets the hero's heart, but encouraged by friends' advice, nocturnal visions, and divine oracles, however, he gains so much strength that he not only persists in his resolve, but in spite of losing his helmsman, steers the ship by himself as it surges in the dark waves, that is, bemoaning in the murky mist of this unstable and uncertain life the carelessness and misfortune of others, yet without abandoning the helm of reason. This is particularly evident in the uncertainties and dangers, until he reaches the inner Italian shore, namely, the gulf of Cumae and Baiae in which, unless I am mistaken, Virgil surpasses the Greek poet. After bathing in a river that he has come upon, to

---

* *Anna ... annosa* is P.'s pun.

rid himself of the caked dirt of mortal life, which is harassed by many misfortunes, he goes to the nether world under the guidance of a prophetic soothsayer, where fictions are numberless and boundless. There he comes to know as much as can be known about the state of the next life, and conceives an immense hope of famous progeny; he now continues more confidently and happily, yet does not forget his usual kindness toward his nurse. Then he sails by Circe's mountain to teach by example that the evils that cannot be overcome must be shunned. Finally, coming upon the mouth of the Tiber, he arrives at the spot where Rome now is, that is, the toilsome and perilous field where he was to seek Glory. Once he has overcome all obstacles and snatched her from her lesser suitors, he makes her his own in everlasting marriage, from which he begets the most celebrated offspring and posterity, the founder of the greatest empire, guardian of peace, merciful to the humble, and conqueror of the proud—inasmuch as the father of this girl, whose marriage is fought over, is the mind, and her mother the flesh, that is, the mind's bride since glory is usually born from the actions of both. But although the Fates had destined this girl for foreign sons-in-law, that is, actively penetrating the difficult and the unknown, still the mother, being weaker and incapable of deliberation, fusses to unite her daughter with a relative born nearby—that is, to carnal desires and earthly endeavors—so that sometimes with her womanish begging and nagging she pulls her husband over to her way of thinking. But in the end, he is swayed by admiration for the foreigner's all-conquering valor, blames himself like a penitent and changes his mind. The maiden's mother, thinking that it is too late to do anything about the son-in-law, hangs herself on the gibbet because when the flesh understands that glory has been awarded to virtue and sees that there is no longer a place for its passions, it does away with itself in accordance with what the Apostle Paul says, that he has been crucified for the world. Although you did not ask about this, although, too, I have failed to answer some of your questions, nevertheless, since I have come to this point in speaking, I shall briefly continue the subject to the end in order not to break the thread of the story I have undertaken.

Therefore, when the flesh, naturally loved and cherished too much, does away with itself of its own accord, and virtue is energetically directed to a desired end, the inferior suitor is deprived of the assistance of his dear mother-in-law;[*] and hearing the sound of hostile arms everywhere, and seeing from the very chariot of mutable and recurring cares, where he is standing, the tower (that is, the loftiest portion of the soul) set on fire by the heat of virtue rising to heaven, he is appalled and confounded by the changing look of things; and though unequal in strength, he still decides to tempt fortune one last time. Rejecting his sister (that is, obstinate hope), with a headlong charge he leaps to his native ground and rushes on foot into battle, since even after the inclinations of the flesh have been vanquished and quenched, the internal spark still does not subside, but now does battle more slowly, and consequently the sword breaks at the first trial. But his immortal sister supplies him with another; she will not stop supporting him in battle until a hellish terror by Jove's command blocks her, sad and groaning.

Aeneas, on the other hand, has been struck by an arrow and his knee gives way, meaning that a man, however well-armed with virtue, is sometimes wounded by temptation so that he limps toward his goal, and no doctor's hand nor any human art whatsoever, while professing to heal, can remove the arrow lodged in his bones, but only the intervention of divine mercy. More boldly yet he sets forth for the fray, and as both armies—that is, the forces of good and evil—look on, he attacks, hurling in the first assault his spear at the enemy with great force. In its flight it strikes the trunk of a bitter olive tree, penetrating so deeply that no human hand can remove it either—that is, when the cutting edge of the mind is directed against carnal desire, it finds something bitter. For if pleasure is sweet, its opposite must be bitter; and it sticks so much that the shot cannot be repeated because the natural hardness of the target itself prevents it, nor can the actions leading to that state be repeated, and a like number of wounds, as it were, inflicted upon the adversary until Venus—that is, the enjoyment of the deed and good, honest pleasure—removes the spear. Her arrival signals the attainment of the habit, as Aristotle terms it, which results in an easy repetition of the action. Such a state, born of difficult actions, soon produces easy actions, so that what used to be done with sadness is done with joy. Then Aeneas, the foreigner (that is, virtue or the brave man victor over the flesh), grabs with his hand the spear that is now easy and pliant, and hurling it with greater success and precision at his native rival [Turnus], knocks carnal passion to the ground. He would

---

[*] P.'s *amata* is a play upon the mother-in-law's name, Amata.

perhaps have spared his suppliant foe, since lust is natural and thus excusable, had he not seen the emblems seized from his Pallas, the noble youth that his foe had killed. To avenge this, Aeneas slays Turnus and—with him out of the way—rules in peace, leaving his son as heir to the throne; following death, unavoidable for a mortal, he obtained the reputation of divinity, and becoming the subject of poets, he lives on in the mouths of man.

Here I have pursued the subject to the very end. Though you would have let me stop far earlier, an impulse bore me on; and driven by your diligenece on one side, drawn by the sequence of events on the other, in order not to unravel the train of thought, I have exceeded the bounds of your request.

Now I turn to what remains, namely, the conflagration of Troy and Dido's banquet. To begin with the latter where Maro started, even if we did not know first of all that Dido, from other sources the founder and queen of Carthage, was a chaste woman, Jerome provides good authority, thoroughly familiar not only with sacred letters, but with secular ones in that book, crammed and packed with a thousand stories, which he wrote against the heretical Jovinian. But Aeneas and Dido were not contemporaries, nor could they have seen one another, since she was born three hundred years or thereabouts, after his death. All those who have any acquaintance with chronology or with Greek or Punic history know this, not only those who have read commentaries on Virgil, but those who have read the the books of the *Saturnalia*. In the second book of his *Confessions* Augustine remarks that Aeneas never went to Carthage. The entire story of Dido and the origin of Carthage is told in the eighteenth book of the history by Pompeius Trogus, or Justin. But why am I seeking authorities for something so clear? For who, except some of the multitude, who anywhere, I ask, is so uneducated as not to know that the story of Dido and Aeneas is fictitious, and that it has gained the status of truth among men, eager not so much for truth as for beauty, through the loveliness of the subject and the poet's sweetness and art, to the point that sadly and unwillingly they hear the truth and are deprived of the forbidden possession of the sweet lie? I know whereof I speak. For I was the first one, or rather the only one, in this age and this place to shatter this lie. So entrenched was it that the delicate ears of many—above all, the one against whom the letter you inquire about was written— scorned to hear the contrary, as not only heresy, but an affront and mockery. Therefore, when I said this as a young and unknown man, they screamed as though I were accusing Virgil of ignorance. And when I maintained that he was not ignorant of this but knowingly playing, they were astonished and asked the reason. Of course, why should the poet who is the best and most learned of all have invented this—for it is certain that he did—why, when he could by all rights have chosen anyone else from the number of heroines or easily formed a new character, should he choose this one woman, worthy of eternal praise, who he knew had laid down her life to preserve her chastity and widowhood? Yet he made her out to be obedient to lustful love. One can ask, but doubt will still remain. What I feel or think about this, because you will hear it from me personally, I omit here so as not to pile up more now. With this interjection, I come to my theme.

Whatever, then, the reason for Virgil's fiction, Dido herself—it is established—was a not a native but a foreign queen, through whom human power is symbolized by the royal name. To be sure, all power that occasions pride in men is temporary, since all mortals have been brought equally naked into this light. An exile from her home, bearing riches with her, she settles on a foreign shore. For we are all exiles and foreigners, with no permanent city here. Coming into this exile, however, we have brought various wealth, a quantity of silver and gold—namely, eloquence, intellect, and natural gifts. She seeks and enlarges with marvelous ability the place to build her citadel. And it is evident with how much skill, how many deceits we too build in enlarging our narrow confines.

To answer your question, she offers a banquet because it is the way of kings and rulers to nurture their subjects, whom nowadays they strip and devour. At this banquet, or this human association over which kings preside, three kinds of men recline at their ease: first, the kings themselves, zealous for wisdom as much as for eloquence; these are figured in Iopas, who talks about the secrets of nature, befitting a philosopher, but, long-haired, he celebrates them with song and lyre, which is the office of a poet. Next are the lustful and greedy who are figured in the draught of Bitias and the cup handed to him by the queen; for lust, as a stream from a spring, is poured down from kings to their subjects. So again we return to the three kinds of lives mentioned earlier.

Reclining at this noisy banquet, a brave man feeds on pride in his accomplishments and delights those listening with a magnificent speech. For when bidden to speak, he begins as if forced, but puts an end to the indistinct chatter of the guests. Then he tells the story as they listen in silence. What do you think he speaks about if not fortune's blows, men's deceptions, the conflagrations of this life, and the ladders of passion clinging to the walls of the soul? He speaks of the idle dream of those who sleep amidst perils, of schemes frustrated by adverse fate, of truth given to false counsel and withheld from the true; he speaks too of the portal shattered by the battering ram of sins, of the enemies that break in while the soul's guardians are wiped out on the threshold; he speaks, in short, about all of life as though it were the one final night spent by blind mortals amidst mindless pleasures and of the deaths of kings, mingled with a crowd of the righteous and the pious. In the midst of these, with immense danger, he barely got out alive, leaving behind the comforts of his native land and losing his first wife (that is, the habit of lust to which he was yoked from his younger years); at first, he was alone in spirit, armed with his virtue, but later, as others rallied to his leadership, he was no longer alone, but carried his aged father on his shoulders while leading his little son by the hand. He was destined to arrive at the place we have mentioned, remarkable for his loyalty to both, and fortunate in the outcome. And this is the tumult, the madness, the peril in which the pleasure-loving city perishes by the flames of lust and the sword of wrath—that is, by the wounds of its twofold passion.

It was fitting for this to take place at night, because of the shadows of human error and the endless gloom of a city buried in sleep and wine—that is, of minds wallowing in oblivion and drunkenness. Once the city's walls were breached and the fortification split and neglected through lack of all foresight, which is the only solid wall for souls and cities, an enormous horse laden with armed enemies had crept into the city in the early hours of a ferocious night, signifying the onset of civic discord, which is ever pregnant with armed emotions, hidden hatreds, and sources of hatreds. This ill-omened device was built to destroy the fatherland by Ephebus or by the law-abiding youths and adolescents, the one battering-ram for overthrowing the city.* The old holy man, Laocoon, forbidding it to be brought into the city, is caught in serpents' coils and the venomous knots of envy, and crushed. With his demise, the insane mob hastens headlong to its own destruction, and installs the ominous monster within the holy citadel, as the place of reason is usurped by appetite, the shortest path to ruin.

Thus, at last, the fatal horse opens, and the many evils hidden

---

* P. has confused Epeus, the mythical builder of the Trojan horse, with *ephebus*, the Greek word for a youth, which was also used as a personal name.

within break out: among others, Ulysses, signifying hostile cunning; Neoptolemus, signifying arrogance and the urge for revenge; Menelaus, signifying jealousy and rancor and the memory of offenses; and finally Sinon himself, the guard and pestilential advocate of that fatal hiding place, signifying dissimulation, perjury, and fraud breaking into the open with all their wiles and concealed evils. In that vast whirlwind of events where, as I have said, kings and sons of kings are brought low along with the populace, only a hero escapes either to rest, as Antenor does, of whom it is said "Untroubled rests he there in peaceful calm" [*Aen.* 1.249], or to go on to glorious labor, as Aeneas did, of whom it is written "he'll wage a mighty war in Italy" [1.263], and again,

> And you shall raise aloft to the stars of heaven
> Great-heart Aeneas. [1.259-60]

Now, wandering about the walls of the burning city, he spots Helen, the root and cause of all the woes, in the light of the flames (that is, vexation); as he prepares to kill her and avenge his dying country, although that section of the divine poem has been removed, Venus again appears to him, excusing Helen and Paris. And why should Venus not excuse the venereal acts, since even unbending moralists are often indulgent about carnal love? What is more, she warns him that it is too late for what he has in mind, concentrating on the cause after the final effect, since no longer is there any room for remedy and the judgment of God is inevitable. In the end she urges him to think of flight rather than vengeance because it does more good in desperate straits to yield rather than to oppose fortune. And she promises to be his companion in flight until safety is reached, signifying that even heroes love to be rescued from dangers, provided they have not been at fault in anything that has happened; they enjoy being saved.

With these words, Venus too retires. For lust, the friend of secure and idle leisure, has no place amidst the perils and harshness of life. Although she later returns, as he is leaving, to accompany him, now she is not lust, but the innocent delight born of escape from danger; and upon Venus's departure, he immediately beholds the angry faces of the gods Neptune, Juno, Pallas, and at last Jove himself, because the Greeks conquered the Trojans through their nautical skills, power, wisdom, and finally through what is the most powerful cause—the favor of the supreme god. This he had already realized, where he says,

The gods all, who this empire had sustained,
Withdrew, abandoning their shrines and altars.
                              [*Aen.* 2.351–52]

But what he was thinking then, he stares at here, since the soggy
cloud that had covered his eyes and blurred his mortal vision has
been lifted. For according to Plato's famous affirmation, reverently
embraced by Augustine and many others, nothing so distracts the
human mind from the contemplation of divine things as Venus and
a life dedicated to lusts. Doubtless Plato could have absorbed this
true and weighty lesson from another* man, less well known but
nevertheless a great man and a friend of his, as his letters show—
namely, Archytas of Tarentum, especially in what is recorded as his
most authoritative dialogue with Gaius Pontius Herennius, the
wisest man of his era, father of that Pontius who, as the Samnite
commander, trapped the Roman army at the Caudine Forks and
forced it to march under the yoke. According to Cicero, Cato
testifies that Plato himself was present at the colloquy, and that
among the many memorable things said is this: there is no room for
temperance when lust dominates, and in the realm of pleasure
virtue simply cannot exist, and finally lust extinguishes all the light
of the mind. Rightly, therefore, when lust leaves and mental blindness is discarded,

        To Troy appear the gods' dire faces, nodding
        Askance in mighty hate. [*Aen.* 2.622–23]

This is what I put together in answer to your question. With your
lively mind, you will think of similar things in other passages of the
poem. Farewell.

Pavia, August 23 [1364–67].

---

* We emend *alto* to *alio*.

Sen. V, 1.

To Giovanni Boccaccio,* a description of the city of Pavia.

You did well to visit me at least by letter since you either did not wish or were unable to visit me in person. Having heard that you had crossed the Alps to see the Babylon of the West [Avignon], worse than the other one because it is closer to us, I had remained in suspense about the outcome of your journey until I heard of your return; aware of the difficulties on that road which I had frequently traveled, and thinking about how heavy you are, both in body and spirit, which is fine for scholarly leisure but not for such worrisome business, I have not passed one day or night untroubled. Thank God, who brought you back safe and sound. For the more serious the danger of the sea from which you have returned, the sweeter and more welcome is your return.

Surely, unless you were in a great hurry, it would not have been difficult, when you reached Genoa, to make a detour here; it was no more than a two-day journey, and you would have seen me, whom you always see wherever you may be in the world, and you would have seen what I believe you have not seen—the city of Ticinum on the banks of the Ticinus [Ticino]. Our contemporaries call it Pavia, meaning admirable according to the grammarians, and it was long the famous capital of the Lombards. I find that earlier, before their time, Augustus Caesar was here during the German wars in order, I believe, to be closer to the action, evidently to encourage his stepson, whom he had sent ahead to Germany and who was gaining the greatest success and glory there; as from a watchtower Augustus could keep track of him, and if—as often happens in wartime—something adverse were to happen, he could immediately come to the rescue with all the imperial forces and with the majesty of his name.

You would have seen where the Carthaginian general gained his first victory over our generals, the field where a Roman general was snatched from enemy weapons by his son who was barely in his teens, and saved from the clutches of death, a sure presage of the greatest general to come. You would have seen where Augustine

* See I, 5.

found his tomb, where Severinus found a suitable dwelling for his exile and the end of his life; and they now lie beneath the same roof in twin urns, along with King Luitprand who actually brought Augustine's body from Sardinia to this city. A devout and pious company of illustrious men! You would think that Severinus followed in Augustine's footsteps while he was alive, with his intellect and his books, especially those he wrote on the Trinity after Augustine, and, when he passed on, with his limbs and his tomb. You would wish to have been laid to rest near these men, so holy and learned.

Finally, you would have seen a city most celebrated on men's lips for its antiquity. Nothing written about it before the Second Punic War, which I just mentioned, occurs to me at the moment; or rather, unless my memory fails me, not even then does Livy mention the city, only the river. The similarity of names—Ticinus the river and Ticinum the city—may itself have caused the confusion perhaps; but to avoid what is doubtful and to stress what is certain, you would have seen a city with a most healthy climate. Already I have spent three summers here, and nowhere else do I recall such frequent and heavy rains, such mild and infrequent thunderstorms, so very few spells of heat, such constant and gentle winds. You would have seen a city with the loveliest setting. The Ligurians hold a large part of Cisalpine Gaul, a people powerful in olden times and at the height of power today; the city lies in their midst, located on a moderately elevated and dominant site on a gently sloping riverbank; with an array of towers it rises into the clouds, while the view is so unimpeded and clear on all sides that I doubt if any city on the plains could have one more sweeping and pleasing.

Almost without turning the head, before the eyes are the Alpine vine-covered ridges in one direction and the leafy Apennine hills in the other. The Ticinus itself, winding gracefully as it speeds to join the Po, glides along, licking the foundations of the walls; and "it makes the city joyful," as is written [Ps. 46:5], with its current, while a stone bridge of outstanding workmanship unites its two banks. This clearest of all rivers, as fame declares and facts prove, is also marvelously swift, although by the time it reaches here, it already seems wearied by its course and slowed somewhat by the proximity of the more celebrated river, and has lost some of its native purity because of its tributaries. In sum, it is most like our transalpine Sorgue, except that this is larger while the other, because of the nearness of its source, flows cooler in summer and warmer in winter.

What is more, you would have seen one of those things that so interests you, and me perhaps too much: in the middle of the main square an equestrian statue of gilded bronze, which seems to be pressing on at top speed to the summit of the hill, which, as rumor has it, was seized long ago from your city of Ravenna. Experts in this art and in painting maintain that it is second to none. And you would have seen something that is last not in the order of importance, but in time—an enormous palace in the citadel, a truly remarkable and costly structure. It was built by the magnanimous Galeazzo Visconti, the younger, the present ruler of Milan, of this city, and of many others in the area, a man who surpasses others in many things and himself in the magnificence of his buildings. Unless my love for the prince deceives me, your refined taste would have judged this work the most majestic of all modern creations; and next to seeing your friend—which I know, and do not just hope—would give you the greatest pleasure, you would have been delighted, I believe, by many admirable sights certainly not of lesser things, as Maro says, but of noble and sublime ones. As for me, I confess they charm and captivate me, except when my mind is preoccupied elsewhere by its cares. Therefore, I am now leaving, but not unwillingly, yet I shall spend the summer months here sometimes, if fate grants me some more summer months.

Since things have happened that kept you from my embraces and from me because of the effort involved and because of your lack of confidence in your strength, as you yourself admit, or because of the lack of time and the bidding of your country that awaits your return, I would have liked you at least to see my dear Guido [Sette], Archbishop of Genoa, and in him you would have seen me likewise; for I have lived with him since childhood in perfect harmony of will, and all else. Believe me, you would have seen a man who, though weak in body, is so sound of mind that you would say you never saw anyone more lively, and you would appreciate that a great tenant could dwell in a frail, decrepit abode. In short, you would have seen the good man that we seek, uncommon in any age, I believe, but never rarer than in ours, and so I am sorry you did not. This I ascribe not so much to your negligence or forgetfulness, as to that of our common friend who ought not to have let you pass by those fine sheepfolds of outstanding flocks without greeting the shepherd.

But to conclude my complaints on a cheerful note. I was happy, by Jove, to hear that in that very Babylon [Avignon] you saw the friends whom death has left me, especially the one whom you truly call my father, Philippe [de Cabassoles], Patriarch of Jerusalem, a man I could describe in few words as fit for his title, and no less fit for the Roman title if ever an honor worthy of his merits were given. According to your letter, in the presence of the Supreme Pontiff [Urban V] and the startled cardinals, he gave you, whom he had never met before, a long and tender embrace of true love, as if you were another me; after affectionate kisses, pleasant conversation, and anxious questions about my state of health, he finally begged you to have me send at long last that book, *De uita solitaria*, which I had written at his country home and dedicated to him when he was bishop of the church in Cavaillon. His request is certainly fair and my delay unfair since I completed it ten years ago. But I call God, who sees everything, to witness: ten times or more I tried to send it in such form that at least the calligraphy would please his eyes, even if its style would not please his ears or his mind. Yet, against my enthusiasm and my promise stood the bad faith of scribes about whom I complain so many times, as you know—a trade that is not the least of the plagues that we creative minds endure. People will scarcely believe me when I say that over so many years I was unable to have copied a work written in a few months. You can imagine the great torment and despair over my major works.

Now finally, after so many false starts, as I left home, I put it into a priest's hands to be copied. Whether his hands, as a priest, will have been devoted to writing or quick as a scribe's to deceive, I do not know. It has been reported to me, however, in friends' letters that what I had ordered is already done. As for the quality, the manifest habits of scribes make me doubtful until I see it. Strange to say, instead of what they have been given, they like to scribble something or other; such is their ignorance, laziness, or scorn. So this book, which I expect any time now, I shall immediately send to him, whatever its condition. Let him blame the scribe rather than me. But to you, along with this letter, I am sending one dictated last year. In your last letter you demanded it with a bitter-sweet complaint, as though in despair of ever receiving it; with it I am including, without your asking, another one written this year. If anything seems left out in that ancient polemic that once drove me to write four invectives against those monstrous men who boast that they heal but really butcher, you will say it is now covered, to convince you that I have not changed my opinion. Both of these letters were written in someone else's hand, which I had never before done with you. When you receive them, you will realize how very weary or busy I am, to be forced in such an unusual fashion to talk to you, or rather to myself, through an interpreter—so to speak. But let us continue.

Before I set out from Venice, I began reading what you sent me of Homer, in your own handwriting. Delighted as I was by your favor and devotion, I was all the sadder for the unnecessary labor that I would never have imposed on you, had I known then what I know now. For I had no wish to know what went on in the Greeks' hell; it is enough to know what goes on in the Latin hell. Would that it befall me to know it only through reading or hearsay, and never by seeing it! But I did want to know how Homer, a Greek or an Asian, and—what makes it more miraculous—blind too, described the remote places of Italy, such as Aeolia, Lake Avernus, or the Mount of Circe; but since you have decided to earmark for me that entire incomparable work later, perhaps I shall find there what I am seeking. But my hope is weakened by your writing that you have sent all of the *Iliad* but only one part of the *Odyssey*. What I would like to know is in that book. I wonder why you sent all of one and only a part of the other. Perhaps you did not have it in its entirety. Whatever the case, I shall see when my destiny brings me home, and I shall have it transcribed and returned to you, whom I could not bear to deprive of so great a treasure. Once again, I thank you; I am a little angry with our Donato [Albanzani], who, while writing me often of lesser matters, wrongly remained silent about this one which he knew I would appreciate the most, considering what was being sent and who the sender was. Farewell.

Pavia, December 14 [1363–66].

Sen. V, 2.

To the same person, concerning the obsessive appetite for first place.*

To use the Savior's words, sinner that I am, I have something to tell you. You are waiting to hear what that something may be. What do you think, other than the usual? Prepare your mind for patience and your ears for a dispute, for while nothing anywhere suits me better than your mind, so nothing, alas, is less compatible at times than your actions and resolutions; often I ask myself the cause for this not only in you but in several of my friends about whom I feel the same. I have been able to find only one explanation for this: those whom Mother Nature has made alike, habit, which is often called second nature, makes unlike. Would that we had been able to live together; then habit itself would have given us a single mind—so to speak—in two bodies.

Perhaps you now think that I am about to say something grand. It is a mere trifle, and why should it not be, when the author himself disparages it, even though everyone likes his own the most? Thus, scarcely anyone is a fair judge of his own. Nearly everyone is deceived by love of self and his own creations; you alone of so many thousands are deceived by hatred and scorn, not love, in judging your creations, unless I am mistaken, attributing to humility what is really pride. And what I mean by these words you will hear at once. You know the vulgar and banal breed that makes a living on words not its own; they have spread among us to the point of nausea. They are men of no great talent, but great memory and great drive and even greater effrontery, who frequent the palaces of rulers and powerful men, devoid of anything of their own, yet dressed in others' verses. Whatever someone has neatly said, especially in the vernacular, they declaim with inordinate emphasis, seeking the nobility's favor, money, clothing, and gifts. The stock in trade for this kind of life they get from miscellaneous others or from the writers themselves, sometimes by begging, sometimes by paying for it, if the seller's greed or poverty ever drives him to it. The Satirist too was aware of the last point when he said,

> He starves unless he sells Agave untouched
> To Paris. [Juv. 7.87]

---

* See I, 5.

How many times do you think they are rude, wheedling pests to me, to others too, I believe, although less often to me than it once was either out of respect for my age and my shift to literature, or because I snub them? For often, to keep them from making a habit of annoying me, I turn them down sharply, and refuse to endure any pestering. Sometimes, though, particularly when I know the beggar's poverty and humility, a kind of charity compels me to furnish some kind of help for their livelihood, which is useful to the recipient for a long time but burdensome to me only for a moment or two. There have been some who came away from me successful in their entreaties, with just what they wanted, but otherwise naked and poor; shortly thereafter they would return, dressed in silk and laden with riches, and thank me because they had shaken off the heavy burden of poverty with my backing. Sometimes I was so touched that, convinced that it was a kind of charity, I resolved not to say no to any of them until, overwhelmed again by distaste, I broke my resolution.

When I questioned some of them as to why they attacked only me for this, and not others and you in particular, they gave this reply about you: that often they had done what I said, but never to any avail. And when I wondered why you were so generous with things, so stingy with words, they added this too: that you had burned whatever you once had of vernacular poetry. This did not check my astonishment, but added something to it; and when I asked the reason for your action, all professed ignorance and fell silent, except one who said that he believed, or perhaps even had heard, your intention was to redo the ones you had first let loose in your teens and then in your twenties—now that your talent is solid and seasoned. Although he and I both thought that you are too certain, too confident, of prolonging this uncertain life, especially at this age of prudence, even greater was my wonderment at this plan to burn what you wished to revise so that there would be nothing left for you to revise.

For a long time my astonishment stayed with me; eventually when I arrived in this city and conversed intimately with our Donato [Albanzani], who loves you and cares for you more than anyone else, I learned the facts that I had long since known, and their cause which I did not. For he tells me that in your early youth, fascinated solely by the vernacular style, you devoted the most time and care to it until, in the course of your research and reading, you came upon the vernacular compositions of my youth in that genre. Whereupon your urge to write grew cool; nor were you subsequently satisfied with not writing any more in that vein—you had to express your hatred for what you had already written; intending not to revise but destroy, you burned them all and deprived yourself and posterity of the fruit of your labors in this genre for no other reason than you judged them inferior to mine. Such undeserved hatred and unmerited fire! This is the ambiguity, however: I do not know whether it is a self-deprecating humility or a pride that feels superior to others. It is for you who know your own mind to judge where the truth lies; I go around guessing, as though talking to myself, as I often do, I were talking with you.

I commend you, therefore, for thinking yourself inferior to those to whom you are really superior, and I would rather choose this error than the one whereby someone thinks himself superior when he is really inferior. This topic reminds me of a passage in Lucan of Corduba [Cordova], a man of lively talent and intelligence, which is the pathway to great heights as well as the precipice. When he felt himself already quite advanced in his studies, though still young considering his age and his initiatives, and elated over the success of his works, he dared compare himself with Virgil. Reciting part of the book about the civil war [*Pharsalia*], which he left unfinished when he was cut short by death, he said: "What will it take for me to match the *Gnat* [*Culex*]" [*Vit. Lucani* 1.2]?* I am uncertain whether one of his friends then answered this insolent question, or what the answer was, but ever since reading it I often answered that arrogant fellow silently and indignantly as follows: "My good man, nothing prevents you from matching the *Gnat* but a great deal indeed from equaling the *Aeneid*." Why, then, should I not appreciate your humility which prefers me to you in your opinion more than the boasting of that writer who put himself above Virgil or equal to him?

But there is something else that I miss, something so subtle that it cannot easily be expressed by my pen. I shall try, nevertheless; I fear that this fine humility of yours is pride. The epithet *proud* applied to humility is new to many and perhaps startling. If it shocks the ears, I shall say it differently. I fear, then, that something of pride may be mingled with such great humility. At a banquet or a meeting I have seen someone seated in a place of insufficient honor suddenly rise to seek of his own accord the last place, on the

---

* P. misunderstands the anecdote. Lucan was not boastfully but wistfully acknowledging that he fell short of Virgil's least distinguished poem.

pretext of humility, but it was really the urging of pride; I have seen another leave. Despite their seemingly mild manners, the cause of their behavior is either anger or pride, even though there is something gentle in it. They behave as though whoever does not get first place, which one person can have, and no more, could not deserve anything, or only last place, although there are degrees of glory as of merit.

Because you do not claim first place for yourself, it is humility, whereas some people unequal to you in intellect or eloquence have dared to hope or canvas for it, and have often stirred up in me gall mixed with laughter; they rely on the votes of the crowd, which I pray will cause no more prejudice in the forum than on Parnassus. Take care lest it really be pride that you cannot endure second or third place, or that I should surpass you when I wish to be your equal, or that the master of our vernacular literature should be preferred to you. Do you bear it so ill to be thus outdone by one or two men, especially fellow citizens, or at most very few? Take care lest this be more conceited than coveting first place. To aspire to the highest can be viewed as magnanimity; to scorn what is next to highest somehow seems like conceit.

I understand that the old gentleman from Ravenna, a competent judge of such matters, always likes to assign you third place whenever the subject comes up. If this is too lowly, if I appear to block your way to first place, which I do not do, look, I gladly yield and leave second place to you; but if you spit at it, I am inclined to call you insufferable. In fact, if only those at the very top are illustrious, see how numerous are the ones in the dark, and how few are those reached by that light.* You see, often second place is both safer and more advantageous. Ahead of you is someone to absorb envy's first blows, to show you the way at the risk of his own reputation, whose steps will teach you what to avoid and what to follow, someone to rouse you or shake off your numbness, someone for you to try to equal or to wish to surpass, so as not to see him always ahead of you. These are the spurs of noble spirits who have often enjoyed amazing success. For, obviously, anyone who can put up with being in second place will soon be able to earn first place. But he who cannot tolerate it will become unworthy of the very place he has rejected. And surely, if you search your memory, you will find scarcely a great general, philospher, or poet who was not driven by

_____
* *Aduertere pronum* is corrupt.

such spurs to achieve that height. Just as for virtually all men first place has been a source of pride in them and of envy from others, so for many it is the cause of slackening. Envy arouses the lover and the scholar. Love without a rival, merit without a competitor languishes. A poor worker is better than a lazy rich man. It is better to be weak climbing through the study of Virgil than to rot in vile sloth after setting foot on the summit. It is better and safer to rely upon the support of active virtue than to count on the praises of idle fame.

It seems to me that you have a case for not disdaining second place. What if it is third? What if fourth? Will you become angry; or have you forgotten that passage of Annaeus Seneca who defends Fabianus Papirius against the opinion of Lucilius? After preferring Marcus Tullius to him, he adds: "For something to be smaller than the biggest does not offhand make it tiny"; and when subsequently he preferred Asinius Pollio to him, he says: "It is quite a big thing to be behind the first two." Finally, when he added Titus Livy, he says: "See how many he surpasses who is beaten by three, and by the three most eloquent ones" [Ep. 100.9]. You too, my friend, see whether these words may not appropriately apply to you—with the exception that whichever place you may occupy, and whomever you see ahead of you, in my own judgment I am not the one.

Have mercy on your works, then, and spare them the flames; but if perchance either you or the others are totally persuaded that I, whether I like it or not, am ranked above you in greatness, does it pain you and do you think it to your discredit to be numbered next to me? Allow me to say that if you do feel this way, you have long fooled me, and you have neither that modesty of spirit, nor the love for me that I hoped. For true lovers always gladly prefer to themselves those whom they love; they wish to be surpassed by them and feel the greatest pleasure if they are. That this is so, no loving father will deny to whom nothing is more welcome than to be surpassed by his son. I hoped, as I still do, to be no less dear to you than you yourself are; I won't say no less dear than a son, and I hoped that my name would be dearer to you than your own. I recall that once, moved by a sweet, friendly spurt of anger, you reproached me about this. If your words were sincere, you ought to have joyfully seen me take the lead, and not to have quit the race because of that, but to have pursued it more obstinately, taking care, too, lest any of the runners in this field intrude between us and snatch your standing away from you. For a friend who is sitting or walking with a dear friend is concerned not about how he ranks, but how close he is to him. Nothing is sweeter than the desired nearness and the great love. Among friends there is practically no rank; the last are first, and the first are last, because they are truly one.

So much for the accusations: now comes the justification for what you have done. Although I know this from your admission and from our good friend telling it to me, I am still trying to find some fitting explanation other than yours, inasmuch as the same act is sometimes praiseworthy, sometimes blameworthy, depending on the doer's intention. What comes to mind? I shall tell you: "It was not arrogance, which is furthest from your kind character, nor envy of anyone, nor impatience over your lot that made you destroy your own works, thereby harming them and yourself; rather it was a noble, glorious indignation that made you wish to snatch any judgment of your talent from a worthless and arrogant age that understands nothing, corrupts everything, and—what is even more intolerable—scorns everything, for, just as with the sword Virginius once freed his daugher from shameful derision, so did you free with fire your beautiful inventions, as though they were the offspring of your mind." Well, what do you say? Have I not perhaps arrived at the truth with a hunch? Certainly I have sometimes had the idea of doing the same with my vernacular writings, few though they were—that is why I guess this about you; and perhaps I would have done so had they not long ago escaped from my control by being so far-flung, although at times I had also had the self-contradictory idea to devote all my time to vernacular pursuits since the loftier Latin style—both prose and poetry—had been so highly polished by ancient talents that now my resources, or anyone else's, can add very little. On the other hand, this vernacular writing, just invented, still new, showed itself capable of great improvement and development after having been ravaged by many and cultivated by very few husbandmen. Well then, this hope so attracted me and at the same time the spur of youth so urged me onward that I undertook a great work in that style; and having laid, as it were, the foundations of that edifice, I gathered the cement and stone and wood; I then began to observe attentively our age, mother of pride and laziness, and to notice the great talent of the show-offs, the charm of their elocution, so that you would say the words were not being recited but torn to pieces; hearing this once, twice, many more times, and repeating it to myself more and more, I finally came to realize that it was a waste of effort to build on soft mud and shifting sand, and that I and my work would be torn to shreds by the hands of the mob. Thus, like the runner who stumbles upon a serpent in the middle of the path, I halted and changed my mind, taking another pathway that I hope will be straighter and higher; although those brief and scattered vernacular works of my youth are no longer mine, as I have said, but have become the multitude's, I shall see to it that they do not butcher my major ones.

Yet why censure the unlearned multitude when my complaint is all the more grave and just against those who call themselves learned? Aside from their many absurdities, they have added that hateful thing on top of their ignorance—the utmost pride. That is why today they tear to bits the reputation of men, bits of works they once said was a great feat to understand. O inglorious age, you scorn Antiquity, your mother, the inventor of all the honorable arts? And you dare not only to match her but to consider yourself superior? I am leaving aside the dregs of mankind, the multitude, whose words and opinions deserve ridicule rather than refutation. I leave aside the soldiers and generals who do not blush at thinking that military science has reached its zenith and been perfected in their time, whereas in their hands it has undoubtedly perished and utterly collapsed; with them nothing whatsoever is done by skill or intelligence, but everything by negligence and happenstance. They go to war as if to a wedding, spruced-up, undrilled, dreaming of wines, dainties, debauchery, their minds on flight rather than victory, their goal and their skill not to strike the enemy but to surrender, not to frighten the foe but to dazzle the eyes of their lady friends. Ignorance and complete lack of learning excuse their mistaken opinions.

I leave aside the rulers who view themselves equal to their betters in valor and glory, as though royalty lies in gold and purple, in a scepter and crown. Ensconced on their thrones for this one thing, to rule (whence derives their title),* they do not really rule but are ruled—and by whose counsels, the facts prove. They lead nations, but are subjugated to pleasures. The kings of men are slaves to lethargy and lust. Their ignorance of antiquity, the brilliance of their present fortune, and their vanity, that constant companion of excessive prosperity, somehow excuse them.

But what, I ask, will excuse men of letters? While they ought not to be ignorant of antiquity, they partake of an identical blindness of opinion. Know, my friend, that I speak of this with indignation and bitterness. Dialecticians arise these days who are not only ignorant but insane, and like an army of black ants from the recesses of some rotten oak they burst forth to plunder all the fields of true learning.

* The noun *rex* 'king' is related to the verb *rego* 'I rule'.

They condemn Plato and Aristotle, they ridicule Socrates and Pythagoras. And this they do, good God, with what foolish authorities! I do not wish to make a name for those whose accomplishments have not, although their madness may do so on a huge scale; I do not wish to place among the greatest those whom I see among the least, and yet the fools gush over them and follow them, deserting reliable models. For all I know they may learn after death. Certainly while alive, they have neither knowledge nor any reputation for knowledge. What shall I say of the men who scorn that bright sun of eloquence, Marcus Tullius Cicero? What shall I say of those who despise Varro and Seneca, or those who shudder at the style of Titus Livy and Sallust, as though rough and uncultivated? And, what is more, they rely upon new models whom they should be ashamed of. I was once in their company when Virgil, the other sun of eloquence, was being criticized. Marveling at a scholar of such unfettered madness, I asked him what he had found deserving of such infamy in the works of such a famous man; listen to what he answered, his face uplifted in contempt: "He uses too many connectives." So go on, O Maro, get to work, and with the help of the Muses take up your poem which has been raised to the heavens; polish it for the time when it will fall into such hands!

What else can I say about that other monstrous breed of men in religious garb, profane in their actions and thoughts, who call Ambrose, Augustine, and Jerome great talkers rather than great spirits? I know not whence these new theologians come who have no respect for the doctors [of the church]; soon they will not even respect the Apostles, the Gospel itself, and eventually will come to speak boldly even against Christ unless He, who is their target, comes to bridle these wild beasts. This is now usual among them and has turned into a habit so that each time these venerable and holy names are mentioned, they either shake their heads silently or else say with impious words, "Augustine saw much but knew little." Nor have they anything better to say about others. Here in my library recently was one of them, not in religious garb (but true religion consists in simply being Christian), one of them, as I was saying, who philosophized in the modern fashion, thinking that nothing is accomplished unless they bark something against Christ and Christ's heavenly teaching. When I cited some passage from the sacred books, he said, foaming with rage and deforming his face, already ugly by nature, with anger and contempt, "You can have your so-called doctors of the Church. *I* have someone to follow, and I know whom I believe." I replied, "You have used the Apostle's words; would that you would also make use of his faith!" "That Apostle of yours," he said, "was a sower of words and a madman." "Philosophers, you are doing fine; for your first reproach was lodged against him by philosophers long ago, and your second one by Festus, Governor of Syria. He was, in fact, a sower of a very useful Word. Cultivated by the saving plow of his successors and watered by the sacred blood of martyrs, we see what an abundant harvest of faith he has produced." At this he said with a sickly smile, "You be a good Christian; I believe none of all this. Your Paul and your Augustine, along with all these others whom you extol, were long-winded fellows. How I wish that you could stand to read Averroes in order to see how much greater he was than these triflers of yours." I flared up, I admit, and could scarcely keep my hand from that foul and blasphemous mouth. "This is an old argument," I said, "between me and other heretics. Now get out and do not return, you and your heresy." Thereupon, grabbing him by his cloak, I put him out the door, more forcibly than my manners, though not his, called for.

There are thousands of monsters such as these against whom nothing avails—not the majesty of the Christian name and reverence for Christ whom weak, wretched mortals insult while angels bow before Him in obedience; not even the fear of punishment nor the armed inquisitors of heresies, prison, or the stake restrain their petulant ignorance or heretical daring. These are the times that we have fallen into, my friend, this is the age in which we live and now grow old, among such judges, bereft of any knowledge or virtue and inflated with a false opinion of themselves, as I complain and rage about so often. For them it does not suffice to have lost the books of the ancients, they must vie with their genius and ashes; and happy in their ignorance, as though what they do not know were nothing, they give free rein to their greasy, swollen intellects, they introduce new authors right and left, and exotic disciplines.

If then, you have snatched your works, having no other recourse, with aid of fire from the clutches of these judges or tyrants, I do not disapprove of your action and approve of its cause. I almost wish I had done with all of my works, while it was possible, what I did do with many of them! For seemingly there is no hope of fairer judges, and the license and number of these others increase daily. Not only do they fill the schools, but even the largest cities; they so crowd the streets and squares that I often reproach myself for my anger against these last years of retribution [the plagues] and for my lament over a world that has been emptied, I would perhaps admit, of its real men, but I dare say a world more full of vices and mere men than any other age. In sum, I do believe that if I had been of this mind even in those days, I would have absolved the daughter of Appius Caecus. Now farewell; this, nothing else, is what I had to tell you for the moment.

Venice, August 28 [1364–66].

Sen. V, 3.

To the same person,* on the boldness and the pompous routine of physicians.

I am glad that you approve of my advice and make use of it. Ultimately that approval is real which is put into practice, for many have learned to extol with words what they despise with their minds. You wrote me—I forget when, since I remember the contents but not the time—that you were gravely ill but were healed through God's grace and a physician's work. I answered then, for this I also recall, that I was utterly astonished at the paths by which that vulgar error penetrated such a lofty mind, for God and your fine constitution had done it; the doctor had done nothing at all, nor could he have except what a loquacious dialectician, rich in boredom and lacking in remedies, can do. But now you write that you had not summoned a doctor for your illness. No longer am I surprised at your speedy recovery. There is no quicker way to health than to do without a doctor; this sounds harsh to inexperienced ears. But for those with experience, it is all evident, clear, and very true. They profess to be nature's assistants, but often they battle against nature itself in behalf of the diseases. The less bad ones take a middle road, awaiting the outcome of the case; truthful and trustworthy men, they become the spectators of sick people's struggles, and, following fortune, join their idle banners to the winning ones and steal a share of the glory. Good God! How many are like Mettius Fufetius without any Tullus Hostilius! Long was the world without this human monstrosity, especially when it was in better shape—Rome at her peak was without it. The great Cato, who earned the name of wise among our ancestors, foresaw this scourge and gave warning to avoid it, but his useful advice was badly received, a common fate for those who give the right counsel. In great numbers the healers broke into our world. Would that they had been healers and not, under the guise of healers, enemies of healing, armed not only with true ignorance and the name of knowledge, but also with the irrationality and credulousness of the patients, who are so influenced by their overwhelming desire for health that whoever promises this quite recklessly is Apollo himself. Heavens, none of them has lacked this recklessness and a very effective weapon for deception: impu-

* See I, 5.

dence and a straight face unshaken because their lies have turned into an art and a way of life.

To this must be added the boastfulness of aristocratic dress to which they have no right: bright purple garments embroidered with various colors, dazzling rings, and gilt spurs. Whose eyes, even those of a sane man, would not be offended by such brilliance? There is astonishment and bafflement in cities, especially our own, at this sight, because no Tarquinius Priscus, nor anyone whatsoever of our own princes, is furious at such boldness and defends the nobility by passing a law prescribing penalties to bring the enormous license of these craftsmen under control. For if they presume all this because of the mere exercise of a plebeian skill, why should farmers, weavers, and other practitioners of like arts not dare to do the same, except that no craftsman would have such audacity? Yet if they usurp such insignia for themselves in the name of philosophy, you know whether they are entitled to appropriate this name for themselves; and if they consider them apt for their profession, their shameful self-deception should also be noted, not only by those who know them to be craftsmen, not philosophers, but also by those who recognize the dress of true philosophers and a rich mind under a poor cloak, a mind scornful of all things except knowledge or virtue, scornful above all of vanity and boastfulness, in which these craftsmen of ours are the leaders. What else can we assume as the cause for their daring all this, if not the immeasurable and well-known madness of the multitude? They count upon this; and widely victorious over the wretched mob and its follies, parading the pomp and spoils, and weighed down with booty and proud of their slaughters, they put on their triumphal vestments.

For what, I ask, do they lack except white steeds and purple-draped chariots? In fact, they do not even lack horses, nor the golden ornaments for them. As for the chariots, they will soon arrive. They cannot all have killed five thousand men, which is required for a triumph by ancient Roman usage; let it suffice that they have killed as many as possible. Whatever is lacking in numbers is compensated by the quality of those killed. For there they did away with enemies, here it is citizens and friends; there the victors were armed, here they are civilians, so that rightfully a lesser number is enough for a triumph. Both match exactly in this: just as the military commanders who have perpetrated the most massacres—and the greatest massacres—are held in the highest esteem, so too among the doctors, those who have killed the most and gained experience, dangerous and uncertain though it may be, through the deaths of unfortunates, are the leaders of the whole profession and singled out the most. "He has seen a lot," they say, "and learned a lot," which is nothing else but acquiring self-confidence about killing through long practice.

One thing is new for them and far different: those generals triumphed only over enemies, these fellows only over citizens, which is forbidden by the very same Roman law and custom. But since these are allowed to kill citizens with impunity—or rather not only with impunity but actually receiving a fee for killing!—why would they not be allowed to break those very laws and customs? Or who would deny the masters of human life power over everything else? Thus they triumph over the citizens, and you think you are playing a game with them who, having gained control over you by virtue of their profession, hope to gain money because of your illness, and experience from your death. After offering you a lethal drink based on some authoritiy or other from Cos, Pergamum, and Arabia, learned perhaps but utterly ignorant of our constitutions, they sit around idly awaiting your end, while you with a mysterious poison circulating in your veins and chest hope in a remedy from a man ignorant of your ills and unable meanwhile to help himself when attacked by his own ills.

One doctor will say to avoid fruit, and other herbs and vegetables, without which food is disagreeable for many people, particularly ours, no matter how expensive and fancy a feast. Nor indeed is our zeal for agriculture and grafts of various saplings sought from other lands understandable if fruits must be avoided by those who plant or cultivate them. We have indeed heard of certain harmful plants and poisonous herbs, but who, I ask, has ever planted them in his own garden except to harm others, and who has not relentlessly uprooted them when they grow wild? Yet this fine dictator made them disreputable and suspect for all mortals because, insofar as he was concerned, they either did not appeal to him or did him no good.

Another doctor, perhaps the same one for all I know, anemic and half-alive (a large part of the populace suffers from this), teaches that the blood must be frugally preserved like a treasure. But I feel, even at my present age, that if I were not bled profusely every spring and fall, this Greek treasure would have long ago conquered me. But these private secretaries of nature, omniscient as they are, condemn for everyone else what they do not approve for themselves or their own folk. Thus everything is reduced to their own, oriental standard.

Another doctor, perhaps an imbiber of hot wines, such as the Achaean or Gnosian [Knossian] shore or distant Meroe produces, and thereby a hater of water, has condemned it in a well-known epigram: "I have found water of no help except when taken for high fevers." Oh, what a noble aphorism! But, aside from high fevers which I have so far not experienced and hopefully I never will, I know many benefits and many fine uses of water. All joking aside, to speak seriously and to pass over thousands of the strongest and the healthiest people for whom water is the only drink, agreeable and wholesome at that, I testify about myself; had I not often drunk a great deal of cold water, now too during these winter nights, I would not be alive, believe me. Is it then a matter of little or no importance or need when a man's life would not continue if you took it away? And how many other things are similar to this? Yet the multitude considers not only as solid dogma but divine prophecy whatever pronouncement on the subject of nature flows, however rashly, from the lips of these heaven-sent men.

This then was that noble art of the Greeks that the wisest man among our ancestors feared they would export to us. They did, and now it is so deeply entrenched in public misconception that the hand of Cato himself could not easily uproot it, were he to return as Censor. These doctors do not really surprise me, for whoever sets out to fulfill his intention, even though he may deviate from virtue, does not stray from his goal; nor does the public surprise me, for he who does what he is used to doing affords no new ground for admiration or blame. I am, however, surprised at well-established states and their magistrates, and amazed at the kings; their eyes can look upon craftsmen dressed to match them. How can their spirits endure it?

But to return to my initial point: if you kept them from your bedside while you were ill, what you did was not lucky but sensible, for they probably would have killed you. To show you how much confidence they themselves have in their trade—I am speaking of those who have some kind of decency which is admittedly rare—I call God and my memory to witness that I once heard a doctor with a great reputation among them say the following: "I know that I could be called an ingrate for deprecating an art from which I have gotten wealth and friendships, but truth must be placed above all feelings. This, then, I believe and declare: if a hundred or a thousand men of the same age, constitution, and way of life were simultaneously afflicted by one disease, and if half were then to follow the advice of doctors such as they are in our day, but the other half took care of themselves without any doctor by following their natural instinct and their own discretion, I have no doubt that more of the former group would die and a more of the latter would live."

During a friendly discussion with another man of greater learning and fame, when I asked him in wonderment his reason for using foods other than the ones prescribed, he answered with a straight face and no hesitation, "If a doctor's life were like his advice, or vice-versa, he would suffer either loss of health or money." Who does not see that these words contain a clear confession not only of ignorance but of bad faith? If it is dangerous for healthly people to have anything to do with these pests, what can sick people expect if not the end of all dangers? Certainly no one will be surprised that he who harms the healthly will kill the sick, for it is not easy to dislodge a well-rooted tree, yet once dislodged it is easy to knock down.

Recently I asked still another man of great fame and knowledge not only in this art but in many others, a man with closer ties to me than the usual acquaintances, why he did not practice this art as do the others so inferior to him; he gave me a grave, sad, amiable frown that carried conviction, and said, "As God is witness to the deeds of men, I fear to commit this sin of fatally cheating the gullible multitude. If they knew, as I do, the little or no good a doctor does for a sick person, how often he does much harm, the army of doctors would be smaller and less decorated. Well, let them do it since the sinfulness of the doer and the gullibility of the sufferers is so great; let them abuse the people's simplicity, promise life, and do away with it and make money; I am resolved not to deceive or harm anyone and have no wish to become wealthier from anyone's trouble; this is my reason for shifting to other arts that I can practice without so much guilt." I can hardly tell you the extent to which this reply made me love him, or enhanced and strengthened the opinion I had always had of him.

That is what they said. In friendly and unguarded conversations with them, that old conviction of mine was confirmed; I cling to it tooth and nail and will not give it up since it is true. I am happy that you too have arrived at the same conclusion; I also approve of your conduct, and if poverty, as you yourself say, gave a reason for not summoning a doctor from afar, there being none in your solitary location, I applaud your solitude and your poverty, which has been useful to you as it often is to those who suffer it unwillingly. Perhaps you would have sent for a doctor—albeit an executioner—not so often on the pretext of health as politeness, which has driven many people, dodging a false danger to their reputation, into a real risk to their lives; to avoid the stigma of avarice they have hired someone to do away with them. You yourself also do not disguise how much faith you have in doctors, by saying that they usually make their patients' holdings slimmer and their sickness greater, and that they are better at emptying the purse than the stomach.

I follow this policy in my own affairs. I once had more doctor friends, but of them all only four are still left—one in Venice, one in Milan, but two in Padua; all are learned and courteous, able to converse extraordinarily well, to argue vigorously, to make quite powerful and sweet-sounding speeches but in the long run capable of killing quite artistically; and even excuse themselves quite speciously, often mouthing Aristotle, Cicero, Seneca, and even—this will surprise you!—Virgil. I know not by what luck or madness and sickness of a mind gone astray it happens that they know everything better than the one thing they profess. But I leave this aside; this truth has long ago brought me enough hatred and trouble. Whenever my health is threatened, I who delight above all in friends, receive them as friends and not as doctors; for I find nothing more conducive either to maintaining or restoring health than my friends' presence and conversation. If they prescribe something agreeable to my way of thinking, I obey and give them credit for it. Otherwise I simply listen and do what I had in mind; I have given my people orders that in the event of anything serious they are to let nothing be done to my body, but let me be left in the hands of nature, or rather of God, who created me and set boundaries for me that cannot be exceeded.

So that this attitude, now both yours and mine, may now be even more acceptable to you, know that it was held by the greatest men not only in that uncorrupted age that spurned all softness, but even later ones when doctors, perfumers, and troupes of dancing girls and drug-vendors, pleasures and delicacies overcame the Roman world. And lest in my haste I be distracted by a many-sided investigation, three or four illustrious examples that come promptly to mind, should suffice. In Suetonius Tranquillus we read that the Emperor Tiberius used his own judgment without medical aid or advice in looking after his health, which was fine, hardly impaired, throughout most of his reign. The same writer says that Vespasian did absolutely nothing to maintain his health, which was excellent too, but massage his limbs and fast one day each month. And about Aurelian the historian Vopiscus of Syracuse wrote thus: "He never called in doctors when he was sick, but cured himself mainly by fasting" [*Hist. Aug.* 50.1]. Albinus [Alcuin], the preceptor of Charles (who won the surname of Great among the Gauls), said in his history that Charles had often been afflicted for several years before his death with recurring fevers; he then added, "He did more things following his own judgment than the advice of doctors, whom he held almost in contempt." But our rulers dare neither to belch nor to spit without the doctors' permission, and yet they live neither better nor longer than the ancients did. Furthermore, doctors preside over the kings' tables, and using that authority acquired through habit, they command, forbid, threaten, terrify, censure, lose their temper, and impose on their masters rules that they are the first to straddle, yet when observed by their masters make their lives short, as we see, and their illnesses long.

I know many are persuaded—or rather it has been implanted in them—that I am a public enemy of all doctors because of my notorious quarrel against them in Gaul. Aside from the fact that my friendships with doctors are and were well known, this idea is so absurd in itself that it cannot be deemed credible about anyone, however foolish, unless he be utterly mad. For who, I ask, would hate a doctor unless he loves diseases? On the other hand, what man would love diseases unless he hates his own health, his life, and himself? But if they are true doctors, they doubtless assist nature, fight against disease, and restore health to sick bodies, keep the healthy ones well and strengthen the wavering ones. Who is so mad, so unaware of nature, or so hostile to himself as to hate his deliverer? I too am a mortal man, I too have inherited a frail dwelling place, and have been endowed with a certain love for my body in spite of myself. How, then, with such a disposition, could I hate medicine or doctors? I love them, yet I do hate certain quacks who, not armed with a subtle dialectic but entangled in it, prate rather than heal; they not only subject those who are well to boredom but harry the sick to death. These I hate, I confess, and a numberless horde they are; but I do love the others who are very scarce.

Nevertheless, to come to terms even with these quacks—if it is possibile—and not always to speak against this kind of technician, with Greek names of remedies and diseases they like to make those who believe them get sick in Greek. Let them at least make them get well in Greek too! In fact, they do promise this. For why should they fear to promise when there is profit in a promise, and no shame or punishment for a lie? There are a thousand examples of this; I shall relate only a very recent one applicable to this place or time. For I have all the ingredients at hand now: the sick man, the doctor, the promises, the lies.

There is a man quite advanced in age, born in those shaded,

chilly valleys nestled among the Alpine precipices through which flows the still narrow Rhone (which is why the region itself is called Valais in the vernacular). Born in that barbarous land, he gained a reputation because of his long life, the uncivilized country, and the inhabitants' ignorance, not only among his own people, but, through their loquacious and false testimony, also among foreigners; and as distance favors a big lie, he began to be known as another Aesculapius. Why drag it out in words? In time his fame reached the present lord of Liguria who hoped the man's advice would help in treating his gout, which it is known he has suffered for years with great anguish to him and no little inconvenience to his people. How many times do you think he invited that poor man with enticing pleas and great sums of money, who was dear to him for his skill and even dearer, as happens, for his foreign origin and the unfettered falsehood of fame. Either aware of his ignorance or puffed up by his fame, the man behaved like a great personage, as if the one summoned were worthy of being summoned, and remained unmoved until this time; he had not confessed his ignorance, which he either did not realize or concealed for fear that his reputation that was enhanced through a lie would be diminished by the truth; but he used now this commitment, now that one as a pretext or an excuse. Thus the desire and opinion of the lord who invited him grew more and more until this past summer, when the poor man fell into the hands of some enemy or other who demanded a large ransom for his release. Seeing himself trapped, he wrote to this lord that, if ransomed, he would come and bring some new remedies for his old illness—as one who had not read or had forgotten or had scorned Ovid's famous verse that even children know,

Medicine knows not the cure for knotty gout.
[*Pont.* 10.101].

But this nobleman, whose magnanimity made everything appear small, and whose desire for health made everything appear delayed, was glad to hear this, either because he felt he would recover his health or because he now wanted to try too the nonsense of foreigners after having tested the opinions of Italian doctors. So, he immediately sent men to pay the ransom and bring him back. And so that you may know the whole story, aside from the expenses of the journey, which were lavish, and whatever else seemed suitable for the magnificent arrival of the new Hippocrates (no one is more generous in such matters, no one further not only from avarice but from stinginess), the ransom alone came to 3,500 ducats, which are minted in our city, a huge price not only for a doctor but even for a general of the armies. Furthermore, on the day the poor old man, who was bought for so much, came to Milan, I happened to be dining with the lord when a breathless courier arrived in advance, announcing that the doctor had disembarked from the ship. Delighted, the lord gave orders that he be met and received joyfully and hospitably, as was his custom. He sent on ahead an escort, horses, and servants, including for the overweight old codger a steed that I can praise from personal experience, whiter than snow, swifter than the wind, gentler than a lamb, steadier than a mountain; on him the Teutonic Galen entered the Italian city through an astonished crowd that expected an instant resurrection of the dead. Already before this, through the same messenger who announced his arrival, he had ordered on his authority as a doctor, as they usually do, that fresh eggs be procured, and I do not know what else, and that with these a concoction be prepared and given at once to the lord. Everyone marveled at hearing this, some thought him a man of God. But I was nauseated and cursed the barbaric recklessness that had dared to prescribe medicine offhand for such an illustrious patient whom he had not yet seen, or rather, had never seen.

Meanwhile, having returned to Pavia, I do not know what he ordered in his fashion on the following days, or what he did, except that shortly thereafter things began to go badly for himself, and worse than usual for the lord. Not much later, having exhausted either his hope of curing him or his shamelessness in making promises, he declared that what he had in mind could not be done by medical art, and that therefore some magic books or other—he himself calls them sacred—had to be sent for. In these lay the last hope for a cure, and so he ordered a search for them in some land—I know not where, nor do I think even he knows. He is completely absorbed in this; now everyone's hope, and especially his, since he is primarily responsible, is cooling down. Thus, that Hippocratic reputation and that fretful waiting and that premature, untimely search for remedies have turned into farce and magic. I have decided therefore to expose this man, so famous in Transalpine Gaul and Germany, that through the renown of his much-heralded title he has lost his own name, and is known simply as the Doctor from Valais. Without his asking or indeed without his being in a position to know, or even if he did know, without his thanking me, I have thus dedicated this idle part of a sleepless night to clarifying what one can hope for from inglorious, obscure doctors and their promises when this is the confidence to be placed in one who is most highly praised.

To return to our subject, they all make the same promises; they make promises, I say, but they will fulfill their promises, as Augustus Caesar used to say, on the Greek kalends—that is, never. In fact, the patients' need and the deceivers' promise are Greek, as are the names of their herbs and leaves and roots: balaustium, reubarbarum, calamentum. Everything is done in Greek, and what is even more troubling, in Arabic, so that the more far-fetched a lie, the more it is credited, and the more foreign a remedy, the more it costs; the minute they gain admission, they give the Greek name of the disease or, if necessary, invent one. This, they say, is *epilepsia*, this is *apoplexia*, this is *erysipelas*. Who would not be charmed by such sonorous names, and who would not like to know what the disease that the Latin patient suffers is called in Greek, although there are neither Greek nor Latin remedies. But we have joked enough; in the past I have seriously said much about our doctors; take what I have said today as incidental.

But about Leontius [Pilatus], once our Leone, who would rather be called Thessalian than Italian, I have not changed my opinion, well founded as it is and confirmed in the end by your judgment. Never will he be invited back by my letters or my messengers, even were he to ask. Let him remain where he chose, and where he haughtily emigrated, let him live sadly. Let him who has scorned Florentine luxuries with so much conceit (which is ugly under any circumstances, but particularly when poor) now suffer the poverty of Byzantium with as much groaning; finally, let him who has condemned the fields of Italy grow old, with my permission, in the Thessalian forests, and be food for Greek worms. Or if he feels like it, let him go back to tending the Cretan Labyrinth where he once spent many years, which you probably do not know, but I have on good authority. This man would otherwise be no hindrance to our studies if he were a man and had not made himself a wild beast by his uncommon rudeness and a passion for novelty—why, I do not know, unless his savage nature forced him or perhaps he seeks fame along this path, as we know many have done. Anyway, let him go and have his own way, his beard, his cloak, his hunger, and let him reap what he has sown, grind what he has harvested, and finally eat what he has ground. There is a place where human error is punished by others. There is also a place where it punishes itself, and brings its own punishment along. Farewell.

Pavia, December 10 [1364–66].

Sen. V, 4.

To Donato Apenninigena [Albanzani], grammarian,* how much faith one should have in doctors.

By chance it happened that of your two letters reaching me at the same time, I read first the one written last, and thus learned your illness had gone away before I knew it had come; and so I was freed from the task of writing my usual words of cheer, which is not as difficult for me as it is distasteful; for I shall tell you something that I believe will surprise you. At the very hour your letters arrived, my mind as well as my fingers were busy working on my little book, *De remediis*. I am hurrying so as to bring it to you finished, if I can, and now I am very near to the end. It so happened that I was then working mainly on the treatise that is about the loss of hearing. And thus there was no toil except to transcribe what I had dictated there. Thanks be to Him, who is the bestower and preserver of our senses, for having made you not need my remedy and me wonder whether to rejoice that it happened to you for a time, so that God's gift [of health] to you might be all the more welcome and you forever more grateful to God, since enjoyment of ease is sweeter after a critical and frightening experience. What one feared that he had lost becomes dearer, whereas things in one's possession without worry are not so precious; prosperity is unappreciated when adversity does not threaten it. Opposites are reinforced by opposites, not in reality but in men's opinions. Just as the recollection of past goods exacerbates present evils, so the memory of evil is a most welcome seasoning to the good.

I also count it no trifle that you see from this brief trial what you have long known: how much you should trust in doctors. You have had experience itself as a teacher. It has made you from now on no mere supporter but the standard-bearer and champion of that old, widely known opinion of mine about this breed of men. So that you may daily reinforce your conviction, I am sending you the three letters that I addressed to our Giovanni [Boccaccio]. Odd and harsh to say and to hear, a certain simpleton, charmed by the sound of the

---

* A respected Venetian grammarian and admirer of P., who often addressed him as Apenninigena because of his birth in the Casentino. He was godfather to P.'s grandson, and was instrumental in helping P. obtain a translation of Homer. P. dedicated to him one of his treatises, *De sui ipsius et multorum ignorantia*.

words, like a donkey with long ears by the lyre, has held onto them, as you can see, for the greater part of this year, always insisting and swearing that he had sent them back; nor would he ever have returned them, had I not—finally torn by anger and indignation and surmising the truth—informed him that I would no longer bear this impertinence of his in silence. When he heard this, whether it was shame or fear, he sent them back, half-mangled by his rough touch. Covered with dirt, but joyfully, they have returned to me, having at any rate slipped out of their chains and jailer's custody. So now, you will make sure that at long last they arrive where they would have originally gone, had they been allowed; and put into your own words the excuse for their tardiness. For although they may be untimely, they cannot be refused. The one to whom they go has great love for me and a yearning for anything from me.

Accordingly, one of these letters will so strengthen my opinion for you—once you have read it through—that you too will take it to heart and bear it to the end; you will say that whatever was missing in my invectives has been amply filled in, if I now add this: recently one of that illustrious group, a most famous man respected for his knowledge, age, and virtue, whom I am not naming lest I turn his colleagues against him, confessed aloud to me that he agreed with my view. Among the many things that I want you to know, he said, "My teacher, whose equal I have never seen in this profession, often used to say that a knowledge of medicine is as delightful as all the others based on skill and rules, but the practice of medicine is based on chance." So go now, and put your faith in chance!

What then must be done? What else but pray to God? And if there is some cloud blocking the pathway of our prayers, it must be dispelled with pious sighs and broken by prayers and tears, so that He who is the fount of life may grant us everlasting health of mind and body, so long as He sees fit. Not only is there nothing to be hoped for from doctors, but there is something to be greatly feared. But far be it from me to dare condemn thus all doctors in this curt and rash judgment of mine. For I have known many good ones who truly love me; they are eloquent and well educated, learned in many arts, but ignorant only of medicine. Shocking indeed, to know everything except the one thing you want or ought to know.

Among the many things that occur* to me to write about, this rich and varied subject comes to mind now. Once in my teens, just

---

* We emend *occurrit* to *occurrunt*.

recovered from a very high fever, I wrote to a friend a short poem and gave all the credit for the cure to a doctor, a truly shrewd man, bound to me in the camaraderie of youth. At that age I felt ready to challenge and conquer not only a fever without a doctor's help, but if I may say so, death itself. What shall I say now, or how can I glue together things that directly contradict each other? But if you will stop and think, I need not say much. I wrote it when I was young, in fact very young; that is all. My mind was still rambling and indiscreet; I found pleasure in praising a man who was dear to me, but whom I had not thought about very much. With no other way to praise him, I made him the savior of my health—of which God alone is the savior. Then as I daily pondered more closely and took many things into consideration, observing at times the outcome of others' illnesses and at times my own, I began to look down on that doctor I had praised, let alone others; and with reason and experience as guides I reached this contrary opinion, which I wish were not so true. These things I want to say, lest that short poem lure you, perhaps more than anyone else, to great admiration. Therefore, read that as something by a boy and this as something by an old man.

Now let there really be an end to this dispute. Let them argue, but let us, while in good health and fully aware of human vicissitudes, laugh on the one hand at the credulous folly of the sick, and on the other at the obstinate ignorance of doctors. As for my book, *De uita solitaria*, which you righfully demand, almost in anger, I have already written to my priest friend in Padua, that he should send it to you. I give you permission to read it as you will, but forbid you to copy it until I have come, for I have added still another word to it. You know my ways; I am a second Protogenes, I do not know when to take my hand from the tablet. Farewell, and give my greetings to your devoted wife and the boys she has borne for us, my Antonio and your Solone.*

Pavia, September 1 [1366-67].

* Antonio was Donato's son and P.'s godson, and Solone was Donato's second son.

Sen. V, 5.

To the same person, concerning the inconstancy of youth,
*and how praise is beneficial to the wise man, but harmful
to the fool.*

What happened to me yesterday I would not put last among the
wearisome things of life and injuries of fortune. Our young man,
whom you some time ago and I recently had adopted as a son
[Giovanni Malpaghini, P.'s scribe], whose praises from our mouths
hither and yon had filled not only the ears of friends who are
present but even the eyes of the absent ones, for we raised him to
the stars with tongue and pen, mindful of the very famous, very true
saying I must often repeat, that glory is an enormous spur for noble
minds; that young man whose stay here would, we hoped, be profitable for me but more so for him, convenient for me but more so for
him, reciprocally bound with the ties of mutual advantage, and
therefore lasting; he through whom I was relieved of no small part
of the labor in transcribing my works, while he seemed likely to
improve himself from day to day by reading, writing, practicing,
imitating, and to go on to the peak of high renown; he whom I at
table, on the road, in gatherings, in conversations, not only open
but secret, in jest and in earnest, treated not as a poor relation but
a dear companion, not as a stranger but one born of our blood; he
whom, as you already know, so that, being free of secular cares, he
would be attached to me and be my very own, I had arranged to
have advanced to clerical status (none, it seems to me, is more
secure or more tranquil) through the bishop of his city, by whom he
was trained—with what precepts, how holy and grave!—to attend me,
and love me, and obey me, and never to be parted from me if he
could help it, and to recognize God's gift in this most of all, that He
had brought him at this age into my hands, which he himself knows
who has quickly spurned the advice and words of so great a father;
he whom, finally, as you learn now for the first time, I had just the
other day encouraged with the definite hope of an ecclesiastical
benefice, not so much to lighten my own burden—which I bore
eagerly—as the embarrassment in paying for his books and clothes
and the unaccountable expenses of adolescence while I was ponder-

* See V, 4.

ing still greater things for him, if my life were prolonged and my fortune more propitious; that young fellow, I say, so beloved by me and so pampered, comes to me last night, changed in looks and spirit. He says that he no longer wishes to be with me, that he wants to leave immediately. But touched, or rather shocked, by his words, I brushed aside my paper, pen, and other concerns to which I was tending, and as if awakened from a heavy sleep, staring at him fixedly as he spoke, I silently began marveling and no less pitying that fickle heart and that most wretched time of life, although for fools and wretches no age is sweeter. When at last I read his intentions quite clearly on his face, I asked him to explain himself: whether I, or any of my friends or servants, had done anything or overlooked anything that had made him get this idea. He frankly said no, adding that he was not unaware that nowhere was there a more peaceful and honorific abode for him than with me. Tearfully he said these things. It seemed to me, then, that he was not pretending, because not many days before, among some copies that he returned to me as usual, I found hidden a small note, the draft of a short letter written in his hand, in which—so far as I could make out—his answer to some friend of his, God knows who, that urged him to leave, was that it was bad advice and to no avail. For he had perfect peace of mind since he lacked nothing to live well and happily; and he had found a father as well as a master. I say nothing about the rest that his sincere love prompted him to say about me, and truth itself to say about his situation.

As I compared these words of his with what he had written, my amazement and pity grew more and more. "Well then, my poor unhappy young fellow," I said, "if this is so, if nothing is lacking that you want and nothing here bothers you, what then is driving you headlong, where are you rushing?" With tears now practically gushing, he answered, "Nothing, except that I cannot write any more." With a laugh that it so happens arose from anger, I said, "What then? Do your hands tremble, or your eyes blur?" "Neither," he said, "but my enthusiasm for writing has not only cooled down but frozen stiff; now there is nothing that can induce me to write." To this I said, "You are getting your just deserts, for often, when I warned you not to work so continuously at writing, you would not listen. See now that excess has done what it usually does: it has made you feel satiated and disgusted. So, drop this urge to write, give your mind a rest, do what careful farmers often do. Just as fallowing is very good for depleted fields, so too for weary minds, except that fields need a full year, while a month or a couple of weeks, and often a single day, is enough for the mind. Allow time to pass. That philosophical saying holds true in almost all matters: a day wounds, a day heals; get rid of the disgust that comes from monotony. Change and variety will best heal this illness. Lay aside a routine that pressures you. Turn your mind to other interests. Think about something else; do something else. That will make you miss this. What used to please displeases, and what displeases will please. The appetites of men, especially of youths, are fleeting; pleasure in turn becomes suffering, suffering becomes pleasure. Be patient and wait; believe me, after a brief pause you will find that you like work and hate idleness, and you will consider holidays most unbearable, and against all the onslaughts of insidious boredom you will first call upon your pen for aid."

As I was saying all this and about to say still more, he indignantly interrupted me with a rather sad countenance. "Never," he said, "shall I write again, by Jove, for you or for anyone in the world." I answered, "So be it; do not write. What does it matter? Why such a drastic separation? I did not take you in as a scribe but as a son. If you will not write, you will read, converse, keep me company; you will honor this little house as it will perhaps honor you and make you worthy of a nobler one." "You are wasting your time," said he, "I shall never endure being in a household where I am of no use to anyone. I am too proud to eat the bread of idleness; you press me in vain. I intend to leave; I ask your leave to do what I would do even against your will." To this I spurted out an answer, "You poor man, do you so look down upon yourself that unless you are a writer, you are nothing? I had certainly had more hope than that for you. For, in case you do not know it, this calligraphy of yours, which was not careless nor frivolous in the letter strokes but restrained, excellently controlled, and sober rather than fancy, I considered not as the fruit of your talent but as the blossoming and prelude of great knowledge. You deceived me; I believed it was a pledge, it was all that could be gotten and expected from you, since obviously when that is eliminated, nothing is left. But what, I ask, since you reject me, will you say to our Donato [the addressee] who donated you to me and me to you?"

"What," he said, "have I to do with Donato?" "O you ingrate," I said, "thus do you respect the father of your talent, thus do you remember his teaching and fatherly affections? Then you have become utterly shameless! Surely when he sees you alone, he will exclaim, 'Where have you left your father?' And he will think either that I am no more or that you are crazy. Nor will he be wrong, for you are crazy, and you are destroying yourself." To this I added something that perhaps would have been seemlier to leave unsaid, but those whom neither ambition nor vainglory would have driven to boast have often been driven to it by anger and grief. Anyhow, I told him urgently to remember his mentor's words that he would perhaps live more opulently elsewhere—more honorably and suitably for what he was seeking. He should consider, he should examine, he should mull over whether our relationship did not seem comfortable enough for him while I live, or munificent enough after my passing, were he to survive me, as his age, if not his countenance, can assure him; posterity perhaps would not hold it against him to have been in my household a friend, or rather a son begotten of my judgment, so to speak, and the chosen successor to my talents, however poor, and my name. He said, "You are accomplishing nothing, you will not catch me in these verbal snares." So he immediately rushed out, and in short went directly to the harbor; nor could shame for himself nor love or respect for me have restrained him, were it not that this city, encircled by a double wall and twin rivers, has a rein whereby it curbs the fools and the wicked, but guides the good; precautions had been taken that he should not leave the place without my permission. And so, lest anything happen to him while alone and reckless, I shall have him kept there until my return, which I shall move up because of this.

I have begged him to disclose the true reason, offering to let him go if he did this, and offering him a letter of recommendation to friends wherever he might choose to go in our part of the world, as well as money for his journey. For I said I was more deeply hurt by his lie than by his departure. But he stuck to his original point, swearing solemnly that there was no other cause than the one given. Still it is my opinion, and that of several others, that he is spurred either by a new hope of greater gain or by madness. Which of these is truer, is in doubt. They both contain some semblance of truth; for, having been praised by me, he had begun to be liked by many. What is more, hope can spring to him from the first and madness from the second. I was not the only one to notice that his eyes were staring more than usual and more prone to tears. This prompted whoever observed him to guess either way.

Amidst so much sad news, you will hear one thing so amusing that you would laugh, [even] if you are angry; already he is beginning to be pointed out; for he had been known here for some time, and through God knows what leaks the affair became public, for nothing that servants know is hidden from the rabble. There were those who would say in hushed whispers, "You see this young man?

He has gone mad from reading." And there were those who said this to me. In disgust I replied to them that neither this young man nor literate people go mad because of reading, but rather they are free from madness since causes generally bring to fruition effects like themselves and do not prematurely bring forth the opposite ones; what is commonly said is false: that some go mad from reading. The truth is rather that they are thereby protected from madness. Although this charge has often been leveled against many, especially the Apostle Paul, still our young man has gained even now, as a reward for his untimely rebellion, the title of a man of letters along with madness. Many may want this title for themselves at any price; so great is the aura of learning that not only does it seem to some people worth seeking through the clouds of insanity, but even the reputation for it, however false. I totally disagree with such people. I would rather be, I will not say Benedict or Francis, holy and unlearned men, or another type such as Marius, a brave and unlettered man, but my old steward, ignorant and rough, yet faithful and diligent, than Empedocles who, not mad from reading but, as a man of letters, mad in the eagerness to seek fame, hurled himself into the flames of fiery Etna; or than Lucretius, his equal whether in learning or madness, who stabbed himself with his own blade because of his impatience with life, and with the same hand that had written so many outstanding verses he thrust out his gifted rather than happy soul.

There you have the story—disturbing no doubt, and justly so since you were the first one to nurture his mind, to form his character and encourage his talent; and you seemed to have made progress not only for yourself but for everyone, and for me above all; as things turned out, you wasted your effort, we were all mistaken. Oh, how hard it is to fall from lofty hopes! I who had determined never to grieve over anything, could not help grieving over this, I confess. Although you who sowed the seed in this intellect, and I who had followed you in your labors, have lost the noble hope of a great harvest, no one's loss is greater than his who was puffed up with our praises (which we gave him not to inflate but to incite his youthful mind) and with a false opinion of himself; while he could amount to something, he believes that he has accomplished it almost before he has begun. And so, the same will happen to him as to many others: in the belief that he has already arrived, he will never arrive where he is headed. This error has indeed blocked from the goal of their race to glory an infinite number of mortals who were stopped in mid-course, content with their present false joy and forgetful of their purpose.

I had already written more than half of this letter when I heard that this young man of ours has decided to travel around the world, madman that he is, heedless of his own strength, and—to say nothing of the greater dangers of the roads—ignorant of what it is like to fall in with strangers, or rather enemies. His is a good age, however, for this. He will find out, and learn at his own expense what we learned at ours. First, it is said he will head for Parthenope [Naples] to raise, I suppose, from the Mantuan ashes a new Virgil from Ravenna. But just as books are full of that man's memory, so will he find the tomb long since emptied of his bones. Let him go then, and may his journey be happy and favorable for himself and for the Italian Muses. And from the fount of his abundant talent may he restore Latium, arid and thirsty through lengthy barrenness. Let us place no obstacle in the way of the public good. After I in person have returned him to you, let him then break forth and be borne on high and fly away. Since he is so ashamed of our nest and sorry to be here, I hope that he, who believes himself something special, will understand the first time he unfurls to the wind his still unfledged wings what he is doing now, and will remember, though late, Icarus and Phaethon.

But let the discussion finally turn back to us. Although the proverb may be ancient—that the lesser of two or more evils must be chosen—I do not see how the choice of an evil is praiseworthy, since the lesser evil is undoubtedly still an evil. So I believe it better to say that greater evils must be avoided with greater effort, so that if all of them cannot be avoided, the lesser ones may be more easily tolerated, not through choice, but through patience, equanimity, and moderation. Let it rather become a proverb taking the form of Cicero's advice: from evils we must extract whatever good may be in them. This will hardly seem surprising to the one who realizes that not only from the bitterest roots and herbs, but even from certain poisonous animals, as rumor has it, come remedies for diseases.

If I am not mistaken, there is inherent in this evil a double good: first, let us not praise in the future anything except a man of firm and resolute mind and proven virtue. For him, virtue grows when praised, as Naso says. But in others, it is pride, vanity, and madness that grow when praised. And no need to look elsewhere for proof: we have ruined this boy of ours with praise. Second, let us never trust that age, although it may display modesty, promise, constancy, and loyalty, and finally feign seriousness and simulate prudence; and let it always be for us a certainty what that great man says in Lucan: "A high level of trust requires mature years" [8.282]. Farewell.

Padua, April 22 [1367].

Sen. V, 6.

To the same person,* on the same subject.

Frightened for a while by my outcries and those of my friends, that
fellow [Giovanni Malpaghini, P.'s scribe] had hesitated through the
modesty of his youth rather than of his nature or through the power
of reason; quickly what he had in mind was revealed since he smashed
the bolts with a surge of madness and left, as you saw, very unsettled
physically but even more so mentally, as one moment he thought of
Parthenope [Naples], the next of Calabria, either for Virgil's tomb or
Ennius's cradle, and the next he sighed for Byzantium, dreaming of
something or other. And what did his restless head do? Physically he
could not be in different places at the same time; mentally he was in
all of them, and in such a way, if we believe Annaeus, that he was nowhere while being everywhere. It is astonishing and almost unbelievable that a young man, bred under the rod, lacking good health and
money, should have so suddenly imbibed such license and wantonness, like a lethal and quick-acting poison, that today he disdains you
and me and all his friends' warnings and advice with the same ears
that yesterday dreaded hearing not only you but the voice and lash of
the tutor you had appointed. And indeed the sole reason, which you
often heard from him, he gave for his rash move was not the labor
and boredom of writing with which he often justified himself at the
outset, but his sudden love for Greek letters, really remarkable for a
man who so far lacked a great deal—practically everything—of Latin.
When I tried to cast this like a bridle upon him as he grumbled, I
added the many hardships of the roads and of the whole enterprise,
and especially his lack of money, as well as having to do without my
help since I loathed his folly. When I added to all these objections the
ancient downfall of Athens—how ever since Ovid's time it was nothing
more than a barren name—and finally the indisputable ignorance of
the Greeks nowadays, he chomped at the bit, aroused by secret spurs.
For a while he hid behind the veil of a more respectable excuse, yet
the real reasons were others that he painfully disclosed at last. But I
shall not reveal them, lest I seem angry at something worse than
youthful extravagances.

The very first and greatest thing about him was his mental instability, which might perhaps have affected others differently, but the

* See V, 4.

experience with this madness is not wasted, for he has accomplished this with me: in no man ever have I seen fickleness equal to his, nor heard or read of it. I saw a thousand different and contrary things troubling him in one little heart; you would say that there was not one but a thousand minds all in disagreement and vying among themselves. Nothing in him was constant for the space of an hour, no one thing except this: inconstancy. This alone, amidst such great instability in thinking of what to do, stood firm. Finally, the outcome of his conflicting desires turned him westward. Never had there been a word of this, I believe, nor a thought; he scorned my letters to friends in which, eager to help him along, I undeservedly commended his mad impulse as curiosity: he said that he wished to visit the Babylon of the West [Avignon], and with those words, rushed headlong into his journey. What you have read thus far you know; what follows is new.

He left and crossed the Apennines as nature buffeted his obstinacy with constant rainstorms, and to any acquaintance he met on the road he would say I had sent him, as if he were beginning to awaken and feel the shame that accompanies a lonely stranger. Because of this lie, which I learned about later, some had an unwarranted compassion for him and a false impression of me. Finally he came to Pisa and the Tyrrhenian coast, where he stayed to await a ship that he could board in all his madness, hoping to fill a wayward stern with his frivolous cargo. When one failed to show, and the poor fellow's boredom grew from day to day and his money dwindled, he hastily recrossed the Apennines. But I pass over the accidents and dangers he underwent, of which he alone is aware. But it is so easy to guess: a mere weakling, untried, alone, the hem of his tunic dragging on the ground over mountain summits, over so many slippery, rocky, rugged, steep places, through so many valleys, rivers, torrents swollen by winter rains, not knowing the road or the people, weighed down by himself and his drenched clothing, he made the crossing with frequent stumbling and the risks of mountain climbing. Finally, upon regaining the Ligurian plain, barely wading across the river Taro at Parma, which is nearly as unpredictable as he is, he was caught in its swift rapids and whirled about between the sand and the rocks; half of him was going back to where he had set forth, the other half going on to undergo the labors of Ixion, or rather to carry a new wheel of torment into hell, if a certain man who took pity on him had not grabbed him by the heel and drawn him from the water. Thus snatched from death, but carried ashore and worn out by hunger, and short of money, exhausted from struggling and pale with filth, he arrived here where he either thought that I had already arrived or knew that I would soon come.

When my Francesco [P.'s son-in-law]—there is no better young man (that is your judgment, for love may be deceiving me), as full of charity and constancy as that other fellow is devoid of both—saw him dazed and stunned by the memory of his recent misfortunes, he did not recognize him at first. For he seemed a thin shade rather than a man, "Such shapes, 'tis said, flit about after death," according to Maro [*Aen.* 10.641]. Then barely recognizing him and taking pity, he comforted him as he heard the account of his wanderings and all his sufferings, and encouraged him—sad and mistrustful of everything—to await me at my home. Out of fear and shame, at first he said no to such urgings, but later, overcome by necessity, he nodded. Many days later, when I had learned of the affair by letter and was returning, he and some friends ran into me at night right in the middle of the Ticino, and I cried out in jest those well-known words of the poet: "Is it your true face? Bring you me true news" [*Aen.* 3.310]? Do you want to know what follows? When I noticed his embarrassed silence and downcast eyes, I embraced him in my usual fashion, but not with the usual feeling of love, I must confess. Now I have no faith in him or his character; when time has overcome his shame and rest his fatigue, and forgetfulness erases the traces of danger, I can see him coming to me once again with a different countenance to say goodbye. I have therefore already accumulated and laid aside the money for his journey, so that his madness may have no delay whatsoever. He will find it all counted out, me silent, and the door wide open.

I know from experience what to expect from this fellow; if I did not, I am learning it now from your letter and advice, to which I fully subscribe and which I intend to follow to the letter, as they say. But what my mind tells me, my heart contradicts. You know me. No hurt is so great that I cannot easily forget and forgive. No enemy is so bitter that I cannot take pity if he repents and blushes, and that I cannot love if he continues in that state. In this case, then, I act not on his merit, not on a friend's advice, but on my own habit of inconstancy which has often, I admit, been costly, but never, I hope, shameful. I prefer that the fault be all his rather than any of it mine. I would rather he be called unsteady than difficult; if perchance he were ever to come to his senses, which I scarcely hope, let him recognize his true self and me, and the friends' advice that he scorned, let repentance and grief be his punishment. Otherwise, let him live by his ways, and me by mine. Farewell.

Pavia, July 11 [1367–68].

Sen. VI, 1.

To Giovanni Boccaccio,* the tragic misfortune of a wretched friend.

The three huge letters I sent you last year at the same time as I was leaving Pavia—they were not written at the same time—have finally reached you, I trust, although they were long held up a for some untoward reason. I really felt as though I had poured out all my thoughts in them. And so, there is nothing new except that, after I had reached Venice in the middle of the night, our Donato [Albanzani] came alone to see me early in the morning. We talked about many things then, as friends do who are all the more eager to talk after an absence, but most was deservedly about you, and at the same time about the Homer which, according to your letter, you had sent. Find out there what happened to it, for I want you to know that it has not arrived here. In another letter I complain of having complained unfairly about Donato concerning this.

But the mention of Homer reminds me of that man who translated him into Latin. Oh, what a sad, what a horrible end has struck Leontius [Pilatus]—shall I say, 'our' Leontius? For pity and deep compassion force me to speak now without gall about him, of whom I have already said much with gall. My attitude has always changed with that fellow's luck which, though wretched before, is now hair-raising. The unhappy man, whatever he was, loved us, though he was the type that had learned to love neither others nor himself; and having entered this world under sinister omens, he left under even more sinister ones, without having seen, I believe, one serene day. In recalling him to mind, I often wonder how even a slight whiff of the Pierian spirit and celestial music had penetrated such a sad and somber soul.

The wretched man begged me at great length to send for him, admitting his error, which appeases angry minds the most. But I was afraid of his instability, which I know too well, and his intractable age, which had become even more stubborn with his changing ways, and above all I relied on your advice, which I like to follow trustingly in any matter since it is illuminated by the two torches of intelligence and loyalty, the sign of a good and sound adviser; so I ignored his entreaty and gave no answer to his letter. Finally a more

* See I, 5.

ardent yearning for our company seized him, and shame that he was so ill-acquainted with Italy; and he trusted in my character, rightly thinking that, although unworthy of being invited, he would hardly be kept away from our doorstep if he came on his own; and so, he set sail from Byzantium this past summer despite Aeolus and Neptune and the entire army of Phorcus. Oh, what can I say? You will hear something wretched and terrifying. He had already crossed the Bosphorus and the Propontis as well as the Hellespont, and the Aegean and the Ionian, that is, the Greek seas; already, I imagine, at the sight of the Italian landscape he rejoiced, I would say, if this were not contrary to his nature; but at least he was less sad as he plowed the Adriatic, when suddenly the sky and sea changed, and a fierce storm arose. While the others scattered to their stations, wretched Leontius stood clinging to the mast—the mast (*malus*) indeed, and the last of the evils (*malorum*) that cruel fortune had saved for him after much suffering throughout his life.

My pen shudders to relate my unhappy friend's downfall. In short, amidst many noisy threats of the heavens, Jupiter brandished his thunderbolt. The sail-yards broke into pieces, the burning sails were reduced to sparks, flames from heaven engulfed the mast, yet while everyone was thrown to the deck and terrified, our friend alone perished: this was the end of our Leontius. O unforeseen human fate! O death, more renowned and more resounding than I could imagine! I never thought that to the name of Capaneus, the Argive champion, or of Tullus Hostilius or Carus—the one a king, the other an emperor—would be added the name of Leontius, a humble man not unlearned but never very lucky or happy. Always—now I certainly understand, as we understand many things after the fact—always, as I was saying, did that dark cloud and the somberness of his sad face foretell this thunderbolt. His untidy belongings, saved by the sailors' honesty, and his soiled books, saved by their own lack of value, came through it all. I shall make inquiries whether among them were Euripides, Sophocles, and the others that he had promised to find for me. His disfigured and half-burned corpse was thrown into the sea. He whom I, in another letter to you, had destined to be bait for the worms of Greece, is, alas, food for the fish of Italy. But you live happily and farewell; remember me.

Venice, January 25 [1365-67].

Sen. VI, 2.

To the same person,* concerning himself.

I have noticed from your letter to a friend that you are very uneasy about my freedom. I am grateful for your concern, I confess, but it is not new. Lay aside this fear, and rest assured that up to now, even when I seemed subject to the hardest yoke, I have always been the freest of men, and will continue to be, I might add, if there were any certain knowledge of the future. I shall still try, successfully I hope, not to learn servility as an old man, and to be free in spirit wherever I am, although it may be necessary to be subject in body and in other things to superiors, whether to one man as in my case or to many as in yours. I know not whether to call your kind of yoke heavier and more troublesome. I believe it easier to bear one man's tyranny than a people's. Indeed, had it not always been the case that everywhere I have lived free, I would either have lost my life long ago or certainly my serenity and joy of life, and you above all are my witness to the opposite. I am unable to serve any mortal for long, unless willingly and at the behest of love. But then you know the ways of men and the oddities and snares of life, whose intricacies neither an arithmetrician could count nor a geometrician measure nor an astronomer examine. But those who approach such things with their eyes open do perceive them.

That is why I have always liked and often cited that brief but pithy and meaningful saying of the Hebrew sage: all things are difficult [Eccl. 1:8]. Oh, what is he saying? All things, I say, even the ones that seem very easy, are difficult. But among all these difficult things none is more difficult than to live, especially a long time. Every hour and every moment brings something new; every step has its slippery spot, its stumbling block, its sharp edge which is rough to step on and hard to bypass. But where am I being dragged, and why do I waste time on the difficulties of things? It is an infinite subject, well known to you, perhaps even better than it is to me. I leave aside other things. It is a fact that the elder Africanus, as you realize, was cheapened in the eyes of the Romans by long association. How do you suppose lesser men fare in others' eyes? Believe me, it behooves many, and especially the sick, to change their

* See I, 5.

position at times; it is not a sign of inconstancy but of prudence to trim the sails to the changing winds and the storm of affairs. Everything cannot be included in a letter, but if you also knew all that, you would advise me, I am certain, not so much to break away as to distance myself at times and compensate for life's troubles by a change of location. Therefore, pray God that the end of this tale, which we call life, be good and pleasing to Him. As for the rest, do not despair that I will choose either the better course or the lesser evil, as the heavenly light illumines my eyes and points the way.

I close by letting you know that your Homer, now in Latin, has finally reached me—which renews my love for the sender and my memory, my sighs for the translator; it has filled me and all those who inhabit this library, be they Greek or Latin, with wonderful joy and delight. Farewell, my most loving brother.

[1365-67].

Sen. VI, 3.

To Francesco Bruni, Papal Secretary,* on the same matter.

I knew you were a friend, and the assurance of your love has long been imprinted in my heart. This certitude has been implanted within the marrow of my bones by my talkative friend from Bergamo ["Bolanus"], stammering out to heaven with oaths by all the saints that no man loves me more than you do. It is amazing when someone who expresses it so feebly impresses it so powerfully. There are times when eloquence is suspect; since it can befriend a falsehood, it is believed to be the enemy of truth.

But if perchance this man, or another or others, as you write, have with their descriptions so portrayed me, whom you have yet to lay eyes on, that you view me either outwardly or inwardly as having a kind of rare or superior** quality, pray rid yourself of this. I would not say this unless I suspected that my person would sometimes belie my reputation. I would not mind being commended to you, even if falsely; but since perhaps you will still see me, do not keep a mental image of me that you will be forced to lay aside. I mean, rid yourself not only of your image of my face, but of your mistaken assumption, and do not believe in men's words, especially of those who love me. A lover is no more truthful than a hater, although he may be more noble. The tongue has a certain itch and hankering for censure and praise. As long as this prevails, truth must be banished. If Augustine experienced how very dangerous the temptation of human praise was in his own case, how would you think this sinner will feel, to whom the undeserved weight of another's praise does harm even if it delights me, and does good if refused and scorned? But experience with this kind of temptation is much riskier and more trying than any other, since if I want to feel how much I can calmly do without praise, I must live thus, subject to the hatred or to the ridicule and mockery of all. Indeed from the very beginning of our friendship, unless memory deceives me, I wrote that you should believe me, no one else, about me. The way I described myself to you at that time is the way I am, except that meanwhile I have grown two years older or so.

---

* See I, 6.
** We emend *angustam* to *augustam*.

In short, unless you wish to be deceived, consider me one of the crowd, although I am well known for scorning the crowd. And do not make me anything loftier than your friend, provided I may say this without contradicting Tully's opinion which asserts that there cannot be friendship without virtue. I thank you too for the book of Ambrose, the most blessed Father and once my host; you sent me books and literary pleasures while I send you chores and annoyances. Hardly a fair exchange!

As for the oil from my once delightful and peaceful retreat at the hidden source of the Sorgue—I sigh at being kept away from there by a great change in circumstances—that one of my acquaintances brought you a sample of to taste, which you have extolled with wonderfully mystic praises, it is all yours, all of it, not only the oil but the olives, not only the olives but the farm itself; though parched and tiny, never has it been dearer to me, never more fruitful than when it gratifies you. And to please your taste all the more, whatever flows from the saplings were nearly all planted with my own hands. That is all for today, except that I consider your troubles and our country's my own. Farewell, be happy, and remember me.

[1363–64].

Sen. VI, 4.

To [Pietro] Pilleo [di Prato], Bishop of Padua,* an exhortation to remain steadfast.

Although silently every day I converse with you (you who are in age my son, long ago my brother in affection, and now in rank my most loving father), the reason for writing briefly is my unusual physical weakness which has remained with me as a guest outstaying his welcome after an even more unwelcome illness. For your good health and for your much desired return, I thank God. Moreover, I urge you to keep—and in urging I praise—your brave and steadfast spirit. There is no safer armor, no stronger citadel, no stouter helmet or shield in the battles with Fortune. I know that you have magnificently shown this steadfastness up to now and more often at this age than is usual for your years or your station in life, and I marvel at this and am delighted. Nor am I alone: the entire Church rejoices and marvels at your patience, although it marvels and grieves over the troubles you are causing it. I therefore beg you not to stop or tire. Strong blows are apt to be short-lived, Fortune wearies. She never feels shame for the brave and innocent, but God will pity them and put an end to their sufferings. Let your hope be anchored in Him; He will not disappoint anyone who hopes in Him. Clouding the naturally serene state of your mind are mists that will be dispelled by the light breath of divine mercy. And perhaps the recollection of what you are bitterly enduring will be sweet. No luck is everlasting, not even long-lasting, whence it happens that while the wretched must hope, the happy must fear. For although torments seem to last longer, adversity still passes no less than prosperity. The wheel of fortune turns everywhere, equally and unpredictably for all. Our feelings, which are arrogant when we are joyful and sensitive when sad, makes our joys short and sadness terribly long, even though the sum of everything is short; and the difference lies in our judgment and spirit, not in things that are in every way equally fleeting.

I shall say only this about myself. I am yours, as you know; and

---

* Made Bishop of Padua in 1359 and of Ravenna a year later, he was very active in church politics, which caused him many problems and eventually led to a cardinalcy, an excommunication, and a second and third cardinalcy. He eventually became known as the "Cardinal of the Three Hats." This is the only letter to him.

although I know I am of no use to anyone, I can love, and there are some who cannot. If you think I can help beyond that, I beg you, use me to the fullest. Finally, I wish to recommend to your protection my priests, your servants, Giovanni and Paolo, whom I have sent to you along with this letter. And if I may, with no breach of respect, I adjure you not to let the harshness of others deprive one of them of the favor that your goodness granted him by my pleading. To judge another's conscience is difficult. I have known many like Giovanni and Paolo—harsh, uncouth, with an unrestrained tongue—who are better men than the smooth ones who are insincere, flattering turncoats. Farewell.

Venice, June 8 [1366–68].

Sen. VI, 5.

To Philippe [de Cabassoles], Patriarch of Jerusalem, the transmittal of a promised book, and an excuse for the delay.*

I have finally sent you, Father, my little work [*De uita solitaria*], often solicited by you and promised by me, but delayed, as you see, for many years. Long ago, alone, at leisure, tranquil, I lived in the silence of your country estate a life that was nearly happy, had it lasted longer; in order not to make my solitude isolated or my leisure unproductive, every day I would mull over or write something new. And it so happened that I got the idea of writing during Lent for two years two short books befitting the holy season and that place of yours, and partly my condition too: one was on the solitary life, the other on religious repose. The first I dedicated to you, at that time the bishop of that region, because being composed in the same place where you were born and raised to eminence, it seemed more deservedly assigned to you than to anyone else. Nor has there ever been since then a moment when I felt sorry for my decision, or even in the least hesitant, as happens when uncertainty causes one to have misgivings over some new consideration.

If you ask me why I therefore did not send it earlier since it was yours, and could not and ought not to be anyone else's, I shall tell you. There was not just one reason for the delay but several: first, my overwhelming and unending business, and then a certain slowness in getting things done which is part of my character—both reasons very well known to you; unless this is overcome from time to time by the zeal of friends, to whom, I confess, I have neither a mind to deny anything whatsoever, nor the nerve or the tongue. And unless the burning urgency of their pleas had melted the ice of my torpid brain, today many of my writings, read by scholars in scattered and piecemeal form, would be hidden away—and better off thus. As they are, however, they are not really mine, for while I

---

* One of P.'s earliest and dearest friends (twenty-four letters to him are extant), whose diocese included Vaucluse of which he was the feudal lord. Upon the death of King Robert of Naples, he was made Regent until Queen Joan reached adulthood. He subsequently served as Pontifical Legate in Germany, Patriarch of Jersualem, Cardinal Bishop of Sabina, and was appointed Governor of Umbria and Sabina by Gregory XI.

admit that they were born in my house and later just partly re-
worked into another form by a restless, immature talent, they
slipped away from me; I threw them out. Let the reader make of
them whatever he sees fit.

For I have noticed that some people like them better than the
ones I chiseled and polished in my riper years; such people are like
pregnant women who delight in sour tastes. I do not object to their
taste, but hereby declare that I call nothing mine that I have not
specifically signed at the beginning or the end. What anyone says at
any age or for any reason ought not to be accepted indiscriminately,
since things relentlessly follow upon one another, words upon
words, feelings upon feelings. Otherwise there will be hardly any
mortal who has not said a thousand times something that he wants
retracted or unsaid.

Another reason for the delay has been the ever deceitful laziness
and lazy deceitfulness of the scribes. How often I have been fooled
by them, you can well imagine—more times than I can count; but to
forget my old complaints, this very work, which was started ten
times or more although it is brief, was finally finished by a trusty
cleric whose penmanship is not so painstakingly refined as it is
fitting to our time of life and, unless I am wrong, to any other. For
youth, thoughtless in all its actions and foolishly admiring silly fads,
scornful of anything practical, likes to pride itself on small, cramped
lettering that baffles the eye; by heaping and cramming everything
together, it confuses the spacing and piles up the letters, as though
they were riding on top of one another, so that the scribe himself
could scarcely read them, were he to return a little later, while the
purchaser would really purchase not so much a book, as blindness
because of the book.

You will accept it as it is, then, not only patiently, as I know you
will, but even eagerly and joyfully, and consider the ten years' delay
a good thing since it has preserved for you to this day, untouched
and unimpaired, after such a lapse of time an extraordinary pleasure which you experience first from this letter. When things come
quickly, they are cheapened; when postponed, they grow sweeter.
Hope, love, anticipation, difficulty are pleasure's seasoning. Nothing
easy is precious. And those things that are valued highly lose their
value if they begin to be easily attainable.

I am joking with you, dearest Father, and what I did reluctantly
and unwillingly, for which I must ask forgiveness, I am trying to
turn to my advantage; and I am putting the onus on you for something wherein I have perhaps offended you, or certainly would have

offended anyone else. I ought rather to be begging you to forgive me and not to take amiss the very small thing that you have been long expecting for some time; bear in mind the obstacles that constantly beset men's plans and endeavors. By way of an excuse, there is one thing that I want to say before closing, not so much for you since you clearly see the reason for it, but for those, if any, who will wonder why I address you in the opening of a work dedicated to you not with your present title of Patriarch but with that of Bishop, thereby using not your new and current rank but your old one. For while you are more illustrious and elevated because of your recent title, the other still seemed more becoming and fitting for the subject in that book: in the first part I said that it was written at your country residence, and in the last, where there are many things pertinent only to that time and situation, I invited you to the solitude and silence of your nearby country estate. Consequently, if these were applied to your present rank and title, something would have to be either changed or deleted; or surely, if it were to remain, in those sections referring to you or your surroundings, something ought to be mentioned or eliminated, or something added on what you were when I wrote the particulars that have changed since then—all for the sake of avoiding obscurity and of being understood. Indeed what connection could there be between the Patriarch of Jerusalem, however solitary, and the actual seat you held when I was writing; or what interest could he have in the rustic dwelling I lived in at the time, or in Vaucluse rather than the valley of Josaphat, in short, by the Sorgue rather than the Jordan? Such names could perplex the unknowing reader, for whom everything will fit when he finds inscribed in bright red letters, at the opening of the work, "To the Bishop of Cavaillon"; and nothing will be ambiguous or confusing. If he learns of your promotion after that time, he will marvel only at its lateness, not at the advance.

Finally, my hand could not bear to erase that former title of a minor Bishop but a very great man, whom I had so often honored with special verse—even now it sounds so sweetly to me—under whose auspices I wrote many things at various times, especially that book; and as a member of your household I spent so many happy, peaceful days with you in that small but noble city of yours and in that poor but untroubled country dwelling of yours, and under that title I wrote you many friendly letters which could not be changed now. Therefore, let the title of Bishop remain lest, if it be changed, the title of Patriarch would also be likely to change soon.

You would surely have risen higher long ago, had your character, so unlike that of our day, not stood in your way. But henceforth, under this excellent judge of merit (unless hope is deceiving me), it will happen that neither others' envy nor your humility will impede you, and inevitably you will rise higher not out of the fervor of your ambition, since you seek only God and virtue, but for the good of the Church, for your noble labors, and for the respite of many. Live happily, and farewell.

Venice, June 6 [1366].

Sen. VI, 6.

To a friend [Zanobi da Strada],* a stern reproach for an unworthy endeavor.

You have set out for Babylon [Avignon]. I marvel at your setting forth. I am astonished at your staying there. I hate the whole business, but if you have devoted to that horrible hell some of your life, undependable and shaky though it be, in order to get subsistence for your feeble age when you will need the help of others (like the bee or the ant who thinks of winter in the summer), I cannot withhold indulgence for human ways and gullible hope, though the matter is not without grave risk and the squandering of such a tiny, irretrievable good is dangerous. But should you persist in choosing that place for your demise and burial, I number you among the dead and buried from this moment onward. For why, my friend, should I not grieve over you all the more deeply than if I were to see you dead and gone, since a useless life is worse than death? For we must all die; we must not live badly.

But what is it that I hear about you and your studies? Although I may not hear, I see with these eyes with which I may contemplate that infernal city, wherever I may be. Alas, my Cicero, alas Maro—for I am addressing the peerless models of the two styles of eloquence—alas, to whom do you yield, not in fact, but in the readers' unjust judgment which, whether envious or inept, often turns against richly deserved praises? Is any amount of money, then, or any honor worth so much, my friend, that you prefer that undistinguished writer [Berardo Caracciolo, author of *Dictamina*] whose name it would be better not to mention, to Tully and Virgil? Alas, noble intellect, alas, illustrious labors and glorious nights without sleep, where has life brought us that I am seeing you classified lower than his scrivening and his writs, not by any common critic, but by a man such as this?

I believe that the end of the world is already near; behold the increase in evil portents! We shall hear that the anti-Christ is already approaching, that—as certain men have surmised—Nero is alive, and

---

* One of the Florentines whom P. met in Florence in 1350 on his Jubilee journey. Originally a well-known grammarian with his own school, Zanobi became royal secretary at the court of Naples and eventually papal secretary under Innocent VI. The original of this letter, which was never sent, was addressed to Zanobi and spoke of Berardo Caracciolo's *Dictamina*. When P. added letters to his collection, he often removed names so as not to give offense.

other things are happening that our fathers predicted to us as future forebodings of that upheaval. Meanwhile, is it too small a portent or premonition of the world hastening to destruction that you are reading that illiterate, and that your eyes are equal to such a distasteful undertaking, and your mind, accustomed to Pierian meadows and founts, is busy with the old wives' ditties in those scruffy, withered parchments and studying a Babylonian Homer? O instability of earthly things! O incredible revolution of studies! Thus, neglecting the princes of eloquence, scorning the teachers of philosophy, and finally, despising the leaders of the true faith who point the way to heaven, you have in hand a cheap journeyman, a hireling; you know from experience how the incessant reading of him leaves you reeling. I well remember how once, when I was forced to do this, it so upset my brain and stomach that its taste long clung to my throat, as though I had drunk a cup of poison; and whatever I swallowed after that, however sweet and tasty, became bitter; so whatever I read in those days seemed like reading that same author, until more than one night's sleep made my forget that dullness and digest the bitter taste.

I will not deny that his style is useful for those who are given nothing higher. Nor am I unaware that the man is esteemed by those attracted by love of money, not virtue or glory. Their number is legion. But do you want, then, to mix with the crowd? Because ovens are useful for society, should Plato become a baker? Just as there are an infinite variety of things, so with minds. Although no one can make what is naturally bad become good, still it is well known that many things good in themselves are made bad or ugly by some people. In all things the way they are done matters the most, for the character of the doer and the circumstances of an action have a great effect. It is no disgrace to read such things—indeed it may even be appropriate for some—but it certainly does not become you. Just as there is profit in certain losses, so there is knowledge in not knowing certain things. Not every art is fine for everyone. The lawyer seeks trials and courts, the multitude games and plays, the farmer oxen and rakes, the soldier horses and arms, the retailer a shop, the pimp a brothel, the sexton a church, the husbandman a ploughshare, the warrior a sword, the sailor a helm and oars. But the scholar handles pen and books. On this very point the disparity is so great that the book I am speaking about sits well in one reader's lap, but very badly in another's. The laws governing things are fixed and not easily shattered. If ever human obstinacy presumes to do so, there results something unbecoming that cannot be expressed in words as easily as it is grasped by the wise, as nature's indelible track overwhelms human strivings.

In vain do we acknowledge and believe you an outstanding man, unless you withdraw from the common herd. In that city where you became a citizen both too late and too soon, there are many eagerly reading that writer who is unworthy of you reading him; nor is it unbecoming to them even to think him a great man, God-sent, since he opens up to them the road to success, and I do not deny he is useful to those aspiring to it. But practically your entire past life indicates that you are pursuing another goal. Where are you now heading, off to the left? Does the crowd's shouting or the beaten path deceive you? Do you not know that nothing is more brittle than the judgment of the multitude? Except for happiness, which everyone seeks in his heart but not in reality, you will find that in nearly everything else what pleases most people is the worst. If you want proof, consider how many friends virtue has, how many pleasure has! If you apply this to books and to the study of the arts and other things, you will find it true.

But now I may be said to have sufficiently reproved an innocent man, nor am I really censuring him as I am you. For he has done what he could, you what you want. I think you will recall how at my urging you laid aside more humble studies to pursue a lofty career, and found glory and rare distinction that I would frankly venture to ascribe to your own merit. If now, to my disappointment, you were unwittingly to slip back, even though driven by avarice, I would rather you had lain there forever. For the baser the cause, the graver the fault. What, then, shall I urge you to do? Leave. But I dare not do that, even if I do think it best. Never was there less freedom to give advice than in our time. A friend fears to tell the truth to a friend, a brother to a brother, a father-in-law to a son-in-law, a man to his wife. A son cannot hear the truth from his father. In short, any truth is an insult, any advice an offense unless it is in tune with the listener. Have I nothing to fear in regard to you except advising you in vain? I feel you can be more easily broken than swayed. Perhaps I would more successfully beseech you to choose to remain there, like the man who contemplates sweet freedom from a bitter prison, or the man who sighs for a friendly inn while traveling a dark, slippery road. This alone I beg you to do for me and for your reputation that I hold as dear as my own: that the quest for profit never render you unmindful of virtue nor practical books unmindful of the classics. Farewell, and live long and happily.

[1358–59].

Sen. VI, 7.

Against teachers of avarice,* and on the avarice of old men, rich men, and kings.

I know that at home you have a teacher of avarice. On the other hand, I do hope that you are unreceptive to that art. You do not need many urgings from me, but a few warnings. Shortly, as I began to say, you will know where I am heading and where I would like to end. A generous and noble mind is being sent to a school of avarice, and escorted back and forth by the people, best trained in the worst arts, with a hundred mouths and tongues, a voice of iron, a mind of steel, and a headstrong will. And yet, note what hope I have in you: truth will triumph, their expectation will fail, and one pupil will baffle the ingenuity of the teachers.

The advice that the avaricious like to give their sons, their friends, their intimates does not escape me—that income quickly ceases, expenses never; that you have as much honor and glory as money; that once money is gone, loyalty goes; that a poor man is never believed, for even if he takes an oath, he is suspected of perjury. But the lies of the rich, on the other hand, are taken as truth; that virtue is naked without riches, like a body without clothing, a sword without a scabbard, an arrow without a quiver; that a poor man's sense is considered folly, his eloquence is called rashness, his noble family a disgrace, his handsomeness a hindrance, his friendships a burden, his offspring a grief, his marriage a punishment, his life a mockery and toil; that money gives pleasure, honors, the highest offices, clients, friendships with kings, the people's votes, purple clothing and silk furnishings, golden vases, Corinthian vases with trees and animals on them, majestic palaces, heavenly bedrooms, and splendid marriages; that money makes and unmakes laws, protects and crushes those whom it wishes, and, what is by far the most important, wins the reputation of a good man for the worst people.

I am not joking; let Cicero protest as much as he pleases, and pile on the Socratic irony, but rich men are called "good" in public despite being stained with every vice; and no virtue will ever earn a poor man that name. Indeed, if a meeting of good men were called,

---

* In the editions of 1554 and 1581, letters VI, 7–8 are extracted as a separate treatise entitled *De auaritia uitanda*. Addressees are unknown.

never in our cities today will Curius or Fabricius sit next to Crassus. Nor among the Greeks will the Athenian Aristides sit with the Samian Polycrates. Thus has wealth taken the place of virtue; and that saying of Flaccus seems to be true: "Lineage and virtue, without money are cheaper than seaweed" [*Sat.* 1.1.52], as does that other saying of his:

> For everything,
> Divine and human, virtue, fame, and honor,
> Gives way to fair riches. He who amasses
> Them shall be famous, brave, just, wise (that too),
> A king, and whatever he will. [*Sat.* 2.3.94–98]

If this is true, who will marvel at that same poet when he exclaims, however angrily,

> O neighbors, neighbors, go for money first,
> Virtue after the bucks? [*Ep.* 1.1.53–54]

And I ask, who would not concentrate on getting first what he thinks is best, and he trusts will bring him other good things too? In case you distrust a single witness, listen to another one. Solomon says, "All things obey money" [Ecclesiastes 10:19]. And I could cite so many, but this is well known, and there is no need of authorities. The same Flaccus says,

> Gold loves to sneak in between bodyguards,
> And shatter blocks of stone more mightily than
> A lightning bolt. [*Carm.* 3.16.9–11]

Do you hear how powerful gold is? No force, no defense can ward off either one, lightning or gold, so that the saying of the cunning man, as told by Tully, is no less true than it is witty: no place is impregnable that an ass laden with gold can reach. Moreover, there is practically none that it could not reach today: thus has greed leveled every pit and bulwark, and such is gold's power to overcome strongholds and topple towers.

Why say more? Money is all-powerful, they say. This is a little less true in the kingdom of avarice. What remains, then, except that money should be some kind of god. And it is doubtless the god of many, although

                    you do not yet,
O deadly money, dwell in a temple. You
Will have built no altars of coins. [Juv. 1.113–14]

While it was definitely said by the Satirist in these words, nevertheless whether the fact escaped his notice and they were unknown to
him as he wrote this or established later, certainly Augustine places
money among the pagan goddesses. Would that today it were not a
goddess, worshipped silently though not professed outright by, I
would not say the faithful, but those who simply wish to appear
faithful!

These are the tenets of avarice's preceptors, these are the brilliant
counsels of those who raise money—the dregs of the earth—above
the stars. The Apostle was evidently scoring them when he said that
avarice is servitude to idols; while foul in anyone, this vice is especially so in old men, rich men, and rulers. But yet, because of some
blindness or other, this is most common in these very people. No
mortals would be further from it, if they had any true light whatsoever. For others covet things that they perhaps need, but for these
people, things are certainly superfluous; and they are heading
toward a dangerous goal along the path of vice. For wealth is mortal, and often grows through fraud and injustice; when it exceeds
the bounds of necessity, it soon begins approaching a danger point.

I do not know what can be more effectively and briefly said than
what Cicero said. "I do not understand the point of avarice in old
age," he says. "For can anything be more absurd than to seek more
money for travel, the less that remains of the journey" [Sen. 66]?
And, of course, that saying of Seneca that we do not need much,
nor for long; while true at any age, this is most true in old age. Yet,
since we seek not a reason for this evil (for there is none for vice),
but its cause, I would perhaps not call silly what Aristotle writes in
the Rhetoric. Discussing the character of the young and the old, he
called the former magnanimous, adding as the reason that they have
not yet been humbled by life, but are untried by necessities; he
called the latter pusillanimous for the opposite reason, namely, that
they have been humbled by life, and know likewise through experience that it is difficult to grab onto money and easy to lose. While
such reasoning perhaps makes fussy parsimony in an old man
somehow less culpable because of his recollection of need and
hardship, it surely does not excuse that obsessive and burning
covetousness, born of despair and, I believe, of senile fear that
makes him dread lacking everything, when nothing is closer to

running out than life, for which those things are being saved or sought.

What sharper, what weightier accusation against rich people's greed than what Flaccus says:

> Let there at last be no more money-making,
> And since you have more, fear poverty less.
> Begin to quit your toils, now that you've got
> What you were after. [*Sat.* 1.1.92–94]

But different causes of this evil too will perhaps present themselves to different people. Seneca wrote the cause of this that seemed to him most true; I have added another that seemed probable to me. I have considered it superfluous to repeat them because they were [treated] in another place. Anyhow, the one root of this evil is that those who have more, need more, if we believe the philosophers and experience, and what Flaccus likewise says: "Those who seek much, lack much" [*Carm.* 3.16.42–43]. This proves, when you examine it further, the insatiable appetite of the human heart which strives so eagerly, after so much experience, for its own poverty and failure, being certain that it will never be more in need than when it owns a lot.

There remains to say something about the avarice of kings, which is the most unworthy of all. For what, I ask, is more grotesque than a man who is thirsty and parched amidst springs? But such is the avaricious king whose riches were not earned, nor did they have to be, since they were inherited from his family, and will be replenished as often as they are dispersed. To have such a fortune, then, and to be thirsty, alarmed, and worried about money is the ultimate, most desperate misery. In what is known as Aristotle's *Secrets*, we find a threefold distinction concerning this royal disease—to call it by its right name. One kind of king is niggardly toward himself and his subjects: why the Indians have called him a good king, I do not know. Another is niggardly toward himself and lavish toward his subjects: the Italians have called this the least dishonest king; unless I am wrong, that is because avarice toward others cannot avoid being damnable, whereas toward oneself it can even be praiseworthy, and, as it were, a kind of moderation, although in that case, it loses the name of avarice and is more fairly called frugality. Although this may seem contrary to magnanimity, it is allied to temperance. For, according to Seneca, it is voluntary poverty, an honorable state especially for us, since our God loved, praised, and demonstrated it. Nor is it unhonored among the pagans, since Flaccus says:

> The more each one denies himself
> The more he will get from the gods. [*Carm.* 3.26.21-22]

This, I think, moved the Italians not to reprove the king who indulges his subjects greatly but denies himself, although there are some who disagree with both sides and define as worthless the king who is not lavish toward himself and his subjects. But another kind of king is niggardly toward his subjects but lavish toward himself. No one would deny that this is the worst of all. But today nearly all are like that. And so, what follows in that same work is fitting. A reputation for avarice is most unseemly for a king and most unbecoming the royal majesty; today it has almost become the nature of royalty, and avarice is considered a certain part and a special ornament of royal majesty. In fact, the greater the rulers, the more they think it permissible for themselves, and hide an ugly vice under the beautiful veil of royal foresight! This is, by heavens, the glory of our kings, this their majesty!

But let there be some limit upon our talking, although there is none upon their amassing and hoarding riches. You have, then, my thoughts about the various kinds of avarice among men. You are neither old nor too rich, nor a king. On the other hand, you are certainly not a lad, nor a poor man, nor a servant, but in the middle state from which to observe more freely the ugliness of the extremes, and to laugh at those whom either age or riches or sovereignty casts into guilt, from whose dishonor you may understand your own honor. Do not listen, I beg you, to folk wisdom or to its spokesman installed in your house. If you have more trust in me, and I deserve it, lend an ear, and not so much to me but to the wise Ecclesiasticus who says, "There is nothing more shameful than a greedy man. Why are you proud, O dirt and ash? There is nothing more foul than to love money, for such a man has his soul for sale" [Ecclesiasticus 10:9-10]. So that you may know this not more truly but more fully expressed, in *De officiis* our Cicero says about shaping our life: "There is nothing more typical of a small, narrow mind than to love riches, nothing more honorable and more splendid than to despise money if you do not have any, and if you do, to bestow it liberally for the welfare of others" [*Off.* 1.68]. There you hear then, how either to use or to despise money. And to turn once more to sacred writers, see how they all agree on this truth; it is written in the psalm, "Do not hope in iniquity, and do not lust for plunder" [Ps. 62:11]. But lest you perhaps believe that riches willingly offered to you must be refused, rather than you must rid yourself of greed, it continues, "if riches stream upon you, do not devote your heart to them." What he urges upon everyone, your own mind has long since persuaded you to do; just don't let your teacher dissuade you. Farewell.

[No date or place assigned by Wilkins].

Sen. VI, 8.

Once again, on avarice, * as it is cultivated by the talents of many [addressee unstated].*

Is it any wonder if the realm of avarice extends far and wide—if gold is preferred to all things? Not only the greed of the multitude, but even writers of talent, the greatest men, seem to have conspired in its praises, calling golden everything that they set about praising. For who, I ask, would not think something great that he hears is the primary, almost the only decoration of every divine and human ritual, the only and the unending epithet of all things that are praiseworthy, desirable, wonderful?

That certain something, whatever it was, was great and desirable, a challenge for heroes to struggle toward fulfillment or to risk the seas on a crude ship, something untried until that day, of doubtful outcome; they called it the Golden Fleece, as though nothing else were worthy of being sought with so much danger, so vast a sea, so many savage shores, through icy and stormy winds, through unknown, troubled waters, amidst reefs that menaced not only the prow but overwhelmed the stern all the way to the Colchians and the Phasis, grim names at that time, as if the quest were in another world, confronting the vigilance of the sleepless dragon, flame-spewing oxen, and earth-born enemies, but invoking the aid of the magic arts.

If the emperor Nero wanted his famous house to be called golden—it occupied such a large part of the city that it was justifiably said of it,

> Rome will be one house. Move to Veii, Romans,
> Unless that house spreads over Veii too [Suet., *Nero* 39.2]

— I am not surprised because the incalculable expenses and the walls, encrusted with gold and studded with gems, deserved that name. It is surprising that the churches of George the Martyr in Rome and of the Apostle Peter in Pavia have epithets—the former, of the golden veil, the latter, of the golden ceiling—since saintly Ambrose, a neighbor of the Pavians, showed that a ceiling made of gold or entirely of bronze, which was no use against sun or rain or

---

* See VI, 7.

dew, was cursed in the holy books, but his authority did not prevail with the inventors of that golden epithet.

On the western side of Rome near the Vatican there is a hill, in olden times the site of a temple to Apollo, now the first and greatest See of Peter, and another hill in Verona on its eastern side, not far from the walls: each is called "Golden Mount" to lend it nobility. And the most ancient of ages they celebrate with the highest praises, not undeservedly so in my opinion. When compared to the following ages, it will be found ignorant of greed and friendly to innocence. But to summarize all its praises in one word, why did they call it the Golden Age? We know that even the king of that age was called golden by Virgil: "Then golden Saturn spent his life on earth" [G. 2.538]. And the same writer, in describing hair and distinctive clothing, called them golden locks or golden vestments, and adorned milk-white necks with golden chains or golden words. Not only people but horses have the same adornment:

> and the steed stands
> Matchless in purple and gold, [Aen. 4.135–36]

and elsewhere,

> Circlets of gold hang downward from their breasts;
> Covered with gold, they champ gold in their teeth.
> [Aen. 7.278–79]

So it is less surprising if he made the queen's attire golden as in that most famous entrance by Dido:

> Her quiver of gold, her hair in a golden knot,
> A golden clasp binds up her purple robe.
> [Aen. 4.139–40]

What of Penthesilea, "tying a golden girdle under her bare breast" [Aen. 1.492]? What of Camilla?

> How royal grandeur
> Covers her smooth shoulders with purple, how
> A clasp of gold binds up her hair. [Aen. 7. 814–16]

What of the dress of the warrior-priest [Chloreus] for whom she perished when her desire was thwarted?

A golden bow hangs from the shoulders, and
The prophet's helm is gold; his saffron mantle
And rustling linen folds he'd gathered up
With tawny golden buckle. [*Aen.* 11.773–76]

Or those accouterments for the boys' games?

> above the chest a pliant
> Necklace of twisted gold around the neck.
> [*Aen.* 5.558–59]

But why do I speak of the golden attire that is worn by many
indeed? When the same writer in one passage wished to call Dido
herself and, in another passage, Circe beautiful, he called each
golden, just as I noted above that Saturn was called golden rather
than a just and good king, as though any grace of body and mind
could only be understood as golden. I shall not say "engraved in
gold / The fathers' mighty deeds" [*Aen.* 1.640–41], and "a cloak stiff
with golden emblems" [1.648], and "a pearl / Necklace, and double
crown of jewels and gold" [1.654–55], and "smooth greaves of
amber and refined gold" [8.624]. I shall not mention the chalice
"heavy with jewels and gold" [1.728–29], "and mixing-bowls of solid
gold" [2.765], and Bitias "sopping himself from a full golden cup"
[1.739], and "Iopas strumming / His gilded lyre" [1.740], and "to
the victor a gilded mantle" [5.250], and "A smooth-linked corselet,
triple-meshed with gold" [5.259], and "The shirt his mother had
woven with soft gold" [10.818], and

> the gifts that opulent Dido
> Had made—the cloth was woven through with gold,
> [4.263–64]

or

> the huge weight of the belt,
> Which Clonus, Eurytus' son, had coated with much gold.
> [10.496,499]

Over these, I say, I shall pass, and over many similar passages that
appear everywhere in Virgil. Nor shall I search in Statius in the bedrooms of Adrastus for "mattresses embroidered in purple, resounding with gold" [*Theb.* 1.517], and "chains from the gilded lamps"

[1.521], and at his table "a bowl complete with figures and gleaming with gold" [1.540], and the winged [horse] of gold, hovering in armor, and the pale face of the beheaded Gorgon in gold [1.544-47], or "gold overflowing onto embroidered dresses" [6.208]. And along the same lines, endless verses by countless others; for they are very popular, and the use of gold has almost become everyone's commonplace to describe arms, clothing, beds, lyres, vases, and buckles. But what about the "fretted golden ceilings" [Aen. 1.726] of the royal palace of Carthage, newly built? What of the gilded beams of Troy, tumbling down? Or finally, what is more famous than "The doorposts proud in their barbaric gold and spoils" [Aen. 2.504]? It is not enough that man be clothed in gold; but beams and doors—and as I shall shortly show— floors and stones are also coated with gold.

What about the the dwelling of Alcinous, king of the Phaeacians in Homer whose threshold was bronze, the door-frame silver and the doors gold, and gold the handles that opened them, and gold and silver the mastiffs sculpted so marvelously by Vulcan to guard the palace, located on either side of the opulent entrance? It is not enough for the house to be of gold, unless its guardians are also of gold, and gold the statues of youths serving as chandeliers inside. Who would not admit that live men desired gold even in the age of Homer, which antedated the founding of Rome, when in that same author Tiresias stands out in the Underworld with his golden scepter, and Minos, holding a golden scepter, judges the dead, and golden too are the thongs or the bow or the sword of Hercules' shade, which he has put in the Underworld—strange to say, since he places Hercules himself with the gods above?

If all these things are read or seen with respect to human dwellings, who can be surprised to read in Naso, that

> The palace of the sun stood high on lofty
> Columns, ablaze with glittering gold [Met. 2.1-2]?

And that Phoebus's chariot had

> A golden axle, golden beam, and golden
> Rims on its wheels [2.107-8]?

And in Virgil not only the chariot or the palace, but the sun himself is called golden [G. 1.217], as I myself—not to mention others—have done; let me not exclude myself from this stylistic weakness. And the sister of the sun, is also called "golden Phoebe" [G. 1.431] by

Virgil and others; I wonder whether she would not better be called gilded since the golden light that covers her is indirect. In Virgil himself the stars more than once are called golden; or better it is Taurus, the sun's host, who opens the year with his gilded horns. And golden he calls the reins of Mars, so that I am less surprised if poets make Cupid's weapon, with which he inflicts the wounds of love, gilded in order to ennoble it.

That Homeric chain stretching from heaven to earth, which explains either the link between the elements or something greater and mysterious is not of air or of fire, but of gold, and rises into the heavens from everywhere with its heavy gold. Hence when Homer wanted to call Venus beautiful, he called her golden, and he gave Diana a golden throne, and to their mother a golden robe, a golden whip, and horses with golden manes. And to avoid any brotherly envy he also clothes Neptune with exactly the same attire; and in Homer too Juno promises Sleep a golden throne. Diana's neck is described twice as golden, befitting a huntress; but logic would call for the head to be golden rather than the neck, which should be milk-white, unless Homer is convinced that nothing in nature is more beautiful than gold, and consequently gives Diana not only a golden throne and neck, as we have said, but a golden distaff as well. Helen's distaff is also of gold and her basket of silver, although it would, no doubt, have been more fitting for the basket to be of wicker and the distaff of reeds. He also gives Circe a golden cup with which she transformed wretched mortals, and Juno golden slippers. But this is less surprising than the air's luminosity which prompted him to give Aurora a golden throne to the dawn as well. But the reason for all of these is the same, whence Fates award a golden robe to Olympian Jove, and a golden beard to Aesculapius, golden locks to his father, and gilded scales to his grandfather. They also give Mercury a golden wand, and weave golden sandals for him, even though one who flies needs feathers, not gold.

But they delight in making all that belongs to the gods golden, even the gods themselves. Thus, they wish the ones they worship, on whom they pin their hopes, to be only of gold (as though the richer they are, the more inclined to bestow favors); they change their old garments and say with Persius: "Let them be foremost, and their beards of gold" [2.58]; and what follows is true,

Gold drove out Numa's jars and Saturn's bronze,
Replacing Vestal urns and Tuscan pott'ry. [2.59-60]

Nor is the same Persius heard crying out amidst such things, "Say, priests, what's gold doing on holy ground" [2.69]? I grieve that this pagan custom has been adoped by our people against the teaching of God who says, "Make not gods of gold for yourselves" [Exod. 20:23]. Certainly that golden divinity, so to speak, has not turned out happily for either people. Thus Seneca testifies that for them the gods were so much more propitious when they were of clay; and there is not a devout person anywhere who does not know that Christ, our God, was more present to us before we sculpted golden images for Him, since He delights in a pure faith and a devout spirit, not in gold. Furthermore, not only do they receive friends with golden pomp, but enemies as well, whom they treat with respectful cruelty and bind with golden shackles, so that vain ostentation descends even to the extremes of human misery. That wicked traitor, Bessus, did this to Darius, the Persian king. In the same kingdom, King Artaxerxes had previously done it to his brother Cyrus. And long afterward, the victorious Aurelian did the same to Zenobia, that spirited and warlike woman who was led in triumph laden with gold and gems, patient about the chains but often complaining about the precious weight.

What is surprising about gold shining in captivity and in chains, when it glitters even in death, in biers, in tombs? It is the one luxury for every occasion, constant and not only lifelong but outlasting the lifetime of men. In addition, those who would praise outstanding cities with equal brevity call them golden, whence in Maro the Capitol of the city of Rome is golden [*Aen.* 8.347–48], while in Ausonius Rome is golden. Having stumbled into this torrent of ostentatious expression, beside the other lapses, I too who have been censuring this in others, do not acquit myself, however I accuse others; in a certain passage in my *Africa* I called Rome golden, although it was never said so wrongly as in our age, since, alas, it is not gold but a wreck; but I looked at the period about which I was then speaking. What I did not know at the time I wrote was that the reverse of a gold seal of our present Caesar [Charles IV] has Rome on whose gates is written in golden letters "golden Rome," as though Rome were not rather revealed to be of iron and Babylon of gold, both by King Nebuchadnezzar's dream and by the Roman victories and her poverty rich in virtues!

But gold is so close to the heart that they think nothing is praised to the full unless its epithet is gold. I suppose that if they wished to praise poverty they would call it nothing less than golden, and what I surmise in others I know I did myself, for I recall that in a certain letter I wrote "golden want." In fact, wishing to praise abundance and to call moderation the best thing, Flaccus calls both of them golden. Finally, the formula that determines the order of the year and the feast days is called the golden number by our writers to make it seem most beneficial. In short, you will note that in heaven and on earth almost everything is golden. We fall back to the fable of Midas.

But perhaps someone will say that these things are profane, drawn from the books of the pagans. Let my pen then go on to the sacred writers, lest anyone be shocked that pagan writers call Rome golden when, according to the Bible, the towers in Jerusalem are built with gems, the gates gleam with pearls, and the streets and walls are of the purest gold. Let us not linger on this nor on the fact that Jerome, in expressing the highest praise of Cicero's felicity, called it a golden river of eloquence, which Cicero himself had already said of Aristotle, or that the most eloquent of Greek Christians [John Chrysostom] earned the surname Golden-mouthed, as though nothing more fitting could be found to describe the brilliance of his eloquence than to qualify it as golden. But let us hasten on to greater examples. For what should men do on earth, where gold is mined, purified, pounded, and guarded, when God Himself, in speaking to Moses from heaven, orders the Ark to be gilded for Him, and as though this were not enough, added, "with the purest gold inside and out" [Exod. 25:11]?

It would certainly be tedious to pursue all that the book of Exodus has to say on this as He commands there that the golden crown and rings, the bars covered with gold, the mercy seat and cherubim of gold, the gilded table, the encircling rim of gold, the bowls, censers, ladles, candlesticks, hooks, chains, rings and bell, all be made of the purest gold, and the altar itself gilded. What of the book of Numbers, even omitting the silver bottles and cups, does one not read there about the golden altar enveloped in a hyacinthine covering? And in the sanctifying of the Tabernacle and the altar, no offering from the princes of Israel is described without a golden pan so that all together there be as many pans as tribes.

And what of the trumpets of malleable silver which the Lord commands Moses to make in order to summon the people, as though those of brass were not more resonant than the silver ones? And what of Solomon, the builder of the temple, in the books of Kings and Chronicles? Did he not cover with gold the holiest shrine in all the world, as well as the structure in front of it and the altar itself, and fasten even the gold leaf with golden nails? And lastly we read that the floor of the building, both inside and out, was covered with gold, and—not to prolong this—it says, "There was nothing in the temple that was not covered with gold" [1 Kings 6:22]. Go a little beyond this and you will discover the altar not just gilded but golden, the table golden, the candlesticks golden, the lamps golden, the tongs golden, the forks, cups, pans, censers, and hinges golden. What shall I say about the two hundred shields and a like number of spears of gold, and the king's throne of ivory, overlaid with pure tawny gold? Finally, the footstool was of gold, and all the vessels and furniture of purest gold, to the point that in those days silver was considered of no value, as abundant in Jerusalem as stone or wood.

What then, since these are material things, what, I say, if Solomon himself says in Proverbs: "Acquire wisdom, for it is better than gold, and gain understanding, for it is more precious than silver" [Prov. 8:10]. And in the same book, "Blessed is he who has found wisdom and abounds in understanding. It is better to acquire these than to deal in silver and gold" [3:13–14]. And again, letting wisdom speak, he says, "My fruit is better than gold and precious stones, and my buds better than choice silver" [8:19]. You see how often he has repeated one and the same idea. Who therefore would not think gold and silver and precious stones are worth a lot when the wisest man compares wisdom to them? For although he says it is better, still he seems to have found nothing better than gold and silver over which he can prefer wisdom. What if the same man calls the word uttered at the right time golden apples on silver beds [25:11], as though he knew nothing more precious than gold and silver? Does he not also in the Canticles make the beloved's head and hands of gold, as if he could not make them of anything better?

What now remains except for us to have God Himself all of gold too? As I said, there are some who do not so much call Him golden as make Him so, out of zeal not so much for religion as for avarice, which makes a bid also for the divine and, having triumphed over mortals, tries to scale the heavens, if possible. Nor am I surprised if the son uses the father's style; he had heard the father say: "The judgments of the Lord are true, righteous in themselves, desirable above gold and precious stones" [Ps. 19:10–11]. And again, "The law from God's mouth is better than thousands in gold and silver" [Ps. 119:72]. Who could despise gold and gems when he reads about the holy martyrs, the most glorious and bravest of men, "upon their head He placed a golden crown with precious stones" [based on Ps. 21:4]? And what about Ecclesiasticus, where "the firm feet upon the soles of the faithful woman" are called "golden columns on silver bases" [26:23]? And did not David himself and Isaiah foresee that gold would be offered to Christ, and Matthew tells us that it was? What about the books of Maccabees, did they also not have their golden altar and vessels for libations, bowls and pans, and in the midst of enemy incursions did they not decorate the temple facade with golden crowns? And in those same books, did not Antiochus, in writing to Jonathan to give him the priestly and political power over four states, include golden dishes and grant him the privilege of drinking from golden vessels, and to having a golden buckle? Who would not consider great that which could not be used without royal permission? Furthermore, who would not consider real gold to be of great value while awake, when its value is enhanced in visions and dreams? There is no question that when Heliodorus, who was sent by King Seleucus to plunder the temple, was hastening to execute the command as the people wept and prayed, he held back, checked by a sudden, frightening vision of a horseman who came into view to defend the temple. And it goes on to say, "And he seemed to have weapons of gold" [2 Macc. 3:25]. This is surprising, as if the heavenly defender could not protect the holy place against man's wrongdoing except with golden arms.

When, after every [kind of] death, Jerusalem was overcome by civil and external evils, and agitated and poised on the brink of destruction for forty days, there appeared in the air flying horsemen and armed cohorts—how armed? With golden weapons, of course, and clothed in golden robes. Later on, when Judas Maccabeus was about to fight against Timotheus, he with his men put on goat's hair, sprinkled their heads with dirt, and prostrated themselves before the altar, imploring divine aid; when the battle had begun, five auxiliary horsemen appeared, decorated with golden reins, and with their aid they won a great victory. Afterward, when the same Judas, with a few men, was hastening against Lysias's huge army, they entreated the Lord with one voice, crying and weeping, to send them a good angel to save Israel; there appeared an armed horseman before them, and with what arms? Golden ones, of course. And his appearance so encouraged them that they all fought and won. Finally, when Judas himself was about to battle Nicanor, with a like disparity between the armies—because the enemy had countless troops whereas he had few—and was anxious about the outcome, he saw in his sleep the prophet Jeremiah handing him a sword, and what sword? Why, of gold. He said, "Take the holy sword, a gift from God, and with it you will overcome the adversaries of my people Israel" [2 Macc. 15:16]. When he related this dream to his men, they all felt encouraged and fought bravely. And it happened as it had been promised. The few overcame the many, and thirty-five thousand of the enemy were killed. Go ahead, despise gold, which is beautiful to see and praised by the Scriptures, and enhanced by visions and dreams. You hear that the gift of the Lord was of gold, and that the bravest man was delighted with a golden sword, although he used an iron one.

What of the book of the Apocalypse, full of sacred things and mysteries? Is not the angel of Philadelphia urged to buy gold, fired and purified, in order to become rich? Is it not there too that we find gold candlesticks and bowls and an angel standing before the golden altar, which is before the throne of God, holding in his hand a golden censer? Finally, do we not read not only about that Great Whore fornicating with kings, who is adorned with gold and precious stones and pearls and holds a golden cup in her hand (that she enjoys such things is not surprising!), but also about twenty-four elders seated in their places in the sight of God, with golden crowns on their heads, and about seven angels coming out of the temple of the Tabernacle of witness, girt with golden belts around their waists? And then at that point beyond which one cannot go, [do we not read] about the Son of Man, girt on his nipples with a golden belt,* and on his head a golden crown as he sits upon the clouds, and about the holy city and its streets, as it is written, "with gates of pure gold and foundations of precious stones" [1 Kings 7:10; 2 Chron. 3:4, 4:2]? Indeed it says not that it was built of gold but that the city and its streets were pure gold, while its dimensions, which will surprise you, are given in terms of golden reeds, as though it were wrong to measure gold with anything but gold.

There are a thousand such passages, and scarcely any corner of sacred writings that is devoid of gold. Some of them are so insignificant that I hate to mention them. For why cite either the mantles, woven of gold, that appear in that nocturnal apparition of the holy virgin Agnes and that bevy of virgins accompanying her, as though without gold there could be no happiness, even in heaven; or those golden crosses woven in the cloak of that noble, handsome elder who roused the blessed priest, Lucian, to find the body of the most blessed protomartyr Stephen, whereas the cross on which Christ hung and redeemed us was certainly not of gold but wood; we were

---

* P. has conflated Rev. 14:14 and 15:6, and writes *ad mamillas* instead of *circa pectora.*

undone by a tree and we have been redeemed by a tree, and it was not gold but blood that came forth in our redemption, although we were captives in the hands of the greediest enemy. What about the golden wand in the same elder's hand, with which he touched the sleeping man? Might he not have touched him either with his bare hand or with another wand, of maple or beech? But because this is the custom, we neither awaken nor sleep without gold, whence generally we see in the bedrooms of our wealthy people beds of gold. And as we have said, in Statius we read about them in Adrastus's bedroom and in Virgil in Dido's:

> The queen took her place in the midst, reclining
> On a golden couch beneath a splendid awning.
> [*Aen.* 1.697–98]

All this and the like, I would deem, is used in secular letters not because of the writers' conviction but the readers' misconception, condescending to their weaknesses; but in sacred writings I would not doubt that they are spoken with a loftier spiritual meaning, yet still this "golden" way of speaking everywhere, coming from the mouths of learned men, can perhaps, by a sort of authority, incite to a greater thirst for gold the greedy minds of the rabble. But whether we act from external or internal urgings—that is, whether by others' words and examples or by some innate greed—you see into what dangers or what folly the human race is driven by avarice.

I need not repeat how Midas starved amidst his gold, and how Tantalus was thirsty in water. The subject does not require any myths, true stories abound, although there is no need either for stories or for writers' testimony when every square, every street, every home swarms with examples. Who has not seen thousands of oaths forsworn out of avarice, of promises broken, friendships mocked, the rights of blood ignored, the fear of God laid aside, in short, right and wrong all mixed up—to bypass those outrages that are offensive to hear, ugly to see, but now common everywhere among those who sell their own flesh at a low price and wretched profit, or who prostitute their own chastity for others' lust, or sell their sisters, wives, and daughters like sheep. Of nearly all dissension there is no other cause but greed, which would be rare or nonexistent if, as the old proverb has it, the two pronouns, mine and yours, were removed from our midst. But since this is not the case, we see this brief and unhappy life seething with innumerable conflicts because of this reason most of all; and we hear Ovid in the preface of his great work proclaim, "They live by plunder" [*Met.* 1.144]. Behold plunder and greed, the root of evils. But if you want to know the branches, listen to the rest:

No guest is safe from host, nor father-in-law
From son-in-law. Kindness twixt brothers too
Is rare. A man is bent on his wife's death,
And she on his. Dread stepmothers mix ghastly
Aconite. Sons seek in advance to know
How soon father will die. [1.144–48]

And to gather all into one phrase, he adds: "Family love lies conquered." It is conquered just because greed is the conqueror. The entire gamut of evil—cheating, plundering, murder, false witness, impiety, discord, foulness, adultery, corruption—all are encompassed more briefly by Maro who says, questioning and exclaiming:

To what do you not drive the human heart,
O curs'd hunger for gold? [*Aen.*3.57–58]

In fact, there is no evil that is not suggested, coaxed, and ultimately compelled by that hunger for gold about which we have said so much today, whose yellowish pallor so delights the eyes and, what is worse, the mind itself. This did not escape the Apostle either, when he said that the root of all evil is greed. "Some, seeking it," he says, "have wandered from the faith and brought upon themselves many griefs." For, to cite his words, "Those who want to grow rich fall into temptation and into the devil's snare, and the many useless and harmful desires that plunge men to death and perdition" [1 Tim 6:9–10]. And while you may see this in everyone, it is especially so in those who wish to become wealthy in a hurry. This is characteristic of nearly all of them, according to the Satirist:

Whoever wants to get rich
Wants to get rich quick. [Juv. 14.176–77]

But, who will put a rein upon headlong avarice? As the Satirist likewise says:

Whate'er respect for law, what fear
Or shame in greedy men rushing toward lucre?
[14.177–78]

If you do not believe Paul, that many evil desires plunge men to destruction, question Crassus. After he despoiled the very wealthy temple in Jerusalem (which the great Pompey, the most restrained of generals, had left untouched), Crassus, loaded with gold but not yet satisfied, still thirsting and longing for more and driven by the madness of his avarice, hastened to his death, to Parthia; only there was the wretch to find his fill, longed-for but deadly. In his way was a treaty ratified by a colleague of his; in his way were justice, shame, and ultimately divine wrath full of threats, full of terrifying thunderbolts. A monstrous storm like the one that by itself had once kept Hannibal from the enemy's walls did not keep Crassus, even with so many other hindrances, from the territory of friends or, at any rate, of people at peace with Rome. It was only his hunger, or more truly his thirst for gold that spurred his wretched, raging spirit to act against honor and shame, against a very vivid fear. For he was going not to eat but to drink gold, and only a single goad—his avarice, more powerful than hatred and cruelty—prevailed over so many checks. But whence came this madness? Like any other madness, from wrong-headed opinions. It was correctly seen by Cicero, I believe, as the source of all evil. For if anyone were to judge absolutely right, I think that he would act rightly too. A tainted opinion is the root and hotbed that taints actions.

But if one asks what was that opinion, it was that no amount of wealth suffices for the man who would be head of state, unless its income can feed an army, as *De officiis* mentions. Thus the greed of a Roman citizen was grasping at something that was hard for the Roman people, even though it had conquered the world. This was the hook that dragged him, the wealthiest of all Romans—who wished to become the wealthiest of all mortals, yet was never able to be anything but needy and poor in that mental state, even if he had heaped up all the wealth existing anywhere in the world. This is what dragged him not only to seize dishonestly an inheritance conveyed by a false will and, as Cicero jokingly says, not to turn down the trifling rewards of another's crime which he meshed with his own, but also to strip a very sacred temple of God of all its gold by the most blatant kind of plundering, and strip himself first of any faith and justice; but finally he went to strip the richest king, who stripped him of his life; and when he was drained of the breath of life, he filled him up with molten, reddish gold. A worthy end, I confess, to such great avarice, but on the other hand, the wreck of so great an army and a wretched, unworthy fate for his innocent son. But often one man's madness has crushed great numbers.

However, I have lingered too long on Crassus about whom I never suspected it would occur to me to say so much; but I was carried away by impulse, I was carried away by my abhorrence of avarice. I come to others lest Crassus be the only one in this letter—how I wish he were unique among men!

Since there is no counting those who suffer from this plague, I shall deal with them as a whole. Surely the power of avarice was never more clearly seen than in the war with Jugurtha. Well known is the story: that until Metellus there was no consul, no soldier in the Roman army who was not a slave of avarice. It was this that made the treacherous king, who distrusted his forces, equal and often superior in arms, although finally an end worthy of his crimes and his character caught up with him. Who does not know the names of Calpurnius or Scaurus in that war? About the first, Crispus says most eloquently, "For there were many good traits in our consul of mind and body, all of which were thwarted by avarice" [*Jug.* 28]. Who has not heard of the incredibly shameless avarice of the commanders and the entire army? But perhaps this same plague raged more moderately in the destruction of Jerusalem, where not only justice was cast under the feet of avarice but a sense of shame and humaneness were trampled upon and those crimes committed that make the memory shudder and the pen shrink.

But where am I hastening? I must encompass the entire world, unravel every age, reread all history, if I want to catalogue the examples of avarice. I must recall Eriphyle, who forgot her conjugal vows through her craving for gold; I must conduct the funeral of Polydorus once again, transform the paramour into a shower of gold,* follow with laughter and hatred that infamous miser—the vendor of a mouse, the purchaser of death—who was driven to the extremes of starvation in the siege of Casilinum. In order to hide in his terribly greedy bosom a bit of money (the price, however enormous, of that unhappy meal), that trifling creature wasted his life and disgraced his remarkable endurance and honesty because of his shameful avarice. Furthermore, I must go from door to door throughout the cities, and ask what kinds of evil or vices wretched avarice has brought into each home—an endless task! Finally I must review the three whom Valerius mentions together: Cassius, Septimuleius, and Ptolemy. The first, for an agreed price, released the assassins who had been sent to kill him with swords—a beautiful act indeed, had it

---

* P. has confused the myths of Danae and Leda.

been done at the behest of clemency and not avarice. The second had been a friend of Gracchus; but when Gracchus was killed, he cut off his head and carried it through the city on a spear; and they even report that he put molten lead in the hollow of the skull to make it heavier, since forsooth the consul had proclaimed that he would pay its weight in gold. However deserving of death Gracchus was, the greed of Septimuleius was horrid and disgraceful.

The third was a king of Cyprus, who saw imminent danger to his life because of the amount of his wealth; and he decided, when he and his riches were doomed, to snatch himself from mockery and the spoil from his enemies. He set out to sea with the intention of sinking the ship there and burying everything in the waves. But when it came to executing his brilliant plan, his greedy mind was dazzled by the gold; and to save his riches, he did not carry out what he had intended, but changed his mind and returned to land, bringing back to his assassins his throat and the payment for killing him. The avarice of the other two was detestable and hateful, but his was foolish and ridiculous. To use Valerius's very words, "Beyond any doubt he did not own his riches, but was owned by them" [V. Max. 9.4.ext.1]. This agrees with the Davidic sentiment that says, "They slept their sleep, and all the men of wealth found nothing in their hands" [Ps. 76:6]. You hear how emphatically and sarcastically he said not "the wealth of men" but "men of wealth." But let there be some limit to this letter. You be the master, not the slave, of your riches, and as long as you can still find something in your hands, wake up when you have been called three times. Farewell in the Lord.

[No date or place assigned by Wilkins].

Sen. VI, 9.

To Philippe [de Cabassoles], Patriarch of Jerusalem, * that praise on any subject whatsoever is suspect.*

Just as ungrateful pride belittles huge favors with words, so humble gratitude strives to increase even the smallest gift. Thus, my little book, *De uita solitaria*—which, as I have often said, contains in my judgment nothing worth mentioning, nothing noteworthy except your name, and which, furthermore, even if it were most noteworthy, might have been unwelcome by the excessive delay, the nuisance of keeping after me, and the annoyance of waiting for it—you have received with such high praise and thanks that I am compelled to marvel at your kindness, though I know it well, and at the constant, ever fresh, daily renewed strength of your old love which lets you glance at everything of mine indulgently, whereas you have a lynx's eye for everything else. What adds to my amazement was your news that the Supreme Pontiff [Urban V] and the Bishop of Porto [Gui de Boulogne], who ranks next to him, are speaking of the little book and request it with esteem, and the Archbishop of Yverdon [Pierre d'Ameil] and the Bishop of Lisbon [Pedro Gomez Barroso] as well. You quite rightfully make me vouch for how clever the first man is, since I do know him; the second I know only by reputation and your letter, but I take your word for everything. You write that both are men of the richest learning and soundest judgment, and that they read my work with great eagerness and vied with each other to say many flattering things about it. What can I say? You and they will even make me start cherishing something of mine that I despised, for learning that it has pleased such minds, I become more ready with this encouragement to continue my studies and more on fire to write other book.

Nor will you be surprised that the same thing could happen to me as to Augustine, who recalls in the *Confessions* a certain book that he had written for the orator Hierius of Rome, saying: "It was very important to me that my book and my studies be known to that man, and if he approved of them I would be more ablaze, but if he did not, my vain heart, empty of your strength, O God, would be wounded" [4.14(23)]. I am not, however, so deceived by your praises that I do not know who I am, what my capabilities are, and what is

---

* See VI, 5.

the merit of the book you praise. I know myself, and attribute everything you say not to my merits nor certainly to your judgment, but to your love. Therefore, I do not stop here as though I were planning for you something great as you keep saying it is destined to be; but I am thinking about what further payment I can now add that is worthy even of you, and would compensate for such a long delay. Farewell.

Pavia, August 8 [1366].

Sen. VII, 1.

To Urban V,* how the return of the Church to its own See, too long delayed, must be delayed no longer.

For some time, most blessed Father, I was doubtful whether to write to you or what to write. I was prompted on the one hand by the talk that is circulating, on the other by letters from friends, telling many splendid things about you, especially from the one who out of so many friends has now remained nearly my only solace, for a long time far out of sight but always present in my mind, Philippe [de Cabassoles], Patriarch of Jerusalem. Not to let me, absorbed in antiquity, overlook the present, and at the same time to offer my pen a rich and noble subject to write about, lately he has often written me enthusiastic letters all about you, laden with wonderful praises for your character and about the holiness of your apostolic endeavors. Thereby, I confess, he forcefully kindled my weary and languishing spirit. Another old stimulus also came into play, namely, I am in the habit of writing to the great and the humble not only with equal frankness, but the greater the personages I address, the more eager I always am to write, since from them I hope for more favor for whatever I say well, and more willingness to forgive short-comings. It is well known that just as petty, envious minds not only become uncontrollably angry at others' shortcomings, but also clamor maliciously against their praises, so serene, upright minds applaud the praises and feel sorry for their shortcomings. That is why I have been convinced, nor will I change my mind, that he who speaks in good faith can be charged with error but not villainy, and perhaps deserves rebuke but not punishment or hatred.

This belief and this hope impelled me to write to your predecessors, the two Roman Pontiffs before the last one, as well as to the Roman Emperor and to princes and kings of the world, even though often unknown to me. Nor have I feared that their greatness

---

* Guillaume Grimoard, Abbot of a Benedictine monastery in Marseille, was elected pope in 1362 to succeed Innocent VI. P. welcomed his election for several reasons: he was known as a man of exemplary personal character and had never been a cardinal; the election of a mere abbot to the papacy seemed divinely inspired; he had personal knowledge of Italy, having served as papal legate in Naples; and his choice of the name Urban suggested that he considered Rome his proper see. Less than one year after receiving this letter Urban did move the papacy to Rome, though only briefly.

would crush my insignificance. For I did not compare myself to my superiors, nor in words did I put myself on a level with those whom Mother Nature or Fortune had separated from me by so great a distance, but I believed that to use the spirit of freedom in the service of truth was not only allowed, but a duty. Nor did I feel somehow that I myself was speaking, but rather my loyalty, my devotion, my love of country. Therefore, while still in my teens, I wrote to Benedict XII, and in my middle twenties, to Clement VI. Why then would I not write to you in my old age? Youth has, I admit, fervor and daring; but old age has more authority and gravity too—and what some would call amazing, more nonchalance. Hence that reply of Solon's has become very famous: when asked by Pisistratus, the tyrant of Athens, how he had the nerve to stand up to him so steadfastly, he answered, "Because of my old age" [Cic., *Sen.* 20]. Then there is that saying of Marcus Castricius, with different words but the same idea; when the angry [Cn. Papirius] Carbo, consul in name but tyrant in reality, said threateningly that he had many swords, he replied, "And I have many years" [V. Max. 6.2.10]. How pithily, how concisely he contrasted years and swords, as though a man of advanced years could not be hurt even by swords. And in truth what should he fear whose life—for the sake of which people fear everything—is behind him; or what can be taken away from that man who has received all he had coming and put it in safe keeping? A storm does no harm to the sailor who has already entered port, nor hail to the farmer who has his barns full. The ending is usually untroubled, whereas the beginning is worrisome, and generally having one's fill of life means great calmness of spirit. However, my confidence in you, the pinnacle of the Church, originates not from my age but your goodness. For I hear that you willingly listen to the truth, though it be bitter, and scorn falsehood, though it be sweet; nor is that surprising since you are the vicar of the living truth on earth. If you love your Lord, you must love what is His or what is from Him. Augustine says that all that is true is so because it comes from the Truth.

Such being the case, I shall explain what has kept me silent until now; perhaps it will surprise you. Everyone who spoke or wrote to me about you, and especially that great herald of your deeds, the Patriarch, had nothing but the very highest praises for you: how holy was your spirit, how alert your mind, how devout your intentions, how enthusiastic your study of literature, what a memory for things past, what foresight for things to come, how lofty and brilliant your intellect, how sweet and overflowing your eloquence, what love for good people, what hatred of evil ones, what dedication to justice, what religious discipline. Everything that reached my ears or my eyes, from the tongue or pen of friends, was full of this and the like. In the midst of all this I was still hesitant. I knew of course that generous minds are aroused to virtue by true and sincere praises, just as fine horses are to the race by spurs which, while not necessary, are often applied with good effect even to the most energetic horses, and add a burst of speed to their natural fleetness. I was glad to have found the occasion for my lowliness to rise to such a lofty style of communication, and I was delighted to say something about such a broad and happy matter. There was only one obstacle to all this; that the praise of the greatest men, however true and sincere, scarcely ever emerges from the mouths of the humble without some suspicion of being mere flattery.

To hide nothing from you, there was another reason for my silence. I am, I admit, a great observer of outstanding men on whose acts and example depends, I believe, the common weal. I therefore kept observing you, and since you had made such a laudable beginning in little things, I anticipated what you would be in the biggest ones. I heard that you had sent back to their dioceses those prelates who flocked to the Curia, and I say fine, well done. What, I ask, is more absurd and likely to lead to a shipwreck than sailors who, having cast aside all their oars and ropes and abandoned the prow of the ship and fled from the sides, crowd the stern and weigh it down, sneak around the pilot when he is not looking, and, having deserted their post, try to take over his job? I heard how you put a halt to the old evil of self-promotion that had enormously increased because of the tolerance of those who preceded you; you ruled that each should be satisfied with one benefice or with a few, if deserved, for virtue or knowledge. That is fair, I say, and worthy. For what is uglier than to behold someone vomiting the surfeit of what he has gained perhaps by foul intrigues, while on all sides many better men struggle with penury and hunger?

I heard how you devote great care and attention on the correctness of your attire. That I praised. For what eye can bear this mockery that our unhappy age has fashioned for itself when it tries to look attractive by deforming and disgracing itself most shamefully by its own hand? What stomach is not upset by the sight of these monstrosities: horned shoes, plumed hats, pony-tail hair curled to a crisp, men's brows furrowed in female fashion with an ivory bodkin, indecent dress that allows no modesty, midriffs tightly bound and crushed with cords, so that the wretches suffer for vanity what the blessed in the past suffered for truth. Add to these the conceited young people with their backs out of kilter, their drooping faces and stooped shoulders, and the bowels shoved toward the cavity of the chest—one thing that I know not whether posterity will believe; our forefathers certainly would not, were they to hear it. We behold all this with our eyes, and beyond this, anything else foul, shocking, savage, silly, that an unsettled mind, clever to its own dishonor, has either learned or invented. While they are ugly to see everywhere, they are ugliest in your presence, and hateful to all honest, well-disciplined minds. You, apostolic censor of morals, ought especially, through edicts and laws, to crack down and put an end to them; in part you have done so already, as it is reported. Oh, I wish that you could and would have done the same thing in all the world, or at least in Italy where I bear these follies all the more sadly because they clash with our inherited customs and with the gravity of the nation of the toga; and they are sinking to the point where being blind sometimes seems to me enviable, being free from these sights.

I heard furthermore about your unusual concern and paternal anxiety about the University of Bologna, greater than any other pontiff or prince had ever had; with what great privileges, what magnificence, what devotion you are rebuilding it after it was ruined and leveled by the long, unending storms of war. And not only do you restore its former dignity to it, but, if luck is with you, you are even expanding it. This too I considered worthy of you; you owed it to yourself. For who else would help and reform that city which is the mother and nurse of all studies, but especially of law, than the man held to be most skilled in both canon and civil law, indeed the sole source and interpreter of the former? Or who else but you either would or could shoulder this collapsed edifice of learning? In this, if you do not realize it, you have done somewhat more than you appeared to, inasmuch as you have instilled great hope in all of us that you do not forget Italy since you honor one of its cities with such great kindness and favor. Finally, I heard how you, with the wholesome scythe of the most just severity, cut short a pestilential abuse. I mean the one that spared from the clutches of the law and from deserved punishment the guilty men who had perpetrated the most heinous crimes, but who took to fleeing to the homes of cardinals. This too I judged worthy of particular praise, peculiarly yours: that by you, the Vicar of Him who is the true Sun of Justice, justice has been defended and restored to its rights, and that a terrible custom, which more than any other was ruinous to virtue, was cut off or uprooted by your hands. No longer can one find, as there once was, a refuge for injustice and a sanctuary for wickedness in the homes of the model teachers of justice.

Hearing many such things about you, and happy over what I heard and with a natural bent to use my pen, I still hesitated; being uncertain as I awaited the outcome of the event, I still chose silence although it was difficult, for I feared that it might happen to me, in dealing with the greatest of men, as I recalled it had in dealing with great ones, namely, that I would exalt the one whom I would have to rebuke at some time when the truth forced me. And, as happens to inexperienced purchasers of horses when they check them, being pleased by their short ears and eyes and attractive appearance, they fail to examine the firmness of their hooves and the sturdiness of their shins and back. And while gaping at their beauty, they pay no attention to their strength—whether the animal, handsome at first sight, is adequate for work, suitable for war, fit for a long trip, ready for racing or leaping. The same I feared could happen to me in writing your praises, so that after commending you for lesser things, I would be disappointed in great ones, and thus chagrined I would have no one to blame but myself for changing my mind. Inconstancy is indeed natural in a child, but ridiculous in an old man. It is disgraceful for an old man to say something that he is soon going to contradict.

These thoughts stopped me, eager as I was to speak and write. I reflected that there are some men nimble and expert in a number of small things to the point of astonishing the onlookers, but should you pin them down on one paramount essential, you would say there is no one more uncouth, more disappointing, and more clumsy, so that those who appear to be great and to know everything suddenly are nothing, and know absolutely nothing. Very often I have noticed men who come out with wonderful bits about the sciences, the arts, and the deeds of men in detail, but tell them to say something extended, to do something complete—for example, to set forth the secrets of that science or art in which they were showing off, or, better still, not to speak about the art but to do something with it, or even to write books or carry out some military or civic business, and they will fail in both ways, betraying their ignorance in speech, and their weakness or inexperience in action. We call such men dabblers, or still better, botchers; since they are ignorant of the essence of things, they make a show of certain odds and ends like those who, in that game the ancients called Robbers, know some traps and moves known as the odds, but not the rules of the game itself.

But those men are not to be considered great who, while very learned and very successful in whatever field, either neglect or do not know the ultimate purpose of their position. How, pray, can a man be considered a general, who though handsome and eloquent, knowing how to talk about arms and warfare, skilled in horsemanship and very strong, thoughtlessly leads his army, recklessly chooses a place for a camp, carelessly deploys the troops and posts the guards, and finally if defeated scarcely copes with the emergency, or if victorious knows not how to use his victory? For these are the skills of a general, those other things are ornaments; so without them he can be a fine general, but without these skills he cannot be a general at all. Give me a helmsman who is trim and strong, inured to hunger and strain, who can sing and speak sweetly, which relieves the boredom of the sea; if he cannot handle the tiller, turn the sails, keep the rowers in time, avoid reefs, escape storms, recognize shorelines, identify places, make for port, he can perhaps be called a sailor, but not a captain.

There are thousands of such examples. You know them all, and from these few you understand what to think about the rest. There are those whom nature or fortune, or to tell the truth, God himself, the Lord of nature and of fortune, has ordained for the highest rank. Among these, two are the loftiest of all, the Roman Pontiff and the Roman Emperor. To His Majesty who initially did not know me at all, but later became a close friend, I have often said and wrote things which to the best of my knowledge seemed to apply to him. He himself is my witness to the kinds of goads I so often used to rouse, encourage, incite, and reprove him. This perhaps was none of my business—except that things overlooked by my superiors and important to everyone, seemed better said by anyone at all than by nobody. Nevertheless, reckoning not my rank but my loyalty, I considered it permissible and worthy of me, to raise my voice in the midst of such a public disaster; even if it were to no avail for the danger to all, it would still soothe my own anguish and uneasiness. With no one taking upon himself this responsibility, I alone, the least of all men but not, I hope, the last in dedication, wailing and screaming since there was no other recourse, took the side of the deserted commonwealth; I was doing something either for my own grief, as I have said, or, if heaven would second my patriotic intention, for the public grief too. For often a single voice has come to the aid of the many; often it was not the source of the voice but the voice itself that moved minds and exercised its power unseen. Thus, not to linger over examples, a single random voice of a centurion steadied the Roman Empire when it was faltering; a single child's voice, heard among the people, made Ambrose bishop, an occurrence that brought peace to that city and deliverance to the churches of the Occident. That lofty Moderator of all things knows how to elicit even from a sinner's mouth a word that is good, penetrating, potent, effective. What more need I say? While everyone was silent, not to say mute, I considered that it was up to me either to rebuke or to exhort the Roman Emperor, as I believed that keeping silent was for me a sin and would not go without infamy. I therefore chose to have posterity accuse him rather than me, that is, his reluctance rather than my silence. But he, the mildest of princes, always accepted my reproaches so gladly, so gently,* so kindly, as others would accept the praises and blandishments of flatterers, and he expressed it with many respectful tokens in word and deed.

Up to now I have done this with that other light of the city of Rome and of the Roman world. But I have yet done nothing with you, fearing, as I have said, to praise you in small things, however praiseworthy, unless I were soon to praise you in the greatest things. If you were conducting yourself properly, I confess I had decided to shower you with praises then for both the small and the great, and to dedicate all my talent, little as it is, together with my pen and what remains of my life, to your praises, and not to leave your virtue unpraised, since ancient virtue has found so many to praise it. For although I am not unaware that I am unequal to so great a task, I had nevertheless heard and read that great battles often result from small skirmishes, and great effects from modest beginnings. Nor did I lack confidence that, following in my footsteps, certain great talents could also be inspired to celebrate you, and it gave me pleasure to be in the forefront of this endeavor though the last in merit.

Mulling all this in my mind, I waited for you for a full three years. Now, as you see, the fourth year is coming around and the days are passing, and still nothing is being done. I mean none of those things which, because they are the greatest and the best, ought to have been first. I would say to myself and I would say to others: our pastor, on the model of Him whose flock he feeds, has done everything well; one thing he defers, the one essential and the uppermost thing: to lead the flock itself back to its own original fold. He does not do this willfully, but is constrained by the very magnitude of the

---

* We emend *leuiter* to *leniter*.

undertaking. The flock has grown used to foreign pastures and marsh grasses, and is enjoying them with such relish that it has forgotten wholesome grass. Prolonged habit makes a sticky glue, a sticky snare that is baffling to break and hard to spring. His saintly mind, occupied with such cares, has yet to begin carrying out what is all done at the planning stage: small ideas are quickly translated into action, but great ones must have elaborate planning. Between thinking and doing, as they say, lies a great mountain that needs persistence, toil, and time to conquer.

These things I used to say, this I used to believe, this was my reply to the distrustful ones, who now demand that I keep my promise, nor can I find any way to avoid it. Therefore, since my hope, by which I eased my yearning, has been taken away not by you but by the hard facts, I have determined no longer to deceive myself or others and not to keep from Your Holiness any of those things that my faith speaks within my ear. I am therefore now speaking to you with the same reverence as to Him whose lieutenant you are among men, and call upon you from now on to bend your mind to patience and for a moment adjust your ears, accustomed to the flattery that goes with being powerful, to just reproaches, as I believe, although they come from the unjust mouth of a sinner. Nearly the entire Christian world, most high Father, now flatters you with one voice. If your integrity is truly what they say it is, I hope it will happen that among so many flatterers you listen not only patiently but gladly to one critic, and if by chance you hear something more or less than proper, you praise his loyalty and pardon his ignorance. Relying on this hope, I begin.

Everything indeed goes well in Avignon, everything is carried out with great prudence; I have said so, and now I congratulate you. It does become you, wherever you may be, that all things go smoothly and well, and that virtue and prosperity accompany your presence. But tell me, I beg you, in the meantime how is your bride doing? Who is the consul that governs her? Who is the general that defends her? What officers are looking after her? You will reply, or rather not you, who will receive my questions without doubt calmly and kindly, but some lesser and more impatient man: "You lay down the law for the Roman Pontiff, or you allow him only one bride, whereas his bride is not only the one you understand, but the universal Church; wherever he chooses to dwell, there is his own bride, his own See." I do not deny it, most blessed Father, nor do I shrink your See, which I would gladly enlarge if it were up to me, and would bound it everywhere on the oceans' shores; and I wish that the name of Christ were today worshipped as widely as we know it once was from many witnesses but especially Ambrose and Augustine, who in nearly the same words place the borders of the Christian religion farther apart than those of the Roman Empire. If we believe that what they said is what it sounds like, not a pious but a historical statement, who does not see the very great and lamentable change? For if that were the case at present, your See and your holdings would be "the sea and its fullness, the entire earth and all who dwell therein" [Ps. 98:7]. But that is not the case. For Christ as the Lord and Creator of the heavens, the sea, and the earth, is ever the same and His riches remain ever constant. We, because of our sins, have become so poor and are squeezed into this corner of the West, and even this is subject to the insults of the infidels who harass and attack us on all sides. Yet up to the present I do not deny or doubt that wherever the name of Christ is properly worshipped, there is your See. But let no one deny me that among all the others the city of Rome has something unique for you, indeed far more than any other. All the others have their bridegrooms who are, of course, subject to you alone, but they do preside over their churches. She, however, has no one but you. Therefore, while you are the highest in the others, you are the only Pontiff, the only bridegroom in the city of Rome.

I therefore question you about that bride of yours who is bound to you and to no other in spiritual union: what is she now doing, in what condition is she, or in what hope does she live? If you remain silent, I shall answer myself. She is sick, helpless, widowed, wretched, lonely; and clothed in widow's weeds she cries all day and night, singing those prophetic words: "How lonely she sits, the once crowded city! Like a widow has she become who was mistress over nations; the princess over the provinces has been placed under tribute" [Lam. 1:1]. And she repeats verse by verse, from beginning to end that whole tearful song. But more sadly she pauses wearily, her voice broken with sighs, where it is written: "Of all her dear ones, there is not one to console her; her friends have all spurned her and become her enemies" [Lam. 1:2]. And again, "At this I weep, my eyes flow with tears; for far from me is my comforter who would restore my soul" [Lam. 1:16]. Here, I say, she sighs more deeply, referring to you. For who else is her comforter? Who can restore her soul except you, who have all the remedies at hand and know the bride's every need and suffering? And if by chance you lack some information, know that she has no rest with you gone, peace is banished, war is there, both civil and foreign, her houses are in ruins and her walls tottering, her churches are collapsing, her holy rites are dying out, her laws are being trampled upon, justice suffers violence, the wretched populace mourns and wails, invoking your name in a loud voice. But you hear her not; you feel no compunction or pity for such great ills, nor do you see the loving tears of your venerable bride and restore yourself to her, you who are her due; to return their bridegroom to churches that are less worthy and less needy, you have most deliberately emptied your senate. So, while any other people has its bishop, shall the Roman people not have its pontiff? And shall small cities find repose in their bridegrooms' embrace, but the queen of cities forever remain a widow? And what I would call worse than widowhood, will she hear of her bridegroom always living with others, a captive to foreign loves? Can she neither hold nor see him whose presence would make him and her glorious and happy?

How can you—and I beg you, merciful Father—forgive my utter relentlessness; how *can* you, I say, sleep peacefully under gilded coffered ceilings on the bank of the Rhone when the Lateran lies in ruins, and the mother of all churches, without a roof, is open to the wind and rain, when the most holy dwellings of Peter and Paul quake, and when what had recently been the church of the Apostles is now a ruin and a shapeless heap of stones, wrenching sighs even from breasts of stone? If my lowliness deserves no answer to all this, will you and your brethren not at least answer Haggai the prophet, or rather the Holy Spirit speaking through his mouth? Or what can you answer generally? He says, "Is it time for you to dwell in your own paneled houses while this house is desolate?" [1:4]. What follows is terrible and well known, especially this: "Because my house is desolate while each of you runs to his own house" [1:9]. Ponder these words, I beg you, and let those whom this touches even more than you, ponder them, not because in every misdeed of the many the guilt of the leader is not graver, but because, forgetful of the Lord's house, they have each hastened longer [than you] to his own house.

Alas, as I speak, my grief grows, my wounds open afresh when I examine them; well then, the most famous, the loftiest steeple of the Catholic faith totters, and you, the highest lookout of the house of Israel and watchman of the Lord's tower, sit on the bank of the Rhone, which does not need you, yet stands stubbornly in the way of others' need. At any rate, does not that name, which you assumed—it was not imposed upon you—scold you silently? For, I ask, how can you be called Urban and flee the city that is the origin of this name? And yet it was that name that gave me and many others extraordinary hope of your coming. Your holiness and your evident piety promised nothing less than this. Your continual talk, your intimate conversation added to this impression, and in my judgment you ought to stand behind it lest, if you fail in your most serious promise, no one believe you in little ones.

Yet the talk, the rumor is that Rome is always on your tongue, that you are ever wishing in words for that journey, and often even promising; and even more often you have been heard to say that your heart will never be content until you are with your flock in Rome. And to this holy purpose and pious talk corresponds that choice of name, which I have called most appropriate and not accidental. For who could better restore that life-giving and holy city than Urban? I shall say something that perhaps displeases many, but I shall still say it; for I hope that it will please you and the lovers of truth: namely, a greater glory, which will endure for ever and ever, will accrue* to you from this than from any deeds that have been done on the Rhone in our age, and indeed throughout the centuries. Often a place augments fame. What is done on high is seen from a greater distance. And laying aside worldly glory which, though sweet and desirable to many, may not attract the sublime humility of your steadfast and unconquerable spirit, how great a reward do you anticipate from Christ for bringing His Church, after long wandering, back where He established it? His providence—as it is written—never fails in the ordering of what is His; had it been expedient, why would he not have established it on the Rhone? But a more distinguished location was chosen deliberately, so that where the head of an earthly empire had been, there would be the seat of the heavenly empire on earth, founded on unyielding faith and humble holiness, and held fast by the sacred blood of the Apostles and martyrs. Human presumption ought not to have changed this divine work, but it has; and now it is your duty, in case you do not know, and no one else's, to put her back whence she was uprooted. There were five of them in a row, I admit, who preceded you. But upon no one was it so incumbent, for no one was so impiously neglectful and hypocritical as you would be if you neglect and dissimulate, as you have begun to do. I wish most of all at this juncture that I had such a flow of words from Tully's fount to convey my concept, as it is, into your mind through language. But I shall do what I can; and whatever may fail my pen, your intelligence will supply.

* We emend *querebatur* to *queretur*.

You keenly noticed, I am certain, and bear in mind the route by which you ascended to this peak; for it will not do to suspect someone of being ungrateful to God when he is most grateful to men. "There is no power except from God" [Rom. 13:1]. The Apostle does not lie who says this; but this power, which certainly is not from anywhere else, comes from Him in different ways. To accomplish its will, the divine wisdom often makes use of human actions: succession, election, donation, acquisition, and any other ways whereby men reach some kind of power. Where traces of human actions and their effects are evident, the will and disposition of God lie hidden, yet not unknown to the learned and the faithful. And this was the path whereby all before you, within our memory, attained the papacy. There are instances when the very will of God stands out so plainly that even the bleary-eyed and the blind know it. On His own, with no mediator, God shows that He wills something in such a way that men seem to have no role; even those whose tongues or hands He uses as a tool or implement, are unaware of what is being done through them, and are surprised and perhaps sad at the result.

In our time you alone have ascended to your position along this path. Let no one deceive you, most prudent Father, let no one persuade you that any one of your cardinals ever may have thought even once of nominating you for the papacy—let alone, electing you. If perchance someone whispers otherwise in your ear, he is hoodwinking you, and by lying he wishes you beholden to him. In fact, it was God, God alone, I say, and no mortal who chose you; though He used their tongues, as I said, which were disposed otherwise, he turned them to obey His will and—strange to say—made them crave what He wanted. How can I believe that this is unknown to you, the keenest of men, when scarcely any of the multitude is ignorant of it?

But if you want it to be made even more evident now, consider the mind and character of those by whose voices you were elected. Take careful note of their haughtiness; nowhere is there such high regard for their own interest and simultaneously such contempt for anyone else's. Accustomed as they are to high office, they each aspire to the very highest, which hardly anybody believes anyone other than himself alone deserves. But since it is necessary to nominate others, each one nominates another while thinking of himself, so that others will nominate him in turn. Thus, neither can each man nominate himself nor does he wish to nominate another except from the same group from which some benefit can be expected in return. Since, therefore, they are of this mentality and character, how could they have nominated the abbot of a humble monastery, though he be well educated and his life admirable? How could they judge him qualified for that high post or how could it even enter their minds to bestow upon an outsider what each one wished for himself or for his supporters, or to see above themselves one upon whom they had looked down from their heights, or to have as their lord one whom they had employed as their underling? Perhaps I speak boldly, but unless I am mistaken, I speak truly: in their state of mind they could never have willingly allowed anything of the sort, let alone have done it. For it is not men's will, but God's, that matters. It was He who wanted you and no other, and He concealed his choice from those who would not have agreed of their own accord; as they were engaged in the meticulous search, He slipped in your name so secretly that when only the name of the abbot from Marseille had rung out from among the many names ennobled by the cardinal's rank, it provoked grief and fear among the wicked, joy and hope among the good, marvel and amazement in everyone, and yet, with one voice, though with varying sincerity, all moved their amazed lips in praise of God who alone performs great marvels.

And if you would like to hear my opinion about so important a matter, insofar as a bat can gaze at the sun or a poor, insignificant fellow, a sinner, at the divine will, I shall say what came into my mind at the first report and has not yet left me, what I said to many worthy men who were listening to me. How true it was rests in your hands; although, if the result I predicted and believed has not ensued, I would still embrace and maintain that opinion of mine about the divine plan, which goes like this: I believe Christ, our God, is beginning to pity His faithful. As I see it, He wishes to put an end to the many evils that we have seen in these past years; for the beginning of the golden age He wishes to summon His Church, which He has allowed to wander so long because of men's sins, back to its ancient and proper See and to the state of pristine faith. If this is all He wants, He has no need for much advice, as men do, nor of any great exertion or extended period of time to do so. As we know, the ease with which He does things is infinite, and with a mere nod faster than words, He can shift wherever He wishes not only the Curia but that rugged massive rock on which Avignon stands. Indeed, not He alone but those who believe in Him could do so if, as is written, they had faith like a mustard seed. But he has decided to fulfill His decree without public miracles, and to have a man carry back home what He allowed to be carried off by a man. Of all men, you were predestined for this sacred task, which is pious, useful to men, pleasing to God; if you neglect God's will, how would you justify such negligence to Him? And since we ought to do what He has decreed must be done, why would you prefer it to be done by someone rather than you? And as that poor old lady is reported to have said to the emperor Trajan: "Consider what your successor's virtue will contribute to your glory." I know that you understand me, and I am saying nothing you have not often pondered and examined; that is my opinion of your intellect and your holiness. But since not everyone has your intellect, I must speak more openly for the sake of the slower ones, in case they hear this.

Someone, then, had to be chosen for this work who had intelligence, virtue, and practical experience, and above all that rare boon, a free spirit. If you ask why, here it is in brief: almost all those who were advisors to your predecessors, and are now to you, and favor keeping the Church in those parts, lack one of these qualities. Certain ones, mental dullards, were unable to choose what is best in the situation, and these, I say, deserve not only forgiveness but pity. Others, endowed with a keen intelligence, but suffering from a lack of virtue, and overcome by passions, either through some kind of undeserved hatred of Italy or some kind of effeminate attachment to their native soil, heeding not so much their reason as their feelings, and putting private pleasure before the public good, urged arguments contrary to what they felt in their hearts. Still others, deceived neither by an evil intellect nor by a perverted will, but by the inexperience of youth, believed that the Church had nothing finer than the Venaissin region. There were among these some who, it seemed to me, believed Italy to be outside of the civilized world, the sea unnavigable and the Alps impassable, whereas the journey is very pleasant either way and Italy is close by. I felt that to some the air, water, wine, and food are suspect, a suspicion that would cease if either they would ever try these things or learn that the mildness and temperateness of the Italian climate and all the things they fear have always been praised and preferred by the most reliable authors, foreign as well as Italian.

At this point certain things come to mind that are small in themselves but not irrelevant to proving what I say. Once when eels from the Lago di Bolsena—wonderfully large and unusually tasty ones—were sent to Benedict XII, his eyes popped out and he had them divided among the cardinals, keeping a tiny portion for himself; a few days later they came to visit him as usual, and when reference was made to the eels, he said in his humorous, chaffing way, "Had I tasted them first, and known how good they were, I would not have handed them out so generously, but I never imagined that anything like this could come from Italy." Those words upset, both outwardly and inwardly, Giovanni Cardinal Colonna, whom I shall forever remember with a reverent sigh; for I spent my entire youth under him in those places. He was of noble complexion and could not bear anything foul to see or jarring to hear. He flared up instantly and said that he was astonished that such a learned man who had read so much should not be aware that Italy excels in all things. Some years later when I was sent from Italy to speak to Clement VI on Italian business—I could not make my point as I wanted to—I said among other things that the Italians would pay a high price to have him know Italy just as he knew Gaul and Britain. Being very intelligent, he understood what I meant, and answered that he wished for the same thing. And in truth, if, as Aristotle says, everyone judges well what he knows and is a good judge of this, being learned in this particular area, how can anyone, no matter how highly intelligent, judge about things unknown? What Aristotle then adds, "he who is learned in all things is unqualifiedly a good judge" [*Ethics* 1.1.1095a.1–2], would be true if someone learned in everything could be found, but I have no idea where to look for him. It is, therefore, a dangerous and calamitous handicap to have no experience with the things you are going to judge, and especially those things that cannot be learned well except through experience, such as models of statecraft and all that part of philosophy that deals with human qualities; we know that therein those without experience exert themselves to no avail.

This of course does not apply to you who, from daily dealings over the years, know Italy almost as you know your own house, but inasmuch as many of your cardinals who have decisions to make about Italy suffer from lack of experience, I would like no one but you to be the judge. Therefore, I am not surprised if meanwhile they err in their judgment of our affairs. Rather I would be surprised if they did not err. However, being inexperienced, they ought to believe those who are experienced, you above all, and they must lay aside that false opinion that has let them imagine Italy as some kind of desert and a huge cheerless expanse. I am certain they would be ashamed of their age-old error, were they just to see with their own eyes, even once, those lands they despise or hate. For, of course, I should think that no one doubts the beauty of the country unless he were blind either through ignorance or malice or obstinacy of mind. Begging the indulgence of all the peoples of the earth, I will say that nothing whatsoever under the heavens can compare with Italy—if I may repeat to you what I protested in speaking with our friend the emperor. I feel that *I* am suspect in this part of the argument. But love of country is not so great that love of truth ought not to be greater and is greater; yet, if need be, I shall produce great witnesses whom shame itself forbids anyone to disbelieve. But what need of witnesses in your presence when I am going to call on you alone as a witness to those who disagree?

Nevertheless, I shall add another witness, also alive, foreign-born, and famous, Gui [de Boulogne, Bishop] of Porto. I recall, and he himself I believe will also recall, that he was returning in the Jubilee year from that glorious embassy of his, and I, in my lifelong devotion to him, accompanied him on his journey. We had come to the Lago di Garda, the finest lake in the Veneto; he himself was surrounded not only by his men but by a huge crowd of Italian nobles and knights, and he stopped on a grassy knoll. With his quick mind and easy, pleasant manner of speaking, having contemplated at some length the Alps on his right covered with snow in midsummer, and the roughness of the deep, deep lake like the sea, the low hills before him and behind him, and on his left the broad, fertile plain, he finally called out my name and said in the hearing of all, "I confess that you have a more beautiful and a much better country than ours." When he beheld that I was delighted by such a frank admission, and that I approved of it not only with a nod but with words and applause, he added, "But we have a more tranquil state than yours, and we are governed more peacefully." And when, having said this, he was withdrawing as though he had won, I detained him with these words, not wanting to be the loser—or rather it was not I but the truth—what I said was, "Who prevents us from having a government like yours the very moment we begin to want it? But nature prevents you from having a land such as ours." He smiled and said nothing, as though he understood that I had spoken the truth, but he did not wish either to give in to me or to contest the truth. So then we parted.

But now I shall turn to other kinds of errors. There are those who in Italy fear nothing but the customs of its inhabitants by whom they believe they would be held in hatred and contempt. If they remembered that the Church had grown to this height from the humblest roots in Italy and nowhere else, if they furthermore considered that nearly all its temporal power, however much that is, and it is surely great, is located within the confines of Italy, they would then perhaps lay aside their false, groundless, and unworthy suspicion. I recall having this argument with a certain cardinal, a nobleman of transalpine origin, who, as much as I could determine, was very kind and honest. It was in the presence of [Cardinal] Talleyrand, [Bishop] of Albano, who just lately was a bright star of the Church, and who would often interrupt that man's simplemindedness and what he called my cunning with his witty remarks. When the Cardinal asked me whether it would be possible for the Roman Pontiff and the Sacred College to live safely in Rome, I said that not only would they be safe there, but not safe anywhere else, and nowhere else would they be so honored, if only they would resolve to live justly and honestly, something that behooves them most of all. If they did this, they would not only deserve to be cherished but almost worshipped.

He said that he was convinced, but if by chance any of his servants were to do anything that deserved punishment, it would mean trouble for him as the master. I replied that as long as he did not interfere with the law, another's crime would hold no danger for him, and that it would not be to his disrepute but to his glory that he showed himself a friend of justice. And when, during the course of our discussion, as often happens, Boniface VIII was mentioned as though it were the most telling argument that would frighten anyone away from here, I replied that Boniface had been seized not in Rome, but in his country, which he preferred to Rome, nor by the Romans—I did not add, however, that it was by the Gauls; in fact, to be safe and free, as soon as he had it in his power to leave, he hurried to Rome, the stronghold of the Christian faith. Listening to these things and pondering them one by one, he said much that I pass over, but finally, sighing and barely holding back his tears, he loudly called Christ and all the saints to witness that he wished with all his heart to live in Rome and die in Rome. Then the gentleman from Albano [Talleyrand], who was very perceptive, in his admiration for the goodness of the man, whispered to me in a most gracious way, "You have what you wanted. You have drained this man; do you want to hear any more?" I have brought this up to make clear that I have heard this and other reservations of that college from conversations with them too—I am not imagining it.

There remains the fourth obstacle that keeps the wandering Church far from her dwelling place. There are some of them who do not lack a keen intelligence, nor experience, nor the will that is naturally good in itself if it were free, but only freedom of judgment that is often choked and bent by wealth (a heavy burden upon the human mind) and by the carnal passions that at times hold even brave spirits under their yoke. These are—oh, the shame and sadness of it all!—these are, I say, the ones who, forgetful of their own homes and Peter's ancient See, build on someone else's ground; as though they have found not just a Garden of Eden but a heavenly abode, they dwell there thinking they will never have to move, and they put all their hope there, all their yearning. And, good God, in what a place! Well, "among the wild clans of the Rhone!" This is what they are called not by me nor by an Italian poet, but by one from Spain [Luc. 6.145]. There on the banks of the windiest river, which means you live uncomfortably with the wind and would live even worse without the wind. To that wind, as Seneca says, which batters the buildings, the inhabitants then are grateful as though they owe to it the wholesomeness of their air. Nor should I leave out what follows when he says, "When he stopped in Gaul, the divine Augustus certainly" [*Clem.* 3.7.1-2(1.9.1-2)] made the vow and then built a temple. There then, in those places either muddy or rocky and parched, are seen the vast palaces and huge houses of your brethren—or rather, their prisons and chains about which I fear that the ethereal musician sings that frightful song, "Their graves will be home forever" [Ps. 49:12]. What follows is well known.

This, then, most reverend Father, is the tight knot that binds their hearts, this the prison that blocks the view of the better fatherland. How great is the power of old habit has often emerged from actual experience, when those who have been raised on country food cannot endure sumptuous fare and those who are used to a rickety dwelling and foul air cling to it and are not easily pulled away, no matter how much better quarters are offered. I have heard of people who, through force of habit, developed a certain attachment and love for their prison, so that although they had entered therein sadly, they came out almost reluctantly. I am therefore less surprised if your brethren love their spacious homes, but I am surprised that they love them so much, since they were meant to be loved in a way that would not block the threshold of their eternal home, lest their travel abroad make them forget their true fatherland. To be sure, nothing must be so loved that by loving it you come to hate yourself.

For me to have poured forth all this, I know not what it has taken more of—frankness or truthfulness, nerve or conviction. I had to go all the way to my goal, although with long detours. I do know that I could have been briefer, but you can hardly unfold big things in a tight space. If anyone were to measure the size of the things about which I am speaking, he would rate this as a summary. However, so that there may be an end to this section, He who searches our minds, knowing all this and whatever else may be hidden to men that might stall the carrying out of His judgment, has decided that all are to be rescued at the same time, and chosen a man completely free of all these ills, who obviously had an excellent intellect and the finest will, wide experience, a free, untrammeled mind that no vain, worldly deceits* can crush, no purple robes reeking of Tyrian dye, no wealth, no riches, no habit binding the spirit, and no proud palaces can shackle, for that man knows where and what Italy is, how great is the church there. Finally, Christ brought it about that you should be in Italy (something that has all the marks of a miracle) when He decided that you should be absent to those who nominated you but present to Him as his vicar, so that there would be no room for quibbling, but that it appear appropriate to you and to all that you should exercise the office of the supreme pontiff precisely in that part of the earth where He conferred it upon you without your even hoping for it, nor desiring it, nor thinking of it, and not through the vote of men, but solely through the providence of God. And where you rose from your humble state to the highest without intervening stages, there you must minister to the humble from on high, resisting the arrogant, for nowhere else in the world nor in any other city but this can the Roman pontiff more gloriously translate the power divinely bestowed upon him into an act pleasing to the Bestower. For although a good work is praiseworthy everywhere, everyone nevertheless agrees that it can be accomplished nowhere more appropriately than when its doer is in his own seat.

You are the teacher of the orthodox faith and the doer of pious deeds; your seat is where you wish. But as I have said, the ancient and true and proper seat, the one that is useful to everyone and universally advantageous, is Rome. Therefore, I now turn to this, and draw my long discussion to this conclusion: that you, the Roman Pontiff, Urban, should seek the city (*urbem*) of Rome, a place pleasing to God, venerable to men, desirable to the devout, fearful to the rebels when you are there, the right place for reforming and governing the world; it has no equal thus far, nor will it ever, unless my feeling deceives me. So, I beg you in the name of Jesus Christ, grasp this occasion offered to you by heaven, and do not let slip the opportunity for so great an undertaking. For time flies, nor does it return or halt. If you use it well, you will rejoice forever, and eternally give thanks to God, who has reserved this outstanding honor

* We emend *fallere* to *fallacie*.

for you. And you will glory in the fact that you turned your back on the earthly fatherland, whence you come, for love of the celestial fatherland toward which you proceed, that you went onward with your ears closed amidst the Sirens' song and obeyed the command, though unspoken, of the Lord who calls you back.

I beg you, let these words of David echo continually in your soul: "Hear, O daughter, and see; lend your ear, and forget your people and your father's house" [Ps. 45:11]. And what the Lord says to our father, Abraham, consider it said to you, "Go forth from your land and your kinsfolk and your father's house, and come to the land that I will show you, and I shall make you into a great nation, and make your name great, and you shall be blessed" [Gen. 12:1]. If you believe that this has been said to you, to whom it may be ambiguous, why not swear at once to the Lord and vow to God that you will put behind you that fatherland that is called yours, and overcome and trample your carnal feelings, that you will not enter into the tabernacle of your abode, nor climb under the covers of your couch, nor give sleep to your eyes or slumber to your eyelids or repose to your days until you have found a dwelling of the Lord, a tabernacle for the God of Jacob. But if you overlook it, or if you delay it, and meanwhile the allotted time slips by, believe me you will regret it then and will blame yourself when grief will be useless and regret too late. That is, when you arrive where soon one must anyhow, where there will be a single fatherland for all the good, and another for all the bad, what will that earthly fatherland be, I ask you, if not a shame and a reproach for those who for its sake overlooked their heavenly fatherland and were more concerned about where they should be buried than where they would live eternally, truly wretches to whom an abode for their dead body is dearer and more carefully provided than for their soul?

I certainly have no such fears about you; would that there were no more to fear about others. For the greatness of your mind has not been limited to one corner of the earth. You have read that verse, "Any soil is a man's birthplace" [Stat., *Theb.* 8.320]; and that other verse, "Any soil is a fatherland for the brave." I trust that you consider not so much whence you come as where you are going. I hope that when you look at the earth the entire world is your fatherland, but when you look up at heaven, this entire world is an exile. Indeed this hope of mine, or rather this hope of everyone, which your slowness has taken away from me and others, your daily acts and words are now restoring. Whatever you do, whatever you say is a sign of a pious will, disposed to return.

I shall touch upon two instances out of them all to make you realize that there are no dark places that can escape your radiance, and that what you say even in your bedchamber is heard by the entire world far off. The first is that recently when you returned to Marseille, impelled on no doubt by old ties and by yearning to see once again that humble, religious nest from which you flew, as it were, on the wings of Divine Providence and of your virtue, to the heights, the devout people, so fond of you, especially received you with the utmost joy and enormous veneration not as a man but as the God whom you represent through your office; overcome by such a pious spectacle, you may have held back your tears but certainly not your words, which rang in my ears more welcome than perhaps in those of many people there. At any rate, you said, among many other things, that if there were no other reason for going to Rome and Italy except to enkindle the devotion of the faithful, that alone was more than enough. O sacred words, worthy of eternal remembrance! So it is in truth, although the city of Marseille, as histories recount, has always been most friendly to the city of Rome from its very beginnings; and today, as I have noted, being in the meantime privy to both sides, there is between the two peoples the remains of some great love. Yet if Marseille received you thus, how respectfully Rome will, how devoutly, and how reverently! You will not only have the people pouring forth and weeping for joy, and bedewing the holy soil with pious tears, but the very angels of God coming to meet you at the threshold to welcome with ineffable joy and the sweetest hymns the vicar and bride of their Lord, as they return to their proper See and bedchamber.

The second instance is that when this impious band of brigands so hateful to God and to the world, and now so terribly devastating to the Christian lands, had driven you to the point of having to ransom your freedom and the freedom and peace of the Roman Curia with much gold after all other remedies had failed, and you justifiably complained much about this to your brethren, you likened this insult, among other things, to the insult suffered by Boniface, but you made it even greater—and rightfully and truthfully so. For although there is no sufficient reason for a man to commit an offense against the vicar of his God, nevertheless, in truth, Boniface, with a tongue that was more biting and, if I may say so, a spirit more haughty than becomes the vicar of the most humble Lord, suffered whatever he suffered not without cause at the hands of his enemies who were, anyhow, great and famous men challenged and smitten by grave, prolonged harassment, and already so driven to the limit that they had either to dare something extreme or to be utterly crushed. They therefore no longer feared anything worse, since they saw death as the end of their woes, not as a further woe. However, neither was the affair accomplished without the help and favor of another great enemy, nor even then by open violence, but by an ambush at night.

You, on the other hand, the most innocent of men, who never harmed anyone, nor wished to, in your kindness and your humble actions and words, followed your Lord to the best of your ability; but you were trapped, not suddenly, not secretly, by a deployed troop of the vilest thieves. O unworthy and infamous crime! You ransomed yourself with money, something that we know Boniface was neither forced nor required to do. Thus, filled with the Holy Spirit, you added to your most holy complaint the final thought that all these evils derived especially from the fact that you abandoned Peter's See and your own, and that you feared even graver consequences from day to day if that See, which Christ had chosen for His bride, were to be deserted by obstinate minds even now. O words worthy of you, O prophecy full of truth, O discourse with which both earthly and heavenly authorities rightly agree! It is indeed because of this widowhood of the highest See and this contempt that your Curia and the entire Christian world are afflicted; and soon, if a man may surmise, there will be even sharper affliction unless you forestall it. See how new waves of robbers are breaking forth, nor will this be all! Others will arise from these, while those same ones whom you will think you have put to flight will return. For those you thought you had appeased with gold, you actually roused with it, as their lust for plunder is boundless. They have no fear of God, no respect for men, no hesitation in deceiving, and finally no shame; you can in no way hedge or plead ignorance of this matter which you protested so loudly in public.

What therefore is being done? Why the delay? Whence this hesitation? Nearly every mistake of doctors in healing bodies results from their ignoring the cause. You who see the illness and clearly understand its cause, and are able to cure it, why are you postponing the remedy? What are you waiting for? For everything to go to ruin and plunder? I ask, has not everything been plundered enough already? Or are you too waiting for the final calamity, postponing your healing so that you may avail to raise it all up, as Christ raised Lazarus? But your Lord reserved this one thing for Himself while entrusting the rest to you. Or through such long delays are you trying to appear forced to do what you ought to have willingly done long ago? But no matter how good it is, you do not merit praise unless you do it willingly. And yet what remains now for you to feel even more compelled, unless they lay hands on you? Heaven forbid and protect you from the gang of godless men, and, as we earnestly pray on holy days, may He not deliver you into the hands of your enemies! For have you not been besieged long enough and often enough? Have not the pathways leading to the Pontiff of the Christians from all over the world been cut off by robbers? Has not the ransom been exacted for the Father of fathers and the Lord of lords, as if he were a slave? And while what we have suffered is bitter, we fear much worse even now.

Therefore, do as though you were compelled; you will thus be less open to criticism from those pressing for the opposite. But seek again your See most willingly and happily; and once you have touched it and guarded your residence like a brave man-at-arms, all will be at peace that now is at war precisely because you are not guarding your principal residence. Why say more? What has been written about your Lord and the Lord of all will quite properly be said of you—there will be peace on earth when you come and speak of peace to the nations, and your power will be from sea to sea. Do not be frightened because Rome too has lately had her troubles with brigands. The barbaric madness that now threatens the holy but headless city will not dare cast eyes either on Rome or even on the borders of Italy, once she gets back her head. Just as you are weaker anywhere than in your own pastures, so are your pastures always more vulnerable, more subject to harm without their shepherd. I shall not press this any further. I hope that you will do everything with success, and especially that one thing that you are so urgently asked to do, provided you vigilantly apply yourself; forgetfulness of your divine office will not sneak over you if you constantly remember that you were uniquely drafted for this task.

I have no doubt you do indeed have this in mind and have a spirit ready and willing to undertake any pious labor; see to it, however, and beware with watchful eye lest pressure from others—not of course from within yourself—overwhelm you and keep you from carrying out such a glorious undertaking. Persuade your cardinals—for they are the ones I fear the most in this—that Italy is not what they think, but is the best, the finest, the most esteemed part of the world, as all writers of note agree, and that she is, as they attest, and as truth itself confirms, the one country out of all that has hardly anything bad, lacks nothing good, if only peace were not lacking, which can no longer be lacking when you are here.

Teach them that here are the noblest, the most beautiful cities which once seen will make smelly Avignon worthless, and make them ashamed that they did not realize it before, that the climate is very healthy and perfectly temperate, between hot and cold, which certain writers have identified as the cause of the Roman world-empire, since it was so composed of opposites that it subdued southern cunning with physical strength, and northern savagery with mental powers, and so it required the extremes on both sides to give way to the middle which shares in both; that here the lakes are full of fish, the likes of which no region has in such abundance in such a small space; that there are rivers that amble through such different regions and with such charming bends decreed by nature that a large part of Italy—Liguria, Venetia, Emilia, and Flaminia—has scarcely any well-known place that is not effortlessly approached as the waters speed on; that she is surrounded by a double sea with one port after another and with a crown of noble cities, and marked on both sides with river mouths so that with salt water here or fresh water there almost all of Italy is readily accessible and delightful; that where there are no seas, there are the lofty Alps blocking the onrush of barbarians; that running down her center are the greenest hills, sunny valleys, the most fertile fields, and the range intersecting Italy throughout her entire length with wooded peaks, the Apennines, the father of mountains, pregnant with sparkling streams on either slope, and springs with wholesome variety of waters cold and warm, delightful to the healthy, beneficial to the the sick, welcome to the thirsty; and that there are veins of all kinds of metals, herds of lowing cattle, varieties of vessels that now so command those seas of ours that, if the Italians say No, no nation sails this entire stretch of water known as the Mediterranean, except a hit-and-run pirate; that here is an infinite abundance of grain, wine, and oil from trees and fruits that your world does not know, of forests and animals, game and fish and fowl, and all kinds of foodstuff, in case they should fear that they might die of hunger—not you, of course, who know these things and were reared from your tender years in the best austerity, and learned to fatten the spirit by abstaining from meat, and who, habituated to devout fasting, welcome hunger and detest that overfull feeling, but rather those used to the delights of Avignon, who can think of nothing beyond the Rhone, and even if they could, they will not, for so sweet is error flavored by habit and seasoned by the years that the taste for the truth becomes too bitter to the mind's palate, than which nothing indeed is more dismal to those beset with sickness of the spirit.

If they say, as they usually do, that Italy lacks something, I shall not contradict them. If there were absolutely nothing lacking, it would not be an earthly place but a heavenly one, and I would remind those who say this of that verse, "Not every land could bear all kinds of fruit" [Virgil, *G*. 2.109]. At the same time I would add that there is no land that does not lack something, or rather a great deal, but I will confidently affirm that no land lacks less that Italy, and that she, more than all others, most abounds in good things (though I am in the habit of seldom affirming anything). But I believe this to be so certain that it is not unknown even to the Indians or the Ethiopians.

Against my will I now speak at length about a lowly subject, foreign to my tastes, but the matter at hand forces me. I know what people are like. I have often heard them say that Italy does not have the wine of Burgundy. What a grievous scandal and a just reason for abandoning Italy! But does this not seem a childish boast to brag about a few jugs of common wine that some hill or other located on the transalpine side produces, and then to scorn so many different kinds of fine wines with which all of Italy overflows? What is this if not shifting a hatred for the people to the natural elements? They will perhaps reply that they neither scorn nor hate what is in Italy, but that they have chosen a place where they may enjoy their own treats as well as ours, transported there by sea and a navigable river. But if ours can be transported there, why, I ask, should yours not be transported here too either by the same sea or river route? And where goods reach us by sea, why should they not reach us over the Alps, where the route is equally passable and shorter? Let those who doubt that they can live without burgundy come, let them come with confidence. They will discover our wines here, and their own will follow them here with no trouble. Nothing is difficult where pleasure in involved, nothing is closed to it: it crosses seas and even moves mountains with a word. But I hope that after they have reached the Italian slopes they will not miss what they left behind. I say this, assuming that their bodily senses are untrammeled and unburdened by mental derangements, otherwise no novelty, however lovely, will ever remove all traces of some silly old habit; and it will happen as it is reported to have happened to the Roman emperor, Severus, who, when he had reached the highest pinnacle of fortune and was abounding in choice foods fetched by land and sea, still ate pulse from Africa with gusto not because it was either a delicious food or not found in Italy, but because he was of African origin, and his love for his homeland made whatever was grown there tasty. There are certain natural processes that are difficult to overcome; they are curbed by reason, but that great man obeyed his natural desire without, however, forsaking his rightful duty because of it. He loved pulse from his native land, but his love for it did not make him tarry in Africa.

One may imagine something similar happening to other princes, namely Trajan, Antoninus Pius, and Diocletian. The first of these, of whom the Spaniards are proud, was born in Spain but served the aging empire like an Italian; either because of his birth or his upbringing as a child he was able to feel a certain constant love for things Spanish. The second was born in Rome but of a family from Nîmes across the mountains; it cannot be thought unlikely, can it, that he delighted in the wine from his native land which certain men delight in so much today—I wish they would delight in more important things, it would befit them. The third was a native of Salonae in Dalmatia; I know not whether anything good is there but he must have delighted in something. For some hidden power or other and some inherent sweetness of one's native soil, as if by some bond of common origin, ennobles and commends even paltry things; and what nature has made bitter, thinking makes sweet. You will therefore scarcely find anyone except a very learned or unassuming man who does not set his own country above all others. If this comes from weighing the evidence, it is most absurd; if from love, it is praiseworthy, provided it be not contrary to that higher love with which we are now concerned.

For do you not agree that none of those whom I have just mentioned, either because of their affection for their country of origin or because they liked the taste of its produce, chose to live anywhere but in Rome, which was the seat of the empire; and it could happen, and one can still believe, that just as Severus had his pulse brought from Africa, so others had other things from Spain, from Nîmes, and from Dalmatia, which they still enjoyed in the palace in Rome? I pass over those princes who were born elsewhere but wished not only to live in Rome but actually to appear Roman, and who strove by all means to be called and considered Romans, who did not want to hear any mention of their old country, rightfully so, since they had gotten a nobler country by coming to power than by birth, as we read about Alexander and Maximinus—the first was ashamed of his Syrian origin and the second of his barbarian origin. I do not demand that anyone feel ashamed of his birthplace, for that is extreme and contrary to nature.

But I do insist that you, Father, and your cardinals accord to the

Church of the eternal God what those four whom I mentioned above accorded to their temporal empire: I mean that when it comes to mind that this one was born in Auvergne, this one in the Limousin, or in any other nearby city, it should occur to you at the same time that *you* are the Bishop of the city of Rome, that they are either bishops of the Roman countryside or priests or deacons of urban Rome, that it is not proper for the Church and the See of Peter to yield to your birthplaces, but for your birthplaces to yield to her, to follow her, and that it is wrong for Catholics and for men of the church to be dragged from their appointed office by hooks of carnal appetites which the pagans broke and scorned.

Furthermore, persuade them—for I hope *you* have already been persuaded—to move to Rome, where the abundance and quality of things are such that it will easily make them no longer desire things from abroad; or should they perchance desire anything else, they can all be imported plentifully up the mouth of the Tiber not only from their native land but from the whole world. This is why it is written that Ancus Marcius, the fourth king of the Romans, founded Ostia as a colony where the river meets the sea, and so on. Evidently, even then he foresaw that the riches and commerce of the whole world would be delivered there at the seaport of the city. Therefore, let not a few men, humble in Christ and fasting, doubt that they can live where so many proud rulers and many thousands of men, such a multitude of citizens and strangers lived sumptuously. And not to speak of those whose number cannot be ascertained, or summarize all the censuses in various periods, I shall touch upon two points that amaze readers: in the sixth year of the Emperor Claudius, when a census of Rome was made, there were found to be 6,944,000 Roman citizens.* Since it passes belief, the witness is Eusebius of Caesarea in his book *On Chronology*, whereas even earlier in the fifty-fourth year of Augustus there were 9,370,000.

Let some born skeptic now go and predict—I don't mean you, who I would dare affirm are as religious today and as devoted to the frugal life as you ever were in the monastery—that the twenty or thirty reverend fathers with their modest households cannot live where formerly three hundred conscript fathers and so many emperors and armies and people lived. But if perchance there is anyone for whom the lapse of time cancels the trustworthiness of

---

* P. mistakes the number of Roman citizens throughout the empire for the number in Rome itself.

the truth, let him recall what we all saw lately, that is to say, during the recent Jubilee when almost all of Christendom—such a number of pilgrims that I doubt any city could feed for one day—descended upon Rome. And although the fields around Rome were unplowed and untilled, and the vineyards had withered in the ice and frost of the preceding year almost throughout Italy, still there was even a greater abundance of everything toward the end of the year than at the beginning.

Although I have said much about this because of argumentative and insolent men who substitute hatred and envy for reason, still for what I am trying to prove, I do not place great hope of victory on the fact that Rome is both very fertile by nature and infinitely receptive to imported fertility. For I consider it neither worthy nor believable that the successors of the Apostles would, in selecting a See, think about pleasures or comforts or anything at all other than Christ and eternal salvation, and how they would rather be where they could please God and help men, where in short they could live well and die happily.

The time now warns me to add one more thing to so many. Oh, if on this night, which is sacred because of the glorious martyrdom of Peter and Paul, and at this very hour that I am writing this to you so trustfully and no less respectfully in my eagerness, you were present in the basilica of the Prince of the Apostles, which is your own basilica for the divine office now being sung and the matins, what a great and holy pleasure you would experience, what sighs you would give, what tears you would shed, what regrets you would have that the night were not longer! Again I will dare ask you to believe me once more when I say that Avignon, with all its charms, which either are already there or can be brought in or can be imagined, will never give you a like joy; for if all the world's gold, all the precious stones, all the wines, and all the dainties were to be piled up there, there will never be that devotion that makes the soul happy. That what I am saying is true and certain, the whole Christian world will acknowledge at least in this: no place on earth is equal to Rome by its own nature, nor can it become so through any partiality of men. But let this suffice.

I have held back one thing, or postponed it until the end, though it could have been at the beginning. You know the plight of your Christians throughout the East. Indeed the evil is close. Have you not heard how the unsoldierly peoples of Asia, whom our slackness makes valiant—especially the former Phrygians, now Turks—endlessly plunder wretched Greece and ravage the Cyclades that are scattered through the Aegean? Even if the Greeks deserve to pay for their stubborn persistence in rebellious sinfulness, the Turks are nevertheless crossing over from there toward us and true Catholicism. Already Cyprus, Crete, Rhodes, Euboea, and, closer to us, Achaia and Epirus, are being attacked. Already the Calabrian shore hears with trembling ears the sad outcries of weeping Greece; and while the Christian faith is undergoing such dangers as you see in the Orient, you, O supreme leader and pontiff of our souls, are still sitting in the West, whereas in order to meet your responsibilities— correct me if I am wrong—you ought to have arisen long since and gone to confront the problems, and hastened not only to Rome but to Constantinople, even alone (although you cannot be alone). Christ himself will be with you since it is His undertaking, and His forces will follow you wherever you go. A good leader must not avoid danger, let alone exertion; rather he must hasten wherever the loudest outcry of his troops calls.

Christ could have fled the cross, had He chosen to abandon us; not bound by any merit of ours, He wished to die for our salvation. We, having benefited from Him already, shun not only death but any hardship for His glory. Long since every state and every age ought to have taken up arms and cast their anchor of hope in Him who has never failed anyone believing in Him; He gave a wonderful and incredible victory to Theodosius battling with few forces against the immense armies of the barbarians, and made the elements fight for him. About this my fellow countryman, though ignorant of Christ, gave an eloquent testimony to the true God in these verses:

> For your sake Aquilo with icy tempests
> From the mountain o'erwhelmed the opposing armies
> And turned the flying weapons back upon
> The ones who shot them; he repelled the spears
> With a whirlwind. O you so loved by God,
> For you Aeolus from his caverns pours
> Armed storms of winter, and the ether fights,
> And to your trumpet come conspiring winds! [Claud.,
>   *Panegyricus de tertio consulatu Honorii Augusti* 93–98]

We too would be loved by God if we loved Him as we ought; for never has He been far from those who love Him, just as He has at times been even with those who persecute Him. For us too would Christ, not Aeolus, pour forth from His caverns the armed winter storms, for us the heavens would do battle, the winds be our auxiliaries coming at the sound of trumpets! But who would fight for ingrates? Who would bear succor to sluggish, lethargic people? Not only lethargic but lifeless, dead from sin, have we withered in our unending pleasures that have now become second nature. Now overwhelmed and buried in evil habits we have been deprived for this very reason of aid from heaven.

But I return to you; I admit your presence is useful, holy, and venerable everywhere. But I ask, why do the Rhone, the Sorgue, and the Durance need you? Who of your people there need your protection? What enemies there must be subdued? The Ionian Sea, the Aegean, the Hellespont, the Propontis, and the Bosphorus do need you. What then is so untoward here? I cannot ask this too often. There is fighting in the Orient, so what are you doing in the West, you who are the leader of spiritual wars? There is a common error of the lords here, which of course is yours too: they think they are lords for their own pleasure, though it is for the needs of others. If you recall your title, your office, your Lord who made you the shepherd of His flocks, you will not linger there where perhaps the shade or a spring is lovelier, but where the rustler or the wolf is more menacing, where the need of your Lord's flock is greater. Keeping in mind that saying from the Gospel, "The good shepherd gives his life for his sheep, but the hireling and whoever is not the shepherd nor the owner of the sheep, sees the wolf coming and leaves the sheep and flees" [John 10:12]. You are the shepherd, yours are the sheep that belong to your Lord. He entrusted everything to you; he put you in full charge, in full control of the flock. The wolf is growling at the entrance to the sheepfold, and you loiter. If you are not a hireling but a true shepherd, confront the noble, pious risk; recklessly choosing it is imprudent, but weakly avoiding it is not brave or magnanimous.

Take the long view, not only of place but of time: you will see how great is the present calamity there and how much danger lies ahead. As the Comic Poet says,

> That's wisdom for you—seeing not just what's
> Before your feet, but also looking forward
> To what will happen later. [*Ad.* 386–88]

Surely, unless you look forward from here, unless you make haste, it is all over, and we shall hear of the downfall of Christianity in those parts; it will be shameful for us, utterly unworthy and pitiful, and it is, as I said, not Christ's loss but ours—for He is immune to harm—our folly, our shame which is already so great in those parts that I doubt it could be any greater. For as it is, I am not certain whether it is worse to have lost Jerusalem or to possess Byzantium. There, at any rate, Christ is not recognized; here He is hurt by being worshipped thus. Those are enemies, these [Byzantines] are schismatics, worse than enemies. Those openly disparage our empire; these call the Church of Rome mother in word alone, but how devoted they are to her as children, how humbly they accept the orders of the Roman Pontiff, the Patriarch you gave them will attest. Those hate us less because they fear us less; but these hate and fear us with all their guts. It is known that they consider us dogs; and if they were free to speak, they would call us dogs. I was present on a holiday while Mass was being celebrated according to the Roman rite when a certain Greek who was not uneducated but altogether stupid and arrogant, exclaimed, "I cannot bear the nonsense of the Latins," a word which, if it had been understood by the people, would not have gone unpunished, I trust. But that is how it is, how they feel toward us; and when any of our people enter their basilicas, they reconsecrate and purify them as though they had been violated by human blood or by some base crime.

And these things the Roman Church has long known and endured. Whether this deserves to be called apathy or patience, when this disgrace could be so easily washed away, I leave others to judge; the fact remains that a great sea lies between us and our enemies who now hold Jerusalem. So, as matters now stand between us and them, it is no small effort. Hence, perhaps our powerlessness excuses our delay, although there is no excuse for powerlessness that results from nothing but our own discords. On the other hand, nothing stands between us and these petty Greeks except our lethargy and our laziness, since, while they have the utmost hatred, they have no power, and it is a simple matter for any two Italian states that want to [fight]; if you would begin to favor it, I can guarantee you that whether together or just singly they can either overthrow that unwarlike empire or lead it back to the yoke of the Mother Church. So more and more I marvel at our connivance, nor can I seem to understand why such truly great things are overlooked when men show so much concern for trifles. And though this be the general shame of all Christians, still in any army the greatest shame falls upon the generals when a campaign goes badly. Often men have perished under one general when they would have been safe under another. Often troops who were set for victory were defeated through the fault of the general. Often too, or nearly always, public opinion ascribes the fault of soldiers to their leaders.

Consequently, you who are the commanders of all—I mean you and the Roman Emperor—you yourselves know with what determination you must rise up if you wish to avoid the weight not only of your infamy, but everyone's. Nor is it enough to know this; something more, rather a great deal more, is demanded of you, lest you think that you have achieved such greatness cheaply. Through the midst of hardships we go to glory. Anyone who has been touched by the spur of virtue will never rest, but will step from one virtue to another with tireless persistence and climb, as it were, so many rungs of loftier glory; and this toil will be sweeter to him than any rest, and is indeed the only rest for the heart that sighs for the heights; taking a holiday from great deeds is sad toil and wretched idleness. You have read how Julius Caesar calls it a loss for him to run out of wars and is vexed to see the enemy in flight; how Titus, the son of Vespasian, complains of losing a day in which he had done nothing generous and noble as was his wont; how Alexander of Macedon, in his teens, first laments to his contemporaries that Philip, his father, by his many victories deprived him of enemies to conquer and of any occasion or any field for praise in war, and later as a grown man how obsessively and earnestly he kept on the alert lest the enemy slip away, and how, having once dispelled that fear, he slept soundly, as though he feared nothing other than safety and security and the end of his toil. To include something from Holy Scripture, Joshua, the leader of the Israelites, could have rested at nightfall after that victory over so many kings, satisfied with the glory gained, and thereby eased the weight of his sacred toil with a good night's sleep; but being eager to increase both the toil itself and the glory with it, he bade the sun to stand still, and it obeyed. Thus toil is the nourishment and the delight of generous spirits, not for its own sake, but for what can be achieved only through it.

That you too keep all this always in sight and always on your mind, I have proposed not only passionately, but even rudely since I would rather fall short in anything other than loyalty. I have fulfilled my obligation, or perhaps someone else's; anyhow I have stated the truth, which should have been said better by someone with greater authority, but either no one has thought of it or everyone has been afraid to say it. I hope, to be sure, for gratitude from posterity and at least for forgiveness from Your Holiness and from His Majesty [Charles IV]. If, as I have said, such things have always been taken in good part by him, I am confident that they will be received still more kindly by you, inasmuch as the successor of Peter ought to be kinder than the successor of Caesar.

With him I often took up this subject in the past as the situation arose, with you today for the first time. Or more accurately, since often I have silently had this argument with you, I have now for the first time put it in writing. Inasmuch as it has turned out to be short for what I want to say, but very long for your many commitments, it must at last come to some kind of end. O Roman Pontiff, leader of the Christians, with a loud voice Rome calls you her bridegroom and Christendom its leader; you are summoned not to rest but to toil, to which man is born, and not to peace but to wars, which last for a time but in them is the eternal peace of the soul, the salvation of many, and glory for you. It is for you to choose in what state you wish to die. For whether you fulfill your duty gloriously or neglect it ungloriously, there is no doubt that you must die. Your predecessors chose Avignon for their See, for what reason they themselves know best. Since childhood I have known that city much better than my own native city, and I have concluded that nothing extraordinary is there except mud and wind. For were I to believe those who brag about the remarkable variety of food there—the opposite of what I have often seen—and were that city superior to all others in this one respect, in which it is inferior to many, I would still not allow this to be a sufficiently cogent reason for such grave and holy men, in imitation of a flock that goes after rich pasture, to choose a place where they may live more luxuriously, not more honorably.

But if being near their birthplaces influenced them, it was perhaps excusable in them, staring at the ground and meditating on earthly things. But you, however, who were reared far differently and elevated far differently, must feel quite differently. Your fatherland is not this or that part of the earth, but the entire world; or rather, as I have said, it is an exile: heaven is your fatherland, whereas the seat of this exile is Rome, not the only one but the holier one, more favored by Him who will call you back from here when He wishes to your fatherland. Rise up with courage and learn to despise petty things; what you have received is great, and what is expected in return is not small, I admit. For you the Lord worked an evident miracle. Now you work an evident miracle for Him by plucking His Church from so deep an abyss. For it will be no small miracle to pull so many and such deep-rooted minds from there. Yet it will be done without difficulty, unless you too are rooted there. But if you are—may Christ avert such a bad omen!—what difference is there between you and them whose useless delay and empty joy lead only to grief? The diversity among men is measured by their pleasures and actions, nor do they differ from one another in anything more than the variety of their works and the difference in their thinking.

I intended to pass over one thing because it was so close to being a joke. But the pious enthusiasm of my mind has compelled me to hide nothing nor to deprive your holy ears of anything that could hurt your reputation or my conscience. Rumor has it that in your palace there is a section called Rome, and that when you enter it you seem to have returned to your bride and to have fulfilled all the duties of the Roman Pontiff. Do not fool with your Lord. He is not taken in by little tricks; He is the greatest of dialecticians to whom no sophism is insoluble; He is an infallible inspector and profoundly understands all our thoughts from afar, keeps track of our pathways and our guideposts, and foresees all of our journeys. If these are crooked and stray from piety, they cannot be pleasing to Him. Therefore, as He beholds them, to use the words of the Satirist, God laughs and abhors, He smiles at our cant, He abhors our goal. It is written, "Do not be misled; God is not mocked" [Gal. 6:7].

Nor let your good fortune flatter you, or the hope of a long life deceive you; the life of mortals and especially that of pontiffs is short because they are old when they reach this rank, or because the weight of their cares, the unending labor, and the pressure of their business inevitably shorten their lives. The death of both young and old must be considered constantly in the offing, but what is just a guess for the former is definite knowledge for the latter. And while the span of life is brief for both, or rather is nothing, and passes by like a dream or smoke or shadow, still a young man can live for a while, although he may die suddenly and often does die before becoming old; it is certain that an old man must die momentarily.

So when we come before the tribunal of Christ, where you will not be the lord and we the servants, but He alone Lord and we all equally servants, do you not think He will say to you, "I raised you up poor from the earth, and building upon your humility I placed you not only among the princes but above the princes, and I willed that they grovel at your knees and your feet. Where in the world have you left my church which I entrusted to you? Favored by me with many unique gifts, what have you given back to me which is different from others, except that you sat on the rock of Avignon, forgetful of the Tarpeian rock? Do you believe that when I chose a capital of the world, I could not have chosen anything else? Or do you despise my choice and my judgment? And you, who were above all chosen marvelously by me to correct the mistakes of those who preceded you, have not budged at all from their course; and though different at the outset, you were just like the others in your course and at the end."

You could not easily answer this question from me, your servant; what are you going to answer your Lord? Or what will you say to Peter? He will say, "Fleeing because of my justifiable fear of cruel Nero, I ran into my Lord who reproached me, and I returned to Rome to face punishment and death. What Nero or what Domitian has driven you away? What fear of death or punishment has made you an exile for so long? What, I ask, is now going on in Rome? How is my home doing, my tomb, my people? You do not speak to me? Do you not know what I am asking? From where are you returning to me? Did you also go into exile on the Rhone; if perhaps you say you were born there, was I not born elsewhere? But each of us acquired one fatherland by birth and another by rebirth. Thus, being aware of the Lord's will, I put Rome ahead of Galilee, but you preferred the Rhone to Rome."

I meant this to be addressed in pure faith and in humble style, most kind Father, confident that you prefer the bitter-tasting truth to honied flattery. If I was wrong, or if my frankness has offended your holiness, I beg pardon upon my soul's bended knees. But now you must reject your false advisors, and take counsel with yourself, whether you would rather spend whatever time is left in the filth of Avignon, or in Rome, with the very flesh and blood of the martyrs; and would you rather be buried on that rock in that homeland of the winds that you now inhabit or in the Vatican, the holiest of places. In the end, on the day of the Last Judgment, would you like to rise again among the Avignon sinners, who today are the most notorious of all that be under the heavens, or among Peter and Paul, Stephen and Lawrence, Silvester and Gregory, Jerome and Agnes and Cecilia, and so many thousands of saints who either happily rest as witnesses of Christ, or more happily perished for their faith in Christ?

Finally, whatever you may choose, Rome rightfully and mournfully seeks only one thing: that if you desert her, you at least give her back what she—no one knows better than you—is entitled to: her other spouse, her Caesar, whom Innocent VI, as they relate, your immediate predecessor, barred from her embrace by the constraint of an oath. O unworthy divorce, if one may speak the truth, and harmful not just to the couple but to all the neighborhood! You, O excellent Father, most devoted to the common good, remove this obstacle which only you can, and not only allow but enjoin Caesar to be in Rome, lest it appear that out of cruelty you do not wish to be there, and do not wish another to be there out of envy; and if you refuse this too, the present and future generations of Christians will believe this is being said to them through my lips, however vapid, trifling, and ignorant, by Him who cannot lie and who, when He so wishes, makes not only the sinners and the ignorant speak, but even dumb animals: when Rome is widowed of her spouses and deprived of her lights, human affairs will never go well, nor will the bounds of Christendom have peace. If she gets one of them back, it will be well, but if she gets both, it will be excellent, glorious, and happy. May Christ Almighty prolong your days into the distant future, and open your heart to counsels that are not flattering nor perhaps attractive but sound and sincere, and, as I trust, pleasing to God.

Venice, June 29 [1366-68].

Sen. VIII, 1.

To Giovanni Boccaccio,[*] on what is called the critical time of life.

It is customary for young people always to subtract something from their age, and for old people either to add as much or more, simply because one who adds can lie more freely than one who subtracts, and is more likely to be believed by his listeners; but the reason motivating each is clear, though different. For young people it is the conservation and prolongation of life, not to say lust, while for old people it is the striving to acquire authority, and to enhance it. Actually both lie with such regularity that the young, while they have often deceived many, at times deceive themselves too and believe that they are younger because of their lie—fine, if they could also deceive death that awaits them at an appointed time; the old, in order to find support for one lie, fall prey to many others, inventing many things that happened before their time as though they had seen and known them with their own eyes. I intend to shun both pretenses, for the youngster's lie is shameful, the oldster's silly.

Still I will confess, nor will I blush at what you think, that for a long time I belonged to the first group, not by lying but by remaining silent. For I was convinced that, although the number of years is usually inscribed on the face itself by Nature's fingers, in my case a certain liveliness and a life style far removed from youthful debauchery would make a beholder consider me younger than I would have had the nerve to claim by shameless lying. My hope, however, was contradicted by prematurely gray hair which, for some reason, had attacked my youthful head from a very early age, though only here and there. It had come with my first stubble—there was something awesome about my whitish crown, as some people said—and it conferred dignity on a still boyish face; but for me it was still unwelcome because it contrasted, at least there, with my youthful appearance.

But since gray hair is often a false indicator of age—and according to all my contemporaries the change had been so early and sudden that no one could have overlooked or doubted it—I hoped that it would be outweighed by my other features. Nor was I disappointed. Meanwhile I pretend to have the "heavy chin" of King Numa [Vir-

---

[*] See I, 5.

gil, *Aen.* 6.809–10], the "whitish beard" of the young Virgil [*Ecl.* 1.29], the "aging hair of the adolescent Domitian" [Suet., *Dom.* 18], the premature graying of Stilicho, and the untimely graying of Severinus [Boethius, *De cons.* 1.1]. And if I read or heard anything of the sort, it would strongly appeal to my mind, and I found comfort in famous companions. But although, to the best of my knowledge, I have never lied about my own age, still, as so often happened, if anyone innocently would ever say I was younger, I would delight in his untruth. But if, as rarely happened, anyone would make me older, I would be silently angry at this lie. And if at times, either by chance or keener insight, anyone told my correct age, I would be offended and surprised by the truth and feel betrayed. I can scarcely explain the reason for this foible. Nor would I deny that perhaps I shared that folly for a while with other young men. But thank God whose mercy will free miserable me from the body of this death as He did with the Apostle; as regards this part of misery, I believe He has already freed me through Christ our Lord [Rom. 7:24–25]. For many years now, but especially since the Jubilee sixteen years ago, that plague has so completely left me that, though still in my prime, I feel far more loathing for it than the pleasure I felt before. Thus, every time that ugly quirk comes to mind, I shudder out of shame and anguish. Christ my Savior knows I speak the truth, for He was won over by my tears and often gave me His right hand as I wept and groaned, and raised me up according to the poet's words, "At least in death may I rest in peaceful dwellings" [Virgil, *Aen.* 6.371]. Such being the case, why that idea of being young, though false, appealed to me from that time down to the present, I wonder, or rather I am astounded, since from childhood I had read that famous opinion of the elder Cato reported by Tully; and I had always fully agreed, that old age, especially when honored, has so much authority that it is worth more than all the pleasures of youth [*Sen.* 17]. Finally, mulling it over and over, no explanation has occurred to me except a kind of habit which, when it is good, is the best thing in the world, but when bad is the worst. Accustomed to mingling with bands of young people, I was moving against my will into another cohort, although a better one. Having thus embraced fleeting youth, I was clinging to it with great effort. When I could neither pursue it nor be allowed to hold on to it, I was heading toward a new friend—old age—and I found pleasant what I suspected to be miserable; I discovered old age to be as fruitful as youth was flowery. From now on I have no further need to lie, nor for someone else to lie.

I am ashamed to want to deny what I cannot, nor would it become me if I could. If I confessed it, there would be nothing disgraceful, and perhaps something prestigious; not in itself—for there is no prestige in being old—but if there is gravity of mind, steadfastness, the preservation of the senses, and, for one's age, a bodily appearance, which is neither decrepit nor unkempt as is the case with most old people, finally a daily regime that conserves strength, or the merits of time well spent in continual study and worthy deeds, why hide one's gray hair? Why pull them out? Once you start doing so, you must either pull them all or quit the futile effort. Why do we struggle to thwart the course of nature? That is useless; after struggling for a while we will succumb, divine law will overcome the madness of the giants opposing the heavenly forces, and disguised old age will betray itself, death will come unexpected. And to oppose it will only bring us a more blatant defeat. I therefore yield willingly rather than be forced to yield. I say that I yield, and I throw up my hand, not to fortune, as Cicero did, but to nature, which it is not courageous to resist but mad. I would no longer hide in myself what I have always venerated in others, I mean old age, which the philosophers and the laws alike define as venerable in the highest degree; we know that it was always revered and honored in well-governed cities.

I have put it off, I admit, as long as I could, seeing that our Cicero, as I said in a letter to you, places the onset of old age at forty-six, others at fifty; Augustine later than anyone I recall, at sixty, perhaps because his constitution was more vigorous and strong. For it cannot be denied that some people at fifty are older than others at sixty, which results from the difference either in their way of life or in their nature. But what was I to do? I had surpassed all these limits, and by that time I was clearly an old man in the judgment of all these authorities, and yet I hesitated and would say: "Why have learned men set up such different limits, if not because each applies to others what he has experienced in himself? How do you know but what you may be stronger by nature? Certainly so far, aside from that lost bloom of adolescence and agility of youth, which are the first things we lose, you do not feel the onset of any special change. Wait, then, until you can resolve the matter according to your own judgment and experience, not that of the writers, especially when they disagree. When you feel that you are old, then and no sooner will you declare your old age. Meanwhile, keep silent and await what the years may bring."

Thus, dear friend, did I used to think about extending the limits of life and changing its boundaries, as though pushing out further the Pillars of Hercules. Today, which is my birthday, has broken my obstinacy; and as I mentally take measure of the past and the future, it has drawn me to my pen, particularly at this early hour when I first saw the light, as I learned from my parents and those who attended me, whom I trust in this as in many things.

Though you have not asked, I shall of my own accord tell you what I have always kept, even from you, in obstinate silence, while others often asked eagerly, except for one astrologer famous lately for that art, to whom I finally told it. He was very keenly and nervously searching and then attempting to elicit, as he said, whether the tenor and fame of my life suited my "signifier," as they call it, and what developments or what outcome awaited me. I wanted to get rid of him, not that I believed my destiny lay in his books—you know how I feel about this, and I think you agree—or in the stars of heaven. This, as I have often said, and shall always say and hope, is in the hands of God. But this consideration alone—namely, that today is my birthday, as you have heard—would not have had so much influence on me as to make me take pen in hand while I am tied up with other concerns. For my birthdays have often come around, and yet I was never so lulled by the allurements of fleeting things but that I was aroused by the reminder of life's passing to say to myself, "Look, poor fellow, you have become a year older and are that much closer to death." There is therefore another and stronger reason for this confession which, if you do not mind, I shall give you in a few words.

There is an ancient view, astonishing for its very strangeness, but even more astonishing for the explanation adduced to prove it. They say that through long observation it has been discovered that the sixty-third year of life is very dangerous to the human race, either because of an enormous disaster or death, or physical or mental illness. While each of these is grave, the last is the gravest, if there is any truth to it. Many have mentioned this year, but those who now come to mind are Aulus Gellius in *Attic Nights*, Censorinus in the book entitled *On Ages*, and Julius Firmicus Maternus, the astrologer, who, if not truer, is certainly fancier than the others I have read. In his fourth book on *Astrology* he carefully analyzes the problem, presenting an explantion as if people were certain about the fact itself and quite in agreement.

But here is the explanation that seemed extraordinary, as I said before. How weighty it is, let those ponder who have devoted their attention to such concerns, for I confess I disdain the entire matter, and the explanation of it just as much. At any rate Maternus says that for a certain natural but hidden reason the seventh and ninth years of life are dangerous and bring destruction, crisis, a sort of plague to mortals [*Astr.* 4.14]. This is why, he says: since seven times nine and nine times seven make the same product of the two unlucky numbers, turning upon themselves and uniting, a double evil and a twofold risk obtain at that time. Now, since the sixty-third year consists of these numbers, it is infamous, and was singled out with a notorious nickname by the Greeks, and called "Androclas" by the Egyptians, as though it were a saboteur "because it shatters and weakens the human substance" [ibid.]. And the various names of the evils that break out at this time are as follows: "Accusations, snares, dangerous journeys, shipwrecks, conflagrations and cave-ins, loss of patrimony and other money, wounds, sicknesses, mourning and deaths" [ibid.]—all horrible menaces, but the one mentioned above, mental illness, surpasses all horror, so much the worse than all of these as the mind is better than the body; and if it loses its well-being, the loss becomes all the more signal.

Who is so fearless that he does not dread these things? To add to the mass of fears, I could adduce the deaths, striking around this time, of philosophers, saints, princes, and tyrants, but my purpose is to diminish, not increase the terror. There is scarcely any time between adolescence and old age that cannot be blamed for many famous deaths. I therefore do not fear these things, having faith in Him who brought me unknowing into this life and cherished me in the very confines of my mother's womb, who has embraced me in the beam of His mercy, who, accompanying me with equal mercy to the very end, will lead me hence at the opportune time, and who, as He did not abandon me when I was haughty and sinful, will not now that I am repentant, now that I hope in Him, love Him, and pray to Him.

For my part, I believe that what those alarmists threaten will not happen, and for the one who leads a good life, or desires anyhow to do it, and grieves with all his heart for having led a bad life, no year of his life will be calamitous. And if any of the ills were perchance to strike, aside from the last one that I called the most grave, I shall bear them all bravely, even death itself, with the aid of Him of whom it is written: "Though I walk in the midst of the shadow of death, I shall fear no evil since You are with me" [Ps. 23:4], and again, "For although I walk in the midst of tribulation, O Lord, you will give me life" [Ps. 138:7], and I shall endure with courage and count death itself among the acts of nature; for I have furthermore turned to the hope of immortality and resurrection. Of these, all good and learned people have had the first, even the greatest men lacked the second; and yet, dying happily and fearlessly, they showed us by sheer strength of mind that contempt for death is not only possible, but not even very difficult. Considering how much light has been shed on these matters, see how really ugly the fear of death is for a Christian.

On this day and at this very hour I am entering, unworried, that year which—unless I am mistaken, is deservedly infamous, and will not bring either anything new or indeed anything dreadful, if I am a man about it. For let me tell you, and let others know, if there are any who do not scorn knowing about such humble origins, that I was born in the year 1304 of this last age which got its name and start from Him who provides me with this hope, Jesus Christ, on Monday, July 20, at the break of dawn, in the city of Arezzo, on what is called Garden Street. That is a red-letter day for our people, namely because our exiles, who had betaken themselves to Arezzo and Bologna, came together on that day from both places armed as a single army; and almost at the very hour when I was born, before the sun burst over the mountaintops, they came to the gates of their native city to take vengeance with the sword for their exile, if luck were with them. Although the undertaking proved fruitless, it had shaken up everything with such great tumult and immense terror that I still do not know whether to this day the enemy has forgotten it, but until these last few years it was constantly on the multitude's lips. This very day is Monday, July 20. What was then the fourth year [of our century] is now the sixty-sixth. Count on your fingers; sixty-two years have passed since I crossed the uneasy threshold of this life, and on this day and at this hour begins that horrendous sixty-third year, as they call it. Thus, if you usually tell the truth and do not yourself, like young people, subtract some years from your age, I preceded you in order of birth by an interval of nine years.

There you have, dear friend, a description of the first day of my mortal life, and I would gladly describe my last day, but it is unknown to me. In vain do I repeat those words of David, "Make known to me my end, O Lord" [Ps. 39:5]. But just as I entrust all my days to the King of the ages, so do I entrust that one above all. If you, as I hope, live beyond that day, you will know when it has come from these friends of mine who run with me along this race-course, for whom, as Maro says, that day will appear

always harsh,
And always burdened .... [*Aen.* 5.49–50]

And when you compare the end to the beginning of my life, however long it may have been, you will perceive its brevity and you will repeat the words of that afflicted old man: "Man born of woman lives a short while; full of many miseries he blooms like a flower, is trodden down, and fades away like a shadow" [Job 14:1-2]. Rising as is my habit in the middle of the night, these things have come to mind suddenly, and I have hurriedly snatched my pen to communicate them to you as soon as possible; we shall see, God willing, the outcome of this year. If something untoward happens, I have no doubt you will grieve. However, if it is death, provided it not be disgraceful, I beg you not to grieve or to complain, for just as there is nothing more unworthy of a son than to defame his parent, so is there nothing more repulsive in a man than to accuse nature. But if the year brings something more joyful than it promises, I know you will rejoice—and I myself will rejoice with you, if life remains with me until year's end, as once Augustus Caesar, who also alludes to this year, did with Gaius Asellius—because I shall have escaped this crag of old age. You meanwhile observe carefully the outcome of the matter; or learn from my death what you have soon to fear or hope for when your time comes, and how much to rely on that famous idea. And farewell, and remember me whether I live or die.

Pavia, July 20, at dawn [1366].

Sen. VIII, 2.

To his friends,* on his old age, and its advantages.

I have grown old, I admit it. I can no longer hide this even if I wanted to; and even if I could, I would not want to. Rejoice, O you who are my age, whether you are sturdier in resisting old age or more ingenious in concealing it or more prone to trust the vain hope that arises from deceptive and fleeting youth. I do not trust the flatteries of an age that glides by stealthily. Rejoice, O you who still want to look young; I give up. My time has come, and I leave the empty place to you. Hold on to it stubbornly, keep your birth certificate. I am undisguisedly old. I read my years in the mirror, others on my brow. My early looks are gone, and the happy light of my eyes is hidden by a sorrowful cloud, as they call it, but a happy one, as I feel. My hair falling out, my rough skin, and the snowy whiteness covering my head proclaim that the winter of my age is here.

But thanks be to Him who watches over us and guides us from dawn to evening, and from early childhood to old age. I feel that at this stage, not only are my mental powers enhanced but my bodily strength for my own studies and gentlemanly activities has in no way decreased. For I rejoice and strive to become unfit for other things, and I help my age along by fasting, toil, and vigils. Whenever I am so affected by all this that I neither feel like thinking anything shameful nor am able to carry it out, I then consider myself stronger than Milo and Alcides, triumphing over my body, as though it were an old enemy who waged many grievous battles against me; and I seem to be driving a laureled chariot up the Sacred Way to the capitol of my mind, dragging in triumph my rebellious feelings, conquered passions, and that most insidious foe of virtue, pleasure, bound with steel knots and stubborn shackles.

Perhaps someone will wonder therefore—but not those who are so well acquainted with virtue that it has ceased to be a wonder— why to me life never was so beautiful as it is now when it begins being hateful to others. And may God, who has brought me step by step to this age, so bring me from this vain mortal life to that true life everlasting, as I prize more one day of this mature age, which nearly all young people both wish for and hate, than a year of that

---

* Addressees unknown.

blooming period, continually upset by so many moves of other people and fickle through youthful changeableness. I apply truthfully to myself that saying of Marcus Cato in Tully's book, although my virtue is unequal to his: "If some god granted me at this age to become a child once again and to squawl again in the cradle, I would absolutely refuse, nor indeed would I like to be called back from my goal to the stable, as if the race were over" [*Sen.* 83]. Nor will I ever agree with that interpretation of the verse from Virgil in the book by Nonius Marcellus, *On Correctness of Language.* He says that our Maro "very wisely divided the day into parts, and in the ninth book [*Aen.* 9.150] called the first part better, as if it were the day's youth, 'since now the best part of the day has passed'" [2.12 (Lindsay)]. Very wise indeed, I know it, but you do not interpret the verse wisely. For Maro is speaking not of life but of the day whose first part, being free and exempt from stomach upsets and from nightly bonds of confusion, is consequently often said to be more fit for great thoughts, although to sober minds and bodies any part of the day is fit for any good deed.

But what you try to apply to age in general, as though its first part were better, even though Virgil himself elsewhere and many others agree, no one in his right mind, while it cannot altogether be denied with respect to the body, would doubt that it is said falsely with respect to the mind, the most noble part of us, except that perhaps we excuse crazy old people on the ground of their suffering this not through any fault of their own but because of their age. In order to excuse themselves, they often unfairly accuse old age, ascribing the blame for their ways to their years, whereas the true condition of old people is not to rave but to be wise. The fact that some, nay indeed many, do rave is because of their earlier years; taking the wrong path leads to the wrong goal. He who goes where he ought not to, arrives where he does not wish to. Thus, a crazy old age follows an erring youth. All ages are contiguous and connected to one another, and just as each previous age hints at the one that follows, so each subsequent age bears witness to the one that preceded; "Age brings everything" [*Ecl.* 9.51], says Maro's shepherd. One must confess that beyond doubt old age is either adverse or burdensome to the memory, because of the multitude and weight of the things it bears; keeping track of a few things is easy, and having everything at hand is a sign of poverty.

Besides, old age checks the memory, it does not crush or wipe it out; and although a young man's memory is quicker, an old man's memory is tighter, he remembers more, but less promptly, for he has seen more, heard more, read more, learned more, and hidden more as if under lock and key. The owner of many things must overlook many. He has many trunks that long remain untouched, and like a wealthy man does not have at hand everything he owns; they must be looked for, dug up as things that have been put away, not lost. Illness has taken away some people's intelligence and memory, but age does this to no one. Never has a wise youth gone crazy in old age. But often a foolish adolescent has recovered his senses because of old age. Therefore, any foolish and crazy old people you may see were silly youths. It is not the fault of age if it gives back what it received. It deserves praise for sometimes making someone different from what he was, and better. Much could be said at this point, but there is no time. I am expected elsewhere. Nevertheless, while haste prevents bringing in everything, here are a few things out of many, whereby whoever hears or sees this will note the difference between my opinion and that of the multitude.

Among those whom we loosely call friends—if they were as many as they are said to be, life would be better—I once had and still have one, a very entertaining man. One day he came to my house as usual, sat down, and began looking around the house, which was not large but comfortable, at the furnishings not of gold but respectable and at the bedroom not laden with silk coverlets but with clean, white straw mattresses. It was winter, and in a corner there was not a blazing fire but a glowing brazier. Then, when he entered the library and silently began counting the books, for a long time he just stood there, marveling at their value. He certainly was not mistaken in this, if only he had figured something other than monetary value. Finally he stared at a very handsome chest of foreign workmanship, a gift from another friend, and he assumed that it was full of gold, whereas it contained neither gold nor silver but was filled with papers and poems. Whereupon, taking into account my special friendships and the favor of famous men, which he knew I had enjoyed, and putting together each of these things and perhaps others, and admiring me and my good fortune as Damocles had admired Dionysius, at last he said with a sigh, "Ah, what in the world do you lack except one thing, which if you had, you surely would be the luckiest of all mortals" [probably based on Cic., *Tusc.* 5.62]. Although I guessed what he had in mind, I begged him to make known that one thing to me, using in a literal sense David's words, "Please let me know what I lack and what checks my happiness, for if I perhaps began to realize this, I could begin to seek some kind of remedy." To this he replied with a deeper sigh, "It is something that can be supplied neither by your genius nor by any other's. The only thing you lack is youth." Smilingly I said, "Dear friend, if you care for me, do not weep because I am not young; weep because I once was." When I thereupon began consoling and showing him that the age he admired was useless and dangerous, whereas the one he despised was advantageous and secure, the best part of life—if there is anything good in life—he walked out on our conversation, unable to listen to me any longer and upset, just as though I were thrusting a new heresy upon him. At that time my age was robust and forceful but no longer lush and blooming, yet for that good but unschooled man, it appeared wretched to have gone beyond adolescence.

The story comes to mind now so that from the opinion of one I might expose the entire multitude, for the same error is made by all, and everyone feels the same. If they were to call life as a whole wretched, perhaps they would not err; now, through a pathetic error, they consider happiest the one part of this misery that is most miserable of all. But let us leave the multitude with their absurdities, since not only have they committed as many errors as thoughts and words and actions, but their whole life is but error and vanity. Even learned men often fall into this error, and, misled by the multitude's footsteps, they so abandon the right path that they grieve at maturity and dread the rapid approach of old age, which their loving parents have wished upon them with so many prayers. They cling with no less effort to fleeting adolescence and youth; and they are wrenched away against their will, and drawn back by vain longing and the empty sweetness that always sticks to what is behind us.

I shall not deny that perhaps sometimes I too was one of those who yearn for what cannot return. But after I drew nearer, it happened to me as it does to those who are deceived by viewing things at a distance. I saw as fearful what I used to desire, and as desirable what I used to fear. God knows, as does my conscience in recalling things past, how often I was ashamed of having sighed in vain for what could not return, and if it could, I would have had to resist its return with all my might. In thinking it over, then, I forgive the sighs of young people anyhow, except for those who become unworthy of such forgiveness because they have accepted the madness of the multitude rather than the advice of old people—perhaps their own wise kin. But those oldsters whose very experience ought to have made them independent of the advice of others, and who still sigh for their youth—the world is full of such people today—I consider quite unworthy of forgiveness and worthy of loathing.

In sum, not the young but the old should pass judgment upon every age, and of the old not all but those who are sensible and have grown old in their thinking too; for the rest must be numbered among the youth, or even among the children. Therefore, the real elders are the proper judges of the stages of life, since those who are young judge things without being experienced, whereas every old man was once young. On the other hand, no young man has been old or knows whether he is going to be. My very age and—unless I am mistaken—my even temper make me one of the fit judges. I know what I am. I remember what I was when I seemed most happy in the flower of my age, and was pointed out and stared at by so many that I got tired of it. Now too this happens to me more than ever, but in another and very dissimilar way. Comparing the different times, even if each age has its bitterness and its sweetness, weighing it all, I conclude that a peaceful, restful, and honorable old age is preferable to any other age. I have often said and I repeat this, though not unaware that I am speaking against the opinion of many, indeed of almost the entire world. Nor am I unaware of how youth is quicker and stronger for running and jumping, for business, for exertions; in addition it is more lively and enthusiastic, but not more constant or well advised, as even the multitude agrees with me, nor more courageous, though they strongly disagree. If the reason for this is asked, it is right here: a young man has his mind set on taking a wife, begetting children, acquiring riches, friendships, power, fame, enjoying pleasures, being singled out for honors, and living a long time—things that of course instill the fear of death in the mind, foreseeing that for so many varied goals it takes time which can be swept away by intervening death. The old man has all this behind him, whether he has long since had them and, as happens, had his fill of them, or he has either spurned them as worthless, or given up on them as hopeless. As they are no more, his only concern now is to die well, less worried precisely because of the nearness to death. Many things are more frightening from a distance.

Never did I approve, either in my teens and much less now that I am old, of that saying of Caecilius, reported by Cicero and so rightly rejected by Cato, that in old age the worst thing is to feel you are hateful to others because of your age; nor do I agree with those words of Dictys of Gnosus [Knossos] in the third book of his *History of Troy*: "No one can doubt that old age is held in contempt by youth" [3.21]. I do in fact doubt this and feel certain about the opposite, that old age is worthy of praise and is loved, revered, and esteemed, and so I judge these words to be of some worthless and inglorious oldster. He knows he is neither despised nor hated by good people; life arouses no shame in him, nor death any fear. But those who have spent their entire life in misdeeds and lusts, who have placed the peak of their happiness in their body, when in the course of living they arrive at old age, that is, at the age that wears down bodily looks and strength, what wonder if—being outwardly frail and unsightly, empty and hollow inside, devoid of book-learning and virtue, and of no use to any one, like horses and mules with no intelligence whose bodily strength has failed, leading a bestial life that has made them just like those beasts, as though they too, stripped of their gilt headgear, have been reassigned from drawing royal coaches to village buggies—they are mocked and put down, and become the butt and the laughing-stock of youth?

When have you ever heard of King David among the Hebrews being held up to ridicule? Or Nestor among the Greeks, and Fabius or Cato among us? They did grow old, but that part of them where-by they stood out the most had no fear of old age. And since only a few reach such a pinnacle of glory, lest anyone give up on this and stick to a lowly place, think how many honored elders of second rank are in sight every day who guide themselves, their families, their country, and energetic youngsters with their counsel, though they are weak in body and worn out by age, if only they are not sluggish or flabby in spirit. In short, this is, and always has been, my opinion on this matter, but now I am even more qualified to judge, having tested it not only through witnesses but through experience. Therefore, while I have often spoken of this elsewhere, I never did so at length, being fearful of saying a great deal about what I did not know. Although I realize my earlier and present statements may seem superfluous since the subject was very carefully treated in an entire volume by Marcus Tullius, it is still pleasant to speak about myself to myself and to my friends, even though not necessary.

I am not overlooking the objections that can be raised by the subtlety of those who disagree: namely, that I have still not reached the real discomforts of old age; that my age is no longer blooming nor green but still firm and sound; that my tone must change when I come to that point; that I speak bravely because I have yet to grow weak with the years,

While I'm still in the unbent prime of old age,

as the Satirist says [Juv. 3.26], and am not yet bent over, looking at the ground, nor do I walk with the help of a cane, but on my own feet. I know all this, and am not ignorant of the fact that any age is divided into three parts: the first is called green, whence in Virgil "green old age," and the second mature; but the third is called on the brink, as Cicero calls his own. I am at that very age, although mine is not yet on the brink but still green with God's help. And yet it is old age, and no longer youth, whatever terms other score keepers may apply to it.

Therefore, when I reach the brink, if I ever do, perhaps I shall still find it more agrecable than they say. So I surmise from similar cases, and so I have heard from learned old men. But should I find anything different from what I hope, what do you suppose I shall do? Shall I follow Seneca's advice and leap out of the rotting, crumbling dwelling? May such madness never enter my soul! I shall persist and hold firm as long as I can, nor will the craving for false freedom make me jump headlong into true slavery; for such men seem, by means of a voluntary death, to have avoided through a shortcut some real illness or terrible blow of fate, but they fail to realize how much more harm each does to themselves by following such advice than whatever fate has in store. For fate brings nothing but temporal death, but they bring an eternal one upon themselves. Yet this kind of evading disease and taking the headlong path prompted that man of great intelligence to utter this disgraceful opinion: "One finds even men professing wisdom who deny the use of any violence against their own lives, and who consider it wicked to commit suicide, and a good end the one decreed by nature" [Sen., *Ep*. 70.14]. Extremely strange, especially from the mouth of a learned man and a teacher of morals and how men should live. He speaks as though those who say this have discovered something new, whereas no one truly professing wisdom can be found who does not say and feel the same. He nevertheless says that one who says this does not see that he closes off the road to freedom; and that his love of freedom had made him his own enemy.

O how much better was it said by Seneca's friends, Cicero and Maro, and many others, whom he knew most intimately! I marvel all the more that he could have forgotten such men or scorned them; in the first one's works, when the younger Africanus was entertaining thoughts about suicide but was told by his father Paullus, "It is not so, for unless that god whose temple consists of all this that you see has freed you from your bodily prison, you cannot have access to this place" [*Rep*. 6.15], that is, to heaven where the conversation is imagined. I omit the rest, since the passage is very famous. When Maro deals with those

> who, though innocent,
> With their own hands committed suicide:
> Hating the light they threw away their lives
>   [*Aen.* 6.434–36]

he immediately added,

> O how they would now choose in the world above,
> To bear hard toil and poverty. [6.436–37]

So it is indeed—fleeing by a precipice, they rush into greater pains, so that they now must wish for the ones they avoided a little earlier by jettisoning their lives. Yet it is all in vain. For, as the poet continues, "The fates stand in the way" [4.440], and the rest, which is also well known.*

I shall not contrast still other writers to Seneca, especially our own for whom that opinion is so wicked and insane that they would not even deign to hear it. It is enough to have opposed his own authorities to him, not random ones but the princes of Latin eloquence. Somehow the decision to move out of an awful building could be, I do not say wise, but perhaps noble, if you had chosen the place for yourself; but now one that has been assigned by the heavenly King to a transitory soul cannot be abandoned without offending and disdaining the Lord. Therefore, I shall not move either from this abode, however uncomfortable, nor from the harshest bonds, unless He who has bound me frees me; and in this matter I have always preferred the opinion of a spoiled, indulged king to that of a strict philosopher. I refer to Darius, King of the Persians, who, conquered in battle and in desperate straits, was asked as he urged his followers to look out for themselves, why he himself did not avoid by suicide the imminent mockery of his life; he gave his reason in these words: "I await whatever fate has in store for me here; perhaps you wonder why I do not end my life; I would rather die through someone else's crime than my own."

With resolve I too shall await my lot, whatever condition either of body or of other things is in store for me; for I shall see what my King has decreed for me here or elsewhere, and with His help strive to shape my mind so that it will accept whatever will be, gladly if it can, or at least bravely and patiently. Meanwhile, I thus far feel no

* P.'s memory has confused this passage (*fata obstant*) with 6.438, *fas obstat*, i.e. "Fate stands in the way."

harm being done by old age, no disappointments, but instead much that is pleasant. Nor do I agree with Terence's Chremes that old age itself is a disease, unless he were perhaps to add one thing that would make the idea more complete, namely, that old age is a disease of the body, but the health of the soul.

I enter this age briskly, I cross its first frontier; and what Cicero in writing to Augustus, as I have said, calls "on the brink" for himself, I find very level and smooth for me. Still I see with wonder the thousands of complainers there, who yearn to live on and bemoan the fact that they have lived; I alone will grow old without trouble, without squabbling, if I can. Why do I use the verb in the future tense? I am already growing old, I have already grown old, nor have I, in the midst of speaking, as often happens, forgotten what I said at the start. I have, I say, grown old, and I give my thanks to Nature, whether she wants me to complete this journey (although after old age there is nothing but decrepitude and death, the former being part of extreme old age, the latter the end of life) or chooses to spare me the final exertion—wherever the traveler stops, there is his journey's end and his last exertion. It matters not how much further he could have gone, if he went no further. I have assuredly left the judgment of this matter, along with any concern, to Him with whom, it is written, lies the guidance of man's steps, the determination of his end, and the number of his months and days, and a thousand years go by as though it were yesterday. He Himself will call me, and I shall answer Him with, I hope, good and saving faith.

Meanwhile I proceed more happily from day to day, and I say to my contemporaries who are still struggling against it, and to those who will follow us, "Come, do not worry or fear or listen to those dismal old men who weep that they have been released from the toils of evil lusts, the same as it behooved them to weep when they were bound. Do not believe them because of their age which makes them venerable-looking, even against their will. Old age, toward which you draw amidst the storms of life, is not what they say. To them every age was awful. It was the fault of their folly, not their age. For the learned and well-tempered man old age is unshakable, once the mental stresses have been stilled; having left behind the reefs of strife and labor, it is peaceful and protected against the outer churning, as if by a ring of sunny hills of rest and quiet. So go, but make haste, as you are bound to; where you feared a shipwreck, there is a harbor."

O dear old age, venerable above all else, O long desired, in no way to be feared by mortals, and, once known, a happy time of life! Unworthy of reaching you is anyone who fears you, unworthy of having reached you is anyone who finds fault with you! I have always desired you, never feared you. As you have approached, I have come up to meet you as far as I could. I hold you present at last, having sought you in my prayers and anticipated you in my thoughts, and I embrace you; O good conqueror of evil affections, best evictor of the worst lusts, to you alone, after God, am I grateful because you release me from my heavy shackles and from my gloomy prison, allowing me at length to begin feeling free, my own master. My freedom comes late, I confess, but the later, the more welcome. Its loss made my youth sad, its recovery makes my old age joyful. It is an odd spectacle but true that all writers over and over, especially Virgil, call sad what I have found most joyful. Oh, that my Socrates [Ludwig van Kempen] and Lelius [Angelo di Pietro Stefano dei Tosetti] were alive—that is, if they would have agreed with me—and many others who have lived with me since my youth! But many do still survive. If I am lying, there are many who can contradict me. It is well known that my adolescence and youth were saddened and laden with cares, for parts of my soul were at odds with each other and in continual discord; and in a state of civil war, so to speak, they would upset my life and my peace. I never longed for great wealth; I had already learned to love moderation, but not yet to endure it; and I burned with other youthful fires, and became a burden, a toil, a punishment to myself so that absolutely nothing is further from my wishes than to return, even if I could, to those tempests of the spirit, from which I rejoice to have escaped with sound keel—and I recognize the favor of God in this.

The wish commonly expressed for friends in their old age—that they might be young again, with the proviso that the same spirit and the same seriousness should remain, the tranquillity of character, moderation, wisdom, experience, knowledge of literature, in short, all the ornaments that render old age venerable—is doubly futile. Aside from the irreversible advance of age (about which we have read that many have returned from death to life, but none from old age to youth), there is another impossibility: a young man cannot have an old mind any more than an old man can have a young body. Why then do they rather wish their friends a learned, sober youth than a healthy, blooming old age, if not because the restless mind—at least in its thoughts—turns back, when it cannot do otherwise, to the years that were propitious to lusts and to those terribly disturbing passions from which, as from an enemy's clutches, I am as happy to have escaped as I would be not only foolish but mad to want to return to. Reason, incapable by itself of restraining these in me, did so with the aid of time. Then at last I began to feel good for the first time, and little by little I seemed to change internally and externally, as if transformed from a crow to a swan, and my white hair seemed to have brought a whiteness to my spirit.

Friends, I eagerly say these many things to you about this unappreciated age that is now mine, but nothing about myself. I do not know how well I stand in it or what sort of old man I am, and how long I will be, when and how I shall leave it. Nothing about myself, I say, except this one thing: I declare and boldly affirm the following praises of old age to all the listeners who know me—there was no sadder youth nor happier old man than I. You be joyful and unworried as you grow old, and delight in it, and farewell, remembering me.

Pavia, November 29 [1364–67].

Sen. VIII, 3.

To Tommaso del Garbo, Florentine physician,* on belief and fortune, which he had asked about.

You offered me a subject that would have been quite unfamiliar and attractive as well as far-ranging and profound, if on the one hand I had enough ability and time to spare, or on the other you had inquired in such a way as to leave me some room to reply. But inasmuch as you have said masterfully and at great length almost everything that can be said on the subject you ask me about, what have you done but turn me from a respondent into an admirer? You have simply repeated to me what our Savior did in examining the teachers of the law when He taught as he questioned them, if their ears were not blocked to the truth. And, of course, careful questioning or shrewd doubting about any subject by distinguished men always carries a silent, hidden lesson. But they are not moved to do so unless there are major reasons, and as they hesitantly unfold the reasons, they often stir up and instruct those who had not felt any doubt about it. If ever this happened any other time, it happened especially now when you raised the question.

The fine and ticklish question you propose concerning belief and fortune is addressed to me but valuable for everyone in general: which of the two is the more powerful, since you admit that both are very powerful? First you pose the surprising and multiple influences of belief which are so violent that they drive the weak soul hither and yon in opposite directions, to the point where often truth is vanquished and gives way to it. Would that this were not so repeated and widespread, that what has become a byword were not so—that all things are controlled by beliefs. Why else, to say something about myself as well, does one man live poorly amidst the greatest riches while another in abject poverty lives most richly? Why is this, I say, if not because of each one's belief? For the one man it shrinks his riches and brings on the need for more, but for the other it depicts want as wealth and instills in him a contempt for restless avarice; and being content with what he has, he considers

---

* A well-known physician whose father had been famous in Florence. He held university chairs in Perugia and Bologna, and was at times attendant on Galeazzo Visconti, who suffered from an extreme form of gout. This is the only letter to him.

whatever may be added a burden and not riches.

Why do we see that those who are in the best health weep, while those who are ill and out of their minds laugh and exult in joy? How strong must a true belief be, if a false belief is so strong? Why does it happen that a man who has often gone erect through a frail and narrow doorway close to the ground stands trembling on the top of a narrow, solid tower? He has the same feet as before, the same strong limbs, the same eyesight; the place itself where he stands is firmer and more stable. Only his belief is weaker, or should I say stronger, since it can so unsettle an otherwise robust mind that one who stood firm on what was shaky shakes on something firm. You have read about Cassius, one of those who had laid upon Julius Caesar, I will not say wicked criminal hands in order not to judge in passing a question that is still in dispute, but certainly bold hands: when on the plains of Thessaly the furies of civil war again pursued the Roman state, he was so beset and overwhelmed by the most compelling belief that he saw Caesar himself in full armor, bearing down on him and spurring his horse. He had not feared to strike Caesar down when he was alive and in power; but he ran away from Caesar when he was buried and lifeless. He screamed those words full of fright and delusion. One can have doubts about the rapture of Paul since he himself says he did not know whether he was in his body or without. But certainly the stigmata of Francis had their beginning when he embraced Christ's death in such a continuous and powerful meditation that, as he had mentally transferred it over a long period of time and felt as though he himself were crucified with his Lord, eventually his pious belief transferred a true likeness of the thing from his mind into his body.

I pass over that deadly power of beliefs which afflicts and corrupts the whole world: that while knowledge and virtue are held in esteeem by very few, by hardly anyone nowadays, wealth, power, and pleasures are to nearly all mortals the highest and the foremost goods. This belief alone, more than anything else, plunges mortal hearts into these miseries that we see. For what else is this but the infinite perversity of beliefs, which some people consider the source of all evils, and I think they are not mistaken? But why do I seek distant or obscure instances when there is at home, under your very eyes, the best example? You who are, I do not say the greatest lest I judge those I do not know, but without doubt the most famous that the art of medicine has—you know how weakly and childishly a great portion of sick people bear even minor pains. Daily you hear those pathetic voices: "Alas, what crime have I committed to be afflicted this way! What have I done? Who ever endured such agony?" In Tully the complaints of Hercules and Prometheus are lengthy and well known.

But you hear many that neither these fretful characters nor the tragic authors writing about them ever conceived. On the other hand, that greatest man of our sphere, the mighty ruler of Liguria, Galeazzo Visconti the younger (for his treatment your renown fetched you from afar) has been suffering so acutely for a full ten years with the gout not only in his feet—from which *podagra* gets its name—but in the hands, elbows, shoulders and the entire body, that his lower limbs are benumbed; and, being paralyzed rather than just crippled, they fail him not only in walking but even in standing; yet he endures it with a spirit that is so unconquered and unbroken that we who wait on him cannot restrain our tears when we see the extreme, intolerable pains that afflict our beloved sovereign. He alone views his tortured and aching body as if it belonged to some unknown stranger. The extent of his patience amazes bystanders that, like a veritable prodigy, a man of delicate constitution, reared in the utmost luxury, who even now (something that could have added to the resentment and pain of a less brave spirit) is still young and vigorous, and, what is more, when he had the use of his limbs, was proud of his many long journeys, as well as wars and martial exercise and equestrian games—that such a man endures not only with dry eyes but an untroubled brow what makes healthy men sad and groan just to see. Ask those who attend him day and night, and they will tell you that they have never heard a cry of pain from him or a word of reproach from his mouth, but instead always the same refrain: "God has done many great things for me. If with His many bounties He has mixed in this one discomfort, there is no reason for me to complain about my Lord, but very many to render thanks unto Him. Blessed be the name of the Lord!" With such unusual composure and such amazing patience, he would seem to me, I confess, most to deserve sounder health, save that the infallible Presence, weighing all things accurately, often applies the sufferings of the body to the salvation of the soul. And he does not simply display patience amidst such great torments, but also magnanimity, constancy, foresight, liberality, gentle concern in happy circumstances and a spirit unafraid in adverse ones, and—something especially astonishing in his present bodily condition and the many vicissitudes and threats of fortune—an unflagging and enduring cheerfulness and everything of that ilk, which he recognizes as essential to rulers. For this reason those words of the Roman emperor Septimius Severus eminently apply to our leader, namely, that the head rules, not the feet.

So far I have enjoyed speaking with you about him, since we both love his virtue and hate his illness; you are getting him all the help that is humanly possible, while I am doing it in the only way I can, through prayers and vows. I have allowed myself to talk about him in greater detail inasmuch as I deemed that he concerns us and his case concerns our subject. For why such great diversity, that one man bears minor discomforts like a woman while Galeazzo bears grave ones like a man, if not because of belief? That is what we are speaking about, how one is convinced that every pain is great misery while another believes that there is no misery except in the mind into which neither misery nor the passions have any access enter if you hold firm. Keep this in mind: that while these ills affecting the body may be rather bitter, they are exercises for the spirit and grist for virtue, which rejoices in hardships and detests anything unmanly. Lastly, from this derives that final point, that one man dies sadly, as the majority of mortals do, another happily; for evidently while death is the same, beliefs about it are different.

I now come to the other part of your letter, which is about Fortune, whose power you magnify with words, and not you alone; the talents of nearly all agree on this one thing with equal insistence though differing expression. Thus Crispus says that Fortune rules in everything; I wish that he had excepted virtue. Cicero called her the mistress of human affairs. In this matter Virgil disagrees with Homer, whom he follows in many others; while in Homer, so they say, there is no mention of Fortune anywhere because he believed there is no such thing, our poet not only names her and calls her powerful, but in a certain passage Fortune is ever omnipotent. Nor has it escaped me that some of our [Latin] writers, both long ago—though it was quite rightfully refuted by Augustine—and lately, have placed her in heaven as though she were some divinity. I find this shocking beyond words, unless they are perchance repeating the multitude's error, concerning which the Satirist says,

> Fortune, 'tis we
> That make you a goddess—we put you in heaven.
> [Juv. 10.365–66]

But it is shameful that for all their knowledge, the wise men, in order to attract followers, follow in madmen's footsteps, whereas to turn diametrically away from there is, after all, the highest wisdom; there are many all over who put good fortune not only ahead of virtue but even of divine help, and would rather be friends of fortune than of God. Wherefore, it can only appear extraordinary that both the learned and the unlearned feel thus—the human race, which disagrees on so many things, agrees on this.

What shall I say, or what shall I think? Aristotle's little book *On Good Fortune* is not unknown to me. Nor have I forgotten those words of Cicero, "Great is the power of fortune on either side, whether favoring one's goal or contrary to it. Who does not know this? For when we enjoy her support, we arrive at the desired result, and when she blows the other way, we are afflicted" [*Off.* 2.6.19]. Along with this I recall the passage of Lactantius when he tears those ideas apart, "First, whoever denies that anything can be known affirms it as though he himself and everyone else knew it; secondly, he who attempts to cast doubt even on things that are true, has considered true what ought to be especially doubtful to him, since to a wise mind it is entirely false. 'Who does not know this?' he says. I do not know it; let him, if he can, teach me what is that power, or what is that wind of fortune, and that contrary wind. It is therefore shameful that a brilliant man says something he cannot prove if you deny it. Finally, he who says that one ought to withhold approval because giving blind approval to unknown things is typical of the fool, clearly believes the opinions of the multitude and of uninformed men who think that it is fortune that bestows good and bad upon men" [*Inst.* 3.29]. Perhaps I have cited these words of Lactantius too early since they directly contradict Cicero's cited above.

But once again I am not unaware that Augustine, after having often called it fortune's doing in a certain work of his, subsequently refuted himself in order not to be refuted by someone else; for that too, like everything else, is done by design and providence. Otherwise that most holy man, in dealing with things sacred, shuddered not without justification at the profane name of fortune. I, on the other hand, a sinner, long since engaged in secular studies, somehow seem to have inserted that word a thousand times in my scribblings; for I knew that the mouths of the multitude and the books of learned men were full of it. Indeed I had even felt such little misgiving about using it that recently I wrote a little book, *De remediis utriusque fortune*, making fortune not twofold but two-faced. How others view this book, I leave to the judgment of those who have heard or read it. As for me, since it was brought to completion, I have not intensely savored anything from it, nor been able to test how much I was helped by my own advice. Still I have taken more satisfaction in it when I learned that it was very well received and sought by certain great minds.

Fortune is such a trite subject. As I have said here, I have not only mentioned it very often but even written a book about it. To be sure, I did so following ordinary, everyday usage because I would more often address the general public than philosophers. What I truly feel about fortune in my heart of hearts, where I have many a quarrel, as is known, with the public, I have often touched upon briefly, as though aiming the spearhead of whatever opinion of mine at a distant target. And now, since you force me, I must touch upon it more explicitly; about this, as about much else, I admit, I would rather listen, which I think is more profitable and safer; but I could not ignore the request of such a distinguished man. I know, then, as you have heard, that great men have written about fortune, and I know that I, a petty one, have as well, and that this term has been used by secular writers and not left untouched by sacred writers.

I recall that Augustine himself, in dealing with fate, which—for all I know—is either the same as fortune or related to it, said along with much else, "unless perchance we understand the word *fate* from *fari*, that is, from the verb 'to speak,' for we cannot deny that in Sacred Scripture it is written, 'God spoke once.' When it says 'He spoke once,' we understand that He spoke immovably, that is, unchangeably. Therefore, with this reasoning we could derive *fatum* from *fari*, save that this word is now usually understood in another sense to which we do not want men's hearts to incline." In that same book he flatly says, "By divine providence human governments are established. If then someone attributes this to fate because he calls the very will or power of God by the word *fate*, let him keep his opinion but correct his language." If, by heavens, it is understood this way, I too do not deny a certain great and "ineluctable fate" [*Aen.* 8.334], as Maro says, or fortune. For if the precepts of mortal princes are so great and so compelling, how much greater must we esteem the proclamations of the divine mouth. Although it is first a Homeric, then a Virgilian fiction that the Fates cannot be changed, can be delayed, yet they really can in no way be changed or postponed, nor is there any room for force, or escape, or hesitation, or delay. But, as the multitude and no small part of literate people accept the term *fortune*, I frankly confess, nor do I fear the taunt of being called an ignoramus, to believing that there is no such thing.

Perhaps you will be among the first to ask my reason for doing this: writing about something I either know or believe is nothing. I shall answer that in writing nothing about fortune but about remedies against what is called fortune, I included what seemed either to soothe or to inspire the human spirit. Since those things are commonly called "fortuitous," I kept the ancient name lest I frighten the reader by quibbling over the word, and turn him against the book and the writer.

I know that most people are persuaded that when anything happens without apparent causes (since absolutely nothing happens without some cause) it is "fortuitous," and that this is called fortune. For example, the head of a household is about to go on a journey. Trusting in no one, he buries his treasure in the ground, so as to find it on his return. He goes but never returns. Long after, a peasant digging in the ground, or an architect laying a foundation, discovers it. The owner had not had this in mind, nor was the finder looking for it; the former had thought only of hiding the treasure, the second of tilling the field or building the house. They say that it was the fortune of both, of the one to lose it, of the other to find it. I cannot make out this thing which is so clear to many. I know that the one who buried the treasure was a householder, that the one who found it was an architect or a peasant, that what he found was gold or silver, or something like that, that what he found it with was a plow or a mattock, that what he worked the implement with was his hands, arms, oxen, plow-handle, or something of the sort.

Someone goes either to Bologna to study or to Rome to pray; he falls in with robbers unexpectedly and is killed. Marcellus was returning from exile and was joyfully on his way back to his country, but he was surprised by a wicked enemy and murdered. Such, they say, was the fortune of all of these. But I see the young student, the devout pilgrim, and the journey of each one, and furthermore the good citizen unjustly exiled, and Mitylene, his place of exile, and Athens where he was killed, and bandits and lurking enemies, and blades, attacks, blows, and blood, and altogether the happenings and actions themselves, and the actors and the outcome; amidst these things I look for fortune, about which we are speaking, and I find nothing beyond the bare name. For if any sudden and unexpected outcome of happenings is itself called fortune, which is the definition given by some, from this alone, unless I am mistaken, the truth of the matter emerges sufficiently. For what is the outcome of all this and the like, other than the wounds, the deaths, and the robbing, the true movers of which are neither fortune nor fate, nor anyone else than men themselves? Swayed by these and other considerations, I am compelled to agree with those who say that fortune in itself is nothing. Lest I take credit for what belongs to others, the subject has been discussed, I believe, cleverly and conscientiously enough by many writers, among whom are those I mentioned above—Augustine and Lactantius Firmianus in his book *On Institutions*.

Therefore, that was a fine and devout reply by the most zealous of Christian brothers who, when they were arrested and doomed to torture and death for the sake of the truth, and their wicked judge mentioned fortune, and declared in a short, laconic but nonetheless true statement that Christians do not know fortune. The authority of great men supports them. Not to mention the two I referred to a while ago, who very often repeat this very thing, I see that for Ambrose there were no Fates, and for Jerome there was neither fate nor fortune.

In sum, then, I use the ordinary term in order to be understood, but about the thing itself, this is my judgment. If perchance it is not ordinary enough nor philosophical enough, I think it is a pious judgment, and that is enough for me. In the past I have often said and written this, but never more clearly. For I feel that the contrary opinion, about whose power we spoke in the beginning, being fixed in men's minds and rooted in deep error, cannot be uprooted nor the common way of speaking changed, and I will sometimes, to avoid argument, speak as most people do; but I will always feel as do the few. But if perchance I often use adverbs deriving from the word *fortune*, I shall still say that Fortune herself is nothing. If, then, that view is truer—for I do not pretend to be a definer of such great mysteries—that is, the view of those who want fortune to be something, either God's providence, itself controlling and driving human events through causes hidden to man but very well known to Him, or, as others maintain, some handmaiden of Providence and executrix of divine will, I know not how, since it is written: "He spoke and it was done" [Ps. 33:9]. But if all this were so, no one would have any doubt that, although that belief is within man himself while fortune is outside of him, fortune is mightier than belief. I have said that it rules over belief and the soul in which belief resides, and the body, and all things.

This is what has offhand come to mind amidst my many concerns, without books and totally absorbed in plans for a trip; and I leave it to all learned men and to you above all, my friend, to make a firmer judgment about this. If you find out anything and write it up for my guidance, I will embrace it. Farewell.

Pavia, November 9 [1366-67].

Sen. VIII, 4.

To Luchino dal Verme, Veronese knight* who had set out to fight the Turks, an exhortation to return

You remember, I think, that I was never happy with this expedition of yours. For although in itself it was pious and undertaken for just causes, it still appeared from the beginning not to be bolstered by enough reserves or by that planning which ranks first, especially in war. It would not have been otherwise if you were now supreme commander against the Assyrians [Turks] as you lately were against rebellious Crete, but such is not the case. There you were acting under your own auspices, now you are under someone else's. Therefore every day that you are gone, I become more and more worried and upset. I feel a strange, unwonted fear; may the saints dispel it! To tell the truth, it now verges on an evil foreboding. You know the fine thread on which human vicissitudes hang. That climate, that company, that responsibility are not for you.

Return to us and please hurry; every day of waiting is longer than a year. To the eyes of those who love you, give back the light we are yearning for. Free our minds from our longing for you; deliver us, in short, from our constant fear, which I hope is unfounded, but still is grave and certainly too long-lasting; please come. If you left to keep away from envy, as great men have sometimes done, look, it is now keeping away from you; if you were tired of the dullness, you have now moved around enough, and more. But if it was out of a desire to see the world, which some famous men consider necessary for future leaders, you have now had ample experience of distant places and events, as well as your fill of foreign things, it is time for you in turn to be moved by a longing for us. Finally, whatever the motive for your departure, no one at all doubts that your basic purpose was none other than to make yourself better by your daily discipline; now that you have become better, come back. Farewell.

Pavia, December 10 [1366].

* See IV, 1.

Sen. VIII, 5.

To Giacomo dal Verme,* on the death of his father Luchino.

Oh fate of men, which they call Fortune, so often treacherous and deceptive in her flatteries, but sometimes threatening and revealing what she is going to do! This last is the way she has treated me now, whether it was she or a higher power against which one must not complain. Nothing was done that caught me unawares; I admit I had foreseen this blow long before. But it is difficult to escape from things hanging over us, especially those that depend on others, so that no role remains for our intellect or initiative. My mind was haunted by sad forebodings, and trembling all over I would constantly think about the deplorable absence of your distinguished father, and I constantly foresaw and feared what has happened: that the rare glory of our age and of our homeland, whose ethereal part was owed to heaven and has now been returned there, whose earthly part was owed to Italy and to the Adige, should now be bodily taken from us by the Thracian Hebrus and the Euxine.

I did not remain silent about this; instead by letter and messengers' tongues I reproached him and his fatal lingering. But perhaps he could not do otherwise: his unconquerable shoulders were driven by an overwhelming inevitability and the weight of a gathering catastrophe. "Thus was it fated," says Naso [*Fast.* 1.481]; rather it was God's will that, inasmuch as since his earliest youth he had always served in the regular army,** and had undertaken his last expedition in behalf of godliness and religion against the enemies of the faith in the most sacred and honorable of all wars, and the best use of arms, the spirit of the deceased should ascend, armed with virtue and triumphant, to Him to whom he owed many famous victories. And I trust that he has reached heaven and found the happy conclusion of his toils, from which his virtue gave him no respite. Since it no longer becomes my age and my thinking, as it once did, to weep over the deaths of mortals, I express joy over his happiness, and sadly and quietly pass over my loss.

I have read your letter, my son, with a sort of keen and bitter sweetness, repeating the endless sighs I had uttered over such a

---

* Son of the famous condottiere, Luchino. This is the only letter to him.
** This is the likeliest meaning of *iusta arma*.

friend. I wish, and I hope, that you will be just like him. I urge and pray that you exert yourself with the utmost eagerness in this. For thus will you instill in all his friends, and in me especially, the great joy of seeing so fine a father simply returned to us in person in his surviving son. For you, the road to glory is not difficult, as it is for many others; you have at home a guide to admire, follow, and imitate. You have the perfect mirror before your eyes: the memory of that incomparable man and the examples of all his virtues right in front of you. It is easy work to copy from a faultless model. Finally, take my advice, do not have his remains moved again, which, as you have learned, were transported to Byzantium by friendly hands, and there honorably buried. Rather, since his soul rests in heaven, let his remains rest on earth in a regal city. You, dearest son, console yourself and your bereaved household, and, in the footsteps of so great a father, live bravely and happily. Farewell.

Pavia, June 9 [1367].

Sen. VIII, 6.

To Donato Apenninigena [Albanzani], the grammarian,* on repentance and on the best books written by saints to achieve it.

Recently two letters of yours written on different days and, for all I know, also dispatched separately, were delivered to me at the same time. Having read them through with considerable joy, I was inspired to answer at length, but recalling my many obligations I restrained the urge. One of them deals with my private business, to which, having too lowly a subject, I shall reply separately, as is my custom. The other concerned your state, I mean the only state that belongs to you; compared to it, all other things are short-lived and transitory, and depend on someone else's will. No longer shall I attribute it to fortune as I usually do, lest I contradict myself; it is a good thing belonging exclusively to you, and it cannot be taken from you unless you yourself consent. I refer to the state of your soul cleansed through repentance—which is the best news you could send me—and a solemn confession. Holy men long ago wrote many things about this; now perhaps something could be said by a sinful man, if only he had as much time as inclination. So I shall do what is available and peculiar to all those who are busy and poor, and who, since they cannot help their friends with money, do so with advice.

Lend me your ear for a short while; I am not far from you as that wretched nurse once was from the Argive leaders in Statius, but I am your guide to a sparkling fountain of water that leaps toward eternal life. Nor shall I fear that meanwhile my serpent may bite me because I have no Archemorus and I do have the best Mithridatic antidote: contempt. I shall show you where to find what I cannot offer you, and send you back to that most blessed pair of men, so beloved by God, who were linked here by their devout love for each other and are now bound to God by everlasting love. Therefore, I too like to join them together in my writings and speech—I mean Ambrose and Augustine, those most saintly souls and most industrious bees of the heavenly hive and divine eloquence. Each of them wrote books on what we are now discussing, that is, repentance: nothing is more conducive to a safe journey in this life and to hope for the next life than those volumes.

* See V, 4.

There is another work by Augustine, entitled *Confessions* and divided into thirteen books. In the first nine, he confesses all the errors and sins of his whole life from his earliest childhood when he was still a suckling, but in the tenth the remnants of sins and the then-present state of his life, and in the last three his doubt concerning the Scriptures and often his ignorance as well. In this confession, if you ask me, he shows himself to have been nearly the most learned of learned men. If you form the habit of reading this book with an intent, devout mind, I expect you will never be without pious, wholesome tears. This I say modestly but knowingly: so that you may come to this reading more confidently on the advice of someone you love, know that that book was for me the entrance to all sacred literature. As an arrogant young man I long avoided it as humble and uncouth and inferior to secular literature because of my excessive love for the one and contempt for the other, because of my false opinion of myself and, to confess briefly my own sin too, because of my youthful insolence, and, as I now understand and see clearly, the prompting of the devil. That book changed me so; not that I have laid aside all my former vices, which I wish I could even at this age, but from then on I no longer scorned or hated sacred literature, or rather its roughness tickled me little by little and drew my unwilling ears and reluctant eyes to itself. Finally, I began to love that literature, to admire and seek it out, and to cull from it perhaps fewer blossoms but certainly more fruit than from the other literature that I had so loved previously. Nor would it have been fitting for a Christian not to be changed at all by Augustine's eloquence when, as he himself recalls in the third book of his work, Cicero's *Hortensius* had changed him so much.

If you do not find these *Confessions* elsewhere, I shall send you a copy so that I may share in your well-being, even though I believe it is closer to you in the library of that noted philosopher, true theologian, and teacher, whom you mention in your other letter, or in his brother's, his equal in the tenor of life and knowledge. Both are real luminaries of their order that takes its name and its rule from Augustine, and both give unmatched luster to the city of Padua, to whom not my own virtue but their esteemed virtue unites me, and whose opinion of me, not as judicious as it is fatherly, I care about more than the viper tongues and hissings of all my detractors, whom the boiling poison of envy daily incites against my reputation. I have more of them than I believed and in unexpected places where I did not deserve it, unless I am mistaken. But there are many things on this elsewhere that I have said sorrowfully, being forced by the subject matter. Now it came spontaneously to my pen and under the prodding of indignation it kept me from retreating. But from whatever source that book reaches your hands, you can, if you like and if you think it fits, put at the opening of it my distich, one of those I used out of scholarly curiosity as a preface in my own books. It goes something like this:

> Whoe'er needs tears to cleanse him of foul crimes,
> Speed through parched deserts to this spring betimes.

But enough of this.

Many others also wrote things very useful to salvation; I speak not of those things that fill us with knowledge and often puff us up, but rather of those which inflame the human mind with humble devotion, such as the *Readings from the Fathers* and the *Lives of the Fathers.* Some of these, packed not only with piety but eloquence, help and delight the reader in wonderful ways. Such is Athanasius's *Life of Antony,* which many have read through and gone on to imitate. And no wonder, since merely hearing about it [Antony's life] benefited Augustine, as he himself relates in the eighth book of his *Confessions* [8.12(29)]. Such are the lives of Martin by Severus, and of Hilary by Jerome, and by the same author the life of John the Egyptian or of Paul the first hermit, which I understand has pleased you a great deal, as well it might. For the little book is no less charming than edifying. Nor must two very devout books by John Chrysostom in this genre be overlooked. One is entitled *On the Restoration of the Fallen One,* the other *On the Heart's Compunction.* Since it would take too long to enumerate all of them, they will be available to you, whenever you want, in my modest library.

I would like to have you get used to these dainties and feed your mind with such food. For, believe me, none of the aphorisms of Hippocrates contains so much hope for recovery or such guaranteed remedies for the sick. Do not let your delay in following his [Augustine's] useful advice deter you. It is better to see the light late than never; and indeed nothing that is well done is done late. For although there is danger in delay, nevertheless the danger disappears upon applying the remedy, which if effective is surely not too late and puts an end to both the delay and the danger. Mull over those words of a tragedy:

> For the return to good ways is ne'er late:
> He who repents of sins is almost sinless,
> > [Sen., *Agam.* 242-43]

—a statement pious enough to have been said by a Catholic.

You say your association with me and our friendship have helped you toward knowledge, virtue, and finally this new direction in life, the desire for confession and penitence. I wish you were speaking the truth. Perhaps—such is the blindness of lovers—you think it is true, whereas aside from some rare and simple though sincere advice I neither was nor could have been any of these things for you; however, in our hearts there are sparks, covered by earthly cinders and hidden by the veil of the flesh. When the Holy Spirit that breathes where He wishes, blows these into flames fed by the tinder of heavenly love and hope, suddenly a holy fire surges, especially in those who understand their true situation and the dangers of this life, among whom, dear friend, I include you. You call me to share in this divine work; I wish I were useful to you and to my loved ones either by teaching or example. I am neither, and I fear that I may rather be harmful in the latter way. And if the cloud of love, which blinds good judges too, is dispelled for a short while, and you fix your eye on this* through the dark shadows, you will see this as plain as day. I do not like to say this, my dear one, and would have been happier either to remain silent or even to boast, if I could. But nothing is more powerful than Truth; she from one side, from the other my love for you compels me lest, while you are a proper judge of your own affairs, you slip when it comes to me because I say nothing.

Finally, what you said with love driving your pen—that my friendship has also contributed substantially to your wealth—was such as to cause me not amazement so much as laughter. So I have added to your riches! I snatched from you not money but the sources of money: worry, anxiety, time; I often dragged you from city streets into forest solitudes, and from business to leisure; I made every day a holiday for you, and finally I rubbed off on you my lazy nonchalance, living on a shoe-string, craving peace and quiet—in short, all my icy indifference to running a household. Therefore, I am uncertain whether you have said this, and this alone, as a joke or whether you have made quite an error in figuring up your accounts. Surely no one, to my knowledge, has become wealthy, but some have become poor, who would not want to be wealthy again, if they could. But to close with a wish for you, I entreat, O gods, every happiness; yet, if both of us live long—although there is no "long"

* We emend *hoc* to *huc*.

here: I am talking about longevity on the human scale—I fear that in the end you will have a perfect right to say about me what you have read that Diogenes the Cynic used to say about his teacher, Antisthenes: "He made me poor when I was rich, and he made me live in a tub instead of a large house." Farewell; whether you be rich or poor, remember me.

Pavia, June 10 [1367].

Sen. VIII, 7.

To Federigo Aretino,[*] concerning the modesty of well-known men.

Your little letter gave me great delight. It contained the utmost wit and humor, and, much better than that, no slight token of a healthy mind. You are happy and content with your lot. There is nothing more useful in human affairs and no straighter path to salvation For kingdoms and empires, wealth and power are for all to desire, but for few to achieve. To desire what you cannot achieve is nothing but to scorn what you have and to waste your spirit in useless toil.

I therefore praise and commend you for enjoying a modest and even humble state, and consider you richer in character than if you had piled up the useless wealth and fragile power of Croesus and Alexander. For insofar as is possible for a man, you have—to use an everyday expression—blocked Fortune's access to you, whereas those two, as you know, were unable to avoid her blows. Strange to say, she that subdues arrogent power is blunted by humble weakness, like a fire that rages more fiercely the larger the log thrown on it, and can be controlled or even extinguished by removing anything in its path.

Therefore what is called Fortune fears neither treasuries nor fortified citadels nor manned fleets nor the most powerful armies; rather she is piqued and aroused by such things, she recalls how often she has been victorious over them, and hence how she can now have a still more glorious triumph; but she fears frugality, modesty, fortitude, and constancy, by which she remembers being conquered most often.

Thus the life that many scorn and burden with empty complaints, you make not only tolerable but enjoyable and happy through your composure and patience; just as this journey of ours has nothing more pathetic than grumbling, so it has nothing more common. I admit there are few things in this life that give great cause for rejoicing. But for those who were born men, all human things must either be accepted or, at the very least, not wept over. For a large part of mankind, however, nothing at all is pleasing except what they either cannot achieve or cannot hang on to; hence the resent-

* See IV, 5.

ment and the rage and unending self-pity of everyone about their lot. Of course, it is sadder to be unhappy and plaintive amidst delights than serene amidst sufferings or poverty. We have heard and seen that there are many such people. Indeed, amidst so many wretched ingrates the only happy one, grateful to God and well-disposed toward himself, is not he who gets what he wishes or who forever keeps as his own what he has gotten—for that has never befallen anyone—but he who looks upon whatever has happened as though it were the one thing he wished, or thinks of whatever he has lost as though it were better to have lost it.

You therefore do well, and indeed doubly well, to embrace your lot happily; thus you make it worth more and gain peace for yourself; that is how to overcome or to cheat Fortune, if there were such a thing. If she denies you great wealth, she could not stop you from scorning it and enjoying your poverty. She denies you the grab-bag of civic honors, but no one, except yourself, will take from you your delight in a solitary retreat and a rural life. Virtue campaigns with you against her; relying upon it, you can never be defeated in any battle. While you read in our poet [Virgil] that she is omnipotent, you will find her weak and powerless when confronted by virtue. For, by Jove, nothing but human insensibility and weakness makes her more powerful.

O happy you, and in my judgment enviable, who have gotten rid of city streets and put behind you the inhospitable doorsteps of arrogant neighbors, and found yourself and the sweet silence of the groves and fields; you rule over the humble villagers with justice, and praise them with your pen, and justly so. For although to a strict judge "no one is good, all are bad," still your people are either less bad or, if—as agreed—bad in the end, they have been good longer. Therefore, live happily with them as you are doing, and believe that you are being dealt with happily, because you have been freed, at least for a time, from the grim, somber frowns of the wealthy, and especially from the mockery of the monstrous clothing that they keep changing every day. To flee from such things was worthwhile for you, not only to find refuge in the Apennines, the most gentle of mountains, but even on the Atlas or the Caucasus. You see almost all your people dressed alike and content, except that perhaps on feast days a few, who either because of their age or their skill in farming have risen to the top, sometimes wear a brighter color instead of white; you see sturdy shoes, a help to the feet, not a hindrance; you see men's clothing that wards off the cold and covers what nature has taught us to cover, and not this madness of our young people, and, what is even more hopeless, of our elders who cover only their faces and bare the private parts. For these it is not enough to have a mind infected and weighed down by all kinds of misdeeds, but they must also corrupt and weary the eyes of others. These make me angry, and I hope that God, who loves modesty, is also angry with them. I know that it is vain for me to complain about them everywhere, but I cannot stop, so great is my disgust and so nauseated is my stomach at the foul spectacle. For this reason I most envy you your country seat and your peaceful life, and all the more because I often experienced it for long periods of time; but to tell the truth, prompted by sin rather than fortune, I slipped into the opposite mode, and, therefore, unless I am mistaken, I have become a fit judge of both ways of life.

Certainly you now feast your eyes on calm contemplation and your ears on pure sounds. My lot is different both ways: I see citizens and foreigners arrogant and puffed up for no reason and conceited; you behold humble farmers staring at the ground. I hear the squabbles and outcries of madmen, and trumpets and drums; you hear the lowing of cattle and the murmuring of a gliding stream and the cries of birds, and you will be the first to hear Philomela, the harbinger of spring. I am being crushed between the crowds and carriages in cities—none is worse than my Avignon; you ramble idly and at will in the woods and hills amidst harmless flocks, and are soon to see leafy branches and budding vines and laughing meadows when Aries returns. I have the same view all year round—rushing crowds, mud, dust, noise, footfalls, and sewers; these are the delights of the cities. What else can you hope from them? Although not only Aries may return, but Taurus and Leda's naked twins, disporting amidst garlands of roses, vexations in the cities are not removed but simply changed. In contrast, the face of the country is always lovely and worth seeking by noble minds, whether it be the harsh winter with its gentle starkness, so busy with hunting wild beasts and fowl, or the flowering springtime so suitable and inviting for careless frolicking, or the dry summer that gives birth to harvests and welcomes the shade, or the rich, wet autumn that occupies the peasants in varied tasks. In anticipation of the forthcoming winter you have here the busy farmer leading the sheep from their grazing on the mountains back to their lowland haunts, there the ranging hunter and the noisy fowler, and there the silent, motionless fisherman, the springs, the rivers, the choruses of nymphs, and the caves and groves and lodgings of the Muses. In short, that life is the sweetest as much for the quality of many things as for their variety, about which long ago, when I myself was allowed to enjoy them, I wrote quite a bit.

So that you may have nothing at all on your farm to dislike, I would not like to pass over one thing that the end of your letter touched upon quite amusingly. While you get honest, sensible pleasure from everything that is there, one noise, the honking of geese—not only all day but all night at all hours, so I understand—upsets you. I do not deny that this impudence is hard on the ears; the geese and the cicadas buzzing in the branches, and the donkeys neighing in the pastures, and so on, do offend those who hanker for peace and quiet. But more than all these things, the crash and uproar of crowds on the streets are far more unbearable. For there are no beasts anywhere, believe me, more pesky than a crowd of people. Almost everything else is quiet either in the winter or at least at night; certain others are a nuisance at night but they let up during the day. The disturbance from the geese is continuous, but easy to bear, if you recall that once a defender of the Capitoline, awakened by the honk of a goose, warded off the attacking Gauls from our citadel; and for this service, a silver figure of this bird was on display many centuries later, whether to glorify that matchless sentinel or because that creature is without doubt the most vigilant. Again I am uncertain whether November first was the date of that event—and for this reason on this day, as we know, the celebrity of the geese took a fatal turn (it is in any event astonishing if a new kind of reward, death, is the price of their watchfulness)—or whether this happens only because at that time of the year the goose is a richer food and more fit for eating.

But whatever we may think, this will definitely be the most wholesome thought, and the best remedy, for the nuisance. When I recently wrote *De remediis*, perhaps this was overlooked by chance, so that now it could be inserted in this letter to you and be particularly useful to you now, namely that every time that bird makes noise, especially at night, you consider yourself being urged to resist vices and you immediately take up arms. I say not the arms fashioned in Aeolia by Mulciber [Vulcan] for Achilles or Aeneas, but those fashioned by the heavenly Smith inside your soul. Do not consider the snares and challenges of the vices against you any less than those of the Gauls against Manlius. Furthermore, whenever a goose squawks in the night, trust that it is not a goose but an angelic trumpeter, remember that you are besieged and surrounded by the keenest enemies—the world, the flesh, the demons—and go forward armed to face them creeping through the shadows and thickets. More about this another time. For the present let this suffice, with the addition that as often as you are awakened by a goose's cry, and from the nobler part of your mind you resist your enemies with God's help and defend its citadel, you take no credit for it, but rather ascribe it all to Him about whom it is written, "He who guards Israel will neither doze nor fall asleep" [Ps. 121:4]. And again, "Unless the Lord guards the city, he who guards her stays awake in vain" [Ps. 127:1]; and still again, "You have shaded my head on the day of battle" [Ps. 140:8], lest, as vainglory hurled Manlius down from the Capitoline rock, which he had saved, so your awareness of a deed well-done arising from it and the appetite for preeminence, should hurl you down too. Farewell.

[1366-67].

Sen. VIII, 8.

To Giovanni Boccaccio,* on the ill-founded notoriety of the sixty-third year.

It is a year today, and the sun has returned to Leo after its journey through the zodiac, since I wrote you, dear brother, that letter in which, while feeling safe myself, I perhaps made you anxious; although, to tell the truth, what made me feel safe was a continual meditation that implanted within me a contempt for the inevitability of death, rather than the idea that the menace of the astrologers, about which I wrote you then was totally contemptible. I do not mean by this that I have more confidence than I used to in their nonsense; but the recollection of time past, whether true or false I do not know (but unless I am mistaken it is true), and as much personal observation as was possible in so few years, had almost convinced me that what they said was in part true: that the seventh and ninth years in a man's life are troublesome because of the insults of others and the bringing of some new calamity. But that the sixty-third year, which is the product of these numbers was twice as terrible because it doubled the dangers, as they would have it, I was not equally convinced, and am much less today when, thanks to divine mercy, I have experienced the opposite.

Since I was then not completely free of the second part of that astrological superstition, and was concentrating on its outcome, I resolved to await the year's end; and, in order to shorten your anxiety, I postponed sending that letter to you for a long time after it was written and sealed, so that you would not start worrying about me until later. Here now is the conclusion I waited for: let others decide how that fearful year has been or will be for themselves, but for me it has been healthy and joyful. I remember having seldom been healthier in body at any age; nothing adverse has happened to me personally, and two very happy public events have occurred in these days, happy, that is, if the one had been firm and lasting, and the other turns out to be. For the first has passed, and the second is anticipated.

King Peter of Cyprus captured Alexandria in Egypt, a great and memorable event, and a huge foundation for the vast expansion of our religion, had there been as much spirit in keeping the city as in

* See I, 5.

capturing it. Rumor has it that he certainly did not lack such spirit, but that his troops, recruited from transalpine nations, which are always better at starting things than ending them, deserted him in the midst of this outstanding operation, so that those who followed the pious king not out of piety but out of greed, departed once they had collected the booty, and, fulfilling their selfish vow, made him incapable of fulfilling his pious vow.

Furthermore, the Roman Pontiff, and I mean the truly Roman Pontiff, worthy of being honorably named Urban V, whom a year ago, as you might have heard, I had reproached for his slowness in a frank but loyal letter, this year has dug up from the dregs and returned to its proper seat the Church of Christ, which from my birth to the present has wandered among the Bordelais and the Poitevins, and most recently aged and grown numb amidst the inhabitants of Carpentras and Avignon. This was the beginning of a great and manifold boon, unless (and may the Bridegroom of holy Church forbid it!) that enemy of good men, inconstancy, were to undermine it. Nevertheless, as of now, it is all the more welcome to faithful souls because it was so unexpected. I have certainly seen what I confess I had never hoped to see but had always wished for. It is only right that I give thanks in person, with the pious unanimity of the entire Church, to the author of this great boon—I am now thinking about it—and that I free this happy year of its undeserved infamy; and that just as I had promised at the end of my other letter, I should celebrate with you, dear friend, not that I am immortal but that I have survived this frightful year, for it has departed never to return again, leaving me behind. Just as I know that I am mortal, so do I know that I shall not die in my sixty-third year, since today I enter my sixty-fourth. To use the words of Augustus Caesar, as you see, we have escaped the sixty-third year, that common bane of all old people. However, I pray not to the gods, as he did, but to God, that whatever time remains for me, I be allowed to spend with you, my surviving friends, while in the happiest state of the commonwealth, as he says, and above all in the happiest state of our souls. Farewell.

Pavia, July 20, 1367, at dawn.

Sen. IX, 1.

To Pope Urban V,* congratulations for having led the Church back to her See, and an exhortation to persevere.

"When Israel departed from Egypt, the house of Jacob from a foreign people" [Ps. 114:1] there was thanksgiving of the angels in heaven and of pious men on earth. And now, Most Holy Father, you have blessed the Christian people as much as you can. No longer will they wander in search of the Lord or of their Lord's vicar, but will find the One in heaven above and within their soul since both are the abodes of God, the other on earth and in his own See; I mean that See that the Lord chose beforehand where the first vicar dwelt while he lived, and remained after his death. You have made our world peaceful, and like the rising sun, chased away both the chill and the shadows of the long night.

O happy you to know you have done something so outstanding! You did what had begun to appear impossible for a man to do, but God was doubtless with you; for He says to the Apostles, "Without me you can do nothing" [John 15:5]. What is unusual and extraordinary about you is that God, lover and creator of the human race, offers Himself to many, or rather to all, and is rejected by nearly all. The world, the flesh, the demons, pride, pleasure, and profligacy have so oppressed their minds that they cannot rise to God who extends His hand.

You, aware of human weakness, not only did not refuse the aid of the heavenly Lord nor quench the Spirit that breathed inspired advice into the ear of your heart, but also, I know, invoked Him with pious prayers and tears able to move the heavens. When He, who overlooks no one that hopes in Him, had perceived this with His ears and eyes and had come to answer your prayer, you went out to meet Him, and taking your Lord by the hand, you led Him with humble devotion into the recesses of your faithful soul; this you did secretly lest His enemies, and yours, should protest and, upon discovering the arrival of the King of Glory, hinder in their usual way the pious and holy initiative. Thus, in silent deliberation with Him about what should be done, you undertook this great cause under His leadership, and magnificently brought it to a conclusion beyond anyone's hope.

* See VII, 1.

Once again, O happy you, O happy day, which brought you from your mother's womb into the light and gave you to the world like a benign star. Now to me you are the true, the truly highest Roman Pontiff, truly Urban, truly the successor of Peter, truly the Vicar of Jesus Christ. This you were before, I do not deny, in power, in dignity, and in position, but now—and this is very good—you are so in will, in piety, and in deed. For the will cannot be more holy or the piety more pure in anyone than it is in you and has always been, in my opinion. But now the events themselves have made it so stand out that no longer can it be hidden from anyone. Nor could anyone more promptly and prudently transform the will into action, without which it is sterile. Within very few days, you single-handedly undid the negligence of some sixty years or more, and of five popes, your equal in rank but not in spirit.

I beg you, since I crave nothing and seek nothing from you but your blessing, allow me to praise fully, without any suspicion of flattery, that which I feel is worthy of full praise, bearing in mind how frankly I censure what I deem worthy of rebuke. Tiny worm that I am, I have so needled not only the lords of the earth but those two luminaries of the world, those two swords of justice, often in the past, and yourself—one of two—recently, that it was either great confidence or great madness on my part. Which of the two it was I leave to the judgment of others; I know in my heart how confident I am. I wish for human affairs to go well, so that what I saw in the worst condition while alive I may leave in the best condition when I die, if there is any way to do this. I see or hope that this cannot be done in any way except through you—second to God, of course—and the other who controls temporal affairs. Certainly, if I dare to jab, why should I fear to soothe? For both belong specifically to the physician's hand; I do both with equal confidence, although perhaps I am not the right one for either.

Although I have learned little, I have read much; also I recall a great deal that I either saw or heard in this brief course of life; and I call to witness Christ, the God of Truth, that I have never seen or heard anything, and shall I say never even read anything, that has been done in our age to compare with your outstanding deeds, either in aim or in wisdom or in result. A great many princes and—I am sorry to say—a great many bishops, think of nothing but themselves and their personal advantage or their own pleasures. Having nobly scorned and put out of your mind the sentiments that perhaps drew you as a man elsewhere, you alone of all the pontiffs in our time, were concerned with the public welfare. O great man without a peer in our times, or with far too few, so could you love virtue and so scorn pleasure, although for true judges there is no pleasure more delightful than that derived from God and virtue, and, as is acknowledged, none more certain or enduring! But I speak of vulgar pleasure, than which there is nothing more contrary to salvation; that pleasure, with early allurements and carnal enticements, led the five predecessors in your office astray from the straight path. Now they understand how much better it would have been to follow reason than appetite, and to fulfill with deeds what some of them had promised, although the promise to do one's duty is superfluous. How much nobler for them to do what so high an office demanded than what the slippery senses, which perish in a day, coaxed them into, and not to battle against the truth with pretenses and to fool with Him of whom it is written, "You hate all who perpetrate iniquity, You will destroy all who speak falsehood" [Ps. 5:6–7]. Nothing is less becoming than duplicity or pretense in a Roman Pontiff, whose conscience must be purer than the sun and whose constancy more persevering, so that, as even an enemy reportedly said of a certain Roman general, the sun could more easily be turned from its course than he from his goal and from carrying out his pious deeds.

You, true Father of the Church, having promised nothing in words but a great deal within your heart, feeling that the Church herself was sick, and making good use of the counsel of expert doctors, brought her from her dismal exile back to her place of origin and to her own atmosphere. This was not as easily done by you, however, as it is said by me. It took much labor and great determination, enormous ability and marvelous cunning deep in the breast to dig up without bruising so many strong roots with one pull. What am I saying? Rather it was with the harshest bruising and the gravest pain to many, but your gentle, expert hand with its light touch soothes the most painful wounds.

So thanks be to God and to you. Now I am seeing what I always wished for, but, I confess, never hoped to see: I see my mother in her own home where she cannot for long be ill, as long as you are safe, and where, having been brought back at your bidding, she will recover under your care. Now, kindly Father, concentrate upon her all the talent of your sacred intellect, given to you with an abundance of remedies by Him who predestined you to this high office in the crisis of His bride. Correct her ways, relieve her feebleness, curb her avarice, drive away her ambition, restore her lost and rejected sobriety, halt her overflowing lust, prod her listless sluggishness, quell her raging anger. Lead her blind envy back to the straight pathway, restrain her exalted pride and swollen arrogance. Those who were raised amidst such plagues and had made the habit part of their nature, could not have done this; for you, raised amidst the virtues contrary to these, it will all be simple. You have already accomplished what was hardest. Now do the rest. Lead the Church, entrusted to your custody, back to her ancient customs, now that you have returned her to her ancient See, so that she may become, as she once was, irreproachable from all sides, and once again begin to be venerated and cherished by the entire world, which has certainly not been so for a long time—those who are at fault will allow me to say so. You were born to this glorious office; fulfill it successfully.

Warn each and every one of your cardinals to remember that they are mortals, not to think always of pleasures but from time to time of death and eternal life; let them focus their eyes; they will see that nothing endures, that all things are short-lived and more fleeting than the wind, and that all that exists here is uncertain, changeable, shaky, transitory. As though they were setting foot on firm ground, they embark on empty enthusiasms and false hopes, and with silly curiosity they clash over worthless things.

For I hear the saddest and the most irritating thing I could hear: that there are some who grumble that they have no burgundy wine in Italy. Would that those vines had never existed, and I would almost say, no vines at all, if they were destined to produce such a poisonous vintage for the Church of Christ! But if they feel any love for God and for men, if they do love the See of Peter, an honorable reputation, the people's salvation, and their own souls, how little they will care about wine! But supposing they do care—just to think they do is a grave matter—I am ashamed for their sake. If they care so deeply and there is no power whereby this folly, stuck in their hearts, can be uprooted, nor any art capable of curing it, surely the way is clear and straighforward to have what they thirst for so greedily. I wrote enough about it, I believe, in my previous letter to you. If I may add one more thought that I cannot under any circumstances withhold, for grief drives me to it although reverence stands in the way. The first Apostles, whose place they are taking, with pious zeal sought where to shed for Christ's sake their body's blood upon the earth, and therefore hardly any of them reached heaven unbloodied. Alas, how things have changed! The modern apostles have displayed a different zeal, where on earth to pour into their body the blood squeezed from the fruit of the vine. The first mention of this is not only in banquets, where perhaps the place itself deserves our indulgence, but also in serious conferences: not the country which produces good men, but the one which produces good wine is preferred above all; that is Zion, that is Jerusalem, that, in short, is Rome which alone is worthy of having the Apostles' successors live there. If they at least judged rightly which wine deserved the prize, they would not have long preferred Avignon above all other lands, not without grave offense to many noble cities. For there you find nothing good except what is imported from elsewhere, as is too well known to need any proof.

They point to the river, which I wish had dried up a thousand years ago, or rather had never burst from the bowels of the earth if it were to be the cause of exile for the Church of Christ. They tell tales about this river as though there is no other anywhere. And yet, if they would read ancient history, the Rhone is not the See of Roman Pontiffs but of criminals and of those condemned to exile, which for some reason that escapes me they worship as a river of paradise; indeed I know only too well why: it carries their burgundy, the fifth element added to nature.

But you, who were long ago raised on bread and water, and have been all the happier to have vinegar water [diluted water] for a treat, show them a father's wrath. Scold them, censure them, berate them out, punish them, restrain their appetites as you did your own for a long time now. Those who are free from vices are usually the most wrathful ones; he who shares in the fault will scarcely feel wrath against those guilty to the highest degree. Nor can whoever is angry punish; both zeal and power are needed; the monastery, the hermitage, religion, and fasting, have given you these, but most of all, that natural, inborn frugality, about which I hear much to my delight, has made you wrathful against gluttony; the papacy bestows the power to punish. "Hear us, O you who guide Israel, you who lead Joseph as though he were a sheep" [Ps. 80:2]. Do not let your sheep grow wanton, O shepherd of a peerless flock. And remember that these are still the two vices, although others may be more grave, that make human life most bestial and lowly—gluttony and lust. Teach your brethren and your sons to scorn what they used to love, to love what they fear or hate, to hate themselves, whereas they have long hated what they ought to have loved; the saying of Augustine is worthy of golden letters: "No one can love perfectly what he is called to, unless he hates what he is called from;" and a little later, "nor will anyone become what he wishes to be unless he hates himself as he is."

Show to their wayward senses, still eager for the evil dwellings on the Rhone and the swampy countryside, those places of healing where it came to pass that the doorkeeper of heaven, together with the teacher of the world—as the Church sings of both of them—judges of the age and true lights of the world, the one triumphant by the cross, the other by the sword, hold the senate of life and are crowned with laurel. Point out to them, not far from the gates of the great, holy basilica, where Simon Peter was raised on the gibbet of the cross, from which he, the keeper of the keys of the kingdom, joyfully departed to Christ. Show them, a little further, where the Apostle Paul, the light of the earth, with head bowed, was crowned with martyrdom for the name of Christ. For they have sung and read this about their models; they have not seen, I think, the holy places. When they see them and those places take hold of them, I hope they will be ashamed of the profane and infamous places for which they have conceived an unworthy love, not through right judgment but crooked feeling and long habit.

Bid them contemplate and gaze inwardly upon the venerable and most holy elder, Peter, leaving there not out of a desire for foreign wine but a justified fear of death; then, in the middle of the road, Christ facing him, at whose sight and, as they say, upon a single word, he at once returned, dauntless, to certain death. Let them see him shortly thereafter hanging on the cross; through him, unless they are ingrates, as they plant themselves upon their golden seats and ivory footstools, that they have received whatever eminence, wealth, and glory they have. Then let them meditate upon the severed head of the most glorious Paul, the vessel of election, the library of heavenly teaching, the brilliant sun of our faith. Let them hear him with the ears of the heart, calling out, as he died, to Jesus in a loud voice with his very last sighs. There the witnesses to the unique miracle are the springs, the same number as the bounces of his holy head, according to tradition, in the very places where his battered neck touched the ground.

If they will listen devoutly to those voices and drink a pious draught from these springs, they will scorn transalpine orchestras and not ask for the parching trickles hidden along the Rhone; but another thirst will, I hope, take over, and they will forever forget the wine of Burgundy. It was unknown to both ancient and modern authorities and was nowhere numbered among the fine wines, but by these men it has been celebrated with excessive and unworthy praise, as though the nectar of the gods; so it has deserved, unless I am mistaken, my just, though very bitter, censure. Although delicious to the taste, inasmuch as it still is harmful to salvation, it should be—like some sweet poison—hateful to all who thirst for virtue. Furthermore, as I have said, this still can be had with no trouble in Rome too; and you can dine without it not only frugally and soberly but even luxuriously and indulgently; they indeed have before their eyes, unless they are blindfolded, many wines to tickle them with a certain finer taste as they contemplate the glory either of the earthly journey or of the heavenly fatherland.

But since I happened to say many things on this as the subject called for it, and since to cover all the holy wonders of the gracious city is an infinite task, I leave this all in your able hands; and I return to your qualities that I had chosen as worthy of admiration and praise, although, to confess the truth, my mind is quicker to admire than my pen to express. Nevertheless, my pen will rise to the occasion and will write down what the mind dictates from within, and offer it for others to read regardless of style, provided I am understood; I seek here no glory for eloquence. I realize, Most Holy Father, the difficulties and labors you have endured in carrying out your magnificent work. I mean that I feel them as though I had been involved in all of them.

I seem to hear the cardinals' flatteries and murmurings purposely shoved into your saintly ears to dissuade you from your original purpose and draw you back from where they, all together on bended knees, ought to have urged you, had you delayed. I am certainly forced to wonder about their intention; I cannot wonder enough. It is an enormous, monstrous, and incredible shock that the cardinals of the Roman Church thus hate or fear or scorn the Roman city and the Roman Church. For who has there ever been, who did not love his own title, especially a glorious and advantageous one? It is altogether a new and sad marvel to see men of such great reverence and such great wisdom and learning be so hard only on their mother, who deserves the best from them—hard and, if I may say so, impious. In order to spend the briefest, most fleeting remnant of their uncertain time on earth in a terrible but cherished place, they have no concern about what is best for them, for the Church, for the human race, or what is pleasing to God. Aside from a few Italians, who, I believe, were awaiting Israel's redemption, who had lived in exile but wished to die in their fatherland which is everyone's, aside too from your only brother (who was raised with you from infancy, used to admiring and imitating you, and having learned to want everything that you did, and nothing else), all the others dreaded the end of their exile, as though it were the beginning. O force of habit so powerful in all things, you have made the fatherland an exile and the exile a fatherland! I would more gladly have written all this to those involved, as would be appropriate, except that their large number and their arrogant spirits, long known to me only too well, indignantly spit out whatever is put into their delicate ears, making them even more obstinate. I have therefore written to the one who, innocent of all blame, alone has the right to correct others, who considers not the harshness of the style but the truth of the matter, and not the writer's circumstances but his intention.

I go on, passing over those you were able to restrain rightfully or to ignore, likewise rightfully, if they delayed your undertaking; but I have no doubt that you have endured much labor and disappointment, since your moderation even toward such men, their contrary opinions, and inflexible ideas is well known to all. The greatest and best known is your having to convince, gently and earnestly, the kings and princes, toward whom you display your indulgence for the good of the Church, to put aside their promises to your cardinals since they were in agreement with them but in complete disagreement with you. Above all these was His Highness the King of France [Charles V], son of the Church, who, in his desire to have his mother nearby because of his devout but youthful love, overlooked how much better and more honorable it would be for her to be far away. As you thought of leaving, he set whatever snares he could, in order to snare your sacred apostolic feet, always ready for any pious, holy labor. I mean he sent a learned and, so they say, eloquent man [Ancel Choquart] who, in his address to you and all your brethren as they listened, too eagerly, took up the largest part of his oration in elevating his beloved Gaul and disparaging Italy— a great, arduous task, and difficult, not to say impossible, not only for him but for anyone. For men's speech cannot alter things, although it may often cover the truth with a lie.

How I wish I had been there, worthy of an invitation from you, so as to reply to his aspersions by relying on the aid of truth, although I was unequal in eloquence and inferior in rank. Perhaps in your judgment I could have proven to him that the facts are altogether different than he said. Even now, if he believes in his cause and would like to engage in a literary contest, I am willing to do battle, although always busy and now worn out, in a duel in behalf of the truth and the fatherland. Let him write down then what he has said or what he can. I, the least of Italians, shall respond to that Frenchman, and the dispute will be more useful if committed to writing than if oral; for spoken words fade away while written words remain, the spoken word reaches only the few who are present while the written one reaches also the many who are absent, as well as posterity. I hope that with Christ and yourself as judges I will easily prove to that denigrator that what he said was false—not, I guess, following instructions but out of his own head. He was otherwise learned and famous, but in speaking he descended to shameful depths from his ardor and mental excitement. I feel that I know the ripe, seasoned mind of the young king, and I am long acquainted with his unique politeness and courteous language on some great occasions. I can believe he bade the man to entreat you to praise Gaul. But I would almost venture to swear that he did not bid him to slander Italy. Yet it is the custom of some messengers—unless they add something of their own, they think they have not done anything. There are certainly many who do not believe that they can praise what is theirs without slandering what belongs to others.

To summarize everything briefly: the condition and the glory of the Italians and the Gauls, and the differences between them, are so well known that no one with any acquaintance with history can doubt them. To argue about the difference in intellect is ridiculous; there are books testifying to the truth. Tell me, what of the liberal arts, of the natural or historical sciences, wisdom, eloquence, ethics, and is there any part of philosophy in Latin that was not practically all discovered by Italians? For if any foreigners ventured to handle any of these subjects successfully, either they imitated Italians or they wrote in Italy or they studied in Italy. Of the four doctors of the Church two are Italians and Romans; of the other two, one was born near Italian territory, almost within, and certainly reared and educated in Italy, while the other was converted and lived in Italy; all of them are buried in Italy. None is Gallic and none was educated in Gaul. Italians established both civil and canon law, and then Italians have so explicated them that nothing, or very little, remains for foreigners. The Italians far surpass the Greeks in civil law; about canon law there is no dispute. Orators and poets are not to be found outside of Italy—I speak of the Latin ones; they were all either born here or educated here. But what am I doing, why waste words on something so well known? The root of our arts and the foundation of all science—Latin letters—were invented here; so was the Latin language and the Latin name, in which the Gauls themselves glory. They all, I repeat, originated here, not elsewhere, and they have grown here. I could deal with these point by point, but enough has been said for the wise and too much for the others.

And what, I ask, have they to stake against so many achievements in so many fields, unless perhaps as a self-satisfied and self-praising people they stake one thing against all these, their noisy Straw Alley. Furthermore, here all civilization flourished, and if there is any of it left anywhere, it still flourishes in some part of Italy. Here are the two pinnacles in the world, the Papacy and the Empire. I would not speak now of arms, victories, triumphs, military discipline, or finally the conquest of all the nations and the annual tributes, lest I upset the Gallic spirit: as for everyday manners, I confess that the Gauls are witty, polished in their gestures and words, prone to joking, joyful in their singing, heavy in their drinking, and avid in their banqueting. But high seriousness and practical morality have always been with the Italians. And although virtue has diminished throughout the world—which is a pitiful loss—if there are still any remnants, they are in Italy, unless I am mistaken. If there is anything morally crooked, it is among the Gauls. Nowhere are strangers held in such great honor [as in Italy]. And let no one doubt, indeed not even that reviler, that nowhere is the Church so great, whether you measure her power or the devotion not only of the Italians but of all the people believing in Christ, inasmuch as here she was born and here she grew up, here she was raised to the summit of glory, here she will remain forever, God willing and you—I hope—acting.

The Gallic part of the Church, I acknowledge, is wealthy and noble, but that the head of the Church, as of the Empire, is in Italy, no one in his right mind can deny. If any of these men do not believe it, let him change his Roman title for a title from his own fatherland, then he will realize what he was and what he is; and he will understand the distance between the head at the top and the feet at the bottom; it is very hard to owe something great when you do not wish to. If they are so ashamed of the Roman name, let them cast aside the Roman honors and let them prefer their own property and fatherland in their choice of career as they do in words. I would be mad to urge them to cast aside their Italian ecclesiastical honors by which alone they are great and famous, these men who solicit Italian cities that are not theirs and usurp them with unheard-of tyranny to Peter's amazement, and with Christ even marveling and threatening. And unless He from heaven and you from earth intervene, since the Italians are lulled to sleep by the draught of some strange herb, our cause is finished; we shall soon see Italy enslaved, and see the Church militant, as it is aptly styled, or rather up in arms and battling for power and not for the faith; finally we shall see her triumphant before she has reached heaven and its starry vaults, and each churchman triumphantly presiding over a certain city until those who sleep awaken and disfigure and reform everything in a terrible revolution.

But although I well know that they are not about to do what I advise, in the meantime I am still writing what I believe incumbent on me, for you, kind Father, to understand, and for them perhaps to be moved if they listen. And indeed, if they could be persuaded to be content with the good things from their fatherland and to cast away the hated alien burden, this will be a mark of a noble hatred and natural resentment rather than scorning the most what they boast of the most. The brave and generous man will chose to surrender his fief, however rich, rather than to possess it under a hated lord. Take Domitius, the one captured at Corfinium; willingly and gladly he threw away, as though it were a troublesome burden, not his wealth or any dignity, but that which is dearer to a man than anything else—his very life, which he had unwillingly and sadly received from Julius Caesar. He ended it as soon as the occasion for a noble death arose. I was expecting, I confess, our notables to do the same and, urged by hatred and driven by pride, to resign their Italian titles and their loathsome insignia. But I wait in vain, I see; their plan is set, and however evil and ungrateful, it is anyhow not futile. They agreed on their rotten scheme to gnaw away at Italy and to hate her at the same time, to bear down on her and to scorn her; and while setting these traps, they said, "Who will see *us*?" But I will see them, thousands of others see them, everyone sees them. Who anywhere is so blind as not to see such things? They see them, I say, but all are silent, or rather speechless. Unless loyalty to my fatherland and indignation over what was happening forced me to speak out, I too would have remained silent along with others, and perhaps more prudently, recalling that saying of Crispus that is very well known even to children. "To exert oneself in vain and to bring nothing else but hatred upon oneself by one's toil," he says, "is utter madness" [*Jug.* 3.3].

For I know that I speak in vain, and realize that because of it the hatred of great men hangs over me, but surely not of the greatest one, whose hatred I certainly do not fear on this account, but rather hope for his love. Otherwise, I would not speak to you so confidently, nor would you listen to me so patiently, as I know from your letter and from the words of those who have come from you; nor, finally, would you be as your reputation makes you, as the world believes you to be, and as I too know, for I have faith not in words reflecting the diversity of the speakers, but in the facts that know not how to lie. Let others, then, believe you to be however they wish; I know that you are a lover of Christ whom you serve in spirit, and of Peter whom you succeed in office, and of the Church over which you preside, and of the Apostolic See on which you sit, and finally of all Christendom and of Italy in particular. Unless this were so, you would never have led the Church back from that hell that borders your country while so many stood in the way, and overcoming all earthly attractions, brought her back to Italy where, if you live and your holy purpose lives in you, I see nothing for the Church to fear, and nothing whatever that is too much to hope for, including, on the one hand, the recovery of the Holy Land and of the special patrimony of Jesus Christ and, on the other, the restoration of ecclesiastical freedom. Those counselors of yours care little about these two things, if only their ancestral pleasures are secure. This being so, you feel the entire burden of this glorious labor falling upon your shoulders, a great work and a boundless, inestimable reward.

Thus that gentleman, however eloquent, did not pay enough attention to the one he was addressing—which some have said is the first mark of prudence. If he had paid close attention to this, he would not have reviled that part of the world that you fondly love, in which your power and dignity and the Church's is based. For perhaps someone will listen patiently when his own thing, supremely dear to him, is slurred, but no one enjoys listening to it.

What he said about Gallic food and wine clearly involved some offense to the listeners, unless I am mistaken. He believed that he had lured and caught apostolic men like so many fish or fowl by dangling food in front of them. Already this story—oh, for shame!—has been excessively publicized throughout the city, to the effect that in choosing the seat of the Church, the supply and tastiness of luxury food, especially wine, comes into consideration as though they were not deliberating about the Christian religion but bacchanalia. Alas, they do not hear Paul crying out to the Corinthians, or rather to all Christians: "Do not draw a yoke with the infidels. What partnership can righteousness have with iniquity, or what alliance can there be between light and darkness, or what agreement between Christ and Belial?" [2 Cor. 6:14]. In my anger and sadness, I add: what analogy is there between Christ and Bacchus? Can it be that because the sacrifice on the altar needs wine Bacchus will be the god of the Christians, and we will no longer obey the precepts and warnings of Christ but the blandishments and frenzies of Bacchus?

Alas and alack, what is this, what do I hear? At least a reverence for your sanctity, consideration of your moderation, and the obvious authority of your brow ought to have deterred that agitator from speaking such nonsense. But you, as was befitting, answered him with a few grave words, while his master, who had sent him, could be answered in no better way than by the deed itself. Not only did you not delay your planned journey, but you hastened it, recalling that often excessive delays have harmed great beginnings. Indeed, if the king loves you like a son and respects you sincerely, as he does, he will rejoice that you are finally in the place where it will be healthier for you and the world. I am aware that there is something soft and tender within our minds which makes us not want those we love ever to be far away. That often proves fatal for those who love. But this is childish and womanish rather than manly, for men consider not where those they hold dear are but how they are; and they would rather have them absent and well than present and ill, as those who are absent in body are present in spirit. They hear them, see them, and they share in their good prosperity anywhere. But silly women and children want to have those they love always close by, and do not willingly let them be wrenched away. For they do not discern nor consider the goal, but feast only on company and fun and chit-chat. They seek no other benefit from friendship.

I could say many things in reply to that inflamatory, though unknown, defamer of the Italian name; he considered it the best argument for winning his case if he asserted that his country had a greater abundance of foods than Italy, as though he were speaking not to the most religious and supreme Pontiff but to Apicius, the master cook. But I could not bear to dwell at length on such a petty, lowly subject, especially since you would be hearing me. But if I had him to deal with, I could perhaps put him to shame, that a man such as he said so many things in the presence of the Vicar of Truth that are not supported by truth.

In any case, what must not be overlooked is that the Gauls, as it is written, learned the value of the vine and the olive tree when Rome was young. And it is a fact that the same people, drawn to Italy at first by the tastiness of the fruit and especially the wine, brought to us many grave wars with their huge army, to the point of setting fire to the city of Rome which was then rising. But with God punishing their headlong, unbridled gluttony, they were all finally laid low and wiped out, so that no one was left of that people, as an outstanding historian says, who could boast that the city of Rome had been burned down by him.

But if the fellow were perhaps to bring up the change in the times and the situations, I am confident the wealth of Italy and the poverty and many shortcomings of Gaul could be so laid bare and set forth to him that not only would he blush but even feel hungry and thirsty. What compels me to say these things against my will is the spirited petulance and boastfulness of that man. If he had intended to exalt himself and to celebrate small things as the greatest, why did he have to put us down with any insult whatsoever? A lie that hurts no one but is only in accord with the interest of the liar has often won the acquiescence of listeners. But if he were to go in for outraging someone else, he is bound to make enemies. I have undertaken the common cause of the truth and of my country, and I have confined it within these limits, although the homeland has many who would respond to these objections more fully and copiously, and the truth answers for herself, shouting from a thousand books or even without a word from the very looks of things.

Another error occurs to me that must be refuted in turn. Recently, as I was writing this, it was pointed out to me in a story that cannot be brushed aside that some of your cardinals agree that Italy once was something great—this cannot be denied—but define her with too casual, too hasty an assertion as being next to nothing. Good Jesus, why such blindness, why such rashness? What envy is this? What intolerance to hate so much when you cannot see the very thing that you so hate, or to know how worthy of hate it may be? Is this not perhaps that perfect hatred that the Psalmist recalls? On the contrary, it is far different and truly the opposite, for perfect hatred consists of hating evil in such a way that you do not hate the good but cherish it, though joined to evil. On the other hand, to love evil in such a way that you hate the good is an imperfect hatred, and the worst, even if it is great. For such perfection recognizes not the quantity but the quality of the hatred. If they do not believe me, let them listen to Augustine in his commentary on that passage. "To hate with perfect hatred," he says, "is neither to hate people because of their vices, nor to love their vices because of the people" [*Enarr. in ps.* 138.22].

But your cardinals hate us so much that because of their exclusive love of the Rhone they hate and attack whatever good things we have, even our very best regions that are the most beautiful in all the world, nor can they open their eyes to gaze even superficially at this beauty and grace. In short, it is a strange but common evil that one who errs badly in something succumbs to many errors with a slip of the mind. See where a boundless yearning for a muddy river and an unattractive land now drives their spirits, so that with undeserved fondness they look up to the lowliest things, and with malicious repugnance look down on the loftiest ones. And while pressed by their sense of shame, they confess what in some way could be denied, they deny upon the prompting of envy what the actual and compelling truth forces them to confess. For if they deny things past, this detracts from the authority of men and the value of books; but by denying present things they are contradicting the truth itself and the testimony of the intellect and of the senses.

Therefore, to those who knowingly argue against the truth, let nothing at all be said in reply, for it is useless to sing to the deaf, and their will dulled their judgment; to the others, if there are any who could stumble through ignorance, one may answer in this fashion: Rome, the capital of Italy, and not only of Italy, but of the whole world, has been weakened, worn out and almost destroyed by many wars and disasters, I sadly confess, and among other things, by the long absence of her pontiffs and emperors. The extent to which her desolation harms not only Italy but the entire body—that is, the world—and primarily Christendom, everyone sees except those whose eyes are blinded by envy and conceit. But this very city, saved for you from the hands of so many plunderers by heavenly decree, unless you turn it down, is to be restored with the help of divine grace and your genius; and it will bring you eternal happiness in heaven and immortal glory on earth. A worthy artist can wish without arrogance that something be lacking in his materials so as to display his own genius, his art, his excellence.

About the rest of Italy, what am I to say except my old and, unless I am mistaken, my true opinion. I do not mean how much she is now weighed down by the memory of that universal plague, the like of which no age has ever had, whereby for twenty years now the world has been periodically drained and ravaged as though by an annual torrent of woe. It has mangled Gaul no less than Italy; or rather to the attack of the air-borne plague has been added the earthly rage of men and the fury of the longest war, which brooded upon those lands so horribly that when a shaky peace was restored throughout those areas and I was sent on a mission to the king, I beheld on all sides the devastation caused by fire and sword, and could not hold back my tears. For we are not like them; we do not hate everything else through love of our country. But I assert confidently and without doubt that this very Italy was never more powerful in terms of men, resources, and especially sea power than in our age—never, if our minds were in agreement and the head were strong as it used to be, was Italy more ready to recover the world empire and not to endure so many thousands of infidels unworthy of such rule.[*]

I am dropping my pen and my line of thought, in order not to tire Your Holiness any longer on this score, especially since I have complained about this at great length elsewhere. I am not unaware that Taranto, Capua, Ravenna and other cities that were once great, but no longer are, contradict me. But to all of them I will contrast just this one city from which I am writing you, the very great city of Venice, or rather the huge kingdom to which once great kingdoms are subject, a city far different from the others, and, as I like to say, a world apart. In the past it was nothing or very little, although the title "doge of Venice" and "Venetian" for the province, not the city, are very old; the city's name, as I recall, I have not read before the reign of Vespasian. But the fact remains that it grew to its present size not many centuries ago. There are also others I can name: Genoa, once an obscure town, now a famous state; my ancestral city too, most flourishing, as its name declares, though it was not yet founded when the Roman republic was flourishing. What shall I say of your Bologna, which I find was called most prosperous in the age of the aforesaid emperor, and was most properous when I saw her as a boy, if there is any prosperity on earth? Subsequently, as mortal things are reversible, with the passage of time we have seen it less prosperous, then wretched, finally, in these last years, utterly wretched, but now we see her former prosperity restored under your auspices.

At any rate, this and other cities, not very ancient, in the same area were either founded by the Romans or markedly enlarged when the Second Punic War raged throughout Italy, and they began to be what they had not been. Not much later, they were almost reduced to nothing, but they have risen once again greater than before. In a letter to Faustinus, written in a sad, piteous style, Father Ambrose recalled these cities, mourning by name Bologna itself, Modena, Reggio, Piacenza, and other cities that were half destroyed at that time. Today, while they do not all enjoy complete tranquillity, their beauty and integrity still remain. And we must rejoice that the feeling of that wisest and holiest man was wrong in this particular instance; he said that they were overthrown and destroyed forever. In short, this entire part of Italy which lies between the

---

[*] We emend *imperiis* to *imperii*.

gleaming Alps and the green Apennines is much richer and more populous in these days than in antiquity; the other parts, by their variety, bear witness to the way of the world. However, let them think as they wish; there is nothing freer than opinion. Many are driven by force to do many other things, but no one ever to believe. Therefore let them believe, if they see fit, that Italy is nothing, while the whole world has often felt that it is something. Or do they even understand this at least— that in this nothingness is included almost all their excellence, and that it matters not how paltry the money box is that is full of a vast treasure?

Having refuted all these charges, kindly Father, I return to you. Here, then, amidst many obstacles, through sudden storms and contrary winds, you have used well the sail of piety, the rudder of reason, and the oar of diligence, and have put holy and venerable Mother Church back in her own See. But it is unavoidable that the head of a household, returning from abroad to his long-abandoned and uncared-for home, should find many things in need of correction. Concentrate on this, use all the power of your holy talent to repair what has been torn apart, set up what has toppled, reform what has been spoiled, buttress what is shaky, restore what has been used up. A wise man does not abandon his destroyed home, but rebuilds and restores it. But if this is true of individual homes, why is it not true of them all and of an entire city, if the situation warrants? Thus, as I was saying, when the city was burned down a long time ago, although the tribunes of the plebs opposed him and were in favor of relocating, Marcus Julius Camillus was right to have it rebuilt. His oration, worthy of the spirit and character of a good citizen and a good man, is extant.

If this happened when that city was still young and the times undeveloped, what would you advocate after so much growth of religion and heavenly and earthly things? I admit you have a shattered city, but still holy and venerable to the human race, and especially to the worshippers of Christ. She stands out gloriously in everthing divine and human—the mother of cities, capital of the world, stronghold of the faith where the faithful love you, where the unbelievers have reason to fear you, not worthy of being deserted because she is mangled and untended, but all the more to be restored carefully and single-mindedly, the more it redounds to the credit of the restorer. Romulus is praised for founding her, Brutus for freeing her, Camillus, whom I just mentioned, for restoring her; but that is the praise for the earthly empire. The spiritual empire was established there by Peter, enlarged by Silvester, ennobled by

Gregory. I see that the occasion is offered you for transferring all their praises to yourself alone. You will deserve to be compared by an uncorrupted and grateful posterity not to one or the other of these but to all together; for the foundations of both empires and their growth and ennoblement have collapsed, and you are the restorer of them all.

For this reason I am astonished at the suspicion of certain men who say that you, despising and throwing away all this glory and all this merit, want to leave either for that same prison from which you rescued the Church, or for God knows where. There is no place equal either in holiness or glory, none where you can please God and help men so much. These are your two ultimate goals, or more truly your single goal in this life under a double mandate, the goal to which the law and the prophets alike hasten, where they halt and on which they depend. Therefore, I do not accept either the story to the contrary, or the shaky guesses, or the confused rumors. In no way can I conceive that after such a start you would end thus, for it would have been better not to have started. There is nothing in the world uglier than the dark end of a bright beginning; as Flaccus says,

> A woman beautiful above
> Ends in an ugly black fish. [Ars P. 4]

If it is ugly in a picture, it is without question uglier in speech, and ugliest in action.

There are many—nearly all men—who begin nothing glorious but are not in disrepute, for they are not even known. But if a man, who has made himself known because of a glorious beginning, abandons it of his own accord, he will not avoid infamy! You not only began but for the most part completed it; take care that you do not overturn your own work—and such a work!—with your own hands. For that is much more foul than not to have started, or even to have started and then dropped it. For it is common in the midst of an action that a kind of weariness sets in when an apparent hardship intervenes; but certainly, when good things have been consummated and brought to a conclusion, undoing them invites resentment. Therefore, you must never digress from the path you have begun. There is none that goes straighter to salvation. You must never stop; the time is short, the road long; the hope of reward eases the strain of the work. In short, never look back. You know that "no one who puts his hand to the plow and looks back is fit for the kingdom of God" [Luke 9:62]. Nor is it unknown to you how Orpheus, according to pagan writers, lost his Eurydice when he turned back as he led her from the Underworld; and how, according to our own Scriptures, as Lot left Sodom, he is commanded to save his life and not to look back; but his wife, either forgetting or disregarding this, looked behind her and turned into a statue of salt. She left an example for future generations and a fine seasoning to flavor them in like circumstances, lest because of a flat taste people turn their minds or their eyes to what they have rightly put behind them.

This being so, let rumor and the multitude in their way intertwine the false with the true, but no one will change my opinion with mere words. If I hear you are leaving, I shall not believe it unless I see it; and if I do see it I shall scarcely believe it. There are things about which we can scarcely trust our eyes. I have held high hopes about you and your affairs, your holiness, your generosity, your steadfastness, your faith, and your intelligence. I believe that perhaps you console sick minds with a flattering hope, and that you do this so that between the boredom of an honorable sojourn and the hope of an ignoble return the days will pass, and, as usually happens, a yearning that formed over time will in time also vanish.

Do persist, I beg you, O most blessed Father. Do it if you can; you, the Vicar of the almighty Lord, can do everything, beyond men. Make those men, who have built for so long and so eagerly where they do not belong, build where their titles are; the stones will be worthy, so too the beams, the quicklime, and finally their labor, their worries, and their expenses since what has been unworthy* of respect on foreign soil will be worthy on their own soil. It is not my business to define how fitting and suitable it is that Rome, "the most beautiful in the world," as Virgil calls her [G. 2.534], is falling in ruins; the sun has never seen a greater city, while—lest the words of the poet Horace be unfulfilled—a small mean-spirited city rises above the stars, and though scarcely fit to be the tail of the world, becomes the head. Let it be left to the conscience of those who have built golden palaces there, while the mother city of all cities under heaven lies prostrate, and while the roofs of the Apostles, which are also their own, or rather the dwellings of the saints of which they professed to be the caretakers, lie strewn about and shattered, and while the Lord and Judge of all looks on and—for all

---

* We emend *honesti* to *inhonesti*.

I know—even approves. Have them make a start, O most far-sighted Father. Have them just make a start. One pleasure shoves aside another, and it will be over: they will soon begin forgetting their old homes and will no longer admire the Avignon mud. Minds that are infected through long error cannot recover quickly; as I have said, having been injured by time, they will also be cured by time. Not only your mind, but your brow, your voice, your untiring concern, your vigilance, your virtue, your authority will overcome them. Meanwhile the days will pass and minds will get used to truer ideas and eyes to better sights. When they begin to appreciate what Rome is, or rather what faith is, and duty and honor, then if any man or occasion were to force them to return where they come from so sadly, they would believe that they were being driven to death or to a wretched exile.

Nevertheless I know and I feel that your sublime holiness and my loyal humbleness are still exposed to contradiction. There are some who say, and I hear them plainly from here, that the Roman air is unhealthy; and I have already answered them in part. For no city, even the tiniest, or for that matter a tiny house, can be so healthy that its ruins do not make it unhealthy. However pure the air, once it begins to be shut in, it becomes dangerous. These are the things they attack or hold against the city of Rome: her climate, and the purity of her air. One must add her prolonged desolation, her squalid walls, the scarcity of inhabitants; what else, I ask, has brought on all this, but that which I have complained of—the absence of Roman pontiffs and emperors? What else, but their presence, could cleanse all this? There is an old proverb mentioned by Aristotle: nothing fattens a horse better than his master's eye; and so the eye of your foresight and piety will fatten and rebuild your city deserted by its pastors. As Jesus Christ demands, you will view her in her fallen condition, and seeing her you will set her aright. She can be set aright and healed, unless she is abandoned. Therefore, let not this short labor, by which you will earn an eternal reward, deter you. Return to her, or rather remain with her now that you have returned. Restore her head, I say, and you will immediately restore her limbs and her strength, if not her original strength, then great strength anyhow. Only he who does great wonders can restore it. Give her back her population; you will accomplish this by remaining and giving hope of a permanent residence, and by removing all fear of the opposite from Christian hearts. When you have done this, you will soon repair the buildings and improve the air.

If someone believes the air is naturally infected, he is contradicted by that astonishing number of citizens which I wrote you about in my other letter, and by what no author's talent can match: the mental power and physical strength which could not have been born nor maintained except in the best air. He is contradicted by the whole corps of illustrious writers—least of all, the ones from Rome, so that the trustworthiness of their testimony should not be diminished by partiality. For instance, that milk-white fount of eloquence and prince of historians, in whose work it is written: "Not without reason did gods and men choose this place to found a city, and these most healthful hills, the river suitable for transporting grain from the Mediterranean area and receiving maritime commerce, the sea nearby for importing goods, but not too close and thus not exposed to the dangers of foreign navies; that this place, in the center of Italy, is the only one ready-made for growth of the city is proven by its very size" [Livy 5.54.4]. And shortly thereafter he says, "This is the Capitol, where once a human head was found and the oracle said that 'In that place would be the head of the world, the headquarters of the empire'" [5.54.7].

I know what follows, but omit it. I do not want to omit Virgil's famous words, "illustrious" for the Seven Hills, and "blessed in her breed of men," "she'll make her empire large as the world, / her spirit lofty as heaven" [*Aen.* 6.781–84]; but Jerome (since you are better acquainted with him), in writing against Jovinian, has occasion to mention the city of which I am speaking, and says, "The powerful city, mistress of the world, the city praised by the voice of the Apostle." And he continues, "the word 'Rome' means either strength in Greek or loftiness in Hebrew" [*Adu. Iouin.* 2:38]. I pass over other things. But it is not surprising that even the gravest enemy did not blush to admit that it seemed to him a city of kings, or, as others report, a temple, and a senate of kings—that is, standing upon laws. Often indeed the truth drives people to confess it, even against their will.

It is not only astonishing but shocking that this very city, always so venerated by friends and enemies alike and held above all others in honor, is hated and despised only by her sons, the cardinals. As a true father, you will urge them to lay aside these ideas, to put on new ones, to love your bride and their mother, adorn her with their presence and their wealth, so that she will adorn them with wealth and glory; and let them not clothe and feed foreign hussies while such a mother is naked and hungry, nor squander on others what should be paid back to their own mother who is needy and poor.

Let them know it is base for them and hateful to Christ who with His blood endowed the Church not only with eternal, heavenly riches, but with temporal, earthly ones as well. To waste these on something other than His praise and worship is impious and sacrilegious.

Therefore, be vigilant, for it is a master's role to stay awake and the servants' to snore. Homer says, "A man burdened with counsels and responsibility for a people should not sleep at night" [*Il*. 2.24–25]. Aristotle says, "Masters should rise before servants, and go to bed later, and should overlook nothing that needs doing, either by night or day; for to rise during the night," as he goes on to say, "is good for one's health, economy, and philsophy" [*Economics*. 1.6.1345a.13–17]. Your health is not only good for you but necessary to the world; you are responsible not only for your own household, but that of the entire commonwealth, which needs much greater vigilance. You have no time for a false, empty philosophy, but for that true, firm one, for true wisdom, the study of God the Father; all the reasons for rising during the night and staying awake come together in you. I say, stay awake, explore, oversee, which is a bishop's proper job, and consider the total picture; there is need for a flexible, keen, and vigilant mind. The accomplishment of anything great requires sleepless nights and a dedicated spirit.

I feel most confident of your firm, excellent will; but I fear the tough barriers of other wills. It is up to you either to soften or to break them, lest this shame, this stain press upon the forehead of the Church, and lest this be the gossip of present and future centuries; how, at least while you were alive the most holy See of Peter was deserted once again by the leader of such a noble undertaking; and especially for such a cheap cause—wine, which can easily be spurned by a sober man, or, if he cannot, it is easily transported and becomes better by being transported. Indeed, that wine was not produced in the area where they were and where they are eager to return, although it was somewhat closer. Nor is this slightly longer journey anything but a minimal task for sailors to whom no task is great, since they were born for this alone. Nor, by heaven, was any man ever such a drunkard that because of his love of wine he would live in a vineyard. A vineyard is tended, not lived in. And indeed wine is born in a vineyard and harvested, squeezed in a wine press, stored in a cellar, and drunk in a great hall. The first steps fall to the steward, the last one to the master.

Your vineyard and theirs extends wherever the true religion is found; it is watered not by wine but by the red blood of martyrs, its harvest is the salvation of faithful souls. But wherever the vineyard may be, whatever the fields, Rome certainly is the royal palace and the uppermost stronghold of the Church. While some people ignore this, there is no one who does not know it, not even among the Indians, I believe, just as there is no one who will deny it. Let them come back to the heart and stop kicking against Christ's spur, for it is hard; let them not shake off His yoke, for it is sweet and lighter than any freedom. Error is a weakness of the human spirit; obstinacy is typical of demons. There have been enough errors—and more than enough. Let there now be a limit to the errors. There has been enough loss of time. We must struggle not to lose the final round. Let them turn the ears of their souls from the promptings of infernal angels. These are most dangerous; they rage with their invisible flames and darts, and, as Augustine says, we dread them "in our very minds." Let them turn to the precepts of the Lord and open their eyes, and they will see Christ pointing out to them the straight path. Let them hear Him, watch Him, and follow Him. Let their stubbornness and fatal hardness cease. Let them not be ashamed of being won over, for they are not won over by Him, and winning over oneself is the greatest of victories; but I hope they are about to do what they should; and let them start believing in you, and let them think about their last moments, which are already near.

These many things, most holy and excellent Father, to use Cicero's words, "I have said previously and now repeated not because you needed to hear them, but because I needed not to be silent, as it were." For I know that those men speak much against this every day and consider any position not only arrogant but mad. They are indeed great men, but truth is greater; and I do not doubt that they scorn, as though it were their right, any modest opponent and humble critic. But if they remember that they are men, they will not scorn reason, and if they subject themselves to it and not try to rely on bare authority, they will have nothing whatsoever to counter these arguments.

Nor is it worth mentioning, although many keep saying it, that there are those in Rome who desire something evil to happen to you or to the Church (may Christ whose cause is involved here forbid such a thing!) that will make you more inclined to leave; and that is the reason why they were pleased at the minor disturbance in Viterbo, from which they have drawn an unspeakable hope. But I dare not suspect—even the servants, except the vilest ones, not to mention the most eminent masters—of having this base, nay shocking and impious, desire; perhaps it may have invaded the wild breast of some utter gallows-bird. For him, whoever he may be, if anyone can be so evil, I wish that he may come to his senses and be forgiven; if he rejects this, I wish for him the eternal punishment of others' happiness; on the other hand, for prosperity I wish permanence, for the Church peace, for you constancy and good health. And although in myself an unworthy mediator, nevertheless with worthy prayers I beg Him who endowed your mind with so great a purpose to grant you a successful conclusion, and what best consummates good works—perseverance.

[Venice, 1367–68].

Sen. IX, 2.

To Francesco Bruni, Papal Secretary, on the subject of
the preceding letter, and his frequent change of residence.*

I know not by what power of the stars, or inconstancy of my
flighty spirit, or hard, irresistible law of necessity governing human
affairs which, to use Flaccus' words, "drives its adamantine nails
even on the rooftops of royal palaces" [*Carm.* 3.24.5–7], or by what
other reason unknown to me, I have spent almost all my life up to
the present in wanderings. While perhaps I have gotten some good
from this, I have certainly gotten the utmost evil. And if I were
asked, "Then why do you not stop?" I repeat what I said at the beginning: I know not the cause, but only the effect; since I think I
said a great deal about this elsewhere, I shall say nothing more here
except what you just heard: that sometimes these trips have been
profitable, which I do not deny, but more often damaging. At the
source of the Sorgue, across the Alps, where I spent most of my
blooming years, I had an overseer [Raymond Monet] whom I remember with fondness, as I do the time and place, for there is nothing more joyful than that time (if it had not passed so swiftly!), nothing more peaceful than that place (if it had remained so!), and no
one in his class more cheerful and obliging than that man (if he had
not been mortal!). To call him loyal is to disparage him; he was
loyalty personified.

From the time I began to take trips from there, he would say to
me with kindly reproof as I set forth or returned: "I see that you
will often be on the move, but believe me, you will never be rich."
Sometimes he would reckon the expenses of a journey I had taken
or was about to take so as hardly to miscalculate anything; as I left
he would say, "You will spend this," and upon my return, he would
say, "You have spent this." He did this so exactly that he appeared
to be not the stay-at-home steward of my little country place, but my
ever-present traveling companion who had sat down at every inn to
calculate the bill. I would marvel and laugh, though I realized he
had spoken the truth, and now I realize it more than ever. It is an
old proverb of our people: a rolling stone gathers no moss.

But to say nothing about wealth, whose instability no man of the
world has regarded as a liability, and some have even regarded it as

* See I, 6.

an asset, what shall I say about other things? By wandering as I have, I have perhaps made more acquaintances but fewer friends. How could a true friendship, one of life's greatest goods, be gained while moving around, when time and concentration are needed to get lesser goods? Even if I have formed some friendships, even if I have formed many in my travels, it is a sign of how many I would have made by staying put, since my nature is more prone to friendships than anything else. As for the stimulation and education of traveling, it is easy to determine. Of course, I have seen more by traveling than I would have seen at home, and I have added something to my experience and knowledge of things, but I have diminished my knowledge of literature. Think how many days of study these comings and goings have taken from me so that, upon seeing my little library again, I would feel like a stranger, not only among the books of the ancients but even among my own trifles, until, little by little, not without time and some effort, I would be restored to my former intimacy. This is no small loss, considering the brevity and flight of time. Had this fear not possessed me and checked my impulses—such was the spirit of youth, heedless of risks and eager to see things—I would have gone to the ends of the earth, to China and the Indies, and visited the most distant land of Taprobane [Ceylon].

I know what my state of mind was then. At that age no labor of the road, no hardships at sea, no perils would have frightened me; it was the loss of time and wasting of my mind that frightened me, figuring that I would return full of the sights of cities and rivers, mountains, and forests, but not nourished by the dear books that up to that time I had collected with youthful zeal, and what is more, though short of time. Therefore I decided not to travel just once on a very long journey by ship or horse or on foot to those lands, but many times on a tiny map, with books and the imagination, so that in the course of an hour I could go to those shores and return as many times as I liked, to those distant shores, not only unscathed, but unwearied too, not only with sound body, but with no wear and tear to my shoes, untouched by briars, stones, mud, and dust.

One thing, however, can be said in these ramblings of my declining years which I endure more lightly in word than in fact: that with the frequent changes of location I have sometimes lost letters of friends—I mean those who I know to be famous for their learning and eloquence. The letters were like a treasure to me both for their style and for love of the writers, and many things of mine have been lost that would have survived, had I been able to stay put. This is of course the only reason, dear friend, I have just slipped into this lengthy narrative and have thrust you into it when you doubtless are involved and busy with many other great matters. This kind of friendly outburst often weaves long stories out of nothing. If this were not so, I could have started with this: your last letters to me—I received one of them while still staying in Pavia, and the other in Venice—I cannot find now that I look for them in Padua, and I would like to make some reply. For the time I have been talking about has come, or rather already passed, whether the fault is that I am so busy or so slow or on the move, so I have to reply from memory, which is treacherous if it fails me, and since it fails everyone continually, especially old people, it is perhaps because it is more in debt to them, and the more you have on deposit, the rarer the banker you can trust.

To begin with, the first part of your letter, unless I am mistaken, spoke of how gravely shaken and saddened you were by the rumor of my death until a truer message raised your spirits. I have only one thing to say about this. Please do not, dear friend, do not ever be upset again by these rumors. Listen to a truly astonishing fact. It is now twenty-four years since a like rumor first ran throughout Liguria, as though it were not the misfortune of an obscure fellow but of some emperor or king. There were those who then went around singing vernacular songs about the event with such fervor that upon my eventual return I was amazed and embarrassed by such premature and undeserved fame: I was so much more famous in my youth than I am in old age. But I pass over this.

Since that time, hardly a year has passed that some rumor of my death has not been revived at least once, which is surprising since until now I have almost always enjoyed the best bodily health and a modicum of good fortune. Such rumors are usually made up only about the more powerful people whose death may be a cause for an event of some moment. My death would bring no great benefit, I believe, to anyone; to few would it be a loss, and to the commonwealth nothing whatever. Why do they hasten it? Why anticipate it with a lie? Were it really to happen, it would bring them nothing, although perhaps it would do something for their hankering and hostility. I would undertake at this point an examination of its cause, except that already on this subject there is a not irrelevant letter of mine to another friend, a good and learned man who had been shaken some time ago by a similar rumor and shock.

But to put it to you briefly, know that these are figments of enemies. You will wonder how I have enemies, but it is so. No offense or hatred has made me enemies, but envy has made many. And you will also wonder, since there is nothing at all enviable in me; but to petty minds whatever you show them that is less petty will appear most enviable. They imagine what they please—a common habit of fools. But with their contrivances they have yet to shorten my life either by a measly day or one moment, but they have added a great deal to their passion through impatience.

I admit that at one of these times, to mingle humor with seriousness—humor to be sure, but annoying—at one time, as I was saying, I was hurt by their lies; some years ago the Pontiff [Urban V], through no service of mine to him, since he had never seen me and scarcely knew of me by vague reputation, without being asked by me but solely from his liberality and kindness, had spontaneously conferred upon me that very modest prebend which I deeply appreciated because it was where I had been reared from childhood. Aware of my wishes, you had announced it to me, and had asked how I wished to have the official letters prepared. Meanwhile there came along one of those who would have me killed off every year, who wound with the tongue when they cannot with the hand, and he persuaded the Pontiff that I had passed away. It was also widely remarked then that you were deeply stricken by the news. It then turned out, as is common, that the old pest received the reward for his lie and I the punishment for a lie I did not tell.

I said there was one time, but I ought to have said two, for something similar in all respects but much more serious happened three years ago along these same lines with the present Roman Emperor [Charles IV]. When both he and I had heard about it, I joked then with my friends, if one may joke with one's patrons, and I joke now. If indeed what had been given to a live man could be taken from him upon his decease, in the same way it could be restored if he came back to life. I do not say this from any ulterior motive. In the letter you will receive from this same messenger, which is to be delivered to your master and mine and everyone's, you will see what I have agreed upon with him, namely that I neither desire nor demand anything from his hand, aside from his blessing. Nor do I know for certain whether what I long ago and for a long time wished to get is still worthwhile for me to go after. Perhaps with this small addition the yearning for my dearest father, the Patriarch [Philippe de Cabassoles], which has long goaded me, and my love of those places, could draw me back to where my stay was once so enjoyable and peaceful. Now, O unstable human condition, not even staying in one place is safe enough, as I personally know from the experience of losing the little I have there. Therefore, I have said these things because of this one false rumor, and have lightened bitter memories with some light talk. Henceforth, if you love me, let neither false rumor nor corroborated truth upset you in regard to me.

You know, dear friend, that both you and I are not exempt from paying dues to death; we share the obligation with popes, Caesars, or rather, by heaven, with all mortals who are or will be. However, those who have lived and already paid their debt have been freed from this, so that what is equal for all ought not be a hardship for any man. It is inevitable that either you hear this rumor about me or I about you. I would not be saying this if there were any particular order governing what happens to us, as I think it only fair that I who came in the front door of this life first should go out the back door first.

But alas, how often this idea has deluded me! And I hope and pray it may never delude me again. Whenever it happens, if you indeed receive true news of my death, I do not forbid you a sigh lest I appear too stern, but from now on I warn and adjure you not to shed even one little tear, nor to grieve much; or rather, I say, do not grieve any more over my death than you would have over my being born. Therefore, do not grieve at all, do not weep at all. It is neither philosophical nor manly to weep over what is natural. It is no less natural nor worse to die than to be born, and perhaps it is better. Rather pray to God for me, while I am here, that I die well, and, when I have departed, that Christ forgive and forget my sins, and run to meet me. This would be useful for me, noble of you, pleasing to God, while weeping would be none of these. Furthermore, speak of me willingly; keep my name or rather our name on your lips, and me in your memory, where you can keep a man you no longer see. This is the kind of funeral and burial that is most fitting for a true friendship, the rest is empty and doomed superstition.

The purpose of all this is to keep you from bearing not only my death but that of any mortal more gravely than is right. Though I myself have too often been guilty of this, as my many letters of mourning attest—I am now ashamed of them and wish they had either never been written by my pen or erased while it was possible—the softness and weakness of my temperament overwhelmed me in the guise of pity at the death of friends. Now I recognize what nonsense I spoke, and what good came of so many tears and laments I poured forth, while those I bewailed either did not hear them or rejected them.

There is no better guide on a road, however, than one who has often learned it by straying and falling. I do not condemn human feelings and pity, lest my attitude be inhuman and pitiless, but I do find fault with womanish weakness and a sick mind in a man. Whoever lets himself be carried away by them will sink into eternal grief, for reasons to weep and grieve will never be lacking. This is what the royal prophet says: "His life will fail in grief and his years in groans" [based on Ps. 31:11]. Another says: "This is the suffering given those who live long" [Juv. 10.243]. Yet it does not apply to everyone, but only to those who fight an uneven battle with accidental happenings while lacking valor and arms. I use my own phrasing with you, lest by concentrating on some new twist for this idea, I block the pathway of the discussion that I have begun.

I would therefore arm you in advance, strange to say, while I am alive, with these weapons against my death. When at last I have been released from this prison, of which already you have often heard false reports, once you hear the true news—as you must if you live a little longer—you will need no other comforter but to recall that I, while still on earth with you, forewarned you not to weep at my death, but to escort me with happy memory as one who has escaped from the snare of this death and begun living.

I come to something else that I used to say was stored in my memory; and I am delighted that that interminable letter of mine, or you may prefer to call it that short book, has been well received, as you say, by the Supreme Pontiff. Certainly whatever its style, whatever its substance, at least the writer's loyalty was clear, and you can be certain the mind's good will could not be equaled either by the tongue or by the pen. Never have I known myself to be so at a loss for words in any of my dealings. Loyalty drove me to this as no confidence in my ability would have done, so that I dared speak so freely about those manipulators of events. The profound vision of the one to whom my words were directed helped the thrust of my loyal mind and the freedom of my pen; for I was certain that those men were much better known to him than to me or to anyone else. So in broaching their character to him, there was nothing to fear so much as having left out many things.

Divine Providence, infallible, eternal, and awesome in its designs, beyond the grasp of the sons of men, has seen to it that he who had been destined to be the prince of the Church, the savior of an ailing world, would most carefully examine his closest advisers before they had any fear or dread of him, or surmised that he was sometimes to be feared or dreaded. It is difficult to know men's character; the recesses of the human heart are dark and deep under the veil of hypocrisy. And in the dark the color of the mind, as of other things, lies hidden. Now it is too late to cast the cloud of pretense; he saw them from within at a time when they were exposed. It was this that gave me the confidence to speak to him, not that I was or am unaware of myself and of them, and how much respect was due them if they fulfilled what they profess. But alas, almost all the virtue of men is a shadow: the words of ritual, the manner of dress, the way of walking, body gestures, eye movement, the forehead, the hair, the eyebrows, all these things are embellished. The internal condition of the mind is disregarded.

Furthermore, I have not forgotten the saying of Cicero that whoever is ready to speak against another must be free of every fault. It accords with the saying of our Savior who, as He wrote in the sand, urged that he who is without sin hurl the first stone at the sinful woman. But I should like to have Cicero himself, if he can, show me the one who is free of every fault, for I confess I do not know that man; and if we have to wait for him, I think it will be too late for anyone to be accused. What is more, I did not intend to accuse any men, but to decry the state of the Church, although such decrying was not without grave reproof of men. And while I know that I am laden with a variety of faults, still my faults are harmful to me alone; theirs are to the world. For of all men, the ones considered most harmful are always those who through poisonous example, as though with a snake bite, have harmed public morality.

If I aspired to wealth, like the multitude, or to power, I would perhaps not have dared speak the truth lest, as is usually the case, the truth breed hatred for me from them and the damage that goes with hatred. Now that I desire nothing, why should I fear? These two things are usually connected, and the one is born of the other. Greediness and fear are the reins of the mind that often twist it from the straight path. Nevertheless, I would not have written such things to these men freely, nor would I have, as it were, exposed my neck, except that I was saying it all to one who knew. I hoped that the recital of history, though known, would incite his most noble and holy soul, and push it where it was itself hastening. Thanks to Christ and to His Vicar, now we see what we would scarcely have dared wish for, and in no way hope for. Let no one claim for this any credit or glory. No other man had any part in this, except perhaps by wishing and praying, whereas many were most heatedly on the opposite side, but all in vain, as God prevailed. Wherefore my admiration for that Most Holy Father is greater every day, and my devotion purer. He escaped here against overwhelming odds, bearing alone upon his shoulders a sick Mother Church, and their abomination was all the greater for having tried to prevent this with such zeal that they filled the minds of the faithful with the strange suspicion that they worshipped something other than Christ. As a result, although satisfied with the outcome, I did not rest, but even now have poured forth much that is just as bitter, or more so, out of which I have woven a second letter nearly as long as the first.

What indignation enflamed my mind at the new rumors cannot be told; I heard what the unholy travelers on that sacred journey are reported to have done and said against the holy leader of the journey. You know that I am spending part of the year in Venice, whose fleet was among those that accompanied the apostolic journey; anyhow, although it is said without offending the others, the Venetian fleet was the first at least in this, that it came from afar, circling nearly the entire length of Italy, and with the helm of devotion and the oar of obedience penetrated the inner bay of Gaul, and there reached remote Marseille, where the Pontiff was waiting, all ready for his journey. From these I learned many things. How upsetting the sight of them was I measure by the fact that they are so very vexing just to hear.

I shall include just one of many things: there were some present even from that venerable order who immediately, as the wind swept the fleet away from land, gave a womanish shriek as though they were writhing in pain, drawing the eyes of the sailors and passengers to them; and even, so as to preclude the excuse of seasickness, they did not withhold insults, shouting, "O that evil Pope, O that impious Father, where in the world is he dragging his wretched sons?" They cried out not as though it were to the one highest citadel of Christianity, the city of Rome, as future kings of the Catholic Church in their own See, but as though they were being dragged off to Saracen prisons in Ctesiphon or Memphis. Therefore, they were truly wretched sons, so overwrought, but he was truly the happiest and kindest father—to put it plainly—for leading his unwilling and resistant sons to salvation.

So I cry out, or rather the entire flock of the faithful shouts: "O that blessed, excellent Pope, sent by heaven to the world, who dared to free the Church from mockery, and restored her throne and dignity." As I see it, whoever rails at this will never praise anything. He is truly the Pope who not only surpasses others but stands alone in our time; and it is a truly evil and foul mouth that howls against such an indulgent father. God, therefore, justly made a clear and frightening example of that one who was the most outspoken among all these revilers: I mean he died as soon as he reached the sacred city. At the point of death, he is reported to have sent word to the Pontiff that the doctors had convinced him to return to his own country and climate if he wished to survive, and so he would need transport. What the Pope replied upon hearing this—as nothing about illustrious men is altogether hidden—has been brought all the way here by word of mouth. Whether all this is true, you will judge since you are constantly at his holy feet. For I am saying something I do not know to one who does. But this I do so that if these words fall by chance into another's hands, the reply may be known to all, worthy as it is of being carved in marble and read on the city-gates and church-gates, and celebrated eternally in the memory of everyone, but especially of learned and holy men. When the messengers had conveyed their instructions, he immediately said, "Go and tell your master, my friend and schoolfellow, his concern to go to his fatherland is good, provided he knows what his fatherland is. To consider the earthly fatherland in his condition, is untimely and deadly. The heavenly Jerusalem, up there, is our true fatherland. Let him therefore sigh for it, let him raise his spirit to it, but on the threshold let him remember that he has made the two greatest and most powerful enemies, the Apostles of Christ, I mean Peter and Paul. He has resisted their will with all his might; and with all the ingenuity that he could, at the head of all those dissenters, he has delayed me in executing their will. Therefore, let him appease them as much as time allows through repentence of the heart, through tears and prayers, so that he may find them propitious to him, and the threshold of the fatherland unobstructed; let him fasten on this, let him meditate on this, and laying aside all useless cares, let him latch on to this one alone whereby the appeased Apostles may appease Christ and may joyfully open wide the door to the celestial kingdom. Go and report these things to him in my words."

O truly angelic reply! Upon receiving the message, that cardinal, the hater of our dear city, expired not much later—God grant that he died well and happily, believing the sound advice! He received burial in the sacred places that he hated and abhorred, so great is Christ's mercy. As I was saying, I am telling all this without knowing it to one who knows. I have never heard of anything said that is loftier and nobler; if it is true, you shall let me know, and I shall let others know. If it is not, write me, if you have time, the text of the apostolic reply, word for word, so that if need be, I may change the wording in this letter too. If it stands as is, let those who hear this know that the event as recounted by me is confirmed by your testimony and that of the truth, and is just as they read it here. If you write otherwise, it will appear here as you write it; for in any case it is something that deserves to be neither forgotten nor hidden. Perhaps after me will come someone to adorn the event with a worthier style, or I myself may return to it elsewhere with greater effort, not to match with my pen the praise it deserves, but to transmit it to the memory of posterity in a less crude form.

Why should I now add to this the childish complaining, unworthy of men, because they do not have burgundy wine, about which it has been argued to the point of laughter and nausea? O holy Jesus, if they believed in you, would they not also have faith that the urns of water could be changed into the best wine? That wine did not precede them, but—let them rest assured—it will follow them wherever they may go; and it has already, I hear, and am happy, by heaven, if this way they would perhaps quit their taunts. What if the heat was unbearable last summer in Viterbo? Is nature, I ask, to give way to their pleasure? And because they are so rich, do they hope not to feel the cold or the heat? Were they free from the summer heat in that most noble city from which they have departed so complainingly and so sadly? Was I never there, or have I forgotten that place because I have been away for some years?

Although I have not been to Ethiopia or to Arabia, I have certainly visited a good part of our western world (there is no reason to mention the northern countries), and I cannot remember that I felt the summer heat more oppressive anywhere else after the north or northwest winds ceased, which are the only coolness and relief in life. If I am not mistaken, it was the last year of the Roman Pontiff, John XXII, when the heat was so intense there and the rainfall so scarce that almost all the commoners ran about naked to their navels throughout that paradise of their lordships the cardinals, who frantically prayed with loud and pitiful words, beating themselves, for the end of the torment, for rain, and for some cool air. I remember that then almost everyone's face of either sex or age, and their necks and the skin of their hands shed, as it were, a sort of scales, like a serpent's, so that any rare person untouched by that scorching heat was thought to be not of flesh but of iron. I do not know of anything like it happening in this way to anyone anywhere in our part of the world; nor do I believe that these men suffered anything like it in Viterbo. But it is not fun either to love or to hate without restraint. If it were possible for someone to be in heaven against his will and in hell willingly, he would discover something to say against heaven and in favor of hell.

Upset by all this and the like, with the most vehement indignation and with that frankness of mine, which nature had given me, my study enhanced, and my age crowns, I have written much that you will be the first to read. For it is coming first to you to undergo your scrutiny voluntarily. In this I beg you not to let love block the truth, as it often does. Judge severely, and see whether the liberty that I take is too much. The indignation cannot be too much.

Neither you nor anyone else should be disturbed by the fact that I speak to the Pope of Rome, than whom there is nothing greater in the world or rather nothing equal, as though reverence for him ought to have curbed my pen. For, as you see, a great part of my confidence is derived from the idea that no particle of truth ought, it seems, to be hidden from the Vicar of Truth, especially since, even if I wanted to, I could not altogether hide anything from him who knows it all more clearly than if he, the physician of those chronic ulcers, had felt it with his own hands. I therefore told him not so that he should learn it from me, but so that he would know that they were known to me and to everyone, and would bend his efforts all the more either to cure these things or to amputate them, lest the blotches of a few, as the leprosy spreads, infect the body of the entire Church. Although I know that I have little authority, still the truth, coming forth from all sides, has its own authority, which binds and attracts minds with a certain hidden force. What difference does it make whether a pipe reed is made of boxwood or of ivory, or of gold and adorned with gems, if the sound comes forth harmoniously and tunefully?

But once you have silently and by yourself read through what I am even now addressing to the Supreme Pontiff, and have carefully weighed it all, consult with the one you usually do and you know I always wanted to, Agapito Colonna the Younger. He is more honorable and famous than the Bishop of Ascoli.

Finally, assume that everything I said last year about my first letter, which I hope you remember, is said here[*] too. And I would add the other Colonna, Stefano, who is also the Younger, to your consultants; for when I was young I cultivated the seniors with these names, now that I am older I love these juniors. However, I have no slight cause for complaint against this latter one (any offense is serious for one who loves), which I would like not to keep from him if the opportunity allows. On October 31, returning from France, as the news of the Pontiff's return made him change his route, he

[*] We emend *hinc* to *hic*.

visited me with his kind selflessness while I was staying in the Milanese countryside. There we fell at once to reminiscing, as time allowed, about many things during the period of our long separation. Like a rushing torrent, our memories burst forth, and several hours flowed by very pleasantly for me in this conversation. With reluctance we finally parted—he, as it turned out, left me altogether, I only in body, as I followed him with my eyes as far as I could and with my mind until the very end. He went after giving his word that as soon as he arrived in Rome he would write me at length about everything he knew I was eager to learn, and I, like one loving and longing for his beloved, awaited the fulfillment of his promise, counting the days. But thanks to his tardiness I have now been freed from this anticipation; nor would I be surprised that he has not done me a little favor as promised, so easy for him and desired by me, seeing that he has neglected major business, advantageous not to me but to himself and his family. And may I say without offending him—as is my way in dealing with friends—that on this point I cannot and will not excuse him.

Some huge commitment that had required all his attention, or some pressing need to leave, or perhaps, since men's lives are shaky and fragile, some illness unknown to me could excuse his sluggishness, but what could excuse the fact that, having by chance, on that same day he visited me, met a young countryman of mine whom he had never before seen or even heard of, and having exchanged a few words with him in haste, he struck up with him such a close and sudden friendship that he has forgotten all about me? He had promised me, his friend for thirty years, to write about affairs of state, and meanwhile he has considered him, who was born many decades after him and who could have been his grandson, worthy of several friendly and humorous letters? O inscrutable and hidden outcome of things human! Maro says:

Now I begrudge him not, rather I marvel. [*Ecl.* 1.11]

I certainly do marvel at how such a man of his age and stability has that hankering for new friendships and indifference to old ones—but enough said, I shall be happy if you tell him this or read it to him. Do not on this account hesitate to invite him to look over this letter, if you see fit, for he is a man of unprejudiced judgment and great intelligence, and although he may not esteem me highly, he does love me a great deal. I am sorry that my father, the Patriarch [P. de Cabassoles], will be absent; he is an excellent counselor and judge.

Therefore, either alone or with those I have mentioned, or with others, do what you deem conducive to my honor, or rather ours.

I see one thing for my rivals to hold against me. I am profuse in my praises of the Pontiff, and they will say that by this route I perhaps aspire to become a bishop. But let the life I have previously led deliver me from such suspicion; there was no need for such flattery. I could often have climbed to that rank, by invitation at that; it is pleasant for me to boast about this with a friend, and to do so "in the Lord" [1 Cor. 1:31, 2 Cor. 10:17]. I know that for certain Roman generals it was considered glorious to scorn the glory of a triumph; and for this I find praised, among others, Gaius Marius, Pompey the Great, and Caesar Augustus. I have neither deserved nor despised such triumphs, but I thank God for giving me the courage to refuse those things that are sought the most by men of my kind. And lest someone be able to say that this was done once, thoughtlessly, by mere chance, not purposely, this opportunity presented itself to me over and over again; and certainly only in this would I not trust or obey that man whom I ought and wish to obey in all things, should he want to elevate me to the episcopate of some city or other. I am already squeezed enough with my burdens. And if I were not to become involved with someone else's (for a sinner I am well off even to the point, which I regret, of being envied), I would soon begin to be in trouble. I know almost all kinds of men. I have seen many high up and formidable, but no one happy. Every height is either next to a plunge or dizzying from the contemplation of the shaky footing on the brink.

Some might say, "Why then so many praises?" I swear by Jesus Christ and all the saints and my conscience that up to now I could never equal with words what I feel about that man. I reproached him when he seemed to deserve it, but meanwhile I still did not withhold due praise, whereby everyone might understand that I was ready to do either, and that I was concerned not about emotions but about naked truth. When he put his mind wholly to deeds and there was no room left for reproach, I praised him with all my soul, and I shall praise him as long as I can speak, unless—God forbid, and may neither the demons nor demonic men bring it about—he should appear once again worthy of reproach for deserting such a noble undertaking. Words must either conform to facts or be deformed by lying. I praised him as much as I knew how to and could, not as much as I ought to have or wished to; my pen was too weak for his praises. My love for that man, cherished though he be, does not deceive me; nevertheless I have never seen him nor do I know whether I ought to; no recollection of a favor received, no hope or desire for one anticipated, only truth impels me. I celebrate not the man but his virtue. I love his virtue, I am astonished by it, I know it; for while I have not seen his face, I see his deeds. I confess I admire him all the more because of his foreign origin and the array of those around him who tried to dissuade him. For had he not been foreign-born, nor they such hostile-minded and relentless enemies of Italy, neither would my praise nor admiration of him be so great; any virtue is all the brighter the more it is exercised and burnished against great obstacles. A comparison with the lives of the preceding pontiffs could add much to my judgment of him and to his glory. The contrast certainly stands out in things that are close, whereas in faraway things it would escape us.

Where shall I mention one thing that I had entrusted to that Stefano, whom I had occasion to mention a little earlier? But I suppose he has carried this out no better than all the rest. You are waiting to hear what it is all about. When he asked me whether he could do anything for me with the Supreme Pontiff, I asked him to add, along with a humble mention of my name, a short story that he should attribute to Annaeus Seneca in the book entitled *On Benefices*. It goes like this. Drawn by the fame of Alexander the Macedonian, the Corinthians through ambassadors once offered Alexander—to him, who had already acquired the surname Great by his victories in Asia— citizenship of their city, which was like a small city of his kingdom offering it to the great king. So it would be a silly, ridiculous legation to the ends of the earth for such a slight cause, except that what was by its own nature a trifle, was rendered great and valuable by the circumstance that they had never accorded that honor of citizenship to anyone besides Hercules. Out of respect for this, that most magnanimous king, who despised not only everything small but everything ordinary, did not scorn that tiny honor but gratefully accepted it and taught with his example how rarity makes a cheap thing precious. Having said this, I asked Stefano to follow this up by making the point that I am unaware of how mean, how worthless the love of such a nonentity is to the Roman Pontiff, but that still it might please him because none of the other pontiffs, not even one, of our time had had it. And should the Pope ask the reason why I, the last weak sheep, had no love for the shepherds of the Lord's flock, he was to answer that, although certain ones seem to have been generous, others learned and eloquent, and still others to have done well by me as an individual, nevertheless none, unless I myself and many others are wrong, have up to this time shown concern for his office.

Since my passion for talking on and on has come over me now, with your permission I shall, at this point, include something just as ridiculous. By habit I get up at midnight to intone the praises of Christ; although I am a sinner and the Lord would say to me, "Why do you speak of my judgments and take my covenant upon your lips" [Ps. 50:16], I still trust in His mercy that justifies the wicked, and I derive so much pleasure and such sober joy from this that there is no other time so pleasing to me and so fully my own. For I often live the rest of my hours for others but those moments for myself. And of all the divine favors bestowed upon me, which were not few had I not nullified all of them by sinning, there is none for which I feel more tightly bound to God than that He made me one of those who invoke His name with praise and hope. I find the silence of the dead of night most fitting for this. This habit I began a long time ago, and kept up throughout my life to this day, unless a serious illness interrupted it, and shall until the last, God willing. Well then, in the holy season of Lent when my body was worn out by vigils and fastings and my mind exhausted from the longer recital of the divine office, and I was approaching the sleepy dawn and at the same time the end of my nocturnal office, it occurred to me that I must pray for our Apostolic Father three times each day. I swear by our friendship that from way back I had seldom arrived at that page without a wry laugh born of indignation overcoming me, although that was not a time to laugh but to groan. Alas, I used to say silently, I do not pray for my relatives and for my benefactors as often as I do for him who detains the Church of Christ in exile, and allows the See of Peter to stand empty. Still I prayed as I could. But since this friend of God has brought it about that the entire Church, both militant and triumphant, is rejoicing, I am always affected this way when I come to that place in my prayer; and with my head reverently bowed at the Pope's name, I recite the three prayers much louder and more distinctly, as though he were a special saint or even Christ, so that I seem to have said nearly all of the prayers for this one reason alone. I myself sometimes marvel at this change in me, but I cease to marvel, knowing the reason. It is the vast sanctity of the man as seen in his highest works that does this. You know how nothing in our sphere is lovelier than virtue. I do this, not unaware that that most blessed Father does not need the prayers of a sinner, when rather I need his blessing, but I perform my office eagerly since what I used to do sadly I now do gladly, and in praying for another I am helping myself.

Now see, dear friend, how great a part of this day I have snatched from your business, but I find no way to conclude. For I have just remembered something else you wrote: that that Father of loftiest intelligence and richest learning asked you to write him some notes on that very plain, humble letter of mine, and that it certainly filled Avignon with further astonishment. For what else can this be compared to but a powerful, agile leopard looking for a bridge to cross a brook half a foot wide? But it is so, and now I understand what people often say, that not everyone is good for everything, which Virgil said previously: "Not all of us can do all things" [*Ecl.* 8.63]; and just as true is that saying of Crispus, "Whenever you concentrate your talent, that gets the upper hand" [*Cat.* 51.3]. The future leader of the Church by the will of God dedicated himself to studies that were not suited to delight the ears of idle men, but to correct the behavior of people. It is a good thing. You are there; just let him deign now and then to read or to hear these remarks of mine, humble to be sure but loyal; he has a living gloss by his side.

If I remember rightly, the last thing in your letter was that you more than anyone in the world desire my works—how I wish they were worthy of your desire! But this is the way of lovers: they consider not the facts, but the source. To use a friend's words, I am eager to pour into you everything as is—I shall leave it to you to examine it. And if I know what you desire the most out of all that has received the finishing touches, I shall see to it that you have it first, although, to tell the truth, it is very easy to figure out how large are the parts of a tiny whole. I have practically forgotten the one thing I ought to have kept in mind above all. You write that, elevated with vain honors and externals, you are fearful rather than hopeful of all this, but that meanwhile you have faith in the divine goodness. You are right. That is how certain people seem to understand that saying of David, "I shall fear in broad daylight, but I shall hope in You" [Ps. 56:4]. Armed in this way on the one hand with fear and on the other with hope, you will not be raised up by prosperity nor laid low by adversity.

I was about to say farewell when suddenly an unexpected friend arrived on his way from Rome, who, after we exchanged greetings, asked what I was writing, and hearing the gist of it, informed me of something new and welcome: that cardinal whom I singled out above was so contrite while dying that no one could be more devout; he repented so profoundly for his previous stubbornness that he wanted his only heir to be the Church of his title, which he had dreaded more than all the others. He ordered that all his inheritance be spent on her restoration, and wished to be buried there after his death. I understand that the apostolic advice, or rather the advice of Christ, conveyed to him by the holy mouth of His Vicar, prevailed upon him, whereby, although late, the conversion of his soul was not to no avail. Let his colleagues learn from this that while there is time they should bend their obstinate minds toward love of their Sees, and not await the day of death to make wiser decisions. Postponement is a dangerous thing. Finally farewell to you; remember me, and take the erasures that you see as the marks of an old friendship.

[Padua, 1367–68]

36159830R00227

Made in the USA
San Bernardino, CA
14 July 2016